DRAGON RAMPANT

DRAGON RAMPANT

The Royal Welch Fusiliers at War, 1793–1815

DONALD E. GRAVES

Foreword by

Lieutenant General Jonathon Riley
Master of the Royal Armouries

Frontline Books, London

ROBIN BRASS STUDIO

Montreal

Also by Donald E. Graves

Fix Bayonets! Being the Life and Times of Lieutenant-General Sir Thomas Pearson, 1781–1847
  (Montreal, 2006)

Century of Service: The History of the South Alberta Light Horse (Toronto, 2005)

More Fighting for Canada: Five Battles, 1760–1944 (Toronto, 2004)

Another Place, Another Time: A U-boat Officer's Wartime Album (Toronto, 2004)

In Peril on the Sea: The Royal Canadian Navy and the Battle of the Atlantic (Toronto, 2003)

Quebec 1759: The Siege and the Battle by C. P. Stacey & D. E. Graves (Toronto, 2002)

Guns Across the River: The Battle of the Windmill, 1838 (Toronto, 2001)

Fighting for Canada: Seven Battles, 1758–1945 (Toronto, 2000)

Field of Glory: The Battle of Crysler's Farm, 1813 (Toronto, 1999)

The Incredible War of 1812 by J. M. Hitsman & D. E. Graves (Toronto, 1999)

South Albertas: A Canadian Regiment at War (Toronto, 1998)

Where Right and Glory Lead! The Battle of Lundy's Lane (Toronto, 1997)

Soldiers of 1814: American Enlisted Men's Memoirs of the Niagara Campaign (Youngstown, 1996)

Red Coats and Grey Jackets: The Battle of Chippawa, 1814 (Toronto, 1994)

Merry Hearts Make Light Days: The War of 1812 Journal of John Le Couteur (Ottawa, 1993)

Normandy 1994: The Canadian Summer with W. J. McAndrew and M. J. Whitby
  (Montreal, 1993)

Frontispiece: **Wellington Memorial**
A sergeant of the 23rd Foot, Royal Welch Fusiliers, stands guard over the statue of
the Duke of Wellington, his former commander-in-chief, near Apsley House in
London. (**Photograph by Michael J. Ellis**)

This book is dedicated to

The Officers and Men of The Royal Welch Fusiliers
Who Have Served Sovereign and Nation since 1689

and, in particular, to

Captain Jon Latimer, 3rd Battalion
1964–2009
Good soldier. Good historian. Good teacher. Good friend.

ff

Dragon Rampant: The Royal Welch Fusiliers at War, 1793–1815

This edition published in 2010 by Frontline Books,
an imprint of Pen & Sword Books Ltd,
47 Church Street, Barnsley, S. Yorkshire, S70 2AS
www.frontline-books.com, info@frontline-books.com

Published in Canada 2010 by Robin Brass Studio Inc.
www.rbstudiobooks.com

ISBN: 978-1-84832-551-7

A CIP data record for this title is available from the British Library

Library and Archives Canada Cataloguing in Publication
Graves, Donald E. (Donald Edward), 1949-
Dragon Rampant: the Royal Welch Fusiliers at War / Donald E. Graves.

Includes bibliographical references and index.
ISBN 978-1-84832-551-7

1. Great Britain. Army. Royal Welch Fusiliers–History. 2. Napoleonic
Wars, 1800-1815–Participation, British. 3. Waterloo, Battle of, Waterloo,
Belgium, 1815. I. Title.

UA652.R9G73 2010   356'.1130941   C2010-900010-2

For more information on our books, please visit
www.frontline-books.com, email info@frontline-books.com
or write to us at the above address.

Printed in the UK by MPG Books Limited

Contents

Maps and Illustrations

Maps and Diagrams

Illustrations in text

Plates   *(between pages 110 and 111)*

Foreword

Lieutenant General Jonathon Riley CB, DSO, PHD, MA
Last Colonel of The Royal Welch Fusiliers

BECAUSE OF THE SCALE OF THE TWO GREAT WARS of the twentieth century, the long stand-off with Communism that followed, and the turmoil since the fall of the Iron Curtain, we tend to forget the length and depth of the titanic struggle with Revolutionary and Napoleonic France that so consumed the world from 1792 to 1815. Consume the world it did – for the war was fought in a thousand places: from the wilds of North America, to the Caribbean, to Spain and the Mediterranean, to Central Europe and Russia, to India and the South China Seas. Such is the gulf of time that lies between now and then it is hard to remember that this was a life-or-death struggle, a contest from which only one set of beliefs would emerge intact. The sacrifices of those who fought in it are no less, therefore, than the sacrifices made by those who fought in any of our more recent wars.

This book is essentially the story of some of those who made those sacrifices – sometimes to the ultimate degree. Some have become iconic figures of folklore – like the camp-follower and army wife Jenny Jones, or the fictional Thomas Atkins, or the now-neglected poetess Felicia Hemans, or the battle-scarred commanding officers like Henry Ellis and Thomas Pearson. Others just did what they had to do and, as Holy Scripture puts it, have become as though they had never been born. We are very fortunate in the archives of the Royal Welch Fusiliers to have such a wealth of historical material of this great conflict – from both the famous and the obscure. The Royal Welch Fusiliers were present at almost every major engagement fought by the British army in the European theatres of war between 1798 and 1815; it is this which makes the book possible, just as the Regiment's service in the American Revolutionary War made Mark Urban's *Fusiliers* possible. We are fortunate too in having been able to persuade Donald E. Graves to undertake it. With his depth of knowledge of nineteenth-century warfare and his understanding of the Regiment through his biography of the redoubtable Thomas Pearson, there is no one better able to tell the tale.

During his researches, Donald Graves has shed new light on many old problems and increased our knowledge of many things. Not least of these is the degree to which the Royal Welch Fusiliers really became a Welsh regiment during the early nineteenth century, something that had previously been thought had not happened until after 1914. We now know more, too, about the battle of Albuera – one of the bloodiest days of the British army; and about Waterloo. Not one of the greatest battles of the period – Austerlitz, Borodino, Bautzen, Leipzig were all bigger – Waterloo was by far the biggest battle experienced by the British. Because of this, and because it was decisive in that it marked the end of one period of history and the beginning of another, it left a folk memory in Britain that did not fade for a hundred years.

So whether you are a serious follower of regimental history, or a general reader of Napoleonic War history, or a scholarly researcher, or just a military buff there is something in this book for you. I thank Donald E. Graves for his wonderful work, I also thank his wife, Dianne, for being so understanding while he wrote it, and I commend *Dragon Rampant* with the very greatest pleasure.

Jonathon Riley
Master of the Armouries
HM Tower of London

Preface

THE EQUESTRIAN STATUE OF THE DUKE OF WELLINGTON opposite Apsley
House in London is a well-known landmark. The work of Sir Joseph Boehm, it
portrays the duke guarded by four colossal bronze figures each representing a
soldier of one of the peoples that constitute the British nation: an English
guardsman, an Irish dragoon, a Scots highlander and a sergeant of the 23rd Foot,
Royal Welch Fusiliers. It is this latter figure, resplendent in bearskin and armed
with sword and pike that concerns us here, as the pages that follow are the story
of the Welch Fusiliers during the long war that was waged in Europe between
1793 and 1815. In the pages that follow I have often chosen to call that conflict
the Great War with France – the name by which it was popularly known in Britain,
at least up to 1914.

My interest in the 23rd Foot arose out of my biography of Lieutenant General
Sir Thomas Pearson of that regiment, published in 2006 as *Fix Bayonets!* While
working on that title I became aware that the Welch Fusiliers possessed a rich
archive of correspondence, memoirs and other documentation relating to their
history. Having told the story of one Welch Fusilier, it seemed a logical step to
narrate the larger story of his regiment and, as much as possible, I have tried to tell
that story using the words of the officers and men of the 23rd Foot, or of those
who fought alongside them. Regiments, however, are not isolated entities, and
their histories, if they are to be properly written, must reflect the context of the
times in which they served and the community whose values they shared. I have
therefore tried to fit the record of the 23rd Foot during the Great War with France
into the political and social background of the period, as far as space limitations
permitted.

What follows is a true tale of battles, sieges, actions and skirmishes large and
small fought by the Royal Welch Fusiliers against a very professional opponent on
three continents. It is a record of long marches, perilous sea voyages, fever and
other illness, poor or no rations, harsh discipline, and of the importance of good

leadership. The Welch Fusiliers experienced bad times as well as good and, while I have not emphasised the former, both are to be found in the pages below. Actual fighting has received perhaps more than its proportionate share of attention but I make no excuse for that because fighting is what regiments are about. Nonetheless, I have also tried to address other aspects of the Welch Fusiliers' story including the experiences of the women who accompanied them in almost all their campaigns.

The Royal Welch Fusiliers have a long and splendid record that dates back to 1689 and have always taken a keen interest in preserving their history. It is quite probable that more books have been written about the Welch Fusiliers, or by those who served with them, than any other regiment in the British army and the list of authors includes such notable names as J.C. Dunn, Michael Glover, Robert Graves, Wyn Griffith, David Jones and Siegfried Sassoon. I have derived much benefit from the Royal Welch Fusiliers' passion for their history as my work was greatly eased by regimental historians whose research relieved me of much labour. I have to say that *Dragon Rampant* was constructed on the foundations put in place by the following authors and their work: A.D.L. Cary and S. McCance, *Regimental Records of The Royal Welch Fusiliers (Late the 23rd Foot)*; N. Holme and E.L. Kirby, *Medal Rolls. 23rd Foot – Royal Welch Fusiliers. Napoleonic Period*; and E.L. Kirby, *Officers of The Royal Welch Fusiliers (23rd Regiment of Foot). 16 March 1689 to 4 August 1914*.

I would like to make a comment on the thorny matter of the use of 'Welch' versus 'Welsh'. In 1702, thirteen years after it was first raised, the regiment was given the title, The Welch Regiment of Fuzileers. In 1751, the spelling 'Welch' was officially changed to the more modern 'Welsh', but the regiment, which preferred the older form, never accepted this and it agitated ceaselessly until 1920, when higher authority agreed to permit 'Welch' to be used in the regimental title. In *Dragon Rampant*, therefore, 'Welch' will be used when referring to the 23rd Foot and 'Welsh' when referring to the people who reside in western Britain, except in quoted passages. If this is confusing to the reader, I might add that it appears to have been confusing to the Welch Fusiliers themselves as, during the period 1793-1815, they often used both spellings, sometimes in the same document. Furthermore, just to make things even more complicated, since 2006 the official title of the former 23rd Foot is 1st Battalion, The Royal Welsh (The Royal Welch Fusiliers). There is a lengthy story here but I do not intend to discuss it, as I firmly believe there are boundaries to knowledge beyond which it is not wise to trespass.

Acknowledgements

I now have the pleasant task of thanking all those who have assisted me during the three years this book has been in gestation and at the top of the list are five members of the Regimental family whose support has been constant.

I must first acknowledge the help of Lieutenant General Jonathon Riley, CB, DSO, PhD, MA, the last Colonel, The Royal Welch Fusiliers, who encouraged me to undertake the writing of *Dragon Rampant* and put me in contact with many others who have aided my labours. General Riley read this book in manuscript and I should add that he is no mean historian himself, having written a number of scholarly works, including no less than three volumes of regimental history.

Lieutenant Colonel Richard J.M. Sinnett, Royal Welch Fusiliers (retd.), is the historian of the regiment and extremely knowledgeable about all aspects of their history from 1689 to yesterday. We have exchanged hundreds of letters and electronic messages in which Lieutenant Colonel Sinnett brought to my attention many obscure matters of fact and regimental detail, which I would otherwise have overlooked. Lieutenant Colonel Sinnett is also one of the most eagle-eyed outside readers I have encountered in three decades of writing for publication. He read this book twice in manuscript and saved me from many foolish and careless errors of fact, grammar and spelling.

Lieutenant Colonel Nicholas Lock, MA, Commanding Officer, 1st Battalion, The Royal Welsh (Royal Welch Fusiliers) has been extremely supportive of my efforts and has provided much useful information on the history and traditions of the regiment. As *Dragon Rampant* went to print, Lieutenant Colonel Lock and his battalion were deployed on active service in Afghanistan. This is the Welch Fusiliers' first campaign in that wretched and desolate area although they came close to it in 1891 and 1923 when they took part in expeditions to the old North-west Frontier of what at the time was British India and is now Pakistan. May they all return home safe.

Mr Brian Owen, Curator of The Royal Welch Fusiliers Museum, Caernarfon Castle, Wales, and his staff have also rendered me constant assistance, providing copies of documents and illustrations, information on regimental artefacts and patiently answering many queries.

Lieutenant Colonel P.A. Crocker, Royal Welch Fusiliers (retd.), former Curator of the Regimental Museum, was good enough to read this book in manuscript and point out an embarrassing number of matters that needed correction.

Next, I must thank the following friends and colleagues who also read this book in manuscript: Robert Burnham; Major John Grodzinski, CD of the Royal Military College of Canada; Lieutenant Colonel Keith Kiddie, MA, of the Royal Regiment of Fusiliers; David McCracken; Ron McGuigan; Howie Muir; and Dr Rory Muir.

I hasten to add that all my outside readers provided much good and critical comment and if I have ignored it, I have done so only at my peril. Any errors of fact or historical judgement that remain are entirely my responsibility.

I would like to express my thanks to Dr Roger N. Buckley of the University of Connecticut for permission to quote from his excellent book, *The Napoleonic War Journal of Captain Thomas Henry Browne*.

I must acknowledge a particular debt of gratitude to Major J.A. Crook, MA, BA, MSc, for bringing to my attention the memoir of his ancestor, Drummer Richard Bentinck of the 23rd Foot. I am very pleased to state that this interesting and informative memoir of a private British soldier of the period, edited by Major Crook, will shortly see publication.

I wish to also express my gratitude to J.J. Heath-Caldwell, who gave me permission to quote from the memoir of his ancestor, Lieutenant Charles Crowe of the 27th Foot, which, edited by Gareth Glover, will also see publication in the near future.

The art of Peter Rindlisbacher has graced the covers of several of my books but, with *Dragon Rampant*, he has gone far beyond any call of friendship and produced a superb jacket illustration, for which I owe him many thanks.

In the past three years I have received assistance from so many people that, unfortunately, space restrictions preclude me from doing anything more than listing them by name. I owe a debt of gratitude to the following: Richard Adlington; Dr David Atack and Mrs. Alexandra Atack; Dr Andrew Bamford; Robin Brass; Tony Broughton; Christopher Bryant; René Chartrand; John Cook; Guy Dempsey, Michael J. Ellis, Randal Gray; Gareth Glover; Martyn Griffiths; Major Edward Hill; Rupert Hill; Tom Holmberg; Dr John Houlding; Christopher Johnson; Bradley Jones; Peter Knox; Lynne Kyria; the late Jon Latimer; Roderick MacArthur; Gethin Matthews; Dr John McCavitt; Gill Owen; Anne Pedley; Sir Christopher Prevost; Ralph Reinertsen; Digby Smith; Steven H. Smith; Dr Stephen Summerfield; Victor Sutcliffe; Mark Thompson; Dominique Timmermans and the staff of *http://napoleon-monuments.eu*; Mark Urban; Dr Gregory Urwin; Patrick Wilder; Allan Wood; and Dr Robert K. Wright. If I have forgotten anyone, I can only plead overwork and ask for forgiveness.

Finally, there is my beautiful wife, Dianne, who is not only a first rate editor but also my staff officer, paymaster, photographer, quartermaster, adjutant, medical officer, provost and translator. Thank you yet again, darling, for enduring bad temper and absent-mindedness – and for permitting me to let the house and grounds go to ruin – during the time I was distracted by *Dragon Rampant*. Greater love hath no woman.

Donald E. Graves
'Maple Cottage
Valley of the Mississippi,
Upper Canada
St. David's Day, 2010

A Note to the Reader

In Britain during the period covered by this book, the system of currency differed from that in use today. It was based on the pound sterling, denominated by the £ symbol, with £1 equalling 20 shillings and 1 shilling (s.) equalling 12 pence (d.). Sums were written as pounds, shillings and pence and thus £5 1s 6d or £5.1.6 was 5 pounds, 1 shilling and six pence. A guinea, often used to price valuable items, was 1 pound and 1 shilling and thus 45 guineas was £47.5.0.

So far so good, but what would be the modern equivalent value of the £ of the Napoleonic period? Calculating the value of historic currency is a very tricky business, subject to many factors, but one attempt to do so (see www.measuringworth.com) has concluded that the 1800 £ is worth £56.80 in 2008, in terms of retail price, and no less than £837.62 in 2008, in terms of earnings. Thus, when Lieutenant John Macdonald complains about having to spend £8 8s in 1812 for a pair of epaulettes (about £450 in 2008) he has a legitimate complaint. while Drummer Richard Bentinck has reason to be happy after earning £3 (about £2500 in 2008) for helping a farmer with the 1814 harvest.

I have retained standard American and British measurement in this book because the defeat of Napoleon in 1815 meant that the horrors of the metric system have not yet been inflicted on the greater part of the English speaking world – Canada being a protesting exception.

Finally, in the British army of the Napoleonic period, the word "regiment" really had nothing to do with a military unit's organization but was part of its formal title. Those readers who are not well versed in the subtleties of the British military mind, would be advised to generally substitute "battalion" when "regiment" comes up in the text. In 1813 the infantry of the army included 104 regiments of the line, each having at least one and some as many as six battalions, the battalion being the basic infantry tactical unit. In the text, 1/23rd indicates the 1st Battalion of the 23rd Regiment of Foot and 2/17th the 2nd Battalion of the 17th Foot, and so on.

D.E.G

Now's the day, and now's the hour;
See the front o' battle lower,
See approach Napoleon's power –
    Chains and slavery!

Lay the proud usurpers low!
Tyrants fall in every foe!
Liberty's in every blow!
    Let us do, or die![1]

Prologue

Near Merbe Braine, Netherlands, Morning of 18 June 1815

THE COLONEL COMMANDING His Britannic Majesty's 23rd Regiment of Foot rode north up the Nivelles highway. He was returning from a meeting with his brigade commander and the commanders of the other two battalions in that formation. They should have met the previous evening but it had been nearly dark when the brigade had finished a long, hard day of marching and gone into bivouac under a furious downpour of rain. Besides, the situation was somewhat confused – but then, the colonel thought to himself, wasn't it always?

This morning, however, the brigade commander, Mitchell, had some information. It seems that the day before, the brigade had outstripped its orders and was now separated from its parent division, which was stationed some miles to the west. It would therefore act independently. There had been, he added, some scrapping just after dawn between the pickets of the two armies, but it had died away. As for today, the brigade commander continued, the 51st Foot would take up a position to the immediate right of the Nivelles highway, almost abreast of a large château surrounded by gardens and woods, while the 14th would be placed to their rear, close enough to support them, if needed. The 23rd Foot, he informed its colonel, would be on the east side of the road – Mitchell was not sure just where at this point but promised that, when he found out, he would send an officer to guide the regiment to its correct position. As for the enemy, he added, Bonaparte himself was indeed with them, and they were believed to number about a hundred thousand men. All this being said, the meeting broke up as the three battalion commanders had much to do and wanted to get back to their units.

As he rode to his regiment's bivouac, the colonel turned matters over in his mind. So old Boney was at it again – that took amazing nerve with most of the civilised world marching against him. 'Set a beggar on horseback', he recalled, the old saying, 'and he will ride straight to hell.' The colonel, who had been fighting the French for eighteen years in a war that had begun when he was ten, would personally be very pleased to send the French emperor directly to hell, considering that the man had caused so much misery for so many. Mind, he cautioned himself, you've never fought against Boney and he's a good general. On the other hand, he reflected, his regiment had encountered some of the French emperor's best in battle – Marmont, Ney and Soult to name but three – and given them a fine milling for their pains. Napoleon might be good, he thought, but we have Wellington, and the Duke never let us down in Spain. Even so, even so, he again cautioned himself, this will be a long day.

He saw a brigade of artillery coming down the road toward him, applied pressure to the mare with his left leg while at the same time gently leading the reins to the right. She responded, moving quickly off the road and he watched as the carriages and caissons rumbled by. Heavy metal, he noted with approval, 9-pounder guns – that's good because we will need weight of metal today; in fact we will need every gun we can get. After the last vehicle had passed, he resumed the road, only to be forced off it again by a battalion of Germans. Brunswickers he judged by their dark uniforms: look like a bunch of wretched undertakers and about as cheerful. When the undertakers had passed, more infantry came behind so the colonel gave up the highway and rode in the fields alongside it.

The mare nearly lost her footing in a patch of mud but quickly recovered. This drew his attention to the ground. It had rained very heavily throughout most of the night. Around him were fields of nearly ripe barley, rye and wheat, some almost as high as a man, but gradually being trampled into a sodden mass by men, horses, guns, and vehicles. There were troops everywhere: cooking, forming, and marching. Busy place, he thought, and being a Worcester man he framed it in familiar terms – busier than The Shambles on market day. This clay ground, he decided, was nearly as bad as the Severn in spring flood – it will not soak up water and that will make for slippery going, and hard going at that. But harder for the French, he considered, and today they would attack because he was sure Wellington would stand on the defensive – he simply had to, given this army with its motley assortment of British, Germans, Dutch and Belgians, many of whom had previously fought for the emperor. So, this being the case, it was good the ground was wet because Boney would have plenty of cavalry and the colonel respected French mounted troops, having seen at Albuera just what they could do. Bad luck to 'em, he thought, they can slide about the live long day and I hope it's as hard for them as it was for us trying to go up that wretched sand hill at Aboukir Bay behind John Moore in '01: three strides up, slide back two; three up, two back.

On the other hand, with Boney in command, today Jack Frenchman might have more than his usual bag of tricks. Not for the first time, the colonel wished the old Peninsular regiments were here, particularly the Fusilier Brigade in which the 23rd had served – a fine brigade, he enthused, commanded it myself for months in Spain. But it had been broken up a year ago and there were barely a dozen veteran British battalions in this dog's breakfast of an army. He considered Mitchell's brigade: Rice's 51st was good, old Spanish hands, and, of course, there was nothing wrong with his 23rd; but Tidy's 14th were grass green, farm boys, most of 'em fresh from the plough-tail.

Thoughts of the Fusilier Brigade invoked memory of Robert Ross, its last commander, killed by the Yankees outside Baltimore the previous September, and thoughts of Ross led him to his old friend, Ned Pakenham, dead at New Orleans these five months past. And that brought him to Tom Pearson, who had run with him up that sand hill in Egypt – rumour had it that Pearson had been hit in the head by a Yankee rifle ball during the siege of some miserable mud fort in America and was now blind and deaf. As the colonel remembered these good soldiers, a flash of anger swept over him – just once, he thought, just once I would like to take the old Welch in against Cousin Jonathan Yankee; I'd put the cold steel to 'em and wipe the smirk off their silly bumpkin faces.

Concentrate, he told himself, concentrate. Have you done everything to prepare the battalion for action? Have you looked after the essentials? And what are they? The essentials, he answered his own question, are ammunition, food and water. He went over them. Ammunition was not a problem; he had brought his first line supply in carts from Grammont and his company officers would have checked the men's cartridges and flints this morning. Nor was water a difficulty; he had not seen any streams in the area when they arrived the previous evening but there were wells in the villages dotted around and he knew his sergeants would have the men fill their canteens first thing.

Food was his main worry. The battalion had been ordered to march with so little warning that he had not had time to issue rations and most of his men had not eaten for two days despite marching fifty miles. He had done what he could. The previous evening, he had sent his quartermaster into that little town a few miles to the north with its English-sounding name but Sidley had not found enough to feed 700 hungry men. Earlier this morning, he and his officers had turned a blind eye when men slipped away from the bivouac area to forage for something to eat – who could blame them. Why is it, he asked himself, that we rarely run short of ammunition but frequently run short of food? We'll have to fight hungry, he concluded – because there was no other conclusion to be reached – done it before, have to do it again.

I've done all I can, he decided, to get my battalion ready for action – it's up to the men now and today we will give the French a damned good drubbing. As he turned things over in his mind, the colonel's face took on a sombre expression. His was a long and soft-featured face, thoughtful verging on sad, with prominent eyes turned down slightly at the corners, giving them a kindly look. It was a face that women might have found attractive, were it not for several rude, purple scars that advertised his chosen profession: a musket ball in the head at Badajoz in 1812; a graze along the temple received the same year at Salamanca; another musket ball through the cheek received in the Pyrenees in 1813; and a damaged eye acquired at Orthez in 1814. He carried reminders of four other engagements on his body – including a wounded knee earned in the Helder in '99, which was stiff and painful in this wet weather. If I were a private soldier, he thought, I would be on the Chelsea list for I am a walking catalogue of military medicine.

And little to show for it, the colonel contemplated ruefully. In eighteen years of active service, he had collected eight wounds and about the same number of field officer's gold medals or clasps, a Turkish medal for Egypt with a flashy orange ribbon, a knighthood and a large and splendid silver-gilt cup presented to him by the good people of Worcester the previous December. But his estate at Kempsey, just outside that city, was mortgaged to the hilt and, should this day go badly, there would not be much left for Elizabeth and their two sons. He put that thought out of his mind and turned to the business at hand. Concentrate, he again prodded himself, concentrate.

Some distance ahead, he could see his battalion formed just off the left side of the highway. Lieutenant John Enoch, his adjutant, had placed it in company columns facing the road. Enoch, a Welshman from Carmarthenshire, was a good man. In fact, at least a third of the colonel's officers and men were Welsh: there were several dozen soldiers named Jones and Williams, and almost as many Roberts and Morgans. The Welsh were good soldiers – not tall but active and intelligent although argumentative, even quarrelsome, at times. Still, all in all, less trouble to handle than the Irish, he thought, remembering the batch of wild recruits from the Irish militia that had come to the regiment in 1800. Doesn't matter who they are or where they come from, he told himself, in my time I've made soldiers of 'em all.

Enoch and the colonel's two senior officers, Dalmer and Hill, all mounted, were waiting for him in front of the grenadier company on the battalion's right flank. As he came closer, the colonel saw they were wearing – as he was himself – a cluster of black ribbons sewn to the back of their coat collars. It's amazing, he thought, my officers have been sporting this adornment since we were ordered to cut our queues in Halifax in '09 – or was it '08? One of these days, he thought, I am going to have trouble with an inspecting officer over it – but not today.

The colonel greeted the three men and passed on what he had learned from the brigade commander. He had known Dalmer and Hill since they were all teenage officers back in the late 1790s. Just boys, that's all we were, and now look at us: me a brevet colonel while Dalmer and Hill are brevet lieutenant colonels – but we earned our rank, he added for his own satisfaction. Dalmer and Hill were a study in contrasts. Dalmer was a good man, quiet, not at all flashy, but competent, yes, competent. Jack Hill was also a fine soldier but rather eccentric – in fact so eccentric that the colonel suspected he might even be a little mad. Didn't matter, the soldiers loved him – as soldiers will always love an eccentric officer, providing they can trust his judgement – and, crazy or not, it was good to have Jack Hill here today.

He rode down the front of the battalion, Enoch following at a proper distance. Passing Hawtyn's grenadiers, he touched his hat to Hawtyn's salute and looked over the ranks of his company. The colonel knew almost every soldier in his regiment, certainly the men from the old 1st Battalion – know 'em better than my own sons, he thought wistfully, because I've spent more time with them. He recognised faces, remembered names: there was Corporal Ridgway, the North American, good man, soon time to promote him; and there was Private Greyson, the Lancashire miner, who has been with me for at least fifteen years. He noted Private Williams was wearing his regimental medal for Peninsular service. The army did not have medals for soldiers, which was a shame, so the colonel had cast and awarded his own decorations. He saw approvingly that other men had copied Williams's example.

He continued on down the battalion – past Francis Dalmer's company, Walley's, Joliffe's and Farmer's – returning salutes from each commander in turn, noting faces and names, but also casting a trained eye over his men. They're soaking wet; they're cold and stiff; they're tired because nobody got much sleep last night; and most of them are hungry, he thought, but their weapons are clean and that's good. He looked for his nephew, Edward, serving in the ranks as a volunteer, but could not find him – on such a day as this, he wished the lad good luck.

The colonel came to the Colour Party in the centre of the battalion and halted. As was traditional, the two Colours, rolled and encased in their protective oilskin covers, were carried by the most junior officers in the battalion and today that was Second Lieutenants Lillie and Leebody. On the other hand, the colour sergeants standing behind the two officers were most decidedly veterans. He knew them well: Sergeant Rostron had been with him since 1798 and Sergeant Gregory about the same amount of time. Good man, Gregory, he thought, but likes his tipple a little too much – I've reduced him to private twice but he always gets his rank back because he is a fine soldier.

He continued past the companies of O'Flaherty, Johnson, Strangeways and Clyde. In O'Flaherty's company he recognised Private Prosser – gave him seventy-five lashes in Spain for theft and when passing Strangeways's company, he picked out Private John West who got 200 lashes for being insolent to his sergeant. In the same company he searched for and found old Mason leaning on his musket. Corporal Samuel Mason was a legend in the 23rd Foot. He had enlisted in '94, survived Santo Domingo in 95-96 and everything since – Holland, Egypt, Denmark, Martinique and the Peninsula – and was still above ground. Mason, the colonel recalled, had been a veteran soldier when he himself had joined the regiment in '97 and there were very few men here today who could say the same thing. Good to have Mason and NCOs like him. I am blessed with experienced, veteran sergeants and corporals, he considered, and they will steady the younger soldiers – the men who had not yet faced Jack Frenchman, all grin and whisker, advancing directly at them in massive columns, drums pounding hard.

Finally, he came to Lieutenant George Fensham's light company on the left and had a few words with its commander, advising Fensham that today he would probably be detached from the unit. He then wheeled his horse and rode back to the centre of the battalion, Enoch following. As he approached the Colour Party, the colonel saw an officer riding fast – too fast in this mud, he thought – in his direction. He's got my orders and we'll be moving shortly, he decided. The rider, a young officer, pulled up – again, too quickly as he managed to splatter mud all round – and saluted. The colonel held up a gloved hand before the new arrival could speak and the officer choked off his words. Young sprog, the colonel thought, clearly his first time on active service – look at that fine uniform, puppy looks like he just stepped out of Poole's in Brunswick Square – and he doesn't realise that business today won't start for some time, given this awful mud. You were young once, he chided himself, don't make him more nervous than he already is, so he politely asked the officer to wait a few moments.

It will be a long day, the colonel thought, so save your voice as you will need it. 'Enoch', he quietly addressed the adjutant, 'the Colours.' Enoch gave the command, 'Uncase the Colours!', and Leebody and Lillie lowered their pikes, or shafts, so that the colour sergeants could untie and slip off the protective casings. The two officers then gently unfurled the folds of cloth before raising them to the vertical. As they were intended to be the regiment's rallying point in battle and had to be highly visible, the Colours were not small, measuring six and a half feet in the fly and nearly as much on the shaft. The King's Colour, proudly held by Lillie as senior officer, was the Union flag embellished in its centre with the royal cypher and the Sphinx badge awarded for the 1801 Egyptian campaign. But it was the dark blue Regimental Colour that caught the colonel's eye. In its centre was the device of the Prince of Wales – three white feathers issuing out of a coronet and the motto, 'Ich dien' ('I serve') – surmounted by the Battle Honour 'Minden' and below, the Sphinx badge for Egypt. In the upper left quarter was the Union standard and in the upper right was the White Horse of Hanover, symbol of the British royal family. The badges in the lower quarters were linked more closely to the principality whose name his regiment bore, as they were the personal symbols of Edward, Prince of Wales, 'The Black Prince'. In the lower right was the Rising Sun and in the lower left, the rampant Red Dragon of Wales – *Y Ddraig Goch* his Welshmen called it in their difficult tongue.

The cloth of both Colours was in good shape, the colonel noted, but then it should be, because they belonged to the former 2nd Battalion. The Colours of the 1st Battalion had been so torn and ragged when it returned from Spain the previous year, that he had ordered new ones made. They had not been ready when the regiment went on active service so he had been forced to use the disbanded 2nd Battalion's Colours. Soldiers are superstitious and the colonel knew (he knew almost everything that went on in his regiment) that there were many men of the former 1st Battalion who grumbled that they should have brought the old rags when they crossed the Channel. Silly fools, he thought, if they could, they would have even brought the Goat, the regiment's stubborn, four-legged mark of distinction, with them. And given the state of his men's stomachs today, the poor beast might well have ended up in the pot.

The colonel had one more task to complete. His men would expect him to say a few words – but no death or glory heroics – something short and simple was best. He searched for words, found them and stood in his stirrups so that more soldiers could see him. '23rd!' he shouted, and faces turned toward him. 'Now, 23rd', he continued, 'we are going to have a hot day of it and mind you do not lose your character that you have gained before.'[2] Not much, but all a battalion like this needed, and he sat down in his saddle.

He turned to the young officer in the fine new uniform, anxiously waiting to carry out his orders and learned from him (as if he had not guessed already) that he was there to conduct the 23rd Foot to its assigned position. The colonel told Enoch to form the battalion into column at quarter distance, right in front, and by the time the adjutant got to the final commands in the sequence of orders to complete this evolution, the colonel and the guide were positioned at the head of the regiment. 'The battalion will advance!', Enoch shouted ... and then, 'March!'

As the Royal Welch Fusiliers stepped off, Colonel Sir Henry Walton Ellis had a thought. It's been a long road, he told himself, a damned long road, but today we just might be coming to the end of it.

Brother Soldier do you hear the news,
There's Peace both by land and Sea,
No more the old Blades must be us'd
Some of us disbanded must be.

Says the Colonel I am sorry for it,
Says the Major my heart it does ache
Says the Captain I don't at all know,
What course in the world to take.

Says the Drummer long time have I been,
But now discharged must be,
And when they want Drummers again,
The Devil shall Drum them for me.

Says the Soldier I'll to my Trade,
My wife and children shun,
T'is better to trust to a Blade,
Than in Germany to carry a gun.

Says the Soldier I'll to the Highway,
I had better to do than do worse,
And these are the Words I will say,
'Stand now and deliver your purse.'[1]

Chapter 1

'Well behaved and orderly regiment'

The Long Years of a Short Peace, 1784–1793

THE BEGINNING OF THE LONG ROAD that would end at Waterloo in 1815 can be found at Doncaster on 14 May 1784. On that day the 23rd Regiment of Foot, or Royal Welch Fusiliers, was inspected for the first time following its return from North America where it had served for eleven years. The 23rd had crossed the Atlantic in 1773, part of a reinforcement of 7,000 troops sent by the British government because of increasing unrest in the American colonies. It was present at Lexington and Concord near Boston in April 1775 when the first shots were fired in what would later be called the American War of Independence, and had fought in many of the major actions and campaigns of that conflict: Bunker Hill in 1775; operations around New York and Philadelphia in 1777-1780; Charleston and Camden in 1780; and Guilford Court House in 1781. When France and Spain declared war on Britain in 1777, converting what had been a local rebellion into a major war and forcing the Royal Navy to keep much of its strength at home to guard against invasion, the tide inexorably turned against Britain and her Loyalist American supporters. The end came at Yorktown, Virginia, in 1781 where a small British army under Lieutenant General Charles Cornwallis, besieged by superior forces of French and rebel troops, was forced to capitulate. When the remnants of the 23rd Foot, 233 officers and men, marched out of Yorktown to surrender on 19 October 1781, however, two officers managed to save the regiment's Colours by smuggling them to safety concealed under their uniforms. Following the end of hostilities in 1783, the 23rd Foot was concentrated at New York and then returned to Britain in early 1784.

There were just fifteen officers and eighty-six men on parade at Doncaster that day in May and the inspecting officer, Lieutenant General James Johnston, reported as follows:

Colours. 2, bad.

Officers. Those which I saw were very genteel young men, well dressed, with a great deal of airs, saluting very genteely.

Non-Commissioned Officers. The few present were very good looking young men with much air.

Drums and fifers. Very good and some boys soldiers' sons, and a very good band of musick.

Privates. Well looking with a great deal of airs, Light Infantry and Grenadiers remarkably good for their numbers.

Recruits. 20 in number, very unexceptionable promising young lads.

Marching. In very good time, with a firm step and much air.[2]

Apart from Lieutenant General Johnston's predilection for the word, 'airs', this was a positive report for a regiment that had just returned from a period of hard service overseas. Reading between the lines, what he was saying was that the Royal Welch Fusiliers, though weak in numbers, clearly retained their pride as soldiers.

There was reason for that pride. The 23rd Regiment of Foot had been raised in 1689 as Lord Herbert's Regiment, its first colonel being Baron Herbert of Chirbury. It had been re-titled the Welch Regiment of Fuzileers in 1702 when it was issued with the new flintlock musket (*fusil* in French). At a time when most infantry were armed with the matchlock musket, a dangerous weapon around the quantities of black powder generally found in artillery positions, special units of 'fusiliers' equipped with the safer flintlocks, were created to protect the artillery. When all British infantry regiments were eventually armed with flintlocks, the three regiments of fusiliers (also known as fusileers, fuziliers or fuzileers according to the vagaries of eighteenth century spelling) in the British army – the 7th, 21st and 23rd Foot – lost their original function but retained their status as élite infantry. The linking of the 23rd Foot with Wales in 1702 was one of earliest regional affiliations in the British army as it was made many decades before nearly all regiments of foot were given county affiliations to aid in recruiting. The regiment became attached to its connection to the Principality, so much so that in 1747, when its title was changed to the 23rd Regiment of Foot (Royal Welsh Fuzileers), it obstinately refused to give up the archaic spelling, 'Welch'. Although the 23rd Foot had early been linked with Wales it did not specifically recruit there but from across the British Isles. The 23rd had seen considerable action, fighting at Blenheim in 1704, Ramilles in 1706, Oudenarde in 1708, Malplaquet in 1709, Dettingen in 1743, Fontenoy in 1745, Minorca in 1756, and Minden in 1759.[3]

But those glorious days were past and, though their conduct during the American war had never wavered, the Royal Welch Fusiliers were part of an army that had been defeated, albeit through no fault of its own. Unfortunately for that army, the decade that followed was a most difficult time, largely caused by inadequate funding.

At the end of the American conflict Britain was in a parlous financial state. William Pitt, the young prime minister who came to power in December 1783,

Royal Welch Fusiliers, 1790s
The 23rd Foot, as they might have appeared at home in the early 1790s. Note the officer saluting with his left hand – prior to 1914, soldiers saluted with their free hand, not necessarily the right hand. (*From R. Broughton-Mainwaring,* **Historical Records of the Royal Welch Fusiliers, 1889**)

was determined to restore the nation to economic health and, to his credit, he was able to do this as the growing importance of the East Indies trade offset the loss of half of Britain's North American possessions. But Pitt also followed a policy of reducing government expenditure and this fell heavily on the armed forces, particularly the army, as he tended to favour the Royal Navy because of its connection with maritime trade. The result was that in the decade that followed, the army suffered severe problems of administration, recruiting, leadership, and training. As one historian notes, there was a

> conscious reluctance by Government to spend any more than seemed absolutely necessary on an institution whose power Parliament had long feared. Many of the Army's troubles stemmed from this simple fact. Parliament's wary eye kept it low in numbers, held its pay down, and denied it the benefits of being regularly housed in barracks. For a century and more, Parliamentarians had indulged in anti-Army rhetoric, and if by the 1790s the Army's very existence was no longer seriously questioned, the embers of hostility could still be made to glow, and nothing fanned them faster than the suggestion of new military expenses.[4]

The army's strength was kept low. In 1783, it was reduced to an authorised strength of 52,378 men with just under 30,000 to be stationed in the British

Isles and the remainder in overseas garrisons. At no time during the decade following the American war, was this figure ever reached: the army varied from a low of 59 per cent of its authorised strength, or 30,703 men, to a high of 88 per cent or 46,092. By 1792, on the eve of another war, its authorised establishment was 49,470 enlisted soldiers but its actual strength was between 36,000 and 38,000.

Not that the British public showed much concern about the state of their army for the sad truth was that, for a number of reasons, they did not much like it. First and foremost was its involvement in 'aid to the civil power' or police activities, such as riot control and the prevention of smuggling. Riots were fairly common in eighteenth-century Britain and the army functioned as a police force – regular soldiers killed nearly 300 civilians during in London during the Gordon riots of 1780. Since smuggling was a lucrative activity in coastal areas, the army's participation in attempting to curtail it was much resented. Another source of dislike was the billeting of troops on the civilian population. Outside London and Dublin, there were few barracks or buildings in Britain capable of holding a complete battalion of infantry and soldiers were therefore often quartered in private residences. Increasing resistance to this practice meant that, by the 1780s, they were usually billeted in taverns or similar establishments. As an early version of the Mutiny Act – the legislation permitting the existence of a standing army which had to be passed annually by parliament – expressed it, soldiers were to be housed only in 'inns, livery stables, alehouses, victualling houses, and all houses selling brandy, strong waters, cyder, or metheglin by retail to be drunk on the premises, and in no other, and in no private homes whatsoever'.[5] It is not surprising that, with such quarters, the conduct of soldiers was often not the best. To make matters worse, regiments were kept in almost constant motion, being shifted from place to place to undertake 'aid to the civil power' duties, or simply being moved to new billets to reduce friction with the populace. Between 1784 and 1794 the 23rd Foot, for example, served at no fewer than sixteen different stations.

The army's unpopularity and the government's reluctance to spend money also resulted in a low rate of recruiting and a high rate of desertion. Normally carried out in the spring, recruiting was extended year round in 1785-1787 which brought in numbers of men but, unfortunately, the years that immediately followed were marked by serious problems of desertion – at one point, one sixth of the soldiers stationed in Ireland were deserting annually. The problem was the soldier's pay. Nominally a private soldier received £9 2s 6d annually – about three-quarters the average annual wage of a farm labourer – but he was subjected to so many stoppages or deductions for his rations, uniforms, accoutrements and kit that he often received no pay at all and, worse still, went into debt and could not even feed himself. Finding themselves in a desperate situation, men deserted but as one historian has pointed out, this set off an unexpected reaction:

It is literally true that the only alternatives open to the private soldiers were to desert or starve; and desertion, through a curious chain of causes, brought about its own increase. All apprehended deserters were necessarily escorted by road from quarter to quarter, frequently for as far as a hundred miles backwards and forwards; and these long marches necessarily wore out portions of the escorting soldiers' clothing very rapidly. The unfortunate men were obliged to replace these articles at their own expense, that is to say, by further stoppage from their pay, which prevented them from supplying themselves with pipeclay, blacking, and other small matters essential to their proper appearance on parade.[6]

The result was that loyal soldiers, themselves on the verge of despair, also deserted. This madness was only stopped by the direct intervention of King George III, who always kept an eye on the services. In 1790 he asked for an account of the debts of private soldiers and this moved the government to pass a Royal Warrant in 1792 which, in effect, raised the private soldier's pay to £12 and 3½d a year – his first raise in more than a century – but, more important, gave him a basic free bread allowance and the magnificent sum of 18s 10½d per year, paid every two months, which was to remain free from all stoppages or deductions. At the same time a proposal was made to increase the pay of subaltern officers, who had not enjoyed a raise since the early part of the century, but it was not approved.

This brings us to the subject of officers, and any discussion of the British officer of the 1780s must first begin with an examination of the purchase system. During the decade following the American war, about two-thirds of the initial commissions and promotions in the army were obtained by purchase. This system had originated in the late seventeenth century when the Crown, looking both for loyal officers and for ways to offset the costs of a standing army, began to sell commissions up to the rank of lieutenant colonel as a bond against good behaviour. An officer who wished to sell his commission was usually required to first offer it to the officer in his regiment with the most seniority in the rank immediately below him. If that man did not buy it, it was then offered to the next most senior, and so on. The price of commissions was strictly regulated but in many cases an unofficial higher price was often paid under the table. Once an officer reached lieutenant colonel, even by brevet, promotion was usually by seniority. A lieutenant colonel could expect eventually to be promoted to general officer rank if his conduct was good and he would then move up the seniority list of generals as those above him fell off their perches.

Although it sounds strange to the modern reader, the purchase system did have its advantages. Foremost was the fact was that the Crown did not have to provide pensions as, if an officer wished to retire, he simply sold out and commuted his profit into an annuity. If an officer wished to leave active service but keep part of

Learning how to smoke and drink grog
In winter quarters in the Peninsula, officers might occasionally get a little to the lee
of sobriety, as depicted in this splendid cartoon by Thomas Rowlandson. Note the
cheroots, the blanket used as a tablecloth, tea cups for drinking utensils and the pet
dog, of whom there were many with every regiment in the army.
(From **Adventures of Johnny Newcome,** *1816)*

---

his salary and thus his investment, he went on 'half pay' (actually about 40 per
cent), which was a retainer paid to him for future services.

Vacancies in the officer ranks of a regiment that occurred from death, whether
natural or in battle, were filled by appointment. Generally, such a vacancy went
to the senior officer of the next lowest rank but it could be filled by an officer
chosen by the Crown, and this permitted the commissioning of deserving non-
commissioned officers (NCOs) or officers without funds. Promotion through
purchase or other methods was slow in peacetime – leading to the traditional
toast: 'A Bloody War and Swift Promotion!' This toast implies that, if the war was
costly in terms of officer deaths from sickness or enemy action, promotion would
be all the sweeter as it would be by appointment or seniority, not purchase.

The purchase system was, of course, open to abuses and some of the most
flagrant occurred in the 1780s when the post of commander-in-chief of the army
was vacant. Perhaps the worst was the commissioning of infants who were then
'promoted' on paper by subsequent purchases up through the ranks so that when
they were finally old enough to join their regiments, they had enough seniority to
farther accelerate their advancement. A case in point is Major John J. Ellis of the
89th Foot who, in 1783, purchased an ensign's commission in that regiment for
his son, Henry, when the child was only a few months old. After the 89th Foot was
disbanded that same year, infant Henry went on half pay for six years but returned
to full pay in 1789 when he became an ensign in the 41st Foot, in which his father

was then serving. When Major Ellis was promoted lieutenant colonel and commanding officer of the 23rd Foot in 1793, his son later transferred to the regiment and, by the time Henry actually joined the Royal Welch Fusiliers in person in May 1797, he was already near the top of the lieutenants' seniority list.

Army officers were generally drawn from four separate groups. First were the nobility and landed gentry, who possessed money and 'interest' (the ability to obtain patronage from senior officers) and were, as a result, the most upwardly mobile. The second, and larger group, were the sons of lesser gentry, families in the professions, trade or the clergy, and even small independent farmers. Not possessing the advantages of the first group, they would not be as likely to reach the higher ranks unless, through merit or attachment, they attracted the notice of a senior officer who provided the 'interest' to assist their careers. The third group, which in some cases cut across the second group, consisted of officers of foreign birth or origins – including a high proportion of Huguenot descendants, Channel Islanders and, most recently, Loyalist Americans – whose families regarded the army as their sons' natural profession. The fourth and smallest group were men who had been commissioned from the ranks. Possessing no advantages whatsoever, few of this group achieved higher rank than lieutenant but, given their background, were usually content with their lot.

Officers being poorly paid, it was expected that their families, if they could do so, would subsidise their careers until they reached the higher ranks. In 1784, a second lieutenant in a fusilier regiment received an annual salary of £103 4s. This was the same as the average income of a well-off shopkeeper, a small yeoman farmer or a minor clergyman in a poor rural parish. From this, however, there were deductions for the upkeep of the Chelsea Hospital, the widows and orphans fund, agency fees and even deductions to pay the salaries of the officials in the paymaster's department. In peacetime, these deductions could amount to as much as a fifth of an officer's annual salary and, furthermore, he had to pay for his lodgings, his food and drink, his uniforms, arms and kit (the bearskin cap worn by the 23rd Foot in full dress uniform was alone valued at £8-£10) and contribute something to the pay of his soldier servant. The 1780s being a time of rising inflation, many officers without independent means were barely able to keep up appearances (and then probably only by skipping the occasional meal). If a fusilier second lieutenant chose to go on half pay in an attempt to live a less costly life, his salary dropped to just £33 9s per annum, about twice the annual pay of a day labourer – scarcely an improvement. The financial stress that officers suffered in the 1780s was one reason why they pooled their resources to create regimental messes to obtain food and drink – and sometimes lodgings – at reasonable cost. It is no accident that the officers of the 23rd Foot organised their first mess in 1787.

Financial cutbacks, problems in recruiting, desertion, the constant movement and dispersion of regiments all impacted on the army's training. As we are concerned with an infantry regiment, any examination of the infantry's training must begin with a discussion of their basic weapon: the smoothbore, flintlock musket. In the period, 1783-1793, this was the .75 calibre Short Land Pattern musket, first introduced in 1768, weighing 10.5 lbs. and possessing a 42-inch barrel.

The loading and firing of this weapon was a most laborious process. On his right hip, the infantryman carried a leather box filled with cartridges: tubes of strong, greased paper, sealed by pack thread and containing a powder charge at one end and a lead ball, weighing just under an ounce, at the other. To load, the infantryman held the weapon horizontally in his left hand, removed a cartridge from his box with his right, bit off the end containing the powder, shook a small amount onto the pan of the musket and closed the frizzen (a hinged cover that fitted over the pan). Grounding the butt, he next inserted the remainder of the charge, the ball and the cartridge paper, in that order, into the muzzle. He then drew his ramrod from the underside of the weapon's stock and rammed home the round to the bottom of the bore. Replacing his ramrod, he brought the butt to his right shoulder and as he did so, thumbed the hammer, with its jaw-fastened flint, back to full cock. He then presented the weapon in the general direction of the enemy and when ordered to fire, pulled the trigger, which brought hammer and flint down on the frizzen, forcing it open and striking sparks that ignited the charge in the pan and, through a touch-hole in the barrel, the main charge in the bore. A trained British infantryman could load and fire as many as four to five rounds a minute, but in action two to three rounds was much more common.

The musket was a somewhat cranky weapon, susceptible to rain and prone to misfires but its capabilities dictated infantry tactics. Given the complicated loading procedure and fairly limited range of about 100-125 yards, it was only effective if used in mass and the basis of land warfare in the late eighteenth century was the deployment of large numbers of musket-armed infantry against similar opponents. It took very well trained troops to use the musket properly and the armies of the period put much time and energy into training. There were two basic tactical formations: the line and the square. The line of two or three ranks was used to both manoeuvre and fire while the square, in which a battalion was formed so that it could present its muskets on all four sides, was adopted when infantry were threatened by cavalry. The advantage of the line formation was that it permitted a battalion to cover the greatest extent of ground and bring most of its muskets to bear; the disadvantage was that troops formed in line moved slowly because they had to pay attention to their dressing, or alignment. The French army had recently been experimenting with a tactical column, which was actually a thickened line, twenty to thirty ranks deep, which could move more swiftly but bring fewer muskets to bear. In the 1780s, however, most armies favoured the line for both fire and manoeuvre.

In that same decade, a debate raged in the British army over infantry tactics. It derived from the army's experience in North America in 1756-1763 and 1775-1783 where, operating with small numbers on a continent of vast distances and

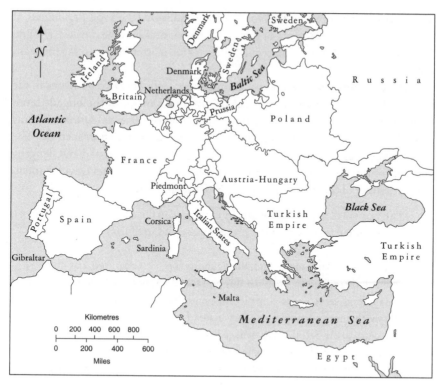

Europe in 1792
Major states only shown. *Map © C. Johnson*

heavily wooded terrain against often poorly-trained opponents lacking mounted troops, British infantry had used smaller units, looser formations and faster movements. Officers such as Lieutenant Generals Cornwallis and William Howe, and Colonels John Simcoe and Banastre Tarleton, known collectively as the 'American' school, urged that these changes be adopted throughout the service. They were opposed by officers of the 'German' school who favoured a tactical doctrine that featured a more rigid form of manoeuvre that would permit the infantry to operate with some chance of success in open terrain where enemy cavalry might be present – in short, to survive while fighting a European opponent on the continent. What was actually needed – although no one could apparently see it at the time – was a fusion of the two schools.

Several factors delayed a resolution of this debate. The first was that, as mentioned above, the position of commander-in-chief of the army was vacant. This officer would have had the authority to carry out experiments that would have proved one or the other school superior (or more likely decided that a fusion was best) and then enforced uniform training by all infantry units. Such training was needed because prior to 1784 British infantry regiments had been using two different manuals: units in Britain had trained according to the 1778 *Regulations* while those that campaigned in North America followed the 1764 *Regulations*, at the same time using elements of the 1778 manual or their own devices. Despite the introduction of an interim regulation in 1786, matters were, to say the least, somewhat chaotic.

Another problem was that in peacetime there were only two garrisons in the British Isles large enough to carry out tactical experiments at the brigade level: London and Dublin. Normally, training camps for brigade-sized formations only existed in time of war as regiments were widely dispersed in peacetime. The controversy was not settled until the Dublin garrison carried out lengthy manoeuvres in 1788 and 1789 using a manual written by Colonel David Dundas, a firm member of the 'German' school. As Dundas put it:

> The very small proportion of *cavalry* employed in the American wars, has much tended to introduce the present loose and irregular system of our infantry. ...
>
> The importance also which the *light infantry* have acquired, has more particularly tended to establish this practice. During the late war [1775-1783], their service was conspicuous, and their gallantry and exertions met with merited applause. But instead of being considered as an accessory to the battalion, they have become the principal features of our army, and have almost put the grenadiers out of fashion. The showy exercise, the airy dress, the independent modes which they have adopted, have caught the minds of young officers, and made them imagine that these ought to be general and exclusive.[7]

It was Dundas's intention to restore sound tactical principles that would permit the army to fight a European opponent with some chance of success. The result of the Dublin manoeuvres was the issue of an interim manual, the 1789 *Irish Regulations*, but this was only a first step to the promulgation in 1792 of a new manual written by Dundas, *Rules and Regulations for the Formations, Field-Exercise, and Movements, of His Majesty's Forces*. This manual was intended 'to establish one general and just system of movement' which was to be used as the basis for 'directing and governing the operations of great, as well as small bodies of troops'.[8] The 1792 *Regulations* were to be the foundation of British infantry tactics for more than a quarter century and when new cavalry, light infantry and rifle manuals eventually appeared, they conformed to the basic principles and movements prescribed in the 1792 *Regulations*.[9]

The training cycle of an infantry battalion consisted of two major phases: basic and platoon. Basic training was for recruits and was usually conducted one on one or in small groups by an NCO. The recruit was taught military posture, movements, the various marching steps and facings. Once he had learned to look and move like a soldier – a process that took, depending on his intelligence, weeks or months, the recruit graduated to the platoon exercises, what today would be referred to as company-level training.

In the late 18th century a British infantry battalion had ten companies. Eight were 'centre' or 'battalion' companies while two – the light and grenadier – were 'flank' companies. Nominally, the grenadier company consisted of the tallest and most experienced soldiers and was regarded as the commanding officer's shock or assault force. The light company provided a skirmishing capability for the battalion, acting as advance, flank and rear guards. Much effort was devoted to its training and it was often combined with the light companies of other regiments to form a specialised grouping, as was occasionally the case with the grenadier company.

Training at either the platoon or company level emphasised weapons drill. The recruit was first taught the slow drill for loading and firing his musket, with many words of command and movements, either individually or in small groups. When he had mastered this, he joined his company for fire and manoeuvre training, either as a company or half company. In contrast to most European armies, the British army placed great emphasis on musketry. British infantry regiments actually practised with live ammunition although the stress was always on volley as opposed to individual firing. Once the recruit had mastered this level, he was regarded as a trained but still green soldier and the rough rule of thumb was that he was green until he had served at least eighteen months. Company-level training was endless in the army – a minimum of ninety minutes to two hours per day – and it should be noted that new officers also went through basic and company training, the same as the ordinary enlisted recruit.

Training was largely the province of the NCOs and great care was taken in choosing them. In peacetime a private soldier usually had to have at least four years of service to be promoted corporal and a further three to four years to be promoted sergeant. At this time, there was no regimental sergeant major, as he is known today. Most of the duties of the modern RSM were undertaken by the adjutant, who was often a veteran NCO who had been commissioned and whose primary responsibility was drilling the battalion for its commanding officer.

Due to the shifting and dispersion of regiments, training at the battalion and higher level was much less frequent. What battalion-level training that was done, was often intended to prepare for the unit's annual inspection, which was conducted, usually in the late spring or early summer, by a general officer. He examined a regiment's 'interior economy' (record-keeping and administration), quarters and messing, disciplinary record and rate of desertion – as a high rate of punishment and desertion could be indications of problems within the unit – but his main task was to review the battalion at drill. The annual inspection was often the one time in a year that a regiment would concentrate its companies and train as a unit.

Like other regiments, the 23rd Foot suffered from the problems discussed above. It moved frequently and, as noted above, between March 1784 and March 1794, a total of 120 months, it served at sixteen different stations in Britain and Ireland, remaining an average of seven and a half months at each place. It was actually very fortunate, however, in spending more than ten months each at six stations: Armagh, Chatham, Doncaster, Dublin, Tynemouth and Windsor and area. Its service at Windsor Castle from September 1788 to July 1789, on what would today be termed 'Public Duties', was probably the high point of the period. On 25 November 1788, in the presence of three of the King's sons, including the Prince of Wales, the Royal Welch Fusiliers mounted guard at the Castle and 'went through' various 'manoeuvres and exercises'.[10] When the King and Queen paid a visit to Windsor in March 1789 the 23rd Foot was 'drawn up before the Lodge, properly officered, in order to testify to their joy on the happy occasion'.[11] During this Royal visit, the regiment, 'posted in the batteries in the Round Tower' fired 'three feu de joys [sic], which had a great effect'.[12] At a review held a few weeks later the Royal Welch Fusiliers attempted to 'carry Windsor Castle by a Coup de Main', demonstrating a fairly high level of tactical expertise.[13] It was probably with regret that the regiment left Windsor in the summer of 1789 to move to Ireland, where it was to remain for five years.

From 1784 to 1786 the regiment's strength was low, rarely more than 200 all ranks. Although the establishment, or authorised strength, of infantry regiments underwent many changes in the ten years following 1783, it would appear that, after 1787, the 23rd Foot's numbers held steady. In April of that year the regiment's strength was 341 men of whom, despite its title, 287 were English in origin. In 1790 when it transferred to Ireland, the regiment consisted of 385 all ranks and two years later, it reported 350 all ranks. The 23rd Foot seems to have been a very steady corps – in May 1788 an inspecting officer described it as follows:

Men. A good body of men well set up, many old soldiers of last [American] war and still serviceable.
General Observations. Well behaved and orderly regiment, only four men punished this year. Have lost fewer men in four years by desertion or otherwise than any regiment upon this [the British] establishment.[14]

The regiment's qualities had much to do with consistency in leadership. Lieutenant-Colonel Nisbet Balfour, who had first taken command of the 23rd Foot in 1778, remained in this appointment for much of the decade following the American War, although he was often away from the unit for long periods because he had other interests, including sitting as a Member of Parliament from 1790 onward. In Balfour's absence, the regiment was commanded by the veteran Major Frederick MacKenzie, first commissioned in the 23rd Foot in 1756. The company officers were also men with considerable experience. The seven captains in the regiment in 1792 had an average of eight and a half years at that rank, most having served with it as lieutenants, and almost all being veterans of the American War.[15]

Good leadership would soon become very important. In 1789 while the 23rd Foot was serving either at Windsor or in Ireland, important events took place on the continent. France, unable to pay the debts she had amassed in the American

War and previous conflicts, was in desperate financial straits. In January Louis XVI acceded to the wishes of his finance minister and called, for the first time in more than a century, the States General, the French parliament, in an attempt to get approval for financial measures, including increased taxation. The sessions of the States General were quickly dominated by outspoken opponents of the monarchy who agitated for political reform. Events accelerated the process – the Bastille, the popular symbol of royal oppression, was stormed in July and by October, Louis XVI and his family were prisoners of a new republican government that became progressively more radical as conditions worsened in the country.

By 1792 France was bankrupt and the republican leaders began to seek an external war as a means of distracting the common people from the internal chaos. When other European nations showed no inclination to engage in hostilities, however, the republican leaders found themselves in a quandary but resolved it by declaring war on Austria in 1792 and, as Austria had an alliance with Prussia, that nation also entered the war. Despite many provocations by Paris, Prime Minister William Pitt refused to be dragged into the conflict, although there was widespread outrage in Britain when the republicans executed Louis XVI and his queen, Marie-Antoinette, in January 1793. Events eventually overtook Pitt, however, as, on 1 February 1793, France declared war on Britain, initiating a conflict that would rage nearly unabated for more than two decades.

Why, soldiers, why,
Should we be melancholy, boys?
Why, soldiers, why?
Whose business 'tis to die!
What, sighing, Fie!
Damn fear, drink on, be jolly boys!
'Tis he, you or I,
Cold, hot, wet or dry,
We're always bound to follow, boys.
And scorn to fly.

'Tis but in vain,
(I mean not to upbraid you, boys),
'Tis but in vain
For soldiers to complain.
Should next campaign
Send us to Him who made us, boys,
We're free from pain.
But should we remain,
A bottle and kind landlady
Cures all again.[1]

Chapter 2

'The army was suffering in a most shameful manner'

The West Indies, Britain and Europe, 1793–1799

AT THE OUTBREAK OF WAR, the British army was in a lamentable state, numbering about 45,000 men, of whom 30,000 were stationed outside the British Isles. The Royal Navy was in better condition: its 113 ships-of-the-line faced 76 similar French adversaries and revolutionary excesses had reduced the French navy to a state where it posed no real threat to British maritime superiority. The army's basic problem was manpower and although from late 1792 onward the government had passed legislation increasing its size – no fewer than 58 new regiments being authorised between 1793 and 1795 – but recruiting was slow and there was competition for men from the militia and fencible units, which were not liable for service outside Britain. The government was forced to turn to mercenaries and 22,000 Hanoverian and Hessian troops were temporarily brought into the service. Progress was made, however, and by 1795, the regular army numbered 126,700 men.[2]

Prime Minister Pitt's strategy was to use Britain's naval power against France's overseas possessions, particularly her West Indian colonies, which accounted for about 40 per cent of French foreign trade. An enemy invasion of the Low Countries in February 1793 derailed this plan when, in May, a small and hastily-raised expeditionary force was sent to Holland under the command of the Duke of York, the second son of George III, to assist the Dutch. It was increased to a strength of 10,000 by drafts of raw recruits, and engaged in two years of profitless campaigning before being withdrawn. The deployment to Holland delayed the planned West Indian operations and it was not until November 1793, nine months after the declaration of war, that a force was dispatched under Lieutenant General Sir Charles Grey, an able officer. It was 7,000 strong, half its planned size, and consisted of eight battalions of infantry and the flank companies of thirteen other battalions. The grenadier and light companies of the Royal Welch Fusiliers, made up to a strength of 158 all ranks, formed part of this force.

A month after the flank companies had departed for the West Indies, the 23rd Foot received a new commanding officer. Colonel Nisbet Balfour, who had commanded it since 1778, was promoted a major general and replaced in December 1793 by Lieutenant Colonel John Joyner Ellis. John Ellis was the adopted son of Henry Ellis, a wealthy and intellectual man and one of the last Royal governors of the colony of Georgia. His father procured a commission for John in the 18th Foot in 1767 and he fought with that regiment at Lexington and Concord in 1775. He transferred to the 89th Foot in 1779 and when that regiment was disbanded, he joined the 41st Foot as a major in 1785 and received promotion to lieutenant colonel in 1790.[3]

Lieutenant Colonel Ellis carried out intensive recruiting and, by March 1794, the strength of the 23rd Foot was 655 all ranks, exclusive of the companies serving with Grey in the West Indies, nearly double its peacetime strength. This increase was offset by turmoil in the ranks of the regiment's officers as some older men, unable to face the rigours of active service, resigned their commissions while others transferred to newly-raised units to obtain swifter promotion. In the first eighteen months of the war, the 23rd Foot lost one major, six captains and twelve lieutenants, a loss not completely offset by the ten new and green lieutenants who joined the regiment. When the Royal Welch Fusiliers set sail from Ireland for the West Indies in March 1794, 655 all ranks strong accompanied by 48 women and 48 children, they were a raw regiment commanded by a small cadre of veterans and a flock of newly minted lieutenants.[4]

The 23rd Foot was destined for Santo Domingo (modern Haiti and Dominican Republic). In early 1794, Grey had taken Guadeloupe, Martinique and St. Lucia but his attempt to capture Santo Domingo had failed when his army was decimated by sickness. Worse still, French forces, which had slipped through the British blockade of France, not only arrived to prolong the fighting but brought with them a declaration abolishing slavery. The result was slave uprisings on most of the West Indian islands and Britain was forced on the defensive to maintain her own Caribbean possessions, the loss of which would have caused financial ruin. The most successful insurrection was on Santo Domingo and by May 1794, when the 23rd Foot arrived on the island, British troops held only the coastal towns while the interior was in the possession of insurrectionary forces who, fighting for their personal freedom, were determined to repel the invaders. In all, the Welch Fusiliers would spend twenty-one months on Santo Domingo and the few men who survived this service would, with good reason, hate the place for the remainder of their lives.

With the exception of two small actions, the 23rd Foot saw little real fighting on the island. On 5 December 1794, elements of the regiment successfully defended Fort Bizothon against insurgent forces and a few weeks later, Lieutenant George Bradford commanded a garrison of mostly black loyalist troops under their leader, Jean Kina, which defended Cape Tiburon against a siege by a superior enemy force. As Bradford reported:

We, to the Amount of 450 Men, counting the Army of Jean Kina, were attacked on the 25th [December 1794], at Day-Light, by the Enemy, from Aux Cayes, with Three Armed Vessels. Their Attention, at first, was chiefly taken up by the King Grey [an armed merchant ship], who defended the Harbour with much Spirit; but their Artillery being landed, and brought to bear from an Eminence, to the Amount of 1 Eighteen-Pounder, 1 Nine, 2 Pieces of Four, and 1 of Two, after Eight and Forty Hours of heavy cannonading, attended with a 50 lb. Shell from an Eight-Inch Mortar, about every Ten Minutes, Night and Day, at length pierced the King Grey so frequently, that she lowered so many Feet in the Water as to render her Battery useless, and a red-hot Shot taking the Magazine, she blew up.

They then turned their Fire on our lower Battery, and very soon dismounted 2 Eighteen-Pounders, the other being burst.

Finding it silenced, they then attacked the great Fort more vigorously than the former Days, bringing all their Cannon to bear on it, with heavy Musketry. They killed and wounded upwards of an Hundred Men, every Shell latterly falling inside the Fort, all our Cannoniers being disabled.

A Shell falling in the Ditch where we had placed some of Jean Kina's Corps, they forced the Draw-Bridge and flew towards Jeremie Road. We then rallied, and forming a Rear and Advanced Guard, putting our Wounded in the Center, retreated in as much Order as the Case admitted of.[5]

Given the rugged terrain, heat and insects, campaigning on Santo Domingo was strenuous. A British officer described what happened when his regiment attempted a cross-country march on the island:

The troops only moved off at 9 a.m., and before that time the greater number of the men had emptied their canteens, for a considerable distance we had to pass through a deep and close ravine, and were half suffocated by clouds of red dust; we had not advanced above two miles when the sergeant-major and thirteen privates of the 67th had expired. Those who had improvidently drunk their grog before moving off were soon seen sucking the sleeves of their jackets for the perspiration that oozed through them; the tongues of several were hanging out of their mouths, amazingly swollen and black with flies; and in my instances, *horresco referens*, the men had recourse to the last extremity to allay their thirst.[6]

To make things worse, there was a general shortage of supplies including medical stores and as one officer commented, 'the army was suffering in a most shameful manner for the want of numerable articles in which it stood much in need'.[7]

The most dangerous enemy in the West Indies proved to be neither the French nor the insurgent forces, it was sickness. The Caribbean had earned a grim reputation in the British army, after several expeditions earlier in the eighteenth century had been destroyed by disease, and operations in the area in the 1790s were made worse by a virulent outbreak of yellow fever. It was particularly rampant on Santo Domingo, which experienced higher temperatures and rainfall during the British occupation and this caused an increased population of mosquitoes, the carriers of the disease. Yellow fever took between three and five days to incubate and the typical victim first experienced sudden lassitude, headache and burning fever, as well as nausea and muscle pains. As the disease progressed, compulsive vomiting began (the dreaded 'black vomit') and this was inevitably followed by higher fever, internal haemorrhaging, coma and death. Mortality varied from 15 per cent to as high as 85 per cent in particularly bad outbreaks.[8]

Within days of landing on Santo Domingo men began to succumb to yellow fever. Because its symptoms partly resembled malaria and hepatitis, medical staff were at first confused, but once they established that they were facing yellow fever, they treated it vigorously by bleeding patients, blistering them, purging them with strong laxatives and building them up with wine. Those few who survived either the disease or its treatment were often so weak that they succumbed to other illnesses like dysentery, malaria and typhus. So many soldiers died that it was small wonder that their still-healthy comrades attempted to remain constantly drunk, believing that 'a sober hour might give the Disease an Opportunity to attack 'and this was not a difficult thing to do as raw cane rum was cheap and plentiful'.[9]

There is some disagreement over the number of British troops who perished from sickness on Santo Domingo before it was evacuated in July 1798. Estimates range from 7,500 to 15,000 men but a recent study has concluded that, of the nearly 20,000 soldiers who served on that accursed island during a five-year period, about 12,700 lost their lives, most from yellow fever, while another thousand, weakened by illness, probably died either on their return voyage or immediately afterward – a horrendous 68 per cent casualty rate.[10] The terrible losses of the 23rd Foot are revealed in the monthly regimental returns and they make grim reading. Of the 655 Welch Fusiliers who landed on Santo Domingo in May 1794, 319 were dead within three months. By December 1794 the regiment had only 231 in its ranks and a year later it had only 131 men. Between 1794 and 1796, sixteen Welch Fusilier officers died in the Caribbean, including most of the young officers who had joined at the outbreak of war and it might truly be said that the West Indies cost the 23rd Foot an entire generation of officers and men. Overall, of the 89,000 British troops who served in that theatre between 1793 and 1801, as many as 45,000 died and nearly as many were crippled by disease. Thus, most of the recent wartime increase in the army's strength was destroyed by these horrendous losses.[11]

*

The remnants of the 23rd Foot, which returned to Britain from the Caribbean in early 1796, consisted of about a dozen officers and not more than a hundred men, many unfit for further service. The task of rebuilding the regiment fell to Lieutenant Colonel Thomas Peter, who assumed command after Lieutenant Colonel John Ellis was promoted in 1795. Peter had served with the Royal Welch Fusiliers in the American war and was one of the officers who had saved the regiment's Colours from being surrendered to the rebels at Yorktown in 1781, by wrapping them around their bodies under their uniforms. He had briefly commanded one of the new wartime regiments before transferring back to the 23rd Foot.[12] Lieutenant Colonel Peter faced a daunting task – on 1 June 1796, he reported a strength of 103 men, about 10 per cent of the regiment's authorised establishment of about a thousand. He immediately dispatched most of his officers and half his men to recruit and such were their efforts that by 1 November Peter could report 229 men on strength, or about 20 per cent of his establishment.

Officers were easier to find than soldiers, and in the eighteen months that followed the regiment's return from the Caribbean, sixteen new officers were commissioned into the 23rd Foot. Among them were five men who would play significant roles in the regiment's history: Thomas Dalmer, Henry Ellis, John Hill, Francis Offley and Thomas Pearson.

Thomas Dalmer from Buckinghamshire was about sixteen when he was commissioned in the 23rd Foot in March 1797 but little is known about his background.[13] Francis Needham Offley, gazetted at the age of sixteen in February 1796, was the illegitimate son of Major General Francis Jack Needham, an Anglo-Irish aristocrat and aide de camp to King George III.[14] Offley was young but not as young as Henry Walton Ellis, the son of John J. Ellis, former commanding officer. As mentioned above, Henry Ellis received his first commission at the tender age of six months and, by twelve had reached lieutenant when he was gazetted to the 23rd Foot in September 1795. When Henry actually joined the regiment in May 1797 at not quite fifteen, he was already well up in seniority on the list of lieutenants. This must have been vexing to men like James Mackenzie, who had taken sixteen years to work himself up to the top of that list but this was the system in place and Mackenzie had no choice but to accept it or leave the 23rd Foot. As we shall see, however, young Henry Ellis would do honour to the Royal Welch Fusiliers.[15]

John Hill and Thomas Pearson were both sons of clergymen. Pearson's father was the vicar of Podimore Milton, near Ilchester in Somerset, while Hill's father served at Hennock in Devon. Pearson was gazetted into the 23rd Foot at the age of seventeen in late 1796 but did not actually join until the following year. John Hill, usually called Jack Hill to distinguish him from another officer of the same name, was at Blundell's School at Tiverton in 1796 when he decided to join the army. Unlike Pearson's father, who was relatively wealthy and, although it was a stretch, could afford the official price of £464 7s 6d it cost him to purchase his son's second lieutenant's commission and the additional £75 to £100 to outfit him with the proper uniforms and kit, Hill's parents were not as fortunate. Economy being the watchword, Jack spent considerable time during his last months at school researching which regiment to join. Being advised that it would be better to purchase a commission in a regiment abroad as it might then be possible to live on his pay, (rarely the case for a young officer in Britain), Hill enquired diligently about vacancies in units stationed in Gibraltar and India but found none. He also looked at regiments stationed in the Caribbean but found that a commission 'may be bought in another Regiment besides those in the West Indies I should think at equally as cheap a rate'.[16] The 23rd Foot being a good regiment in need of officers, Jack Hill joined it at the age of seventeen in April 1797.[17]

At this time the war was not going well for Britain. Although her navy was supreme at sea, and had won a number of major actions, Britain could not hope to fight a land war against revolutionary France without continental allies. Unfortunately, the French revolutionary armies, superior in strength because of conscription and filled with national ardour, drove Austrian, British and Prussian troops out of Holland in 1795 and both Prussia and Holland made peace. In 1796, a brilliant young French general, Napoleon Bonaparte, conducted a very successful campaign against Austrian troops in Italy while Austrian attempts to invade France across the Rhine were unsuccessful. By March 1798, Bonaparte's triumphant armies were just ninety miles from Vienna when Austria sued for peace. Britain had now not only lost her strongest European ally but had also gained a new enemy, as Spain had been coerced by France into declaring war on her. Next, the French government sent Bonaparte, the man of the hour, to the Channel coast to command the 'Army of England', intended to invade Britain and he ordered the construction of thousands of landing craft.

After its return from the Caribbean the 23rd Foot was stationed first at Kidderminster and then Chatham, but in the spring of 1797 it moved to Chelmsford in Essex. In May it formed part of the force assembled to prevent any disturbances arising from the naval mutiny at the Nore. British sailors had long-standing and legitimate grievances, among which was their pay, which had not been raised in nearly a century and had not kept up with the rate of wartime inflation. When bureaucratic ineptitude delayed the resolution of these grievances, there were mutinies at Portsmouth and the Nore, the latter being the more dangerous as the sailors threatened to sail their ships to France. As the nation was under threat of invasion and the fleet was the mainstay of her defence, the government was both shocked and angered but met some of the sailors' demands, although it quelled unrest at the Nore by force. The Nore mutineers had attempted to get the army to join their cause but the men of the Royal Welch Fusiliers would have nothing to do with any such activity. On 6 June 1797, they submitted an address to the King in which they assured their sovereign 'no atrocious [sic] villain has ever yet been daring enough to attempt by Artifice (or otherwise) to seduce the Royal Welch Fuzileers from their hitherto unerring Fidelity'.[18] One happy result from the disturbances in the fleet was that the enlisted ranks of the army, like their naval counterparts, got a long overdue increase in pay.

This raise was one of the positive changes instituted by the Duke of York after he assumed the duties of commander-in-chief of the army in 1795. York took over the War Office, popularly known as the Horse Guards, and, with the power of the King behind him, introduced a number of measures that improved all aspects of that service. He curbed the abuses of the purchase system and gradually restricted it, made officers subject to confidential reports, disbanded the many weak and useless regiments raised in the early years of the war, generally tightened discipline, and not only improved the army's pay but also its clothing, weapons and equipment. Most importantly, York stressed proper training, insisting that all infantry regiments without exception follow Dundas's 1792 *Regulations*, and increased the time spent at drill, both at the battalion and brigade level. To ensure that training was being properly carried out York emphasised the importance of unit inspections, and commanding officers that were found wanting soon heard from the duke. Although it was some years before his measures fully took hold, York's labour eventually transformed the rather amateurish British army into a professional fighting force.[19]

Such reforms were needed, not only to make the army efficient enough to meet a tough opponent with some chance of success, but also to improve the living conditions of the common soldier, which were so bad that desertion was rife. In August 1797, Lieutenant Jack Hill discussed this and other matters in a letter to his parents. Noting that the 23rd had lost nearly a hundred men through desertion in six months, Hill felt that 'Some stop or other will be put to so infamous a practice.'[20] He also noted the increased attention paid to training and the lamentable state of the army's musketry:

> We now have two or three times a week a field-day; we have a curious General here he knows but little of the manoeuvres in the Field: we have two Field Pieces attached to the Regt. lately. The whole Regt. will learn the great gun exercise: we had the Regt. fire ball, some time ago, about 4 in an hundred hit the target: we should make a poor Regt. of Yagers or Riflemen: it is no wonder, some of them do not know how to load their pieces. The badness of the musket, the ball not fitting, the powder some of the best [worst] I ever saw, come from the King's stores, such as you would give 2s. 6d. per lb; all together made a fine business. It seems strange soldiers are not taught to shoot with more precision.[21]

In March 1798 Lieutenant Colonel Peter retired and was succeeded as commanding officer of the 23rd Foot by Lieutenant Colonel Richard Talbot. Although Talbot had served fifteen years in the army, he had seen no active service and had spent much of his career on half pay.[22] He unfortunately assumed command at the same time the 23rd Foot was chosen to take part in a raid on Ostend. Although French attempts to land forces in Ireland and Wales in 1797 had come to a swift and inglorious end, there was still much anxiety in Britain about the build-up of enemy forces along the Channel coast. The Ostend raid was intended to destroy locks on the nearby Bruges canal used by the French to transport men, supplies and boats from the interior to the Channel. The brainchild of Captain Home Popham, RN, this undertaking was not favoured by the Admiralty but the government approved and Major General Sir Eyre Coote was appointed to command the expedition. The troops assembled for this operation consisted of the 11th Foot, the flank companies of the 23rd Foot and 49th Foot, and twelve light companies from the Guards, a total of about 2,000 men.[23]

When he was informed of the decision to include the Welch Fusiliers in this operation, Lieutenant General Sir Charles Grey, commanding in south-east England, queried this choice as the regiment had 'a great many Dutchmen' in its ranks, which he did 'not think calculated for the intended service'.[24] This was a somewhat curious remark and it is rather difficult to ascertain Grey's meaning at this distance. The 23rd Foot might have recruited some of the Dutch refugees who had flooded into Britain after the French occupation of their country although there is no evidence of this in its extant inspection reports. But it might also be a reference to three Welch Fusilier officers whose ancestry was Dutch, although far removed, as these men were termed 'foreigners' in a later inspection report. The three were Major Philip Skinner and Lieutenants Harman Visscher and Jacob Van Cortland, who were descended from Dutch pioneers who had settled the Hudson valley area of North America in the seventeenth century. Their fathers had been prominent Loyalists during the Revolutionary War and their presence in the 23rd Foot was quite likely the work of Colonel Nisbet Balfour, who had many connections among the Loyalist élites. Despite Grey's concerns, the three Loyalist Americans were with the 23rd Foot when it embarked at Margate on 14 May 1798.[25]

Bad weather prevented sailing for a day and even when the expedition put to sea on 15 May, it was not until 19 May when it anchored off Ostend. Although Popham warned Coote that the weather might prevent him taking off the troops from the beach once landed, the general was keen to proceed and the troops were therefore put ashore at about 5 a.m. There was no resistance and a detachment under an engineer officer quickly blew the locks as well as destroying several small vessels found in the canal. The entire force was back on the beach by 11 a.m. but attempts to re-embark were stymied by wind and wave and Coote therefore entrenched, hoping to get away when conditions improved. Unfortunately, the weather favoured the French who attacked the beachhead at dawn on 20 May. They were repulsed but the situation was clearly hopeless as the landing force could not be re-embarked and Coote was forced to surrender, having suffered 163 casualties.[26]

The Ostend raid cost the regiment four killed, eleven wounded and 183 officers and men taken prisoner – over a third of its strength. Among the captured were Lieutenant Colonel Richard Talbot; the senior major, Philip Skinner; the commanders of the grenadier and light companies; and Lieutenant Jack Hill. The prisoners were incarcerated in an abandoned church in Lille and treated well before being exchanged and returned to Britain in June 1799.

In Talbot's absence the second major, Major John Hall, commanded the regiment, which was posted to Guernsey. Its strength was low, only 401 all ranks were on parade when it was inspected by Major General Sir Hew Dalrymple in early October 1798. Dalrymple thought the Welch Fusiliers 'extremely steady, the whole seem to possess the proper *esprit de corps* which leaves no room for doubt, that, in a short time, the regiment will be as excellent as possible'.[27] The implication is that the regiment was not in the best shape and an officer who saw them in Guernsey at this time noted that the 23rd Foot was not 'in very high order'.[28] In February 1799 it was transferred to Eling Barracks in Southampton and was there when the Ostend prisoners rejoined in June. Early the following month the Royal Welch Fusiliers marched to Barham Downs Camp near Canterbury to embark for another overseas expedition.

This time their destination was Holland. In 1798, the ambitious young General Bonaparte, realising that any attempt to invade Britain was impossible in the face of the Royal Navy, convinced the French republican government that a more serious blow could be struck against the island nation if France turned to the east and threatened British trade with the Indies by seizing Egypt. In June 1798, Bonaparte took advantage of the temporary absence of the British Mediterranean fleet and landed with 31,000 men in Egypt, defeated the troops of the Ottoman Empire and occupied the country. In early August, however, a British fleet commanded by Rear-Admiral Horatio Nelson destroyed the French fleet at Aboukir Bay near Alexandria, isolating Bonaparte and his army. The news of this victory caused Austria, Russia and Turkey to declare war against France in the spring of 1799 and thus a Second Coalition came into being. When Austrian and Russian troops were successful against the French in Italy, Britain and Russia agreed to send a joint force – 30,000 British and 18,000 Russian troops – to acquire the Dutch fleet and liberate Holland from enemy occupation. The Duke of York was selected to lead this force and Lieutenant General Sir Ralph Abercromby was chosen as his second-in-command.

The plan was for Abercromby to make the initial landing at the northern tip of the Marsdiep Peninsula, which divided the North Sea from the inland waters of the Zuyder Zee. This was close to the naval base at the Texel where the greater part of the Dutch fleet was stationed. It quickly became apparent that the government would not be able to assemble the required number of troops, so at the last moment, fourteen of the regiments selected for the expedition were reinforced by volunteers from the militia, who were lured by the large bounties. Some of these men had still not entirely sobered up from spending this largesse when they embarked on board the transports.[29]

On 13 August 1799, as part of Abercromby's force, the 23rd Foot sailed from Ramsgate. The fleet was delayed by contrary winds and high seas and it was not until 27 August that Abercromby could undertake a landing at the village of Helder near the northern tip of the Marsdiep Peninsula. The Welch Fusiliers were part of the initial assault force, which rowed through boisterous surf that upset some of the boats, and made a landing on a beach surrounded by sand dunes. Almost immediately, the first units ashore were attacked by the enemy and a desperate six-hour battle ensued before the British infantry advanced into the dunes with the bayonet and as Jack Hill remarked, the French, 'did not like this movement' and shortly 'began to go off in quick time'.[30] British casualties in this beachhead action were about 1,400, with the Welch Fusiliers suffering the highest single unit loss of ninety-five killed, wounded and missing. Among the wounded was 17-year-old Captain Henry Ellis, who had been shot in the knee.

Within days the Royal Navy had procured the surrender of most of the Dutch fleet at the Texel, one of the objects of the expedition. As more troops and supplies landed, however, Abercromby decided to extend the beachhead to the line of the Zuype Canal, but did so very cautiously. This slow advance gave General Guillaume Brune, the French commander in Holland, time to assemble 21,000 men and he was ready when, on 19 September, the two armies met north of the town of Alkmaar. Abercromby attacked, putting the enemy to flight after another hard fought battle among sand dunes, and Lieutenant Jack Hill took part in this action:

> We marched against a large body of the enemy posted along the top of the [sand] hills, with a gentle ascent without a hollow near them within musket shot. We drew up in line just out of musket shot; when I was ordered with the Col[onel]'s company forward – to act as Light Infantry and give notice to the enemy's yagers, to quit their lurking places. The first rifle shot fired from them hit the hairs of the bearskin of my helmet, the third wounded one of the company. We then began firing, when some more companies on the right coming up and, advancing on them, we soon turned them out of a wood, but before this their line had moved off.
>
> We went on skirmishing a considerable way, till we came to a large hollow with a small wood between them on each side the hostile troops were [posted], and the sharp-shooters in the cover between. We were firing near two hours in this situation, when small parties of ours began to get into the wood against the enemy's rifle men. At this time our right was also gaining ground, and the enemy was passing off along the hills just before mentioned. Some troops on our left began to charge.[31]

When the Duke of York arrived to take command late in September, he had about 40,000 men, including a sizeable contingent of Russian troops. York decided to make an attempt on Amsterdam but ferocious storms delayed his advance until 2 October when he attacked the town of Egmont-op-Zee on the North Sea coast. After some heavy fighting he had possession of that place but did not progress much farther. Four days later, York engaged Brune at Kastrikum, a confusing action that ended up drawing in almost every unit in both armies. At one point a British regiment, which consisted mainly of raw militiamen, was in full flight with French troops hard on their heels when it encountered another British regiment formed in line. It was the 23rd Foot and to the delight of the fleeing men, when the Welch Fusiliers 'had given them a volley or two, the French gave way and retreated with as great precipitation as they had advanced'.[32]

Although Kastrikum had more or less been a British victory, York's campaign ground to halt. As it was becoming clear that it would be extremely difficult, if not impossible, to take Amsterdam during the present season, he decided to withdraw to the line of the Zuype Canal and this was duly done on 7 October. But after the Royal Navy cautioned that it might not be able to supply his forces over open beaches during the winter gales, Pitt's government decided to withdraw York's force to avoid a disaster. York signed an armistice with Brune, which restored the 8,000 prisoners his army had taken, but permitted him to retire unmolested, taking the surrendered Dutch fleet with him.

On 29 October 1799 the 23rd Foot boarded some small Dutch warships at the village of Helder. The grenadier and two battalion companies, as well as some military dependants, went on board the 24-gun frigate, *Valk*. On the following day, when the remainder of the regiment got under way, the *Valk* was ordered to remain to take on additional men of the regiment from another frigate, which had been found unfit for sea. The *Valk* finally sailed on 30 October and sighted the Yarmouth lighthouse that night but early on the morning of 1 November, she was blown out into the North Sea by a southwest wind of almost gale force, losing some of her rigging. Unable to make Yarmouth, the *Valk* tried to run for another port only to run aground early on 10 November 1799, about six miles from the shore of the Dutch island of Ameland. What happened next is best told in the words of Lieutenant Jack Hill, who was on board:

> I was asleep, wrapp'd in my great coat, on the floor of the Cabbin and was awaken'd by the shock. The Officer on watch immediately came down and said, 'the ship is aground'. We were on deck scarcely a moment, when she struck a second time, twice beating against the sands.
>
> I went up to the Captain and ask'd if he had any orders to give that could be carried into execution for the Troops, he made me no answer. I then ask'd the Captain where the Ship was. He said on the Lemon and Oares (a sand to the North of Yarmouth). I pointed to a long dark line in the Horizon and asked if it was not land, the reply was 'we are far enough from any'.
>
> A knowledge of our situation was soon after spread through the crowded ship, and a dreadfull confusion took place, for to heighten our distress we had a number of women and children on board; it is impossible for any language to describe this scene. The Dutch sailors gave themselves soon up and applied to acts of devotion [prayer] instead of exertion. There were not many of them indeed who had been a long time

at sea and it was even necessary for an Officer to point out every rope. Latterly some of the British entertained the idea, that Capt. Martinius had betray'd them, and had ran them on shore to destroy them, and were going to throw him overboard, to have the satisfaction as they said, to see him die before them. Lieut. [Henry] Hanson the senior officer put a stop to this, but after it, the Captain did not exert his command, at that moment every thing was hopeless.

Lieut. [John] Hoggard who had some little knowledge of sea affairs was particularly active in attempting to get the sails thrown aback, and when the ship had beaten over one bank was the first person who observ'd it, saying 'be steady boys and obey orders she floats again', and something was said about letting go an anchor. I was now looking over the side of the ship and observed a line of breakers into which the ship was fast drifting broadside on and went up and pointed them out to the Captain, who said 'all is over'. The Vessel was soon in among them and the Mizen mast went overboard breaking with a loud crash about its middle. The Main Mast next went and in its fall destroy'd the long boat. Lieut. Hoggard had got the pumps at work and continued there till the seas began to break over the ship.

The Gunner had been repeatedly called for, but no one could give any account of him. Our guns had been all drawn the night before and had not been reloaded. I went down with Lieut. Decharie to break open the Magazine. A private Grenadier (Love) was of the party, observing my anxiety, he came and put his hand on my shoulder and said 'for God's sake, Mr. Hill keep yourself cool, without it we can do nothing'. By a strict observance of this valuable advice, I conceive I am indebted for my life. The grenadier was less fortunate, he got on shore, but expired on the beach.

Some cannon cartridges were obtained and we proceeded to load one of the guns in the waist, but the violence of the seas wash'd every one from their hold and destroy'd the powder. There were no cannon on the quarter deck, it was with great difficulty I gained a station on the top of the boats from whence I fir'd about 20 rounds of musquetry.

I now heard the ship beginning to go to pieces, and went to the Forecastle, where there were very few people, as the Fore mast in its fall had destroy'd all around it. Having gotten there I laid myself down flat to shelter myself from the waves and was from this situation a spectator of the fate of most of my companions.

The masts were now laying to leeward entangled in the rigging with many people on them. The quarter deck was divided into three parts; with a horrible crash the larboard piece first gave way, and floated to a short distance when it received a check from the shrouds, and shook off the greatest number who were crowded on it, and as it was brought back again close to the ship, the waves breaking over her, fell perpendicular on it, and beat off the remaining few. Captn. Ludovick Martinius and Lieut. Hanson were standing on the deck where it divided and the next sea wash'd them away. Of the whole number who had cover'd the quarter deck only ten persons escap'd with their lives.

About this time, myself and a few others were adhering to the last portion of the vessel which remain'd, but the most had gotten out on the bowsprit, when shortly the bows turning over on its broadside, destroyed them. At this moment there was nothing to be seen but a great number of fragments floating to leeward as the forecastle had turn'd over, it was impracticable for me to stay any longer in my present situation.

I took advantage of a large piece of the wreck that had given way near me, but this proved to be entangled in the cordage and a sea wash'd me from it. By swimming I gain'd a piece on which were two Dutch sailors who were holding on by a ring bolt, but there not being room for all our hands I pull'd off my silk neck cloth and passing it through the ring held on by its ends.

No sooner was this arrangement made, than we were threaten'd with destruction by the Foremast floating beside us, I expected that every wave would throw it upon us as I had receiv'd a blow from it. I determined to alter my situation. After shifting to two or three other pieces which from their ill shape turn'd round and had nearly drown'd me, in swimming I hit upon one which was scarcely above water, large and convenient, being part of the deck where the fires are made, and on this I rested at first my arms.[33]

Fortunately, Hill was washed ashore and rescued by the local inhabitants. Of the 416 souls on board the *Valk*, only twenty-five survived – Lieutenant Hill, 19 Welch Fusiliers and 5 Dutch sailors – while the dead included 265 officers and men of the regiment, 37 women and children, 115 crewmen and a British officer and his wife taking passage. Among those drowned was Lieutenant Harman Visscher, the Loyalist American. By this disaster, the 23rd Foot had again lost more than a third of its strength, requiring another effort to rebuild the regiment, the third in three years.[†]

---

† In November 1999, the Royal Welch Fusiliers dedicated a memorial, constructed partially of ballast from the wreck of the frigate, to the *Valk* disaster on the coast of Ameland. Among the regimental party, which attended the dedication was Lieutenant Edward Hill, the great-great-great-great grandson of Lieutenant Jack Hill.

You people all I pray draw near
Unto these lines pray lend an ear
It is the truth I do declare,
Called Abercrombie's glory.

It was in the year 1801
When first in Egypt war begun.
O there we landed Britannia's sons,
Called Abercrombie's glory.

Thus bold Britons did advance,
Through fire, smoke, sword and lance.
And so boldly made the French to dance,
That was Abercrombie's glory.

Here's a health to George our King
His generals and his soldiers.
Hoping England's rights they will maintain,
That was Abercrombie's glory.[1]

Chapter 3

'Our men attacked like wolves'

Egypt and Gibraltar,
July 1800 – June 1803

ON THEIR RETURN FROM THE HELDER, the Royal Welch Fusiliers were stationed at Battle Barracks in Hastings during the winter of 1799-1800. Some of their recent losses were made up by a large draft of volunteers from the Irish militia who turned out to be very troublesome. On a more positive note, in April 1800 the regiment sent an officer and thirty-six men to Horsham to receive training as riflemen, part of an initiative to provide a rifle company or detachment in fourteen selected regiments of foot. For nearly a decade afterward, there were riflemen in the ranks of the light company of the 23rd Foot.

In June 1800 the regiment moved to Plymouth. That same month they received a new commanding officer when Lieutenant Colonel Richard Talbot was replaced by Lieutenant Colonel John Hall, who had entered the army in 1786 and had transferred to the Welch Fusiliers as a major in 1797.[2] Unfortunately, Hall was not with the 23rd Foot on 1 July 1800 when, 500 all ranks strong, it embarked on the frigates, HM Ships *Naiad* and *Alcimene*, for an unknown destination.

This operation resulted from major events that had taken place over the winter of 1799-1800. In October 1799, Bonaparte had abandoned his army in Egypt and scuttled back to France, where he had staged a *coup d'état* that overthrew the government, and replaced it with a Consulate of three, of which he was the First Consul and virtual dictator. In the spring of 1800, Bonaparte had gone on the offensive in Italy and won a remarkable series of victories against the Austrians. At the same time Russia, ruled by the unstable Czar Paul, had withdrawn from the war leaving Britain and Austria to fight on alone. In an effort to assist her major European ally, Pitt's government decided to send military forces to the continent.

The first and larger component of these forces, which sailed in the spring of 1800, was under Lieutenant General Sir Ralph Abercromby, who had a bewildering set of orders listing no less than seven objectives, many of them either contradictory or impossible. The second and smaller force, which included the

23rd Foot, left in July and was under Lieutenant General Sir James Pulteney, who had orders to either support a royalist uprising in western France or attack the Spanish naval base at Ferrol. In seven years of war, so many expeditions had set forth and returned without having accomplished anything that the British people took a rather jaundiced view of the possibility that their army might actually be successful. General opinion was aptly summed up by the caustic Lady Holland, *grande dame* of the Whig party and inveterate enemy of the Tory government, who recorded in her journal:

> Great embarkations are making at Plymouth of the Guards and other troops. Their destination is not known, but rumour says they go to the Mediterranean. Were I not satisfied how harmless an English military force is against an enemy in battle array, I should wish contrary winds to waft them leagues out of their course, if they are destined for Egypt; but they inspire as little alarm to their enemies as they do confidence in their countrymen, for they are, as one of their commanders in Ireland said publicly of them, 'Formidable only to their friends'.[3]

Lieutenant General Sir Ralph Abercromby (1734–1801)
Abercromby was fortunate to be the first British general in the Great War with France to have enough time to train his army properly. His troops performed very well in the Egyptian campaign of 1801, restoring the British people's confidence in their army. (*From Richards,* **Naval and Military Heroes of Great Britain,** *1860*)

The Royal Welch Fusiliers, along with three other regiments, spent nearly a month on the Isle d' Houat in Quiberon Bay, waiting for a royalist uprising in France that never took place. As the island was only three miles long and a mile wide, this made for very crowded conditions. On 19 August 1800, however, the regiment re-embarked to join Pulteney's main force, which had now arrived from Britain, and six days it was off Ferrol in northern Spain, where part of the force landed. Pulteney captured an outerwork of the defences but realising that Ferrol was too strong to be taken by the force under his command, he re-embarked and sailed for Gibraltar. Lieutenant William Gomm of the 9th Foot, who had gone ashore, recalled that the Spanish 'were very glad to let us off without any obstruction; indeed, I believe they would have lent us boats to row us to our ships if it had been necessary'.[4]

When Pulteney arrived at Gibraltar, he came under the command of Abercromby, who had received orders to attack the naval base at Cadiz. The combined force dutifully sailed for that place where it arrived on 7 October, but when the navy advised that there was a danger of the fleet being blown off the coast, isolating any troops that might be landed, Abercromby gave up the project and sailed for Gibraltar. Unfortunately, a series of gales blew the fleet and transports out into the Atlantic for nearly two weeks and it was only on 24 October that Abercromby anchored at Gibraltar, to find fresh orders from London directing him to invade Egypt. He dutifully set out for Malta, where he intended to overhaul his transports, many of which had been at sea for nearly five months, but was delayed by the necessity of making landings to procure fresh water. It was not until 24 November that the army disembarked on Malta and after their long odyssey around the coasts of Europe, the troops had begun to refer to themselves as the 'Floating Army'.[5]

Understandably, they were not happy with their lot – as one officer remarked:

> If we were doing our country service in lying on board transports in the manner we have done, that alone would remove all the inconveniences we labour under. We should then live sumptuously on salt junk; but rolling about in this way for no earthly purpose whatever, I own, does not suit with my taste. However, I believe we shall still remain loyal subjects. The army will not always be lying on board transports. I hope for the credit of the British army that something will soon be done worthy of them.[6]

At Malta, Abercromby took the opportunity to inspect his units in preparation for the forthcoming operation. He was not happy with the 23rd Foot which, in the absence of Lieutenant Colonel Hall, was commanded by Major James Mackenzie, and expressed 'his astonishment at the state of the Regt. after all their advantages which they had' to drill while on Isle d'Houat.[7] A 'very severe censure' was passed on the Welch Fusiliers and they were removed from Mackenzie's command and put under the direct orders of their brigade commander, Major General John Moore.[8] Mackenzie, a veteran soldier who had served in the 23rd Foot for nearly two decades, must have been crushed by this rebuke but there is reason to suspect that he was not in good health – his brother, Captain George Mackenzie, had observed that since the regiment's return from the Helder a year before he had perceived James waste away 'in a most extraordinary manner' and complain of constant stomach pains.[9] Fortunately, Lieutenant Colonel Hall arrived at Malta and took the regiment in hand. On 20 December 1800, Abercromby embarked his army for Marmoris Bay on the coast of Asia Minor north of Rhodes, where he intended to make final preparations for the descent on Egypt.

Arriving at that place Abercromby was disappointed to find that supplies promised by the Turks had not yet arrived, and this caused further delay. While he waited, Abercromby put the time to good use training his troops – in fact Lieutenant General Ralph Abercromby had the good fortune to be the first British commander to be able to adequately prepare his army for battle in the eight years since the war had commenced. In terms of tactics, Abercromby favoured neither the 'American' nor 'German' schools of doctrine but with the common sense that marked the man, emphasised a fusion of the two, so that his infantry could fight either in close order or as detached skirmishers. He used Dundas's 1792 *Regulations* as the basis of his training but reduced its many complicated evolutions to the basic manoeuvres that would be useful on campaign. Moore was impressed with his superior:

> The Commander inspected the regiments and brigades separately. He gave praise where it was due, and was severe in his animadiversion where ever he observed carelessness or inattention. He became thus acquainted with the state of every corps and the character of its commander. Discipline was improved and emulation excited. Corps were landed daily [from the transports] for exercise. The men were warned of the importance of preserving invariably their order in an open country exposed to the attack of cavalry; and the attention of general officers was called to adopt the simplest and most speedy modes of forming from the column of march columns to resist the shocks of cavalry.[10]

Abercromby also stressed preparation for an amphibious landing and there were frequent live rehearsals:

> This morning the reserve of the Army under the Command of Major Gen'l Moore and the first brigade of the Line under Major Gen'l Coote, with a considerable proportion of Artillery from the different Men of War disembarked for practice; after going through the movements, it is intended they should execute in the face of the Enemy they re-embarked.[11]

Although they worked hard, the army found Marmoris a pleasant station; there was little sickness, provisions were good and the weather temperate. Jack Hill of the 23rd discovered that there was good shooting available and went several times

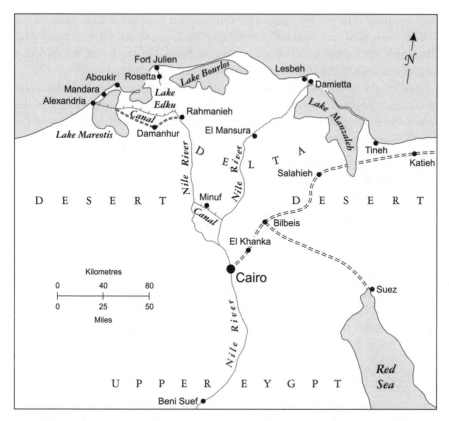

The Egyptian Campaign, 1801
Map © C. Johnson

ashore to hunt woodcocks, but not having proper weapons, he confessed that 'we did not get much to bring on board, we make a grand party soon, armed at all points, as there are a great number of wolves, bears & leopards here on the mountains'.[12]

After six weeks of relentless training, on 22 February 1801 Abercromby's army, 15,000 strong, sailed for Egypt confident in its leader, its training and its abilities.

The chosen landing place was Aboukir Bay, the site of Nelson's 1800 naval victory. Shallow water prevented the fleet from closing the shore and the first assault wave was forced to make a long approach to the beach. In all, it numbered some 5,000 troops and the 23rd Foot, 553 all ranks, formed part of Moore's 'reserve', which had the task of securing the right flank of the beachhead. The troops boarded the boats at 2 a.m. on 8 March 1801 and, after spending several hours getting into proper alignment, commenced rowing the four miles to the shore. 'We rowed very slow with our oars muffled', one seaman later commented, 'the water was very still; and all was as silent as death. No one spoke, but each cast an anxious look to the shore; then at each other, impatient to land'.[13]

As daylight came, the French saw the lines of boats moving towards them and about 1,800 enemy troops, including cavalry and artillery, were positioned on the beach. After a signal rocket was fired to indicate that the boats should close the beach, Moore remembered, his troops:

> ... were fired upon from fifteen pieces of artillery as soon as we were within reach, first with round shot, afterwards with grape, and at last by the infantry. The boats continued to row in steadily, and the sailors and soldiers occasionally huzzaed. Numbers were killed and wounded, and some boats were sunk. The fire of grape-shot and musketry were really most severe.[14]

Despite the heavy French fire, the assault troops were not daunted, comparing 'the fall of the bullets on the water to boys throwing handfuls of pebbles into a mill-pond'.[15] Disregarding their casualties, Moore's men continued to row toward the beach and, as soon as the boats grounded, 'officers and men sprang out, formed on the beach, and landed'.[16] Moore immediately led the flank companies of his brigade in an attack on a sand hill, about 180 feet high that overlooked the right flank of the beachhead. A participant recalled that it was hard going because:

> ... progress was retarded by the loose dry sand which so deeply covered the ascent, that the soldiers fell back half a pace every step they advanced. When about half way to the summit, they came in sight of the enemy, who poured down upon them a destructive volley of musketry. Redoubling their exertions, they gained the height before the enemy could reload their pieces; and, though exhausted with fatigue, and almost breathless, they drove the enemy from their position at the point of the bayonet.[17]

The sand hill taken, as well as four pieces of artillery, Moore halted until he 'could perceive what was being done upon the left, where a heavy fire of musketry was still kept up'.[18]

The two brigades attacking the centre and left of the beachhead experienced a more difficult time. French cavalrymen rode out into the surf to sabre men still in the boats but were beaten off. It took some hard fighting before the beachhead was fully secured. Abercromby had observed the attack on the sand hill from his boat and as soon as he was ashore, sought out Lieutenant Colonel Hall, shook his hand and said: 'My friend Hall, I am glad to see you; I shall never abuse you [the 23rd Foot] again.'[19]

Overall, the assault force lost 748 casualties in the landing, the Welch Fusiliers' share being forty-one killed, wounded and missing. Among the wounded were Captains Henry Ellis and Thomas Pearson, commanding the grenadier and light companies of the 23rd Foot respectively. After the battle was over and the dead buried, Sergeant Benjamin Miller of the Royal Artillery remembered, the British dressed their camp in 'awful grandeur', collecting all the dead Frenchmen's 'hats, caps, and helmets, and stuck them on pikes and poles in front of the tents, some covered with blood and some full of hair, skull, and brains of the late unfortunate wearer'.[20]

After taking four days to unload stores, artillery and equipment, on 12 March Abercromby advanced toward Alexandria, twelve miles distant. During the day his lead elements repulsed attacks by French infantry and cavalry but took heavy casualties from well-handled enemy artillery, forcing Abercromby to withdraw to a good defensive position along a ridge near some old ruins, which the army dubbed the 'Roman Camp'. Again, there was a pause while Abercromby brought up supplies preparatory to a further advance, and this permitted General Jacques Menou, the French commander in Egypt, to assemble 11,000 men with which he hoped to drive the British into the Mediterranean. His plan was to attack at first light, starting with a diversion on the British left flank and when that was accomplished he would make a major attack against the right flank held by Moore's brigade. Moore had positioned his troops in and around the extensive ruins of the 'Roman Camp:' the 28th Foot held a redoubt in front; the 56th Foot held the ruins; the 42nd were stationed outside to the left; and the 23rd was in reserve behind. Suspecting he would be attacked, Abercromby ordered his army to stand to their arms before dawn on 21 March and they were ready when Menou's diversion went in at about 3.30 a.m. An officer of the 42nd Foot recalled the opening stages of the battle:

> For half an hour no movement took place on either side, till the report of a musket, followed by that of some cannon, was heard on the left of the line. Upon this signal the enemy immediately advanced, and took possession of a small picquet, occupied by part of [Brigadier-General John] Stuart's regiments but they were instantly driven back. For a time silence again prevailed, but it was a stillness which portended a deadly struggle. As soon as he heard the firing, General Moore, who happened to be the general officer on duty during the night, had galloped off to the left; but an idea having struck him as he proceeded, that this was a false attack, he turned back and had hardly returned to his brigade when a loud huzza, succeeded by a roar of musketry, showed that he was not mistaken. The morning was unusually dark, cloudy, and close. The enemy advanced in silence until they approached the picquets, when they gave a shout and pushed forward.[21]

In the impetus of their attack, aided by the poor light, a French infantry battalion actually entered the ruins and desperate fighting ensued until Moore ordered forward the Welch Fusiliers. Lieutenant Jack Hill, with Pearson's light company, remembered that the 23rd Foot:

> ... mov'd up to the support of the 58 Regt. and halted about 60 paces from the front face of the ruin'd Roman building, the Light company being in front; the Lieut. Colonels company was on the left flank; the head of a French column was observ'd entering through the broken wall on the left face, the dawn of day shewed their hats, on which I wheeled the company up in silence and gave orders to fire at about 35 yards distance, during the 2nd discharge, Capn. Bradford brought up his company on the right, and the late Colonel Sir Henry Ellis his on the left, when the word 'Charge' was given, the openings [to the ruins] gain'd and about 340 prisoners made.[22]

'Our men attacked like wolves', Hill commented, 'transfixing the Frenchmen with their bayonets against the walls of the building'.[23]

A second French attack on the ruins was also repulsed. Frustrated, Menou ordered three regiments of dragoons to charge directly at the ruins. The horsemen surged around the redoubt of the 28th whose commander, Lieutenant Colonel Edward Paget, coolly ordered his rear rank to face about and put a volley into them, but managed to catch the 42nd still re-forming from the previous attack and rode through them. The Highlanders fought them off:

> Broken as the line was by the separation of the companies, it seemed almost impossible to resist with effect an impetuous charge of cavalry; yet every man stood firm. Many of the enemy were killed in the advance. The companies, who stood in compact bodies, drove back all who charged them, with great loss. Part of the cavalry passed through the intervals, and wheeling to their left, ... were received by the 28th, who, facing to their rear, poured on them a destructive fire, which killed many of them.[24]

Still, Menou would not give up the battle and brought the ridge under heavy artillery fire, while ordering forward a heavy screen of skirmishers who galled the British line. Finally, at about 9 a.m., he realised it was no use and ordered a withdrawal.

French losses in this engagement were about 2,500 while Abercromby lost 1,430 killed, wounded and missing with the Royal Welch Fusiliers suffering twenty killed and wounded. Moore, who was wounded along with Abercromby in the action, summarised the Battle of Alexandria: 'their numbers were superior to ours, they had the advantage of cavalry and a numerous well-served artillery; but our troops seem to have no idea of giving way, and there cannot be a more convincing proof of the superiority of our infantry'.[25] Sadly, a week after the battle,

Abercromby died of his wounds and was mourned by his entire army as, after so many years of frustration and defeats, he had given them several successive victories. Major General Sir John Hely-Hutchinson now assumed command.

The army was troubled much by illness and the 23rd Foot had 116 men on the sick list on 30 March 1801, including Lieutenant Colonel John Hall and Major James Mackenzie. Mackenzie's brother, Captain George Mackenzie, convinced him to go on board the fleet and saw him properly conveyed to the frigate, HMS *Heroine*, but was shocked, within hours of saying goodbye, to receive a note from that ship's surgeon informing him that James Mackenzie:

> … came on board yesterday evening very much exhausted; symptoms of inflamation [*sic*] about the Hypochondria was evident. – This afternoon about 4 the pulse sank, and a mortification of some of the Viscera of the abdomen took place which no doubt occasioned his death – He died about 10 o'clock the same evening.[26]

The next day George brought his brother's corpse ashore in a hastily-constructed coffin and buried him on shore of Aboukir Bay under a palm tree. Lieutenant Jack Hill read the service, which was also attended by Captain George Bradford. Among James Mackenzie's papers George found a memorandum dated 2 March 1801 shortly before the landing, directing that all James's worldly effects and funds should be given to his brother. George gave his snuffbox to Bradford and 'two or three trifling articles to his old friends of the Regt as a remembrance'.[27] James Mackenzie had served in the Royal Welch Fusiliers since 1780.

After the Battle of Alexandria Menou and part of his army had withdrawn into Alexandria while the remainder retreated to Cairo. Leaving a screening force outside Alexandria, Hely-Hutchinson took Ramanieh at the mouth of the Nile and pushed slowly up the river toward that place. The British were now joined by about 4,000 Turkish Mamelukes, whose costume intrigued them:

> They have no uniformity either in clothing, arms, or appointments; I mean as to the colour of their clothing, which is blue, black, brown, red, etc.; every soldier has a gun of some sorts, which Turko carries as he likes best, either across his shoulder, over his arm, or under it. They wear a kind of sash made of a sort of bunting, which passes half a dozen times round the body, and in which everything belonging to them is carried. All of them had a dirk, and a pair of large horse-pistols stuck in his sash, and they will any of them sell all or any part of their arms or appointments. ... Their tents consist of a long piece of canvas without any walls, under which about thirty of these turbaned heroes are either stretched at full length or squat on their bums smoking.[28]

Marching in the relative cool of the night and early morning, the army advanced on Cairo, passing seemingly endless mud brick villages. Sergeant Miller remembered that at one of these villages, the men in the ranks 'heard a great noise, much like the noise of turkey cocks'. As they came closer, the troops saw 'some hundreds of women's heads looking over the walls, warbling their tongues in a very ridiculous manner – their fashion of saluting us, so we displayed our Colours, and the Bands [were] ordered to play'.[29] With reference to the Egyptian women, Lieutenant Thomas Evans of the 8th Foot made a surprisingly modern comment:

> ... melancholy is the state of the female of this country, doomed to perpetual bondage from her earliest infancy, she has no alternative than in a perfect resignation to the tyrannic will of the male, for to no purpose, has Heaven or the soul of its image ... imprest ... these monsters in the shape of men, acting under the influence of a religion ... barbarous in its tenets, deny that women possess souls and consequently consign the wretched mortals, from the moment of their birth, to drudgery, pain and labour; they are required (exclusive of the management of the domestic affairs, and satisfying the sensual appetites of the men) to reap, get together the produce of the land, tend the cattle and perform or superintend every other kind of husbandry, whilst their lords rest in idleness and debauch.[30]

Cairo was invested in early June and after a few days of negotiation the French commander, General Augustin-Daniel Belliard, agreed to surrender the city on generous terms, which included the transport of his army of 13,672 men to France at British expense. Once terms had been agreed, the two armies were quite friendly towards each other, as Evans of the 8th Foot recorded, and a meeting place was created about midway between the two forces 'where a kind of sale is established, at which the French sell or barter whatever they think proper. Mameluke sabres either real, or of specious manufacture (in their possession) are more especially brought up with avidity, and at enormous prices by the English officers'.[31]

Turning over the occupation of Cairo to another British force, which had arrived from India, Hely-Hutchinson's army escorted Belliard's troops down the Nile to Rosetta, their intended point of embarkation. During the march, there were many difficulties with the Turks, who wanted to slaughter the French out of hand and at one point, Miller commented, the British 'were obliged to go between the French army and the Turks, or else they would have destroyed the poor Frenchmen'.[32] Had the Turks attacked, he added, 'they would all have been killed, for our army was drawn up in order of battle, guns loaded and matches lighted.' With Belliard's troops safely embarked, Hely-Hutchinson next turned to Alexandria but Menou, realising his position was hopeless, finally surrendered and 10,524 more French soldiers were soon on their way home, again courtesy of the British taxpayer. Thus, the campaign in Egypt came to a victorious conclusion.

After years of defeat, the victory in Egypt restored the self-confidence and pride of the British army, which 'regained its ancient standing in the estimation' of its own people.[33] To honour their success, the regiments which fought in Egypt were granted a 'distinguished mark of His Royal Majesty's approbation' and 'a lasting memorial of the glory acquired', in the form of a badge to be worn on their Colours consisting of a Sphinx with the words, 'Egypt'.[34] The sultan of the Ottoman empire, highly pleased with the whole affair – as well he might be – presented the Order of the Crescent complete with a garish orange ribbon to every officer who served in the operation. The Egyptian campaign had provided excellent training for a new and rising generation of British officers, including Thomas Dalmer, Henry Ellis, Jack Hill, Francis Offley and Thomas Pearson of the Welch Fusiliers.

When news of the success in Egypt reached Britain in early October 1801, it found the government of Prime Minister Henry Addington engaged in peace negotiations with Bonaparte. Addington had replaced William Pitt when the latter, after nearly twenty years in office, resigned over a political crisis. The British people, tired of high wartime taxes and inflation, longed for an end to the seemingly interminable conflict and Addington gave it to them. For his part, Bonaparte also wished an end to hostilities so that he could consolidate his regime. On 1 October 1801, a ceasefire took place bringing to a close more than eight years of fighting.

When the hostilities ended, the Royal Welch Fusiliers were stationed at Malta. Two months later, they were transferred to Gibraltar, which was not a popular station – one officer calling it 'a wretched hole' with 'no amusement but gaming and drinking'.[35] Lieutenant Jack Hill, always careful with his finances, hated the place because of the high cost of living and complained that it robbed him of five months pay and 'upwards of twenty pound pocket money almost'.[36] At this time the 23rd Foot was very weak – only 290 all ranks were reported fit for duty at the end of December – but officers and men enjoyed Christmas as best they could. After Hill made sure that the men of his company got a good dinner consisting of 'boild beef, plum pudding, potatoes, & a bottle of porter each', he left them as soon as he could, 'as an officer looking on would be a check, and consequently make them less comfortable'.[37] Hill planned to dine at the Fusilier officers' mess, to which his comrades had invited many guests, but having time to write a letter home to his family in Devon, wished he was able 'to look in on you this very moment – here I am with my coat and waistcoat off, my fire out, while you are enjoying your Xmas fire'.[38]

In May 1802 life in Gibraltar got much worse when the Duke of Kent arrived as the new governor. The fourth son of George III, Kent was a disciplinarian of the first order who was obsessed with the minutiae of military life. His father, who rather disliked him, tried to keep him out of Britain as much as possible but as there was concern over the state of the Gibraltar garrison, which exhibited 'laxity of all military rule and insubordination', Kent seemed just the man to correct these faults.[39] His older brother, the Duke of York, therefore sent him to his new post with the instruction that he was 'to exact the most minute attention to all His Majesty's regulations for disciplining, arming, from all of which not the most trifling deviation can be permitted'.[40]

Kent not only followed these instructions to the letter, he considerably exceeded them, turning life in the Gibraltar garrison into something resembling a penal colony. Officers and men were ordered to rise at 3 a.m. in the summer and 5 a.m. in the winter and there were two daily 'minute inspections' when all officers and men were to parade in full equipment, including greatcoats, the officers to check the NCOs and the NCOs to check the private soldiers to ensure every piece of clothing and equipment was 'marked with the Company's Letter, and the whole Set has the same number, that every Man has his own, and that none of the Marks or Numbers are disfaced'.[41] Officers were to have their hair cut by the same barber in each regiment during the first week of every month, 'and no oftener', and the length at the back was not to exceed 'a line formed by passing a packthread' from the back of one ear to the back of the other.[42] Every officer and man was to attend divine service, and while listening to the inspiring words of the clergyman, were to stand in the same position and no other, officers to have 'their left hands placed, with their fingers extended, upon their Scabbards, & keeping their right Arms, at the same time, close to the body, with the fingers of that hand in like manner extended'.[43] Sergeants were not permitted to converse or socialise with corporals nor corporals with privates 'except on Duty under pain of being punished'.[44] The unkindest cut of all was that the men of the garrison were warned that, on Christmas Eve and the national feast days of St. Andrew, St. David, St. George and St. Patrick, traditional holidays which soldiers celebrated, there was to be no 'Intemperance & Indiscipline' and nothing would protect any offenders 'from the Punishment they merit if guilty of excess'.[45]

As one soldier remembered, Kent's 'tyranny was exerted with all the power and force he could suggest'.[46] The duke punished frequently and severely – Sergeant Miller of the Royal Artillery witnessed 'five men tied up and flogged all together by the tap of the drum, for small crimes'.[47] Soldiers became so exasperated with this unrelenting repression that some committed suicide and others deserted to the Spanish. After seven months, and just before Christmas 1802, the men of the 1st and 25th Foot rebelled. As Miller recalled, it was a terrible time as the entire garrison:

> ... was ordered under arms to protect the Duke, whom they intended to kill. Many of the Royals [1st Foot] were shot before they could get their redress. I was Gunner on Waterport Guard. The Captain of the Guard came to me and ordered me to reverse guns that were pointing to the Spanish lines and point them on my comrade soldiers, who but a short time before had been fighting with me in Egypt. This was a horrid

Christmas, for the night after Christmas, we were formed up against another Regiment [the 25th Foot] who broke out in rebellion, and killed many of them. I was at a gun that was formed up close in front of them and expected every man of us would have been put to death, our guns loaded and matches lighted. They frequently cried out 'Charge the Bugars [*sic*].'. 'Fire a volley at the Bugars.' I was more afraid than ever I was fighting against the French, and we found it more dangerous to fight against exasperated British soldiers standing out for their rights. They at last went off to their Barracks and all the regiments in the garrison surrounded them until daylight.[48]

The ring-leaders of this near mutiny were court-martialled: three men were executed in the presence of the assembled garrison, eleven were transported to Australia and many more were flogged. When news of this matter reached the King, however, he removed Kent from the governorship at Gibraltar and, fortunately for the British army, he was never again given an active command.

This being the case, it is somewhat surprising that when Kent inspected the Royal Welch Fusiliers on 4 March 1803, he was full of praise. He found the officers, non-commissioned officers and soldiers to be of high quality although he noted that the officers did not have gorgets or regulation swords and the private soldiers were rather short 'but stout, active and fit for any service'. In fact, Kent was so pleased that he recommended the adjutant and sergeant-major to his brother, the Duke of York, as meriting 'any mark of favour which he may choose to bestow upon them'.[49]

About two months later, on 17 May 1803, the British government, exasperated by Bonaparte's constant breaches of the terms of the Treaty of Amiens signed a year before – and trusting him not at all – declared war on France. A few weeks afterward, the Royal Welch Fusiliers embarked at Gibraltar for Britain.

Come all you ancient Britons of every degree,
Come enter with us in our brave TWENTY THREE,
And a bounty you'll have in proportion to years,
By joining the Corps of the Welch Fusiliers.

Then avoid all bad masters who will not pay your due,
Come enter with us and we will give bail for you,
And we'll make them repent in sorrow and tears
On your joining our regiment of Welch Fusiliers.

Our regiment at Worcester where it now doth lie
Is completing so fast I'd have you comply
And without hesitation join us volunteers
Of the Twenty Third or Welch Fusiliers.

A health unto his Majesty the Prince of Wales also
Likewise to all brave fellows that's not dismayed to go
And fight for their Country like brave volunteers
Along with ancient Britons, the WELCH FUSILIERS.[1]

Chapter 4

'Where are the men to come from?'

1st Battalion, Britain, Germany and Denmark, 1803–1807
2nd Battalion, Britain, 1804–1808

WHEN THE ROYAL WELCH FUSILIERS ARRIVED in Britain in August 1803 the nation was in a state of anxiety, nervously anticipating a French invasion. Bonaparte had massed what he termed his *Grande Armée* on the Channel coast and was busy building landing craft in preparation for an amphibious landing on the opposite shore. Although Lord St. Vincent, First Sea Lord and the senior officer of the Royal Navy, assured his countrymen that a seaborne invasion was impossible given Britain's maritime superiority, many were not convinced and some began to talk of an airborne attack, with Bonaparte's troops being lifted over the Channel in gigantic balloons. The press both attempted to agitate and calm the public. The *Cambrian*, the major newspaper in Wales, advised its readers to 'be on the alert!' but assured them that 'Your native courage, acknowledged proficiency and military discipline, and the recollections of the glorious deeds performed by your illustrious predecessors in former times, will stimulate you to imitate their noble example.'[2]

The entire southern coast England was nervous. After their return, the 23rd Foot were stationed at Freshwater Gate on the Isle of Wight and Jack Hill recorded that when one Sunday morning, 'a vessell with French Colours flying came within musquet shot', the 23rd Foot stood to its arms and 'informed the people in the Fort of it who immediately opened upon her'.[3] When the strange vessel did not reply, an officer was sent out in a boat to investigate and the intruder 'proved to be a prize' commanded by a midshipman who, 'not having any other colours on board, thought it finer to wear French than none' but 'very soon took the hint from the 18 P[ounde]rs. [guns] and downed colours in a short time'.[4]

In September 1803 Hill informed his parents that should the enemy attempt a landing, the Welch Fusiliers would 'give them a warm reception, we are busy entrenching ourselves in Freshwater Gate in this part of the Island'.[5] Like most regular soldiers, Hill was confident that any invasion would swiftly be defeated, as 'François' would have no cavalry if he did attempt to land and 'had better take care how he quits the covering fire of his Gunboats that our Navy allow him to keep'. 'We shall be disappointed', he added, if Bonaparte 'does not come now that we are prepared for his reception'.[6] When there was no sign of the French by December 1803, Hill was puzzled: 'Bonaparte is not yet come, what can he be driving at?'[7] By the time the regiment moved to Hailsham Barracks in Sussex five months later, Hill believed that the invasion was delayed by the internal political situation in France, or as he put it, 'the slippery ground upon which that consummate villain Buonaparte stands only prevents the sailing of the Fleet destin'd for our invasion'.[8] During the following summer, when the Welch Fusiliers were camped near Beachy Head, he reminded his parents that this was not far from where William the Conqueror had landed in 1066 and, thus the 'old Welch are again at one of the posts of honour'.[9]

Perhaps so, but the regiment's strength remained low. On the first day of 1804, Lieutenant Colonel Hall reported only 389 all ranks present, a shortage of 361 officers and men from establishment. After its return to Britain the regiment had as many as six recruiting parties scouring England and Wales for men, but at the end of October an inspecting officer noted that its strength of 550 men was still 200 short of establishment and added that many recruits recently acquired in London had since deserted.

Increasing the regiment's strength was the biggest problem facing Lieutenant Colonel James Losack who replaced Lieutenant Colonel John Hall when the latter retired in November 1804. Aged 49, Losack had first been commissioned in the 43rd Foot in 1773 and had fought in the American Revolutionary War but had not seen much active service since then.[10] The task facing Losack was eased somewhat when rumours went about in late 1804 that the Welch Fusiliers would shortly be raising a second battalion – but as the newly-promoted Captain Jack Hill pointed out, 'where are the men to come from?'[11]

At this point, we will leave the 1/23rd Foot, weak in numbers but strong in spirit, in their camp at Beachy Head near Eastbourne, gazing out at the Channel for French sails, to take up the story of the Royal Welch Fusiliers' new battalion.

The creation of a second battalion for the 23rd Foot was a direct outcome of a severe military manpower crisis. In 1803, when the war resumed, Britain, with a population of about 16 million, faced France, which had 33 million. With the power of universal conscription, Napoleon commanded an army of nearly 450,000 men, many of them veteran troops, and could also call on manpower from his allies and occupied nations which, although not the same quality as the French army, more than doubled that figure. Against this, in early 1804 the regular British army consisted of 150,593 British and foreign regulars, of which only about 90,000 were stationed in the home islands, the remainder garrisoning the overseas colonies. The regulars were backed up by two 'home defence' organisations – the militia and the volunteers – not liable for service outside Britain of which the militia, 89,000 strong in 1804, was by far the superior. Organised by county from men balloted or conscripted for five years, it was armed, equipped and trained as regulars and constituted a useful reserve. Although they numbered over 450,000, the volunteers – part-time soldiers with extremely variable training but usually fantastic uniforms – were considerably less useful. There were, however, enough armed men of one description or another in Britain to defeat any French invading force that might get by the Royal Navy – which was very doubtful.[12]

But for Britain to wage an offensive war was quite another matter because the government could barely replace the regular army's annual losses. Between 1793 and 1801, 226,506 soldiers had been recruited into the army but 145,481 had been lost through combat, desertion, sickness and shipwreck. When war resumed in 1803, it became clear that something would have to be done to maintain the army at its existing strength, let alone increase it. For the next several years, the government wrestled with the problem of how to keep the army up to strength without imposing universal conscription – the best solution – and passed a number of palliative measures that, although they brought men into the ranks, barely maintained the army's numbers. The government knew that the British people would support impressment or conscription for the Royal Navy, the nation's first line of defence, but would not tolerate it for the army, which remained unpopular because of its use as a police force, coupled with its awful losses in the West Indies in the 1790s. Of the various initiatives undertaken to solve the army's manpower problem, two proved most effective: the creation of second battalions for its infantry regiments and massive recruiting from the militia.[13]

On 19 April 1804 the War Office sent out a circular letter to the colonels of nine regiments of foot authorising them to raise a second battalion. This was a departure from tradition since up to this time in the war most British regiments – with some exceptions – possessed only a single battalion. The prime purpose of these new second battalions, which were ultimately raised by most regiments, was to recruit and train men for their first battalions, which would serve overseas although, as we shall see, necessity sometimes saw second battalions sent on foreign service. The 1804 circular set out the establishment of officers and men in each of the new units and permitted officers of the first battalions to 'recruit for rank', that is, they could gain one step in rank if they raised a certain number of men. A captain would attain a majority if he raised ninety men; a lieutenant would gain a captaincy if he raised forty-five men and a second lieutenant might gain promotion if he raised ten men. This being the case, when active recruiting for the 2nd Battalion of the 23rd Foot started during the winter of 1804-1805, many officers of the 1/23rd went on that service to gain promotion.[14]

Among them were Captains Francis Offley and Thomas Pearson and they were later followed by Captain Thomas Dalmer. Jack Hill did not get involved, for not only did he think it impossible to 'raise the numbers specified', he was also angling for a staff appointment.[15] Henry Ellis, on the other hand, now at the top of the captains' seniority list, gained promotion to major when a vacancy occurred after Major Evan Jones was promoted lieutenant colonel to command the new 2nd Battalion at the end of 1804. Despite Hill's claims that recruiting for rank was impossible, both Offley and Pearson reached major's rank by this method during the first eighteen months of the second battalion's existence.[16]

Finding men, however, was not easy. Recruiting parties from every regiment in the army were fishing for new blood across the British Isles. As one NCO who was a veteran of this activity commented, recruiting consisted, in his case, of taking a drummer and fifer and attending 'all Wakes, Races and Revels within twenty miles of London' where they 'had to strut about in our best Coats, and swaggering, Sword in hand, drumming our way through the masses, commingled with glazing clodpolls, gingerbread mechanics, and thimbleprick sharpeners'.[17]

When getting men the three greatest inducements were alcohol, cash bounties and unemployment. The sergeant of a recruiting party, resplendent in his best uniform, complete with sash, sword and ribbons would buy a drink for all and sundry males in a pub of his choice (usually chosen with a prior transfer of coin to the publican), spin a tale of 'Gentlemen soldiers, merry life, muskets rattling, cannons roaring, drums beating, colours flying, regiments charging and shouts of victory!' and try to hook a fish.[18] The cash bounties – between £16 and £17 in the case of a potential recruit for the 23rd Foot – were attractive at a time when a servant was lucky if he made £3 per year and a farm labourer fortunate if he brought home a £1 a month. Of course, what the recruiting sergeant did not tell his prey was that from the bounty he would only receive about £11, as there were deductions for his 'necessaries' or personal kit (including shirts, shoes, pack, leggings, stockings, brushes, black ball, combs, straps for great coats, stock and clasp) and for certain expenses, and that the recruiting party itself would genially assist him in drinking what remained. Overall, unemployment – particularly in the Midlands where thousands of hand weavers had been thrown out of work by the advent of industrialisation – was probably the most effective inducement, the army being the best of a hard choice between military service and the parish poorhouse.[19]

A set procedure had to be completed before a man was legally enlisted. He had to sign the proper forms, pass a medical examination and be 'attested' before a magistrate who would verify that he was sober and then read him those sections of the Articles of War dealing with mutiny and desertion. As both doctor and magistrate were paid by the Crown for these services, recruiting could be a profitable activity for them and many medical examinations were not that diligent, while magistrates attested men reeking of alcohol when legally they were supposed to be sober. Recruiting sergeants always knew which doctors and magistrates could be relied on to easily pass such men and brought them much business.[20]

Changing Quarters, *c.* 1805
This print by J. A. Atkinson shows a battalion changing its quarters in Britain. Units were constantly on the move throughout the war and the artist has aptly illustrated the fatigue, boredom, work and confusion of a change of station. Note the soldier's wife to the left of the mounted officer. *(Author's collection)*

In terms of age and size, so desperate was the need for men that the army took what it could get. Recruiters regularly overlooked the regulations specifying that no man was to be enlisted for the infantry who was above thirty years of age or under five feet, five inches in height, who was 'not stout and well made' or who had 'the least Appearance of Sore Legs, Scurvy, Scald Head, or other Infirmity, that may render him unfit for His Majesty's Service'.[21] By regulation, even boys under age sixteen (euphemistically called 'growing lads') with a minimum height of five feet, four inches, were taken provided they were 'perfectly well limbed, open Chested, and what is commonly called long in the Fork'.[22]

Owing to the competition for men, it took more than two years to raise the new 2nd Battalion. In early February 1805 it had just four officers and 36 men but things improved the following month when its strength rose to 129 all ranks – of an authorised establishment of more than a thousand all ranks. By June it reported only 135 all ranks and, it being clear that the battalion was having difficulties, its establishment was lowered to 400. This did not entirely solve the problem as, even at the end of 1805, it was still short of its establishment by 253 men. For the first two years of its existence, the 2nd Battalion's headquarters were at Wrexham in Denbighshire and recruiting efforts were concentrated in north Wales but when they proved unsuccessful, in December 1805 its recruiting area was extended into the adjoining counties of England. A year later, the 2nd Battalion reported a strength of 400, which showed some improvement, and this being the case, its establishment was increased to 600 and later 800 men.

At this point, the second effective government measure to increase the size of the regular army came into play. In early 1807 the government sought 28,000 men from the ranks of the militia, using generous bounties as an incentive and militia regimental commanding officers as recruiters. Although the bounties were expensive to the Crown, recruiting militiamen proved cheaper than trying to get civilians to enlist, and since most of these men had been in service since the resumption of the war in 1803, they were well trained. The response was good and between 1807 and 1809, 49,313 militiamen – most of them trained soldiers – volunteered into the regular army. This success led to the development of a system that remained in place for the duration of the war whereby second battalions recruited men from the militia, trained them, and then sent them to the first battalions of their regiments as reinforcements.[23] Another incentive was that in 1806 the government permitted soldiers to enlist for limited terms, seven years in the case of the infantry. Prior to that, enlistment had been for life, usually taken as meaning twenty-one years.

The 2/23rd Foot obtained immediate benefits from the widespread enlistment of militiamen, obtaining 385 recruits by this means in 1807 alone. Its strength increased by June of that year, and an inspection report for the battalion, now at Chester, noted that it had 646 men and was much 'improved in point of height and appearance'.[24] Battalion Orders issued regarding training are of interest:

(5) Men to be drilled for one hour in the morning, viz. from half-past seven till half-past eight in squads (when they are to breakfast), and again from two to three in squads or otherwise. The non-commissioned officers to be drilled once a day under the direction either of the adjutant or sergeant-major.

(6) At every parade some manoeuvring or marching is to take place.

(7) The pendulum and taps of the drum to be resorted to ensure correct marching, and pacing sticks to ensure the length of the step.[25]

As its strength increased, the 2nd Battalion began to fulfil its primary function and, throughout 1807, sent drafts totalling 333 officers and men to the 1/23rd. In the autumn when it went to Loughrea in Ireland, the 2/23rd had a strength of 702 all ranks, not far short of establishment.

The 2nd Battalion went through a number of changes of command. Lieutenant Colonel Evan Jones appears to have been frequently absent and Major Thomas Pearson is noted as being in command on several occasions from 1804 to 1806, and Major Francis Offley in 1807. In April of that year Jones assumed command of the 1st Battalion after Lieutenant Colonel Losack retired from service. Jones was replaced as commanding officer of the 2nd Battalion by Lieutenant Colonel William Wyatt, a veteran of fifteen years of service with the 29th Foot, but this succession did not take place for nearly a year and in the interim, the newly-promoted Major Thomas Dalmer commanded the battalion.[26]

One very positive result arising from the creation of the 2nd Battalion was that it initiated a process by which the Royal Welch Fusiliers became a truly Welsh regiment. Although this may sound strange, despite the fact that the regiment's title had first been linked with the Principality in 1702 and it took great pride in this connection, it had only served in Wales once prior to 1805 and that was in 1729 when a company had been briefly stationed at Wrexham. The 23rd Foot had always recruited throughout Britain but now an increasing number of true Welshmen began to enter both its officer and enlisted ranks. In December 1806, an inspecting officer noted that, of the 400 men in the 2nd Battalion, ninety-seven were Irish, eighty-five Welsh, seven Scots and the remainder English – the first time the designation 'Welsh' appears in these particular records.[27]

The process accelerated when widespread recruiting from the militia commenced in 1807. There were thirteen Welsh militia regiments, one for every county in the principality, and it seems clear that – in their own minds at least – they believed in a link with the 23rd Foot as no fewer than five styled themselves 'fusilier' regiments.[28] From 1807 onwards, as the 2nd Battalion received a steady stream of volunteers from these units who were later sent to the 1st Battalion, the number of Welshmen in the 23rd Foot began to rise. In March 1807, it was noted by an inspecting officer that of 991 men in the 1st Battalion, 146 or 14 per cent were Welsh. In August 1808, of a strength of 744 men in the 1/23rd, no fewer than 200 or about 28 per cent were Welsh, while in May 1809, when the 2/23rd was inspected at Horsham, of 788 men, 437 or 55 per cent were Welsh. Over the next five years, while the percentage fluctuates, the extant records reveal that when a 'Welsh' identifier is provided, the proportion of Welshmen in the two battalions of the 23rd Foot varied but was generally between 30 and 40 per cent of the enlisted soldiers. Indeed, by the autumn of 1807 there were so many Welshmen with similar surnames serving in the 1st Battalion that they 'had to be distinguished as "David Davis 3rd", "Robert Roberts 3rd", and "John Jones 6th".'[29]

The intensive recruiting carried out in the years immediately following the resumption of hostilities in 1803 brought men into the 23rd Foot who would serve it well in the hard campaigns that lay ahead. Among them was Richard Bentinck from Bacton, Suffolk, who has left behind a memoir of his service. When his father and two brothers joined the army, Bentinck's mother sent him at the age of eight to earn his 'porridge' but after a series of low paid jobs with long hours, at the age of sixteen Bentinck 'availed himself of that common expedient of the needy' and decided to enlist.[30] He was on his way into Bury St. Edmunds to do so in January 1807 when he encountered the 2nd Battalion marching out of that town and thereupon joined the Welch Fusiliers. Because of his small size, Bentinck was made a drummer and given a bounty of £16, which was just as quickly removed from him, one way or the other, authorised or not.[31]

At first, Richard Bentinck did not much enjoy soldiering, remembering that 'every scrap of leather had to be heel-balled, every inch of piping pipe-clayed, and even the gun barrels were kept bright, for the great suffering of the unhappy warriors'.[32] But what he really disliked was the morning ritual of dressing his hair which, as he commented:

> ... was not indeed a task to be laughed at, under the absurd military fashion then prevalent. In the first place every man had to use at least half a pound of flour a week to powder his hair with, making it look like an unbaked cake clapped upon his head and pressed carefully down upon his face. But this was not all. The curling irons had to be used with great exactitude to make two or three little curls, like those on a drake's tail, on each temple, and woe betide the unlucky fellow who appeared on parade with one of these a shade out of twist. Then a tail of horse hair had to be fitted to the back of the head, bound up with a bit of leather shining like a mirror with 'heel ball' and tied, every hair in its place with string or wire.
>
> Those who could not manage this intricate business and who came in for the punishment drill rigorously imposed for any real or imaginary defect in his work, (and there were many) paid sixpence a week to any dexterous comrade who would do it for them. Which was thus not over paid considering that a shake of the customer's head would subject the artist to penalties.[33]

Samuel Thorpe, the same age as Bentinck but at the opposite end of the military social scale, was commissioned a second lieutenant in the 2/23rd Foot in 1808. Thorpe was actually a rarity among Welch Fusilier officers because he was a graduate of the Junior Department of the Royal Military College at Marlow in Buckinghamshire, created by the Duke of York in 1802 to train prospective regimental officers. It had been a struggle for Thorpe to get his mother to accept his wishes to join the army as she was set on him becoming a clergyman, and constantly lectured him 'upon the pleasures of rural retirement, and, as she termed it, a snug parsonage'.[34] Toward this end, Thorpe was first sent to Westminster School to train for the Church and only liberated after his older brother, a serving officer, managed to get Thorpe's father's consent to him going to Marlow. It was a happy 14-year-old who bade farewell to Westminster as 'caps, black gowns, and fagging ... Curacies, livings, and bishoprics were now lost sight of in more general prospects, while Homer, Virgil, and Ovid gave way to ditches, redoubts, and demilunes.'[35] Just managing to pass the entrance examination, Thorpe became a gentleman cadet and with the other new entrants was:

... were ushered into the Serjeant-Major's quarters; when I was ordered to take off my civil inexpressibles, and was soon braced up in a pair of College titoos, and gaiters; and a polished leather stock was buckled round my neck until I was almost black in the face. The solace, as I thought, of all my woe, the smart scarlet jacket was now produced, and buttoned up so tight that I could scarcely breathe; the large felt cap with the heavy silver plate was placed on my head like an extinguisher; and now being from head to foot in the pillory, or like a boy in armour, I was turned out to the parade, much to the amusement of the monkeys who had seen more of the world than I had. I almost repented my rash choice; I walked about like a marching mummy, and felt almost choked with grief as well as with my most unaccommodating stock; like most new acquaintances we were very stiff at first, but years of intimacy have made us quite easy in each other's company. It was not many hours before I was introduced to the drill squad, vulgarly called awkward, when I was destined to practice the graceful position of the goose step. ...

In a few days my stock seemed less stiff, the jacket buttoned easier, the blues were less tight, drill went on well, and ... I ventured even to write to my father, and tell him how happy I felt, and how much pleased I was with my new profession.[36]

Thorpe remained at Marlow for two years and was promoted a cadet officer. When time came to graduate he was offered a commission in the 2/23rd Foot and, just turned sixteen, joined the battalion at Loughrea in Ireland in 1808. He never forgot the warm welcome he received from Lieutenant Colonel William Wyatt and his fellow officers:

With some difficulty I found out the situation of my new corps, and as soon as the parade was over presented my letters of introduction to my Commanding Officer. The cordiality of welcome to my new profession, and the kindness with which he introduced me to my future companions soon made me shake off all the *mauvaise honte* of a youngster first entering the world, so that it was scarcely half an hour before I found myself quite happy and at home in my new situation. ... My camp equipage was produced (which I had furnished myself with in Dublin), my tent pitched, my camp-bed, table, and stools put up, my canteen opened, my trunks unpacked, and when the dinner drum beat for the roast beef of Old England, I was equipped in full uniform; not a little proud of the two epaulets (then worn by my corps), and the rich gold lace with which the coat and facings were ornamented, to say nothing of the hat and feather.

I was again introduced by the Colonel as a member of the regimental mess. The interior of the mess tent was novel and pleasing: the expensive and elegant plate with which the table was profusely covered (after the simple College board), quite astonished me; the appearance of so many members in rich dresses; and, above all, the martial music of a fine band, completed my ideas of earthly grandeur and felicity. I retired early to my tent, and scarcely slept from the novelty of my situation.[37]

Another young officer, Grismond Philipps from Cwmgwilly, Carmarthenshire, had a somewhat less auspicious entrance into service. Commissioned a second lieutenant in the 2/23rd Foot at the age of seventeen in August 1809, Philipps joined it at Horsham and almost immediately ran into financial problems. As he explained to his father:

> Major [Thomas] D[almer]. tells me that I must have a Bed which I can get here just about £14.0.0, and indeed I think it will be much better buying one at once, than paying 1.6 a night for one in the town. I shall only want a great coat, boots and shoes, and some pantaloons, all of which I can get here, if you send me money.
>
> The money you gave me is nearly gone, I have been obliged to buy different things to furnish my room with such as curtains, for the windows, brushes, blacking, etc. etc. All these little things come to a great deal of money you know.
>
> As to my pay Major D[almer]. says I cannot receive any pay just yet, as we are paid at present by the commander of the districk [sic]. I shall be obliged to pay the mess £3.3s.0d and my servant is to have 1s.0d a week, besides a jacket & trousers to do his work in.[38]

His father sent him the requisite funds, but a month later Philipps reported that his mess bills were expensive as 'it costs me £2 4s 0d every Week, we pay 14s every Week for our dinner, and 1s 6d every afternoon for Wine, and a Shilling for Breakfast, &c. &c'.[39] To assure his parents that he was trying to economise, Grismond enclosed a list of items he had purchased and their cost – the aforementioned bed, as well as boots, shoes, pantaloons, jackets and trousers for his servant, mess fees, great coat, gorget and a plume for his hat – which he managed to add up incorrectly but which came to £33 19s 1d.[40]

Things shortly began to get worse. In October 1809 when the 2nd Battalion was under orders for Colchester, Grismond asked for:

> ... some money to pay my Mess bill and for different things I have had since, which will amount to £20. My mess bill alone coming to £10. My pay is never sufficient to pay my mess bill alone. I shall not be able to leave until I hear from you. I also want about £10 to pay my marching expenses.[41]

His father apparently sent £15 to help out but Grismond forgot to thank him as, in February 1810 after a reminder, he confesses himself 'quite ashamed that I have delayed so long without answering your letter with the £15; but I hope you excuse it, as I have not been very well lately'.[42] Grismond apologised for getting into debt but assured his father that he 'may depend that I shall never trouble you again on that account, as I have now experienced what a miserable thing it is to be in debt'.[43] Easier said than done for less than a month later, we find Grismond writing to inform his long-suffering father that, 'As the Regiment is under orders to march for Guernsey, and as the people of Horsham will not trust me any longer, I wish you will have the Goodness to send me some money to pay them; otherwise I shall be arrested [for debt], which will be very unpleasant'.[44] At this point, the local merchants to whom Grismond owed money went to Lieutenant Colonel Wyatt, who wrote directly to the young officer's father about his son's financial and legal situation. In response, Mr. Philipps assured Wyatt that he would pay Grismond's debts and inquired what an adequate allowance would be for him. Wyatt's response was that, 'from all I can learn from the Officers that Lt Philips's debts have arisen from imprudence and not vice' and suggested that an annual allowance of £80 would be suitable.[45] It is clear that Wyatt had an interview, or perhaps a number of interviews with Grismond, which could not have been comfortable for the young man. It is not certain, however, that Second Lieutenant Philipps got the message, for soon after, he informed his father that

> As I understand from Colonel Wyatt that you will allow me eighty pounds a year independant [*sic*] of my pay, I should be much obliged to you if you would permit me to draw upon you on the twenty-fourth of every month, as all the officers who are allowed anything besides their pay draw it on that day: and it will be much more convenient for me to have it at that time than at the end of the month. ...
>
> P.S. As I was very much in want of money when I arrived in this place, in consequence of my being detained at the Army depot Isle of Wight, I have taken the liberty to draw on you for ten pounds, which I hope you will honour.[46]

Perhaps a more promising new arrival was John Harrison who, at the age of sixteen, was commissioned a second lieutenant in the 1st Battalion in early 1805. Harrison was a Worcestershire militia officer and a neighbour of Major Henry Ellis, who convinced him to join the 23rd Foot. He would serve with the Royal Welch Fusiliers for thirty-two years in war and peace and play an important role in its history.[47]

We left the 1st Battalion in their camp at Beachy Head near Eastbourne in 1804 watching for French sails in the Channel. In the intervening time, major events had taken place on the continent. In early 1805 William Pitt, who had returned to lead the government, managed to create a new Third Coalition of Austria, Britain, Russia and Sweden. Napoleon, who had been crowned emperor by acclamation the previous year, was infuriated when he learned of this alliance and in August, moved his army, 270,000 strong, from the Channel coast into central Europe. In October he surrounded one Austrian army at Ulm and forced it to surrender and then prepared to advance on Vienna. Three days later, a Franco-Spanish fleet numbering more than forty warships, left Cadiz and threatened to enter the Mediterranean where it would tip the balance of naval power in that sea. Finally, in late October, Pitt, anxious to assist Austria in her time of need, decided to dispatch a large British force to the mouth of the River Elbe to try and establish a new front in northern Europe. The 1/23rd Foot was ordered to join this expedition and on 23 October marched for Deal and then Ramsgate to embark.

Jack Hill was delayed leaving Eastbourne and was not with the battalion when they embarked at Ramsgate. He had been having problems selling his horse as potential customers, fully aware he was going abroad, proved to be stubborn bargainers and in the end, Hill was nearly 'obliged to give her away'.[48] He arrived at Ramsgate somewhat the worse for wear, having 'been marching and riding from daylight till very late for four days in the same clothes' and complained that his 'unfortunate old regimental coat is out at the elbows'.[49] The battalion officers, at anchor in a transport, managed to inform him that they had not been given enough time to buy their 'sea stock', and asked for help. The term 'sea stock' requires some explanation. When the army embarked on transports, the soldiers were fed but officers were expected to bring their own victuals, for which they were given a certain amount of money, which was never enough to cover the actual cost of purchase.[50] Since his brother officers either faced starvation or paying an exorbitant price to obtain food from the master of the transport, Hill managed to bring away a leg of mutton and some bread when he was rowed out to the ship.

On 29 October the Elbe expedition, which would ultimately number 26,000 troops, sailed and was at sea when news reached Britain of Nelson's great victory at Trafalgar which, although it rendered the nation safe from invasion for the foreseeable future, brought Britain no closer to defeating France.

The Royal Welch Fusiliers disembarked on 17 November and were billeted on the banks of the Weser. On 2 December 1805 Napoleon gained a major victory over a combined Austro-Russian army at Austerlitz, causing Austria to sue for peace. Although Russia remained in the war, the Third Coalition dissolved, putting the British troops in Germany in an untenable position. Orders were given for them to withdraw and there was great happiness in the 1/23rd Foot, which had spent a cold, wet and miserable winter in North Germany, when it received orders on 13 February 1806 to embark at Cuxhaven for Britain. The battalion landed at Harwich and was stationed at Woodbridge until June 1806 when it moved to Colchester.

Since 1793, the government had steadily constructed numerous barracks to house the expanded wartime army. The buildings at Colchester, fine and newly built, were capable of holding 4,000 infantry and cavalry and the Welch Fusiliers enjoyed a comfortable winter there in 1806-1807. In February 1807 Lieutenant Colonel James Losack resigned and was replaced by Lieutenant Colonel Evan Jones, who moved over from the 2nd Battalion. A Welshman from Gelliwig in Carnarfonshire, Jones had joined the 23rd Foot in 1791 and had fought with it in the West Indies, the Helder and Egypt. He was famous in the regiment for having survived yellow fever in Santo Domingo after his life was saved by a native woman who wrapped him in a blanket soaked in vinegar, which 'arrested the rage of that dreadful malady'.[51] At about the same time as Jones assumed command, a large draft marched in from the 2nd Battalion, which included Majors Francis Offley and Thomas Pearson, Lieutenant John Harrison and Drummer Richard Bentinck. When the 1st Battalion was inspected on 26 March 1807, it paraded 991 all ranks, of which no fewer than 146 were listed as being Welsh.

Two new officers who also joined the 1st Battalion at about this time were the Browne brothers, George and Thomas, sons of a retired wealthy merchant who resided at Bronwylfa in Flintshire. The Browne family possessed a literary streak – the brothers' sister, Felicia Hemans, became one of the most widely read woman poets in early 19th century Britain ('The boy stood on the burning deck') – and Thomas Browne was to leave a detailed and witty memoir of his service with the 23rd Foot. He was a keen observer, witness his account of the annual St. David's Day dinner held at Colchester Barracks on 1 March 1807 when the officers having dined:

> … one of the little drum-boys, rides a large goat, with which the regiment is always provided, round the Mess-room, carrying in his hand a dish of Leeks. Each Officer is called upon to eat one, for which he pays the Drummer a shilling. The older Officers of the regiment, and those who have seen service with it in the field, are favoured only with a small one, and salt. Those who have before celebrated a St. David's day with the regiment, but have only seen garrison duty with it, are required to eat a larger one without salt, and those unfortunates, who for the first time, have sat at the Mess, on this their Saint's day, have presented to them the largest Leek that can be procured, and unless sickness prevent it, no respite is given, until the last tip of its green leaf is inclosed in the unwilling mouth; and day after day passes before the smell and taste is fairly got rid of.[52]

Browne's description of the St. David's Day celebration introduces the subject of that legendary beast, the Regimental Goat. By this time in their long history, the Welch Fusiliers had forgotten just when and why they had first acquired a Goat – perhaps early in the 18th century – but they have had one ever since, informally called 'Billy'. It must be stressed that the Goat is not a mascot and is never called such; he performs an important function at ceremonial parades as, in company with the Goat Major, the soldier appointed to tend to him, he leads the Royal

Eating the Leek on St. David's Day
The Royal Welch Fusiliers hold an annual dinner to celebrate the feast day of St.
David, the patron saint of Wales. In Napoleonic times newcomers to the mess had
to stand on their chairs to eat a leek, the Goat was paraded around the mess table,
ridden by the smallest drummer boy in the regiment. The origin of the Goat has
been lost in the mists of time but the Welch Fusiliers have had one on strength at
least since the early 18th century. (*Painting by R. Caton-Woodville, courtesy RWF
Museum*)

Welch Fusiliers when they pass in review. The scanty evidence available on the
service of the Goat during the Great War with France, 1793-1815, seems to
indicate that he served with the 1st Battalion when it was in Britain. If it went
overseas he transferred to the 2nd Battalion – indeed, the Goat was marching
with that unit when Bentinck enlisted in it – and if that battalion went abroad, he
was put under the care of one of the Welsh militia regiments. The Goat was not
with the 1/23rd, therefore, when it marched out of Colchester for Harwich on
25 July 1807, bound for yet another overseas expedition.[53]

This time the destination was Denmark. In 1806 Czar Alexander of Russia had
concluded a secret alliance with King William III of Prussia to render mutual aid,
but when Prussia declared war on France in October of that year, Napoleon
crushed that nation in a few short weeks before the Russians could mobilise to
assist their ally. He then launched a winter offensive in Poland, which had mixed
results, but in the spring of 1807 the French emperor gained a great victory over
the Russians at Friedland, which caused the Czar to sue for peace. In July the two
emperors met at Tilsit in east Prussia to sign a peace treaty and agreed on a
number of secret clauses, which permitted Napoleon to acquire the fleets of
Denmark, Portugal and Sweden. These, combined with the French and Spanish

navies, would finally give him enough naval power to mount a successful invasion of Britain. When the British government, headed by the Duke of Portland after Pitt's death from exhaustion in early 1806, learned of these clauses, they issued orders for a force to sail to Denmark and attempt to force that small nation to turn over her fleet to Britain for safekeeping until the war had ended.

As the 1/23rd Foot embarked at Harwich on 26 July 1807, Lieutenant John Harrison recalled, they were 'cheered by the loud huzzas of the spectators, which was returned with three times three by the fuzileers'.[54] Harrison was pleased to find that the captain and crew of his ship, the brig *Louisa*, were all Welshmen, 'which is very apropos'.[55] The fleet sailed on 31 July and by 9 August was off Elsinore Castle in Denmark. As by this time the officers on Harrison's vessel had nearly exhausted their sea stock, he volunteered to take a boat to the Swedish town of Helsingborg where, leaving the boat in charge of a sailor, he went shopping and with some difficulty, 'procured a few eggs and potatoes, also a couple of Ducks and Fowls' as well as a sheep for 12 shillings which was smaller than 'an English Tom-Cat' and cost about a shilling a pound.[56] On 16 August 1807 the army disembarked at Vedboek, about four miles north of Copenhagen. Harrison remembered that the men of the battalion were issued with 80 rounds of ball cartridge and two days' cooked provisions and when 'the boats came alongside to receive us I instantly buckled on my Knapsack, and slung my Haversack and Canteen across my shoulder, well stored with Ham, Biscuit and Grog, and took my leave of the Louisa'.[57]

The Danes did not resist the landing and the army advanced south to Copenhagen, a city of some hundred thousand souls. The Danes refused, however, to surrender their fleet although Lieutenant General Lord Cathcart, who commanded the British land forces, warned that he would destroy the city unless they did so. When there was no reply, on 2 September the Royal Artillery began a heavy bombardment of Copenhagen, which continued day and night. With all the enthusiasm of a young soldier on his first campaign, Harrison noted that there was so much light from the burning city that, 'although we are two miles from where the fire took place that you may read or write with all possible ease – it would make an excellent thing for a panorama'.[58] An older, more experienced officer took a less enthusiastic view, writing that Copenhagen:

> ... was in flames a quarter of an hour after the bombardment began, and
> continued so in a slight degree the whole of Thursday. But at night the
> timber-yard took fire, and the conflagration became much more general
> during the whole of Friday; and the wind, which was high during the
> whole of the time, carrying the flames directly over the town, increased it

to such a degree that on Friday night the appearance was rather that of a volcano during a violent eruption than anything I can conceive. The sight was dreadful, but it was truly magnificent; the church of Notre Dame, the cathedral and the church, which made the finest appearance in the town, fell to the ground at five in the morning, and nothing is standing but the bare foundation. Do us the justice to believe that we felt the horrors of this scene in all its extent; and imagine us at the same time redoubling our exertions as the calamity increased, and throwing showers of shells towards the parts where the fire raged most to render ineffectual the means employed to extinguish it. But now, indeed, I believe all human efforts were in vain had the wind continued; and setting this aside, the fire from our batteries was so tremendous that no means could be employed towards checking its progress.[59]

After two days the Danes capitulated and agreed to surrender their fleet. The officers and men of Cathcart's army, although they knew it was a matter of national necessity, were not very proud of their actions and there was much relief in the British camp when it was learned that during the bombardment, 'the women and children, and most of those incapable of bearing arms, had flocked in great numbers to the island of Amager, on the other side of the town, where our fire had no effect'.[60] But civilian lives had been lost – when Harrison and some other Welch Fusilier officers entered Copenhagen to see the effects of the bombardment, they were somewhat embarrassed to encounter a civilian who said to them in 'tolerable good English' that they had 'killed my dear wife, and sweet little child, burnt all my property, and you can do me no other injury'.[61]

It took some two weeks to complete arrangements for the transfer of the Danish fleet and then the expedition started on its return voyage. The fleet encountered very rough weather and both Lieutenants Browne and Harrison recorded some of the perils of period sea travel. During an overnight squall, Browne's ship collided with a smaller vessel and those on board could hear 'cries of distress' which 'sounded most lamentable in the gale, during the short moment we were able to hear them', but soon 'all was silent'.[62] For his part, Harrison's transport became detached from the main fleet in a storm and did not know its position until those on board sighted a coast 'which we took for the North Foreland, but what was our surprise when standing in quite close we found ourselves going into Calais at a pretty fast rate'.[63] 'You may be sure', he added, that 'we did not delay putting about.' Despite these hazards, the 1/23rd Foot returned safely to Colchester Barracks on 28 November 1807.

It now received a new commanding officer – the eighth in fourteen years – and this time it was the newly-promoted Lieutenant Colonel Henry Ellis. Ellis had actually received this appointment the previous February but had opted not to take it up immediately, perhaps because Evan Jones had just shifted that month from the 2nd to the 1st Battalion. Although Ellis accompanied it, Jones

The destruction of Copenhagen, 1807
In 1807, when the British government learned that Napoleon intended to take over
the Danish fleet, it sent an expedition to Copenhagen to demand the surrender of
these warships. When the Danes not unnaturally refused this demand, the city of
Copenhagen was bombarded until they capitulated.
(From Grant, British Battles on Land and Sea, 1897)

---

commanded the 1/23rd Foot during the Copenhagen expedition but now that
the battalion was back, Ellis took command and Jones retired to live on his
property in Caernarfonshire.[64]

Henry Walton Ellis had just turned twenty-five when he assumed command of
the 1/23rd Foot. He was, however, a very experienced officer who had fought in
all the Welch Fusiliers' campaigns and actions since 1797, being wounded in the
Helder campaign of 1799 and in Egypt in 1801. Ellis was also fortunate to have the
assistance of Majors Thomas Pearson and Francis Offley, two relatively young
but seasoned subordinates who had served with him for a decade. Of the five
teenage officers who had joined the Royal Welch Fusiliers in the late 1790s, Ellis,
Offley and Pearson now held the senior ranks in the 1st Battalion; Jack Hill was
third from the top on the seniority list of captains; and Thomas Dalmer would
shortly be promoted major in the 2nd Battalion. These five still young men were
now seasoned veterans and their leadership qualities would be needed, for the
hardest battles were yet to come.

Eyes right, my jolly field boys,
Who British bayonets bear,
To teach your foes to yield, boys,
When British steel they dare!
Now fill the glass for the toast of toasts
Shall be drunk to the cheer of cheers,
Hurrah, hurrah, hurrah, hurrah!
For the British Bayoneteers.

Great guns have shot and shell, boys,
Dragoons have sabres bright.
Th' artillery fire's like hell, boys,
And the horse like devils fight.
But neither light nor heavy horse,
Nor thundering cannoneers,
Can stem the tide of the foeman's pride,
Like the British Bayoneteers.

The English arm is strong, boys,
The Irish arm is tough.
The Scotsman's blow, the French well know
Is struck by sterling stuff.
And when before the enemy
Their shining steel appears,
Goodbye, goodbye, how they run, how they run,
From the British Bayoneteers.[1]

Chapter 5

'The excellence of the Fusilier Brigade'

1st Battalion, Britain and North America, 1808–1809

COLCHESTER WAS A FINE STATION and the officers and men of the 1st Battalion of the Royal Welch Fusiliers were glad to get back to it in November 1807. 'We had little to do', Lieutenant Thomas Browne enthused, 'as the weather was too wet & cold for drills, and the garrison was so large, that duties were light.'[2] Extensive leave was granted to the officers and ten men per company, and many took advantage of it while those who remained busied themselves with enjoying a comfortable winter. The officers laid in a stock of wine for their mess, subscribed to several newspapers and periodicals, had the mess itself redecorated, bought new instruments for the band, and organised a choir among the men. They also gave a ball for the local gentry (actually for their unmarried daughters but parents unfortunately had to be invited) at the Three Cups Inn in town and held a masquerade party in their own mess.[3] Life was also good for the men and Drummer Bentinck never forgot the day when 'a cask of strong ale' was brought into their mess 'in mistake for [the] thin table beer' that was part of the soldiers' ration. Everyone got so uproarious that Lieutenant Colonel Ellis stopped even the thin beer, giving each man a penny a day in compensation.[4] The Welch Fusiliers were having a good time and were counting on 'about six months more of the same laughing careless life'.[5]

Unfortunately it all ended on the evening of 16 January 1808. The officers were lingering over their wine after dinner in the mess when an official message arrived ordering the battalion to march to Portsmouth in three detachments to embark for foreign service – and the first detachment was to leave the following morning. Frantic activity followed as the regiment worked to prepare for the move. There was much to be done: mess silver, regimental records and personal belongings had to be packed, rented furniture returned, bills paid and letters sent to fifteen officers and 100 men on leave, including Lieutenant Colonel Ellis, ordering them to report immediately to Portsmouth. There were 'a thousand unforeseen arrangements to be made', Browne remembered. Officers and men worked through the night to complete them while listening to the 'usual wailings of sweethearts & wives, who were not allowed to accompany their Husbands', which 'resounded in the barrack yard'.[6]

Lieutenant Browne's comment about 'wailing' wives and sweethearts brings up the subject of women in the army and it might be wise at this point, while the Welch Fusiliers finish their packing, to discuss it. Although it seems strange to the modern eye, during this time there were women with almost every British regiment both at home and abroad and they were regarded as rather a mixed blessing. 'Marriage'. stated a period manual, 'is to be discouraged as much as possible' and officers were directed to explain to their men 'the many miseries that women are exposed to, and by every sort of persuasion they must prevent their marrying if possible.'[7] However, men and women being what they are and a man in uniform being attractive to many young ladies, the army permitted a certain number of men to marry and have their wives with them in barracks. A private soldier wishing to marry had first to obtain the permission of his company commander, who would inquire into 'the morals' of the prospective bride and ascertain 'whether she is sufficiently known to be industrious, and able to earn her bread'.[8] If the officer approved, a married soldier was 'indulged, as far as can be in the power of Officers to extend their favour, whilst his behaviour, and that of his Wife deserves it'.[9] If the officer discovered, however, that a prospective wife was of a loose character, 'which too often is the case of those, on whom the Soldiers fix their affections', he was to strongly discourage 'a connection, which, must, in a short time, inevitably destroy the ease and happiness' of the man.[10] If the soldier persisted, the officer had the power to prevent the wife from living in quarters or having any access to his pay.

Only women on the married roll of a regiment – the authorised wives – were permitted to reside in barracks. It was not the most private arrangement as military couples lived and slept with the single men in the same room and only had a screen of blankets or canvas separating them. Inevitably, babies appeared and grew up into children who were not raised under the best of circumstances – one author has characterised soldiers' children as 'stunted, gnome-like little creatures' roaming around 'wearing cast-off army garments, tightened tunics and cut-down trousers', who could be seen 'pulling at evil-smelling short clay pipes ... and swilling frightening quantities of ale, porter or canteen beer'.[11] When they were of age, the boys usually enlisted while the girls married soldiers.

Soldiers' wives were supposedly subject to military discipline. A wife could be turned out of barracks for drunkenness, foul language, fighting, sexual promiscuity or theft. Punishments could be severe – a woman was ejected from the garrison of Gibraltar after being 'whipped through the streets of the town for theft, receiving one lash every fifty yards'.[12] Keeping discipline among the regimental wives was easier to do in barracks than it was on campaign as the single greatest punishment a commanding officer had was the power to turn a problem wife out on to the street for bad behaviour. On campaign, however, it was harder to keep good order among the women, who formed a somewhat intractable element in every regiment to which they belonged. Young officers, many of whom were just teenagers, often found the task of dealing with the regimental women a particularly difficult one and the more intelligent did what a good officer should do under such circumstances – turn the matter over to an NCO and walk away. One lieutenant remembered a particularly difficult wife:

> Early in the afternoon the Serjeant of my 5th Company came and earnestly requested me to go and quiet the woman Fisher, wife of our Fifer; for she was mad with excessive drink ... I instantly ordered him to give her in charge of the Guard. But he assured me he had thrice done so; and she had forced her way out. I sent him for the Fifer to meet me at the Guard-house ...
>
> I met the frantick demon – I never witnessed anything so atrocious!! I desired the husband to control her, but he declared his incapability for she had knocked him about like a ninepin. And the poor fellows face and clothes confirmed his assertion. He begged of me to quiet her if I could anyhow; but that he would not go near her. It was very evident that something must be done; but I knew not what.
>
> Thinking my rank and authority would check the fiend's fury, I tried to reason with her; but she showed fight, and made such desperate blows at me, that I was compelled to beat them off with my sheathed sword in my left hand. I then fixed a very stern and steady look on her and by my orders some soldiers closed around her and forced her into the guard house. I made the Drummer take the sling from his drum and unbraid it: I very soon whipt the cord round and secured the woman's legs; carried it up and tied her hands behind her – but could not affix it to her tongue – her yells and vociferations were quite deafening! – to stop this nuisance I was obliged to put a drumstick across her mouth and bound it behind her head. ...
>
> I walked about outside and the Serjeant of the Guard informed me that she was nearly asleep. I gave him orders to remove the drumstick when she was in sound sleep: and if, on her awaking she was become quiet, to release her. About three hours after I received a report that Mrs Fisher was gone to her billet quite subdued.[13]

Women like the redoubtable Mrs Fisher could create problems but army wives often proved to be an asset, both to their husbands and their regiment. They supplemented their families' diets, either through gardening or purchasing food with money from gainful employment. It was noticed that married soldiers ate better than their single counterparts, an important consideration since it was believed that a good diet corrected 'drunkenness, and in a great measure prevents gaming [gambling], and thereby Desertion'.[14] Many wives were hard working and skilled improvisers – simply because they had to be – a British officer on campaign in the Peninsula admired the women of his regiment who created a 'piggery, to have a little nice winter bacon, and I have heard it said, that they go so far as to have a bit of garden to furnish greens for ditto'.[15] Since soldiers' pay was low and often in arrears, many wives sought employment to improve the lives of their families. They worked as cleaners and servants, took in sewing and sometimes assisted in the preparation of meals in the cookhouse.[16]

The most popular employment for wives – and most engaged in it – was to work as laundresses. This labour was usually well regulated with prices being fixed by the regimental commander – one example was 2½d to wash a shirt – and steps were taken to ensure that women were paid promptly. Less commonly, some were employed as nurses and regulations for military hospitals provided for 'one decent, sober woman nurse, who shall receive at the rate of one shilling *per diem*, whose duty will be to prepare the slops and comforts for the sick, and occasionally to assist in administering medicines, cooking the victuals, washing, &c. and for every ten men confined to bed by fever, an additional Nurse and Orderlyman should be allowed'.[17]

Difficult as life was for the wives, it did offer some security in the form of regular pay and rations (at a reduced rate for women and children) and for this reason most wives tried to accompany their husbands if a regiment was posted overseas. When a regiment was in Britain, legal wives 'on the roll' could live in barracks, but when serving abroad, their number was strictly limited. Before 1813 the maximum number of wives permitted to accompany a regiment embarking for foreign service was six per company. In that year a new General Order allowed up to twelve women per company to embark for foreign garrison service but only six per company if a regiment was ordered 'for active Field Service' or none at all, 'according to the nature of the Service for which the Regiment may be destined'.[18] The number of women to be taken was usually left to the discretion of a commanding officer of a unit. He might decide to take none but if he did decide to bring wives, he was advised to select only those 'of good Character and having the inclination and ability to render themselves useful'.[19] Since there were always more wives wanting to accompany their husbands than the regulations would permit, and despite the advice given to commanding officers about choosing them, the selection was usually done by publicly drawing lots – pieces of paper marked 'To Go' or 'Not to Go.' Naturally, wives dreaded this procedure, which was often delayed as long as possible to give them some hope, and was usually supervised by the NCOs, many of whom were married men.

For those left behind, quite often the majority, regulations provided for them to receive a stipend if they chose to return to their home parish. To qualify, a wife first had to obtain from her husband's commanding officer – Major Thomas Pearson in the case of the 1/23rd in January 1808 as Lieutenant Colonel Ellis was on leave – a document with his signature certifying she was 'the Wife or reputed Wife of a Soldier in his Regiment, Battalion, Corps or Detachment'.[20] Having shown this to a magistrate, she then received a second document, which stated her intended destination, the route to be travelled, and an amount not to exceed two pence per mile to the next town. As she travelled, a wife was required to present her papers to the 'Overseer of the Poor of any Place' through which she passed, in order to receive funds to get her to the next locality within a radius of eighteen miles.[21] When she finally reached her destination, the wife surrendered the certificate to the overseer of the poor and all too often, both she and any children ended up in the parish poorhouse. Regulations were strict that any wives who did not comply with these requirements were to be 'treated as Vagrants'.[22]

The lot of a soldier's wife left behind when her husband went overseas was not a happy one – as a song of the time put it:

> Poor wives they think a month longer
> Than they used to think a year,
> Because they've lost husbands and fathers
> Who cannot their children hear.
>
> Children prattling to their mothers,
> 'When will father come?' they cry;
> Which sets the tears a-flowing
> From each tender mother's eyes.
>
> Ask relief, then the parish grumble,
> It's the truth you really do know;
> And when they can't keep house no longer
> To the workhouse they're bound to go.[23]

With this in mind, it not surprising that the 'usual wailings' were heard at Colchester Barracks during the night of 16 January 1808.

Those wives permitted to accompany the 1/23rd Foot were with the battalion when it embarked at Portsmouth. As usual, the pressing necessity for the officers was to secure provisions for the voyage and Thomas Browne recalled that:

> … two Officers of each ship, were appointed to purchase and lay in sea-stock. We subscribed about twenty pounds each, the government allowance of Bat[†] and forage money to subalterns, (twelve pounds ten,)

† 'Bat' or 'bât' was baggage. When they went on active service, officers received an allowance for bat, baggage and forage, to pay their soldier servants who looked after their baggage and for feed for their horses. Officers often used this allowance to purchase their sea stock. In 1811, the bat and forage money for a lieutenant proceeding on a foreign posting was set at 6 d per day up to a maximum of 200 days and a single grant of £3 15s, see Charles James, ed., *The Regimental Companion, Containing the Pay, Allowances and Relative Duties of Every Officers in the British Service* (3 vols., London, 1811) vol. 2, 213-214.

being insufficient for that purpose. The most useful articles, were tea, sugar, coffee and biscuits. We had a tolerable quantity of port and sherry and spices of all kinds. Live sheep and pigs, fowls and ducks, with plenty of potatoes made this part of the business very comfortable. Some oranges and lemons were added in case of illness, nor was bottled porter forgotten. We purchased tin plates and dishes, and cups to drink from.[24]

Lieutenant Colonel Ellis, having travelled hard from his home near Worcester, arrived to find his battalion embarked but managed to get on board before the transports got under way. Ellis need not have hurried, as the ships did not actually sail until 13 February 1808.

Their destination, which was officially kept secret, was British North America. The Welch Fusiliers were on their way to the far side of the Atlantic because of growing tension between Britain and the United States caused by the war in Europe. Following his defeat at Trafalgar in 1805, Napoleon had decided to wage economic warfare against Britain's maritime trade. In 1806 he passed a decree stating that any British goods found in French-controlled territory would be subject to seizure. Britain responded with Orders-in-Council proclaiming that any vessel carrying cargoes to or from a French-held port would be subject to seizure and Napoleon promptly countered with a decree that any vessel which obeyed the Orders-in-Council would be seized. This war by proclamation harmed the United States, which had a very large merchant marine that traded with both nations. Even more annoying to the republic was the habit of Royal Navy captains of boarding American vessels and impressing any crew member they believed to be a British citizen. In June 1807 HMS *Leopard* fired into the unprepared American frigate, USS *Chesapeake,* when the latter refused to be boarded for an inspection, killing or wounding several people. Britain apologised for this act but the United States was understandably outraged and such were the calls for armed retaliation that the British government decided to reinforce its North American garrisons. In January 1808, therefore, four strong battalions (the 1/7th, 1/8th, 13th, and 1/23rd Foot), nearly 4,000 men, embarked at Portsmouth for North America.

Although supposedly a secret, most officers seemed to have guessed their destination. Captain Jack Hill was one of them and assuming that there would be good shooting on the other side of the water, had carefully brought along a personal arsenal, which included hunting rifles, 150 lbs. of shot, 12 lbs. of powder, and 300 flints. Hill's big regret was not having time to send for Linquo, his favourite retriever, from his parents' home at Hennock. As the convoy sailed west past Devon, he could recognise local landmarks through a spyglass and was very tempted to try and collect the dog but that, of course, was impossible.[25] Leaving behind Cornwall, which was most unusually covered in snow, behind, the convoy cleared Land's End on 17 February 1808 and then steered south to pick up the prevailing winds. On St. David's Day it was far out into the Atlantic and the Welch Fusiliers, unable to hold the traditional celebration, did their best to mark the occasion by having all their food 'dressed in Onions, and drank an extra glass of grog'.[26]

The transports were crowded. Browne recorded that his vessel, the *Royal Yeoman*, had:

> ... *eight* Officers and 200 men on board, besides her crew. The cabin was very small, and we slept in wooden partitions, just long and broad enough for one, fixed one above the other. There was a table in the middle of the cabin, fastened to the floor, and round it, just room for a wooden chair, which it was necessary to move, to enable us to step into our berths. The whole cabin was the most uncomfortable concern that can readily be imagined, but it was scarcely possible to be ill-humoured at it, as it produced so many ludicrous occurrences.[27]

This was luxurious, however, compared to the quarters of the men below decks, which were two-tiered bunks, actually large platforms with half a dozen men sleeping on each. Regulations were strict about married couples, who were not permitted 'to make separate Births [sic] *all over* the Ships, by hanging Blankets, which obstruct the Circulation of the Air', but were directed to have 'adjoining Births in one Part of the Ship if possible'.[28]

On each vessel officers and men were divided into three watches, which were to be on deck during fine weather. Soldiers (and their wives) had to rise at 7 a.m. and be in bed by 8 p.m., an officer being assigned to ensure that they were. Three parades were held each day, more for sanitary purposes to ensure that the men were clean, than any military function. The men also received physical training, with round shot being used 'as Dumb-bells'. as well as other 'Diversions calculated for the Purpose of bodily Exercise'.[29] The great fear was sickness, and regulations stressed that the privies or heads were to be sluiced frequently 'to prevent the Soil from sticking to the Sides of the Ships' and that bedding was 'to be brought upon Deck every Morning, if the Weather will permit, by Seven o'Clock; and to be well aired'.[30] Nor was the men's spiritual health neglected:

> Divine Service to be performed on every Sunday that the Weather will permit; selecting, where there is no Clergyman on board, an Officer whose Manners qualify him for the Duty. Independent of the strong Reason which, in a religious View, demands the Discharge of so important and sacred a Duty, the regular Performance of Divine Service has ever been found to produce and promote Cleanliness and good Order among the Soldiery.[31]

As there was no chaplain on Lieutenant Browne's ship, one wonders which Welch Fusilier officer was considered qualified to read Divine Service, in view of the fact that card playing was the primary amusement of his comrades. The stakes often got high, to the point that:

... two Officers of the regiment carried their game at Cassino so far, that one lost every sixpence he had, and all his clothes and appointments; he was retiring from the table in despair, when, being a man fond of good eating, he suddenly recollected that he had a jar of pickles left, which he staked against a dollar with his comrade; luck took a turn, and he literally won back everything he had lost.[32]

The convoy reached Bermuda on 21 March and anchored long enough to send the 13th Foot ashore before heading north for Halifax, where it arrived on 8 April 1808. As the ships came up the Eastern Passage into the commodious Halifax basin, one of the finest natural anchorages in the world, officers and men commented on the great forests of pine and, where the woods had been cleared for small farms, the novel sight of split-rail wooden fences which could only exist 'in a country abounding with wood'.[33] The town of Halifax, one British officer recorded,

... is prettily enough situated on a hill-side, at the top of which there is a citadel and block-house. The houses are all built of wood, and in general painted white or yellow, which has a very pleasing effect, particularly in summer. ... There are also two churches, both very neat buildings of wood, and one or two meeting-houses. There is a square in town called the Grand Parade, where the troops in garrison parade every evening during the summer; and where all the belles and beaux of the place promenade, and the bands remain to play as long as they walk.[34]

As Major General Sir George Prevost, the new lieutenant-governor of Nova Scotia, had travelled with the convoy, its arrival was enthusiastically greeted by the Haligonians.

One ship, however, was missing – the transport *Harriet*, carrying the companies of Captains Jacob Van Cortland and John Leahy. She had separated from the convoy shortly after leaving British waters and had not been seen for more than a month. As the days passed without her appearance there was fear that she had foundered or been captured by French privateers but, in fact, the *Harriet* had suffered a number of mishaps and her progress was hampered by her captain who remained in a constant state of intoxication. Private Richard Roberts from Denbighshire recorded that shortly after the unlucky vessel sailed, a fire broke out on board:

The smoke burst through the hatches. In a moment all was disorder and consternation. The women and children were screaming; the crew distracted – shouting, cursing, bawling; none to direct and none to obey. It was a frightful scene, such as I must not attempt to describe. We were far from land and not a sail was to be discovered in our track. The fire was rapidly gaining upon us, and at length got so near the magazine, that I expected every moment to be blown up. There seemed to me to be but one alternative; fire or water so I stepped up to the forecastle and just as I put my foot on the bulwark, in the act of jumping over, a comrade got hold of my skirt and pulled me back.[35]

Roberts's saviour pointed out that the fire had been contained and therefore it was better to stay on board than swim the Atlantic. A few weeks later, the *Harriet* encountered a heavy storm but

> Still, however, we were in no absolute danger; and the transport being a stout-built vessel, though not stoutly manned, promised to carry us safely, if not pleasantly, through the tempest. In another moment, however, a cry was heard, 'the helm-rope is broke!' On hearing this, our drunken captain clasped his hands, and exclaimed 'God be with us; we are all lost!' It was the only prayer I ever heard him utter.[36]

Fortunately, the first mate was able to make emergency repairs and the *Harriet* sailed on, reaching Halifax on 13 May, five weeks after the remainder of the regiment and three months to the day since she had left Portsmouth. As Roberts noted, the two companies of Welch Fusiliers on board were only too glad to 'escape from a faithless sea and a drunken skipper'.[37]

To their dismay – as Halifax looked like a lively town – shortly after they arrived, the Welch Fusiliers were sent to man outposts around Annapolis Royal in the Bay of Fundy. It was another four days of sailing before they could finally get back on dry land but they then spent a very pleasant six months during which, as military duties largely comprised only ninety minutes daily drill before 8 a.m., they risked becoming settlers. Jack Hill enthusiastically recorded the officers' pastimes which included shooting, fishing, farming and assembling a menagerie that ultimately comprised four cats, two ducks, a pet fox, three porcupines and a bear, not to mention twelve dogs brought from Britain. Hill bought a twenty-foot sailing boat for fishing and also had the men of his company construct a weir in the nearby Minas Basin which has some of the highest tides in the world and was shortly able to provide them with plenty of fresh cod, haddock and halibut. Lieutenant Colonel Ellis, Major Offley and Lieutenant Edward Thornhill purchased a sixteen-acre farm for £110 and, using the labour of the soldiers, produced vegetables and raised livestock for the regiment. Farm life seemed to suit Francis Offley, who had a reputation for being quick tempered, as according to Jack Hill he was now 'not quite so violent as formerly, he has turn'd a great farmer here for the mess, we have 40 sheep, bullocks, etc'.[38] Lieutenant Thomas Browne, whose post was nearer Halifax, had his men dig a large garden, substituting an hour of labour 'instead of having an evening Parade', and soon had three acres under cultivation.[39] Browne struck up a friendship with a Mi'kmaq

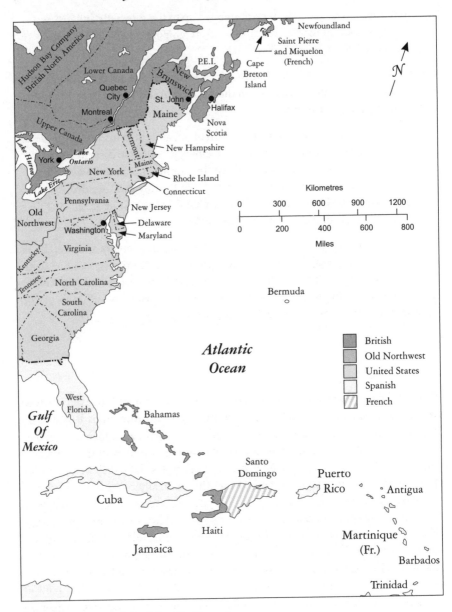

North America and the West Indies, 1809
(Map © C. Johnson)

warrior named 'Whisker Tom', who taught him how to row a birch bark canoe and guided him to inland lakes brimming with trout. For his part, Captain Jacob Van Cortland engaged in a profitless correspondence with American authorities to get compensation for the extensive family property seized after the War of Independence.[40]

While the Welch Fusiliers fished, farmed and shot, the war in Europe continued. After Britain removed the Danish fleet from Napoleon's grasp he began to put pressure on Portugal, one of Britain's largest trading partners, to either declare war on the United Kingdom or face war with France. When the Portuguese government tried to play for time, Napoleon sent an army across Spain with the connivance of that nation but it arrived too late to capture the Portuguese fleet, which sailed to Brazil. The French emperor now began to eye Spain as a possible conquest although she was his nominal ally. Decoying both the Bourbon king and his eldest son to France and forcing them to abdicate, he then sent his armies over the border to place his brother, Joseph, on the Spanish throne. This led to a Spanish national uprising, which began in May 1808, and Britain immediately came to the insurgents' aid, sending an army to Portugal under Lieutenant General Sir Arthur Wellesley, who had made a name for himself in India. During the summer of 1808, Wellesley inflicted two humiliating defeats on the French at Rolica and Vimiero while the Spanish surrounded and forced to surrender an entire French army at Bailen. These encouraging events, which demonstrated that Napoleon and his legions were not invincible, thrilled all Europe.

On the other side of the Atlantic, meanwhile, the tension between Britain and the United States, which had brought the Welch Fusiliers to North America, gradually subsided. 'The politicks in this part of the world', Hill commented, 'are that we are not to have an American war.'[41] Like many British soldiers, Hill did not have a high opinion of 'Cousin Jonathan', the British and Canadian nickname for Americans, the implication being that they were uncouth country bumpkins: 'They really have been flattering themselves that Europe could not do without them, but have now found England has not given them much satisfaction and that France has not condescended to pay any attention to them, things remain in much the same state as when we came here.'[42]

Throughout the summer of 1808, the 1/23rd Foot remained dispersed. When Major General Prevost inspected it at Annapolis Royal on 10 August, only sixteen officers and 271 men were on parade, while no fewer than twenty-three officers and 744 men were 'on command' or detached, making a total strength of 1,054 all ranks. In his report, Prevost noted that 200 of the men were Welsh.[43]

In the autumn rumours began to circulate that the battalion would be going to the West Indies. When no movement orders came, Browne recorded that 'we began to pay little attention to them, and perhaps the less, as there was no particular disposition in the Regiment for West Indian service', which is is not surprising considering the 23rd Foot's disastrous experience on Santo Domingo in the 1790s.[44] In November, however, Ellis received orders to concentrate his battalion at Halifax and on the 27th of that month, the 1/23rd embarked, along with the 1/7th and 1/8th Foot, for an unknown destination. As Hill noted, 'many are the speculations: Martinique, Cayenne and the city of St. Domingo are mentioned' but 'the object of the attack is a profound secret, perhaps wishing to keep our [American] neighbours on their guard & put them to expense'.[45]

The Royal Welch Fusiliers were bound for Martinique. By 1808, Britain had taken most French possessions in the West Indies except Guadaloupe and Martinique, which provided protected bases for enemy privateers. Lieutenant General Sir George Beckwith, the military commander in the area, was ordered to reduce these two strongholds and Major General Prevost was sent with a force from Halifax to assist him. It was not until 6 December that, under naval escort, the convoy weighed anchor at Halifax and headed for the West Indies. It took just over three weeks to reach Bridgetown in Barbados, the selected assembly point for the expedition and it was a fairly pleasant voyage, although at one point lightning struck one of the transports, killing one man and injuring several others. A few days later, one of the naval escorts hailed a merchantman, which passed across newspapers. These contained the interesting information that Lieutenant General Sir John Moore had replaced Wellesley in the Iberian Peninsula and had been joined by reinforcements, which included the regiment's 2nd Battalion.

The 1/23rd Foot had a long wait, nearly a month, at Bridgetown while plans and preparations for the attack on Martinique were completed and in the interim the officers were permitted to go ashore. Before doing so, they received many 'very sage instructions' for 'the care of their individual health', particularly 'to avoid exposure to the great heats of the day and the damp of the evening'.[46] After listening to this medical advice, Browne remembered that he and his fellow subalterns, being young and therefore immortal:

> ... selected the hottest sun of noon-day for our expeditions on shore, and I remember being saluted by some half naked black women in the Market place of Bridgetown the Capital of Barbados, with 'Ah Massa Johnny Newcome go back to Shippy, too hot for him here, kill him.' In the evenings we behaved with equal prudence, landing about seven o'clock for a dinner at 'Nancy Clarkes', the principal hotel keeper there, where we used to eat the highest possible seasoned meat, drink Sangaree & Madeira in considerable quantities and adjourn to a dance at some other hotel which usually began at midnight.[47]

The Martinique expedition, numbering 12,400 troops, sailed from Bridgetown at the end of January 1809. Beckwith's army was organised in two divisions: that commanded by Prevost, which included the troops from Nova Scotia; and a smaller formation commanded by Major General Sir Thomas Maitland. Martinique was defended by 6,250 French regular troops, sailors and militia concentrated in and around Fort Royal, the capital, on the south coast and Fort

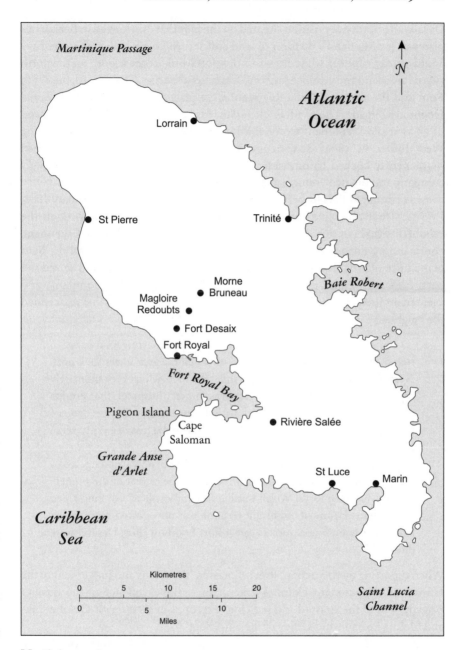

Martinique, 1809

As part of General Prevost's division, the 1/23rd Foot landed at Baie Robert and advanced to Morne Bruneau and the Magloire Redoubts where they fought some stiff actions. For the rest of the campaign they screened Fort Desaix, the French stronghold in the interior, which ultimately capitulated. *(Map © C. Johnson)*

Desaix, an impressive position situated on the hills that overlooked it. Beckwith's plan was for Maitland's division to land and secure Fort Royal so that the navy could offload supplies while Prevost's division would come ashore on the north side of the island and advance on Fort Desaix from the rear. The 1/23rd, the 1/7th Foot and the 1st West India Regiment were placed in Major General Daniel Hoghton's brigade. The 1/7th Foot, a fellow fusilier unit, was under the command of 30-year-old Lieutenant Colonel Edward Pakenham, who had served in the West Indies in 1801-1803, acquiring a neck wound which left his head permanently cocked to one side. Pakenham and Ellis enjoyed each other's company and the two young battalion commanders became close friends.[48]

After landing at Baie Robert on the north side of the island on 30 January 1808, Prevost's first objective was to secure Morne Bruneau, a pass through the mountains that ran down the spine of Martinique. On 1 February Pakenham, commanding the advance guard consisting of his own 7th Foot and the light companies of Hoghton's brigade, drove away French outposts and seized the pass. Ellis then came up with the Welch Fusilier grenadier company, and Lieutenant John Harrison, serving in that company, commented that it ascended the heights:

> ... and drove the enemy across them and down a narrow road between two sugar plantations, at the mouth of which the grenadiers took post. Here they were soon assailed by a superior force, which they ultimately repulsed. The contest, however, was most obstinate; the French repeatedly returning to the attack with drums beating. The grenadiers, however, maintained their ground, though with the loss of twenty-six of their number killed and wounded.
>
> The remainder of the battalion [1/23rd Foot] now came up, and a sharp action took place, which terminated in the retreat of the French, and in which the Royal Welsh Fusiliers had upwards of 100 men killed and wounded. A most important position was now gained, from which all the subsequent operations against Fort Bourbon [Fort Desaix] were directed.[49]

When reporting on this action, Prevost praised 'the valour and judgement of the Honourable Lieutenant-Colonel Pakenham, ... the excellence of the Fusilier Brigade, and of the spirited and judicious exertions of Lieutenant-Colonel Ellis and Majors Pearson and Offley of the 23rd Foot'.[50]

On 2 February, Prevost continued his advance but encountered two strong French earthworks sited behind a swamp, each armed with three 12-pounder guns and surrounded by an abbatis. With Pakenham in the lead, the 7th Foot attacked these positions but, suffering heavy casualties from artillery, were forced to fall back, covered by the grenadier and one battalion company of the Welch Fusiliers. At this point Lieutenant General Beckwith approached Ellis to ask whether his men could take the French position. 'Sir', replied Ellis, 'I will take the flints out of their firelocks and they shall take them.'[51] Beckwith would not allow the attempt, however, and that night the French withdrew to Fort Desaix. A General Order was issued praising the efforts of both fusilier regiments but cautioning that 'their spirit and determination', if tempered 'by less impetuosity', might lead 'to the happiest results'. During the fighting Pakenham had been beneficially wounded – hit on the opposite side of his neck from his previous wound, the injury had the result of permitting him to again hold his head upright.[52]

While he waited for the Royal Artillery to bring up heavy ordnance from Fort Royal, which had been taken by Maitland's division, Prevost loosely blockaded Fort Desaix. During this time Major Thomas Pearson of the 23rd commanded a scratch battalion, comprised of the light companies of the division, which ringed the place and experienced heavy skirmishing with French detachments that sortied from it. Hampered by heavy rain and poor roads, it was not until 19 February that the British began to bombard the fort and over the next five days, the hardworking gunners fired 14,000 shot and shells at its defences. On 24 February 1809, the French commander surrendered and the garrison marched out, drums beating and colours flying, having been accorded the honours of war. Two French regiments, the 28th and 82nd Line, surrendered their eagles to the victors, which caused much excitement, as they were the first trophies of their kind to come into British possession. Thomas Browne, who examined one of these items closely, rather unkindly noted that they were screwed on their poles, 'so that in case of reverse, nothing was easier than to unscrew the Bird, pocket it and save the disgrace which its capture would bring with it'.[53] The eagles were taken back to Britain and laid up with great ceremony in Chapel Royal at Whitehall.[†]

The Martinique campaign of 1808 cost the Welch Fusiliers twenty killed and 102 wounded. Lloyd's Patriotic Fund voted £250 for the wounded of the grenadier company and much of it went to place a memorial in St. George's Church, Halifax, to commemorate the company's fallen.[54] The Welch Fusiliers did not linger in the West Indies – on 15 March 1809 Prevost's division sailed for Halifax. Ten days later one of the escorting frigates hailed a passing ship to learn that Moore's army 'had retreated from the interior of Spain to Corunna' where a battle had been fought that had cost his life and that his army had then been evacuated to Britain. 'This news', Browne commented, caused 'considerable gloom' in the 1st Battalion as it became anxious about the fate of the 2nd Battalion, which had been under Moore's command.[55]

---

† The Martinique eagles were later transferred to the Royal Hospital at Chelsea where they remained until after the Second World War when they were presented to the Royal Regiment of Fusiliers (late 7th Foot) and Royal Welch Fusiliers. The eagle of the 82nd Line is now on display in the Royal Welch Fusilier Museum at Caernarfon Castle.

Now lonely I sit 'neath the green spreading willow,
The loss o' my Johnnie in tears to deplore.
Loud blows the wind o'er the white, foaming billow,
But the wild howling storm can awake him no more.

Oh, blirty and blae was the day when we parted,
And sair blew the blast on the bare, naked tree;
But mild was the storm, compared to the tempest
That raged in my bosom, that blinded my e'e.

Bravely he fought on the hills of Vimiera,
Was doomed at Corunna with Moore to lie low;
But bravely he fell, his brave comrades declared,
While bravely he pressed on the ranks of the foe.

Fondly, but vainly, he strove to cheer me,
An' spak' o' brave days when again he'd be free;
But oh, never mair shall the sight o' my Johnnie
Bring joy to my heart or yet gladden my e'e.[1]

Chapter 6

'At every league dropped hundreds of our comrades'

2nd Battalion, Spain and Walcheren, September 1808 – October 1809

THE PARTICIPATION OF THE 2ND BATTALION of the Royal Welch Fusiliers in the Spanish campaign during the winter of 1808-1809 derived from events that had taken place the previous summer. Following Lieutenant General Sir Arthur Wellesley's twin victories at Rolica and Vimiero in August, he had been superseded in Portugal by Lieutenant Generals Sir Harry Burrard and Sir Hew Dalrymple, who accepted a French proposal for an agreement that would permit the enemy to evacuate their forces. As the orders of the two British commanders had been to expel the French from Portugal as a prelude to assisting the uprising in Spain, they signed the Convention of Cintra, which provided for the transport of the enemy's army, complete with its arms and equipment, on British ships to a French port. Unfortunately, the convention also permitted the French to take with them such 'property' as they had legitimately acquired during the campaign and this was stretched to include a massive amount of plunder. When word of this transaction reached Britain in early September 1808, the public outcry was so great that Burrard, Dalrymple and Wellesley were recalled to face an inquiry. Perhaps the best thing about this sorry business was that Lieutenant General Sir John Moore – a talented commander and trainer of troops whom we have encountered before – assumed command in Portugal.

Moore arrived in Lisbon in early October and shortly afterwards received orders from the government to advance with 20,000 troops into northern Spain to aid the Spanish insurgents. Moore began his movement a few weeks later but a lack of local knowledge and a shortage of transport caused him to split his forces. He sent his artillery on a circuitous route to Salamanca that he had been assured was a more suitable road for vehicles while he moved with most of the infantry on a more direct route. It would be six weeks before Moore would be able to re-assemble his army. To reinforce him, the government decided to send a second force of some 17,000 troops under Lieutenant General Sir David Baird directly from Britain to northwest Spain.

Lieutenant General Sir John Moore (1761–1809)
A very professional soldier, Moore was a gifted trainer of troops who believed in rewarding good behaviour in his subordinates rather than punishing bad. He was the only general officer in the Army whose abilities matched those of Wellington and he was universally mourned after his death in 1809.
(***Richards, Military and Naval Heroes of Great Britain, 1860***)

___

Lieutenant Colonel William Wyatt's 2/23rd Foot, stationed at Cork, was chosen to join Baird's force. On 9 September 1808, knowing only that it was being sent on foreign service and nothing more, the battalion embarked at Cork on five small collier brigs, with a strength of 37 officers and 634 men, as well as 40 women and 20 children. It sailed to Falmouth, the rendezvous for Baird's force, and here Wyatt learned his battalion was bound for Spain. On 8 October the expedition departed for Corunna and Captain William Gomm of the 9th Foot recalled that, when the order to weigh anchor was given on his vessel, it created a 'hullabaloo' and much apparent confusion with 'all talkers and no hearers, ... hammers going as hard as they could, directly overhead' and 'the little midshipmen running about helter-skelter, like so many imps of darkness, enjoying the whole catastrophe'.[2] The fleet made a swift crossing of the Bay of Biscay and arrived at Corunna on 13 October.

Much to Baird's surprise, he was denied permission to land by the very people whom he had come to assist. With the collapse of its central government, Spain was ruled by a patchwork of juntas, or councils, and the officials at Corunna, having had no advance notice of Baird's expedition, refused to let him disembark until they had learned the wishes of the 'Supreme Junta' in Madrid. This took nearly two weeks to arrive but, after a few days, the Corunna authorities did permit a limited number of officers from each regiment to make day visits to the town.

When his turn came, 16-year-old Lieutenant Samuel Thorpe – whom we last met just after he joined the 2nd Battalion the previous January – was excited by his first visit to a foreign place where 'everything was new and extraordinary', so much so that he knew not what 'to gaze at most'.[3] It was not long before the young man's eyes fixed on 'the beautiful form and graceful step of a Spanish Señora' and although her face 'was unfortunately veiled', Thorpe noted, 'the handsome foot and well-turned ankle gave sufficient warrant for the beauties that were hid; and we indeed soon found that the praise we had so often heard in England of Spanish beauty was but just".[4] Fuelled by an omelette 'in which garlick and oil predominated' and a bottle of 'tolerable *vino blanco*', Thorpe's imagination was truly set ablaze when he attended the theatre and saw a fandango, during which 'a very pretty girl in very short petticoats made some pirouettes that would have graced the Italian Opera'. Such movements, he wistfully remembered, to 'a lad of sixteen just escaped the strict rules of a college, were rather dangerous' and it was as well that young Thorpe returned on board with his comrades.[5] For his part, Captain Edwin Griffith from Flintshire, an officer of the 15th Light Dragoons, was much less impressed by Corunna. He thought the place filthy, dark and gloomy and much too noisy, as the Spanish always conversed 'as if they were in a violent passion' and this, combined with 'the braying of the mules & asses; the dreadful screams made by the wooden axletrees of the little carts which are never suffered to be greased', the 'horrid *Arree-bo!*' which the drivers continually bellowed at the oxen, made 'altogether an uproar in the streets that may be imagined but cannot be described'.[6]

On 25 October 1808 permission came from Madrid for Baird to land his troops. He faced tremendous difficulties obtaining provisions and transport as he had received no funds for this purpose but with commendable energy he overcame these problems. It was not until early November, however, three weeks after his arrival at Corunna, that he began to move his army forward by detachments to Astorga, some 200 miles distant.

As part of Colonel Robert Craufurd's brigade, the 2nd Battalion of the Welch Fusiliers marched out of Corunna on 11 November 1808. Although their route lay through the Galician Mountains, it was not an unpleasant journey as the weather was fine and the Spanish people, having overcome their earlier suspicions, became increasingly friendly. Griffith recorded that by the time the 15th Dragoons were nearing Astorga they were greeted with applause and shouts of '*Vive Los Ingleses!*' and '*Vive Jorge Tercero!*'[7] It became clear, however, that things were not well with Britain's newest ally as, frequently the 2/23rd encountered small bands of 'the dispersed and fugitive armies of Spain, who designated themselves patriots; and upon the appearance of any straggling disorderly troops', the fusiliers would cry out, 'Here come more patriots!'[8] By early December 1808, Baird's troops were approaching Moore's army, which had now come up from Portugal.

The situation in Spain, unfortunately, had changed for the worse since Moore had left Lisbon in October. Late in that month Napoleon, angered by the resistance of the Spanish and the capitulation of a French army at Bailen the previous July, had crossed the border with 130,000 troops. In a series of battles, his experienced marshals swept aside the Spanish armies, whose commanders refused to co-operate with each other and, by 4 December the French emperor had taken Madrid.

Moore, meanwhile, had reached Salamanca, sixty miles northwest of Madrid, on 3 December. News of the French invasion and the numerous Spanish defeats had come to him while on the march, and deciding that any farther advance would be suicidal in the face of French numerical superiority, he ordered Baird to withdraw towards Corunna. No sooner had these orders been issued, than Moore countermanded them after he received the false information that Madrid had not fallen but was holding out against a French siege. Furthermore, the Marquis de la Romana, one of the more competent Spanish generals, assured Moore that he had rallied the remnants of several defeated forces and would soon be ready to go on the offensive with 23,000 men. With this intelligence in hand, Moore decided to mount an audacious but risky operation – he would move north, join with Baird and advance, in conjunction with la Romana, toward Burgos in north-eastern Spain, thereby threatening Napoleon's communications.

Snow was falling on 15 December when the 2/23rd, marching with the advance guard of Baird's force began to approach Moore's army. The Welch Fusiliers were in good spirits and their 'joy was great' when a detachment of the 5th Foot, one of Moore's regiments, joined them near Valderas.[9] Moore's troops, however, took a more jaundiced view of the newcomers. Private Benjamin Harris of the 95th, noted that Baird's men 'looked fresh' with clean uniforms and accoutrements while his comrades, having recently marched nearly 250 miles were 'gaunt-looking, way-worn, and ragged' with 'faces burnt almost to the hue of an Asiatic's by the sun' and 'accoutrements rent and torn; and many without even shoes to their feet'.[10] Moore now had about 33,000 men under his command and he carried out a major re-organisation. The 2/23rd – along with the 1/6th, 1/9th and 2/43rd Foot – were placed in Colonel William Beresford's brigade, part of Major General Alexander Mackenzie-Fraser's 3rd Division. It took some days for this re-organisation to be completed and in the meantime, the Welch Fusiliers kept moving forward.

On the morning of 21 December 1808 the 2/23rd Foot was approaching the village of Sahagun when firing was heard in front. Lieutenant Colonel Wyatt immediately gave the order, 'Off hammer caps' which, Thorpe recorded, 'caused a thrilling sensation of delight, expectation, and ten thousand other thoughts and feelings impossible to describe'.[11] This was followed by the command, 'Prime, and load!' and 'the ramrods rattled gaily in the barrels, bayonets were fixed, and, as if their musical jingle had raised the spirits of all', the battalion moved forward at the 'double quick', eager to see action. Unfortunately, by the time the Welch Fusiliers reached Sahagun, the firing had ceased. They had missed an action in which the 15th Light Dragoons, under the command of Lieutenant General Henry, Lord Paget, had routed a superior force of French cavalry.

That night the Fusiliers heard all about it when they were billeted in a convent with some of Paget's men, and their prisoners. Thorpe thought the Frenchmen were 'fine soldier-like fellows' and admired their 'brass helmets surrounded below with leopard-skin, with a crest, from which drooped large curls of black horse-hair' which caused the Spanish peasants to call them '*los diablos*' ('the devils'). He spoke with a British corporal who had fought in the action and who 'complained much of the defensive armour of the French, their brass helmets, and scales on the cheeks and shoulders', remarking that he had 'picked one chap out when we charged, and I hammered him like a tinker for ten minutes; but if it had not been for my pistol, I should never have done no good'.[12]

Sahagun was the opening move of Moore's threat against the French communications. He had now learned of the fall of Madrid but resolved to continue moving forward against Marshal Nicolas Soult, who commanded some 30,000 troops spread out around the town of Carrion. Unfortunately for these intentions, Napoleon had learned the position of Moore's army – which he had believed to be retreating to either Lisbon or Corunna – and had decided in turn to attack with a view to destroying what he termed 'the hideous leopard' which 'contaminated by its presence the peninsula of Spain and Portugal'.[13] Ordering Soult to fight a delaying action to occupy Moore's attention, on 22 December the French emperor left Madrid for the north with 70,000 troops.

That same day, Lieutenant Colonel Wyatt's 2/23rd Foot was at the village of Santa Marta where it met its new brigade commander, Colonel William Beresford. A tall, powerful man with a ferocious appearance created by a dead eye, Beresford ordered the brigade to form square around him. He told his four battalions that they would soon see action and advised them, when they did, to remain cool and steady, and make 'as much use of the bayonet as possible, and, above all, not to throw away their fire until so near as to be certain of doing deadly execution'. On hearing these words, the brigade began to cheer but Beresford chided them: 'I know, my lads, you will do your duty; don't cheer; but remember the proof of the pudding is in the eating.'[14]

On the night of 23 December 1808, the brigade moved under arms toward Carrion. As Beresford expected to make contact with the enemy, its women and children were left at Santa Marta 'much against their wishes'. When Baird had landed at Corunna two months before he had tried to send the women and children – what one of his officers termed an 'everlasting clog' to the army – back to Britain, but the women had insisted on accompanying their menfolk.[15] Letting them go into action was quite another matter, and since the women rarely obeyed any orders given to them, Beresford formed a guard across the road to prevent their joining the line of march. After several hours of trudging in mud and snow, his brigade did not encounter any enemy, only their women 'who had with the perseverance of their sex out-manoeuvred the guard, got a Spaniard to guide them by a nearer route, and were quietly waiting our arrival in the morning at the turning of a cross road'.[16]

Moore had expected to open his attack early on 24 December but, during the previous evening, he had received reliable information that Napoleon was advancing rapidly toward him. Outnumbered more than two to one and in danger of being surrounded, he had no choice but to order a retreat toward Astorga. This order had a very adverse effect on the morale of his army, which had been high because it believed it had ended its interminable wandering and would soon see action. One officer remembered that 'solemn gloom prevailed through the ranks' of his regiment when the orders were given out and the only sound to be heard was the clatter of muskets being 'thrown down in despair'.[17] 'In my life', another commented, 'I never witnessed such an instantaneous withering effect on any body of living creatures'.[18] Not understanding the reason for the change the army reluctantly faced about and began to move west to the River Esla.

As part of Mackenzie-Fraser's 3rd Division, the 2/23rd Foot crossed the Esla by the Castro Gonzalo bridge and reached Benevente on Christmas Day 1808 after a miserable march under heavy showers of rain and sleet along roads knee deep in mud. In honour of the day, young Samuel Thorpe and his fellow officers were anxious 'to have extra good cheer' but, far from that, they did not receive any rations and so, 'dinnerless and supperless we turned into a convent'. Fortunately, Thorpe's hunger was 'appeased by a cake of chocolate bestowed by one of the friendly monks'.[19] The army was in a black and savage mood – as a medical officer described it:

> Weary and disheartened, in want both of rest and food, disappointed in all their fond hopes of victory, and indignant at being compelled to turn their backs upon an enemy whom they despised, and would so eagerly have met in battle; it was no doubt a relief for them to vent these their feelings, in transports of rage, upon the only objects within their reach. In this frame of mind they commenced a scene of plunder and havoc as they went along; and the officers, many of whom already murmured loudly at the excessive rapidity of the retreat, and were discontented with the stern silence which the commander-in-chief maintained respecting his future measures, did not exert themselves, as they ought to have done, to prevent these excesses.[20]

Considerable looting took place at Benevente and when Moore arrived there on 27 December, he issued a strongly-worded General Order condemning such acts, which he attributed to the 'negligence and inattention' of his officers.[21] As for complaints about the retreat he added that, when it was proper to fight a battle, he would do it, but would 'choose the time and place he thinks most fit'.

The 3rd Division marched for Astorga on 27 December. On this same day French cavalry attempted to cross the Esla but were rebuffed by Moore's rearguard, commanded by Major General Edward Paget. Over the next two weeks Paget's troops, termed the 'Reserve', would fight a series of notable defensive actions against the pursuers, keeping the enemy at a distance.

The Welch Fusiliers entered Astorga on 28 December under the impression – along with much of the army – that now they would halt and face the enemy. There was so much confusion and crowding in the town, however, that the commissariat found it impossible to make a regular issue of rations and many soldiers went hungry. When Moore issued orders, therefore, to destroy the provision and ordnance stores, it became clear, as one officer commented, 'that we were not only retreating but actually flying before the enemy'.[22] It also 'gave signal', another officer noted, 'for all the bad passions of those who witnessed them, to let loose, and, mortifying as it is to confess it, the fact cannot be denied, that from that hour we no longer resembled a British army' but 'rather a crowd of insubordinate rebels, in full flight before victorious soldiers than a corps of British troops moving in the presence of the enemy'.[23]

The work of destruction took nearly a day. When the 2/23rd left Astorga on the morning of 29 December, rum from the liquor stores was running down the streets and the Fusilier officers had difficulty preventing their men 'from remaining behind and getting intoxicated' and 'those who had shoes slipped them off their feet, and filling them with rum and mud drank it off at a gulp' while 'others filled their caps for the same purpose'.[24] There were more incidents of looting and Moore issued another General Order stressing that the army must behave properly, and directing general and commanding officers to 'adopt such measures, both on the march and in the cantonments, as will ensure it'.[25]

As if he did not have troubles enough, Romana's Spanish army – in retreat after being defeated by the French at the Battle of Mansilla on 30 December – intersected Moore's line of march at Astorga, causing much confusion. The Spanish 'Patriots' were a miserable sight, one British soldier commented, as they 'wanted clothing, accoutrements, arms, ammunition and even food' and the 'soldiers under arms little exceeded in number the sick borne on carts and mules and, as they passed slowly along, enfeebled and emaciated by disease', they resembled 'an ambulatory hospital'.[26] After some discussion, Romana agreed to retreat to Vigo, leaving the road to Corunna free for Moore's troops.

When the 2/23rd Foot marched out of Astorga, it entered the Galician Mountains. In the first twelve miles the road climbed nearly a thousand feet and much of it lay through the long Sierra Sevada pass. The weather grew worse, the

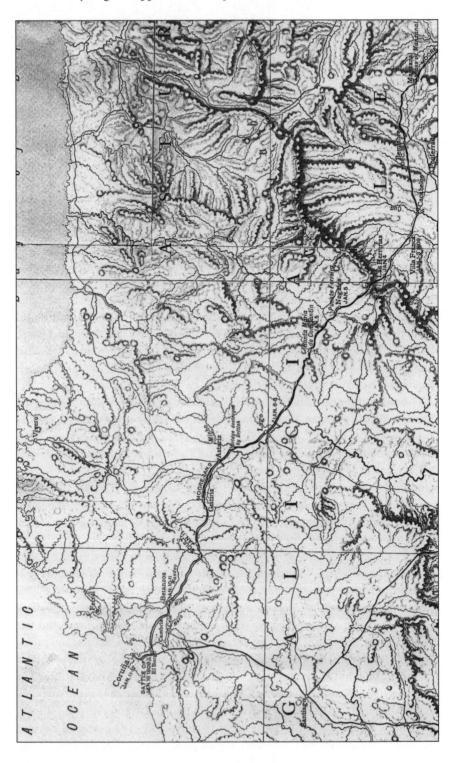

rain turning to sleet and then snow, and one man remembered that the silence in the ranks 'was only interrupted by the groans of the men' or when 'the report of a pistol told the death of a horse, which had fallen down unable to proceed'.[27] After a cold and hungry night in Mazanal, a miserable village huddled on a mountain top, the 2/23rd departed on 30 December for Bembibre, fifteen miles away. They now descended some 1,500 feet along a road that wound back and forth so much that it appeared that the column was making absolutely no progress.

Unfortunately for the army's discipline, which had earlier slipped its bonds, Bembibre – characterised by one officer as a 'wretched, filthy little hole' – was the centre for the local wine industry.[28] It was not long before unruly soldiers discovered the vats and the result was disastrous. Lieutenant Robert Blakeney of the 28th Foot, who marched into Bembibre with the rearguard on 2 January, recorded that 'Rivers of wine ran through the houses and into the streets, where lay fantastic groups of soldiers (many of them with their firelocks broken), women, children, runaway Spaniards and muleteers, all apparently inanimate, except where here and there a leg or arm was seen to move, while the wine oozing from their lips and nostrils seemed the effect of gunshot wounds.'[29] It was estimated that nearly a thousand soldiers and camp followers were prostrate but despite all the efforts of their officers and the rear guard, they could not be roused from their lethargy and had to be left to the enemy cavalry, which was pressing on the heels of the army. The French had no sympathy for these miscreants and galloped through them, slashing at them with their sabres 'right and left, regardless of intoxication, age or sex'.[30] Some of the survivors found their way back to their units where they were paraded through the ranks as examples to their comrades.

On New Year's Day 1809, Napoleon reached Astorga. Realising that Moore had eluded his trap, he turned over the pursuit to Soult and prepared to return to France as intelligence had reached him that Austria was preparing for war. Never a man to let the truth get in the way of good propaganda, however, Napoleon informed his minister of police that:

> The English have abandoned the Spanish is a shameful and cowardly manner. ... The English, it seems, had sent for 10,000 horses, so as to escape more quickly. Have all this shown up in the newspapers. Have caricatures [cartoons] made, and songs and popular ditties written; have them translated into German and Italian, and circulated in Germany and Italy.[31]

Left: The route of Moore's army from Astorga on 30 December 1808 to Corunna, which was reached on 11 January 1809, lay through the snow-covered Galician Mountains. (*From J. W. Fortescue,* **History of the British Army**)

That same day the 3rd Division departed Bembibre for Villa Franca, twenty miles distant. The weather grew worse with heavy snowfalls, intermixed with rain and sleet, and the weak and sick began to fall out by the side of the road. One officer thought this part of the retreat was 'terrible and heartrending' because:

> He who could go no further, stood still; he who still had something to eat, that ate he in secret, and then continued marching onwards; the misery of the whole thing was appalling – huge mountains, intense cold, no houses, no shelter or cover of any kind, no inhabitants, no bread. Every minute a horse would collapse beneath its rider, and be shot dead. The road was strewn with dead horses, bloodstained snow, broken carts, scrapped ammunition, boxes, cases, spiked guns, dead mules, donkeys and dogs, starved and frozen soldiers, women and children.[32]

The men and women in the columns, wet, frozen and weary, moved like automatons. While marching at the head of his regimental column Captain Charles Steevens of the 20th Foot fell asleep on his feet, only to wake up at its rear, forcing him to have to run forward to regain his proper position.[33] The seemingly endless marching was all too much for teenaged Samuel Thorpe, who became so exhausted that he fell out of the ranks and lay down in the snow. As he later wrote:

> The idea of becoming a prisoner caused me, however, to make great exertions, but the utmost I could do was to walk on half a mile, when the rattling of wheels announced the approach of our retiring artillery dragging through the snow. I now leant over a league-stone by the road-side, and looked a farewell as the guns passed, as at things I was about to take leave of for ever: the last passed by; several Officers cast a pitying look at me as much as to say, 'Poor fellow! would we could help you!' In the rear rode an Officer: at the first glance I found him to be an old brother collegian [from the Royal Military College at Marlow]: he dismounted and offered me every assistance in his power, and finding I could not proceed on foot, he kindly offered, even at his own personal risk of disobedience to orders, to place me in the forge-cart attached to the brigade. With gratitude I accepted his kindness, and soon found myself seated upon the forge-bellows, and screened from the observation of any general Officer by the low painted canvass tilt; he also, when able to speak to me without being observed, brought me biscuit and a little wine, with which I was so much refreshed, that –- after a march of between twenty and thirty miles, in a conveyance sufficient to dislocate every limb of a man in health –- yet when in the evening I entered the town [Villa Franca] in which my own corps was halted, I was so much recovered that after thanking my kind preserver most cordially I took my leave of him.[34]

The Sevadon Pass, 1809
A drawing by artist Robert Ker Porter, who accompanied Moore's forces, shows the retreating army snaking back and forth over a mountainous region south of Lugo. The roads in this region were abysmal and the weather was worse.
(Ker Porter, **Letters from Portugal and Spain,** *1809)*

The retreat continued. On 3 January the 3rd Division marched from Villa Franca for Lugo, sixty miles distant where, it was rumoured, not only were there large stocks of food but that the army would stand and fight. Immediately out of Villa Franca the road began a continuous back and forth ascent for about fifteen miles as it crossed the seven-mile wide Monte del Cebrero. It was bitterly cold and strong winds swept a heavy fall of snow into the faces of the marchers. As they neared the top of the height, some looked back to see 'the rear of the army winding along the narrow road' with 'the whole tract marked out by our own wretched people, who lay on all sides expiring from fatigue and the severity of the cold – while their uniforms reddened in spots the white surface of the ground'.[35]

It was now that most of the remaining women and children began to die. Before ordering the retreat Moore had tried to send the army's women to Portugal but, 'after being absent a few days, they again made their appearance' in the ranks.[36] Their fate now, one officer thought, 'was dreadful to behold' as some:

... were taken in labour on the road, and amid the storms of sleet and snow, gave birth to infants, which, with their mothers perished as soon as they had seen the light. ... Others in the unconquerable energy of maternal love, would toil on with one or two children on their backs; till on looking round, they perceived that the hapless objects of their attachment were frozen to death. But more frightful than this, was the depth of moral degradation to which these wretched followers of the camp were frequently reduced. Nothing could be more appalling to the heart, than to hear the dreadful curses and imprecations which burst from the livid lips of intoxicated and despairing women, as they laid them[selves] down to die.

Robert Ker Porter, a civilian artist travelling with the army, 'saw the body of a woman lying in a situation, that for misery', he thought 'unequalled' as 'two little babes, to whom she had just given birth, lay struggling in the snow'. Ker Porter was happy when the newborn were 'given in charge to a woman who came up in one of the bullock carts'.[37]

After spending a cold, hungry and miserable night in a small and barren mountain hamlet, the Welch Fusiliers marched into Lugo on the afternoon of 4 January to find a scene of the 'most dreadful confusion'.[38] The townspeople were 'praying, swearing, and screaming, and carrying out their beds, furniture, and valuables to the country, alarmed by the firing and near approach of the enemy' and the streets were 'filled with stragglers, Spaniards as well as English; the dead horses and mules blocking up the streets; pistols and carbines going off at intervals as the dragoons shot their horses ... when by fatigue and weakness they could urge them no further'.[39] The battalion did not pause long, however, as Major General Mackenzie-Fraser received orders to march his division to Vigo for embarkation and it took the road to that port. Moore, however, wisely deciding his exhausted men needed a rest, sent orders to Mackenzie-Fraser to return but unfortunately, the dragoon rider entrusted with this message got drunk on the way and Mackenzie-Fraser did not learn of the change of plan until his division was nearly a full day's march in the direction of Vigo. When the order caught up with him on the evening of 5 January, his weary men turned about and marched back to Lugo, where they arrived two days later, leaving behind a great number of stragglers.

Having collected his army and knowing that Soult would shortly be appearing, Moore decided to risk a battle. He assumed a good defensive position a few miles east of Lugo and issued another stern General Order demanding that his officers 'exert themselves to restore order and discipline in the regiments, brigades, and divisions which they command'.[40] Stressing that he was tired of giving orders, 'which are never attended to', Moore attributed the many 'crimes and irregularities' that had occurred on the march to a breakdown of discipline which it was the officers' responsibility to maintain.[41] He also informed the army that it would shortly face a battle with the French. The effect of this information was almost magical – one soldier remembered that insubordination ended, 'stragglers hastened to join their regiments, worn frames became reanimated with vigor, and the promiscuous assemblage of disorderly soldiers became again invested with all the attributes of a disciplined army'.[42] Thorpe commented that the Welch Fusiliers, 'although wet and hungry, with scarcely a leg to stand upon', gained heart at the prospect of 'thrashing the enemy'.[43]

The army waited but hour after hour passed without any action on the part of the French. Having only one day's supply of rations left at Lugo, Moore reluctantly decided to resume the retreat. During the night of 8 January, the 2/23rd 'received orders to procure as much fuel as possible, and make fires along the line at dark, as if intending to remain upon this ground during the night'.[44] When darkness had fallen, the army stood silently to its arms and withdrew along muddy roads under a heavy fall of rain, heading for Betanzos, some fifty miles distant.

Its hopes for battle dashed, the army again became dispirited. At this point, straggling grew to epidemic levels – with the exception of a few regiments and the faithful rearguard, which was kept in hand by Moore and Paget. 'Our men', one officer wrote, were 'quite mad with despair' as their fatigue 'and the consciousness of their disgrace, in thus flying before an enemy whom they despised, excited in them a spirit which was quite mutinous.'[45] Many fell out to plunder and 'so irresistible was the tendency to drunkenness amongst the men, in their now exhausted condition, it was even judged better to expose them homeless to the cold and rain of a severe night, than, by marching them into Betanzos, the next town, allow them to enter the wine-houses'.

As the marching columns moved down from the mountains into the foothills, the weather began to moderate but it was still a gruelling march, one portion of the road consisting of 'upwards of thirty zig-zags, apparently parallel for two miles'.[46] Along with many others, Samuel Thorpe was literally on his last legs and on several occasions, Lieutenant Colonel William Wyatt gave up his horse to the young officer and walked along by his side. Thorpe remembered that:

At every league dropped hundreds of our comrades; many falling dead from fatigue and exhaustion; others sinking into the mud and mire, where they perished from cold or suffocation: a general feeling also of delirium, more or less violent, seized on all, occasioned, I believe, by want of repose; some imagined they had arrived at home, and ran to salute their friends, and fell headlong over the terraced sides of the road; others had different but equally unreal visions. I myself several times thought when passing over bleak heaths, that I saw a noble inn with a roaring coal fire, and a substantial breakfast; and had it not been for a comrade with whom I had made a treaty of mutual assistance, I should several times have diverged from the road as thousands did, never to return. Shortly afterwards I was enabled to render assistance in a similar manner; for my friend himself

The retreat to Corunna, 1808–9
A detail from a drawing by Adam Neale showing a column marching through the mountainous country. Note the soldier with the sack slung over his musket and the woman with two small children. Unfortunately, most of the women and children who participated in the retreat died in these mountains.
(*From Neale,* **Letters from Portugal and Spain,** *1809*)

being quite overcome, told me abruptly that it was no use to try to go any further, but that he must rest upon this broken gun-carriage; and down he plumped upon a poor fellow who had lost his last shoe, and was groping for it [in] a pond of mud. With trouble I again got him on his legs, after hundreds of falls, some of many yards off the sides of the road, which was regained with the greatest difficulty.[47]

For his part, Soult was deceived by the night withdrawal from Lugo and when the 3rd Division, followed by the remainder of the army, reached Betanzos on 10 January, the French were lagging behind. Moore therefore granted his men another day of rest and made intense efforts to restore discipline. By this time a considerable body of British soldiers was moving between the two armies – some were stragglers who had fallen out because of exhaustion, while others were marauders who had deliberately left the ranks to plunder. The rear guard, posted a few miles outside Betanzos, observed these men, nearly 1,500 in number and 'formed in tolerably good order', actually repel a French cavalry charge, after which the enemy left them alone.[48] Major General Edward Paget ordered his rear guard to search the stragglers when they approached his position. Any money believed to have been acquired by dishonest means was removed from the miscreants and distributed among the rear guard while any plunder was thrown by the side of the road.

On the morning of 11 January, the army set off for Corunna, twenty miles distant. On this leg of the retreat Moore took the opportunity to speak personally with every regimental commander, emphasising that their eyes 'should be every where' and that straggling could be prevented by their activity.[49] His efforts paid off and the army resumed a tolerable state of order. About midway between Betanzos and Corunna, the columns ascended a hill, from which the soldiers could see the ocean and, as the exhausted men gained sight of 'the distant element in the midst of whose bosom was placed their beloved country', Thorpe remembered, they began to cheer.[50]

There was considerably less rejoicing when the 2/23rd Foot arrived at Corunna that evening to find not the fleet they had expected, but only a single warship and many were the 'maledictions' heaped on the Royal Navy.[51] Moore inspected each regiment as it entered the town. Some units were barely more than a rabble, others were in good order – particularly the two battalions of the 1st Guards, each still 800 strong, who entered Corunna, 'in columns of sections, with drums beating, the drum-major twirling his staff at their head and the men keeping step, as if in their own barrack-yard.'[52] Beresford's brigade was overjoyed when it was sent to do duty in the walled medieval quarter of the town, which they called the 'citadel', as it was the best billet they had enjoyed for months. Thorpe noted that the townspeople, who were 'all confidence and boast' when the battalion had landed there three months before, were 'now all panic, fear, and confusion, the streets filled with inhabitants flying they knew not whither, others hastening to the ramparts to prepare for defence'.[53]

While he waited for the fleet, Moore prepared to embark the army. Military stores and equipment that could not be issued were destroyed, including two magazines containing 4,000 barrels of powder that were detonated on 13 January. The resulting explosion broke windows all over Corunna and was so powerful that many of the inhabitants, believing 'that an earthquake was going to swallow them up, dashed out of their houses with despair written on their faces, and shouting like maniacs, tore their hair from their heads'.[54]

On the following day, 14 January 1809, Thorpe, somewhat recovered from his travails, made his way with several fellow Welch Fusilier officers to the ancient Roman lighthouse on the heights north of the town. Ascending to the top, they used their telescopes to keep:

> ... a watchful and steady eye along the waves of the distant horizon. A single speck was seen in the west: all eyes were directed to it as it increased and seemed to be nearing the coast; the hull gradually appeared; she was square-rigged, and three-masted. An old tar who had been sent to look out, exclaimed, 'She's a man-of-war, I can see her teeth' (guns). In a moment after he exclaimed, 'There's a fleet astern; look at him; he's telegraphing his commodore; he has got the signal for land flying at his mast-head. ...
>
> Other specks appeared along the margin of the view, and in the course of three hours some of the most mighty engines of British power passed within a few cables' length of where we stood, rounding the point to enter the harbour, our old nautical companion explaining with the highest interest the achievements of each line-of-battle ship. 'There, look how that was done (as a majestic first-rate handed her top-gallant sails); that there's the Ville de Paris; the old Tonnant couldn't a' done it better; but look at that there ship, that's just tacked for the harbour; that's the one as took her; that's his own ship; look, my boys, that's Nelson's ship' (it was the Victory).[55]

The transports came in at dusk and the embarkation, beginning with the sick, wounded and non-essential personnel, commenced the following day. It was none too soon as Soult, with three divisions, more than 16,000 men, was investing Corunna and French artillery batteries were bringing portions of the harbour under fire. Sadly, there were no special horse transports with the fleet and the army reluctantly destroyed most of its animals, lest they fall into the hands of the French. Steevens of the 20th Foot was horrified to see the killing of 'our fine English horses; many of them were brought to the edge of the rock over-hanging the sea, some shot, and others stabbed, and then thrown down; of course very many of them reaching the bottom alive, and there lay on the sands, poor things, where there were men placed to despatch them, frequently with a hammer'.[56]

The embarkation of non-essential personnel continued on the following day, 16 January, and Moore planned to have the entire army on board by nightfall. In the morning, however, seeing Soult massing in the hills around Corunna, he deployed for a defensive action on a series of low ridges nearer the town. About noon, Thorpe commented, Beresford's brigade, 'was ordered in much haste, by Moore in person, to quit the town and take up their place in position' with Mackenzie-Fraser's 3rd Division on the right flank of the army, guarding the road to Santiago, where it remained unengaged.[57] Around 2 p.m., Soult commenced a series of heavy attacks on the left flank of the British line, which pushed back Moore's outposts and threatened to take the ridge held by the divisions of Lieutenant Generals Sir David Baird and Sir John Hope. As the French began to work around the flank of the ridge, Moore ordered Paget's division forward and it broke up the French attack with disciplined musketry, following that up with the bayonet as it pushed the enemy back. Moore was planning a counter-attack when he was hit by a round shot which tore open his chest and left shoulder, exposing his lungs. Mortally wounded, he was carried to the rear but died shortly afterward. In the words of one of his senior officers, Sir John Moore was 'a brave and high-spirited' soldier who 'preferred the honour of his army to its safety; and by preserving the one, he provided for the other also'.[58] The fighting died away at nightfall and the French pulled back. It had been a hard-fought action, with much credit and heavy casualties on both sides, but it ensured that the British embarkation would be unmolested.

Baird had been seriously wounded in the battle and command now devolved on Lieutenant General Sir John Hope, who decided to continue

The keys to Corunna
Unable to find a Spanish officer to take the keys, Captain Fletcher brought them back to Britain, where they are now on display in the regimental museum. The metal tag reads 'Postern of the Lower Gate'. (*Courtesy RWF Museum*)

the embarkation that night. Major General Mackenzie-Fraser's 3rd Division, with the 2/23rd Foot, had not played an active part in the action and was therefore chosen as the last division to go on board. As a small, sorrowful party buried Moore by lantern light in a bastion of the medieval city, the army, brigade by brigade, leaving a line of fires in their positions to confuse the French, marched down to the port. The process of loading continued throughout the night and into the following day but was not seriously hindered by the enemy, although Soult's gunners fired at the fleet causing a number of transports to run aground, and these vessels were abandoned and set on fire to deny them to the enemy. The people of Corunna behaved very creditably – one soldier remembered that from the shore, the women waved their handkerchiefs at the soldiers in the boats 'whilst the men manned the batteries against the French, to cover our embarkation'.[59]

Beresford's brigade was the last to go on board and the 2/23rd Foot was the last British unit to leave Spanish soil. It was late on the evening of 17 January when Captain Thomas Fletcher's company, the battalion rearguard, left its post. Fletcher had the keys to the postern of the gate in the outer wall of the city nearest the harbour, but when he attempted to lock it behind him, the key would not turn. One of his corporals inserted a bayonet into the loop of the key and the two managed to secure the door before making their way to the waiting boats at about 1 a.m. on 18 January 1809. Finding no Spanish officer to receive them, Fletcher pocketed the keys and they can be seen today in the Royal Welch Fusiliers Museum at Caernarfon Castle in Wales, complete with their steel identification tag inscribed 'Postigo de Puerta de Abajo' or 'Postern of the Lower Gate'.[†] Their departure lit by the flames of the burning transports, the Welch Fusiliers sailed for Britain and, while out at sea on the next day, they 'could hear the heavy discharges from the Spanish works, directed, no doubt, against the advancing columns of France'.[60]

The troops from Corunna landed in almost every port in southern England, most of the 2/23rd coming ashore at Portsmouth. The survivors, Lieutenant Blakeney of the 28th Foot noted, 'were ragged, displaying torn garments of all colours' and British civilians, 'never having seen an army after the termination of a hard campaign, were horror-struck, and persuaded themselves that some dreadful calamity must have occurred'.[61] Moore's army had escaped the trap but the cost had been high – it has been estimated that, of the combined total of 33,234 men under his command, no fewer than 7,035 men were lost. The Welch Fusiliers paid a heavy price – of the 634 men of the 2/23rd who had left Cork the previous autumn, only 418 returned to Britain, although most of the missing men, 150 in all, were prisoners of war. There is no accurate information about the fate of the 2nd Battalion's 60 women and children and sadly it must be presumed that most perished.

Many of the survivors were ill with typhus and dysentery and about 6,000 were hospitalised. The army and navy's medical staff was overwhelmed and an appeal for assistance was made to medical students in London. The response was enthusiastic for, as one of the volunteers remarked, besides getting useful practice, the students received 'the privilege of dissecting those who die' without charge – a real bonus, considering that in London, they 'could not get a dead body under three guineas'.[62]

For his part, Lieutenant Samuel Thorpe made his way to his uncle's house, where his widowed mother resided, to take some leave. Because of his appearance the servant who answered the door did not recognise Thorpe and refused him admittance. After he had established his identity, the worthy servant 'burst into an agony of grief and filled the house with his cries', before shepherding the young

† In May 1979, through the good offices of the British Ambassador to Spain, the Royal Welch Fusiliers presented the Mayor of Corunna with exact duplicates of these keys.

man into the drawing room where his family was assembled. Thorpe sat in front of the fire while his loved ones sadly contemplated his ruinous state, which was so changed that even a favourite dog did not know what to make of him, but finally 'settled the doubt by a piteous whine' and jumped up on the teenager's knees 'to seek a caress'.[63]

Leaving 109 men in hospital at Portsmouth, Lieutenant Colonel Wyatt marched the remainder of the 2/23rd Foot to Horsham Barracks in Sussex and immediately commenced recruiting to fill his ranks. This seems to have been partially successful as when Lieutenant General Lord Charles Somerset, commanding the southern district, inspected the unit on 11 May 1809, it had a total of 788 men on its rolls, although about 250 were listed as either prisoners of war or in hospital. Somerset reported the men as being 'young and stout, rather tall than otherwise' and noted that there had been few regimental courts martial with the unit 'not having had a man punished since its return from Spain'.[64] Overall he found Wyatt's unit to be 'a very good steady battalion, well commanded and well officered'. Somerset also noted that no fewer than 426 of the men were from Wales, about 55 per cent of the total.

It was also in May 1809 that the Horse Guards asked Somerset whether the 2/23rd Foot was fit for active service. This query arose from a wish on the part of the British government to assist Austria which, encouraged by a restive mood throughout Europe against Napoleon's tyranny, had declared war on France in April. After much discussion, the government decided to make an attack against Antwerp, where Napoleon was constructing a fleet that was viewed as a potential threat. Remembering sad past experiences, however, it was determined that this expedition, to be commanded by Lieutenant General John Pitt, Earl of Chatham and brother of late Prime Minister William Pitt, would be as strong as possible and, eventually, Chatham received command of nearly 40,000 troops. Throughout the spring and early summer of 1809, the chosen units made their way by land and water to Deal in Kent, the rendezvous for the expedition. Hope, meanwhile, soared throughout Europe when word came of a major Austrian success against Napoleon at Aspern-Essling on 22 May, the first serious setback he had personally suffered since assuming the French throne five years before.

The 2nd Battalion, being judged fit for service, received orders to join Antwerp expedition. Given his strength, however, Lieutenant Colonel Wyatt only marched a half-battalion or five companies, 456 all ranks, to Portsmouth in late June where, after the usual wait for ships, they sailed for the Downs off Deal, arriving there safely on 27 July. A traditional rendezvous for overseas expedition, the Downs presented a marvellous picture of Britain's maritime power – there were so many warships and transports, nearly 300 sail, at anchor that it resembled 'an immense forest'.[65] The embarkation was a thoroughly splendid affair, one officer remembered, with bands playing the National Anthem and plentiful applause from the large crowds of civilian spectators, including many 'superbly dressed women'.[66] 'Many beauteous fair', he fondly recalled, 'whose smiles were rendered yet more brilliant by the intrusive tear, waved their handkerchiefs in the breeze to the fond objects of their fixed regard' as they were rowed out to the waiting transports. Not all the women present were happy, however, as owing to the miserable fate of the wives and children who had perished during the retreat to Corunna, orders had been issued severely restricting the number of dependants allowed to accompany Chatham's army. According to Private Harris of the 95th, the women left behind raised a 'terrible outcry' and 'some of them clung to the men so resolutely, that the officers were obliged to give orders to have them separated by force'.[67] Even after the men 'were in the boats and fairly pushed off', he commented, 'the screaming and howling of their farewells rang in our ears far out at sea'.

Unfortunately, the delay of more than two months in mounting the expedition proved fatal to the government's plans. Recovering quickly from his check at Aspern-Essling, Napoleon had engaged the Austrians at Wagram on 6 July, gaining a qualified victory that two days later resulted in a temporary armistice. News of this event reached Britain just before Chatham sailed, but hoping that this setback was temporary and that Austria would retake the field, the operation went ahead.

Making excellent progress, the fleet was off the mouth of the River Scheldt on 28 July 1809. To reach Antwerp, however, Chatham had to take his army nearly sixty miles up that shallow and treacherous waterway, which was divided into two channels – the East and the West – by the islands of Walcheren and South Beveland. Chatham's first step, therefore, was to either capture or get past the forts and batteries on these islands, which guarded the channels. A more aggressive officer would have moved swiftly but Chatham, although not without ability, was a cautious man who proceeded in a methodical fashion by first occupying the islands and then reducing the fortified positions, one by one. This gave the French, who had been taken by surprise by the sudden appearance of the massive British force, time to bring up reinforcements.

Bad weather delayed a landing until 30 July 1809 when the first troops – the five companies of the 2/23rd among them – came ashore on the north side of Walcheren. It was two days before Chatham's forces, having crossed the island and accepting the surrender of Middelburg on the way, appeared before Flushing, which commanded the West Channel. The enemy commandant refused to surrender the town and Chatham ordered batteries to be constructed to bombard it. Much of Walcheren had been reclaimed from the sea and was below sea level, and as the island's dykes had been cut on Napoleon's specific order, the boggy ground made it very difficult to haul heavy ordnance from the landing place on the north side of the island into the required position.

Despite the hard work, Chatham's army was impressed with what it could see of Holland. Captain Charles Steevens of the 20th Foot observed that there was hardly 'a piece of ground uncultivated; as for the towns they were remarkably clean and the houses very neat'.[68] Gomm of the 9th Foot was particularly impressed with Middelburg, which was 'neat that it gives you more the idea of the model of such a place, made of paste-work, than the town itself'.[69] The major complaints concerned the flat, uninteresting and flooded terrain, and the hordes of mosquitoes which descended on the army.

For nearly two weeks, soldiers and sailors laboured to construct batteries and to emplace heavy ordnance in them. Chatham was rarely seen but his senior staff visited the works daily and were always well turned out 'with brand-spanking new epaulettes, and snow-white feathers'. Unfortunately, their visits often resulted in new and contradictory orders 'as if for the sole purpose of displaying superior knowledge and individual importance' until it got to the point that, when the tars of the naval shore parties saw these officers ride up, they would nudge each other and shout, 'here comes the long feathers to undo our day's work'.[70]

The bombardment of Flushing commenced in the early afternoon of 13 August and young Samuel Thorpe thought it 'tremendous' with hundreds of guns firing on land and from the warships, 'as well as mortars and Congreve rockets all firing at the same time'.[71] It continued on into the dark, the night sky 'brilliantly illuminated by the flashes of the guns, the bursting of shells, and the streams of fire from the rockets.'[72] The Royal Marine Artillery detachments manning the Congreve rocket launchers had to take great care with their rather cranky weapons, as the back blast of these missiles often burned their hands and faces, and many thus 'exhibited a strange appearance' with 'no hair on their heads and their hands and shoulders severely scorched'.[73] On 16 August, having delayed Chatham for nearly two weeks, Flushing surrendered and the British entered the battered town to find whole 'streets had been thrown down or consumed, and the balls and shells had riddled the houses that remained standing, and broken all their windows' although the 'congreve rockets appeared to have caused more terror than absolute harm, most of them having fallen short'.[74]

Flushing had fallen but the army now encountered a new and more deadly enemy than the French when malarial fevers struck with remarkable swiftness and severity. Harris of the 95th saw parties of soldiers in the streets of the town 'shaking with a sort of ague, to such a degree that they could hardly walk; strong and fine young men who had been but a short time in the service seemed suddenly reduced in strength to infants, unable to stand upright'.[75] The fever spread rapidly – by 3 September 1809, Lieutenant Colonel Wyatt had 244 men on the sick list, about half his strength, and a week later there wasn't a single man fit for duty in the 2/23rd Foot. The malaria itself was not necessarily fatal but when combined with the more traditional scourges of typhus and dysentery, the result was a lethal epidemic that killed men in great numbers.[76] The Welch Fusiliers did not have enough healthy men, commented Samuel Thorpe:

> … to perform the honours of the funeral ceremony over their deceased comrades, nay, not even men to carry the coffins to the churchyards. To prevent the inhabitants knowing the extent of our losses, the bodies were

taken after dark, seven or eight in a waggon, to their long homes [i.e. graves]; and as the chaplains were all sick, the duty of reading the funeral service devolved upon those of the regimental Officers who were sufficiently well to perform it. A most melancholy duty it was. To be surrounded by the mortal remains of those who a few weeks, nay, days before had been our gallant comrades, while reading the awful and impressive service by the dim light of a horn lanthorn held by a non-commissioned Officer, who himself looked the picture of dissolution –- with the recollection that the very man who was now a corpse before you officiated on the last similar occasion –- caused feelings of a sad and melancholy nature mixed with gloomy forebodings for the future.[77]

Hospital facilities were almost non-existent. Major General William Dyott, Wyatt's brigade commander, visited the thousands of sick men in the extemporised military hospitals on Walcheren in late September and wrote that 'the miserable, dirty, stinking holes some of the troops were from necessity crammed into, was more shocking than it is possible to express'.[78] In vain, the government requested Dr Lucas Pepys, the physician-general of the army, to go to Walcheren and take charge of the medical services but Pepys declined, on the rather amazing ground 'that he knew nothing of the diseases of the soldier'.[79] Many invalids were shipped back to Britain but the sick list continued to grow, with an average of twenty to thirty men dying each day. 'Something must be done', Chatham's second-in-command, Lieutenant General Sir Eyre Coote, wrote him on 29 September 1809, 'or the British nation will lose the British army – far more valuable than the island of Walcheren.'[80] The government, however, delayed ending the operation because it hoped that Austria would resume hostilities with France. When news came in November that Vienna had signed a peace treaty with Napoleon with terms so harsh it cost her nearly a fifth of her national territory, orders were given for an evacuation that was completed in early December 1809.

The Walcheren expedition was an unmitigated disaster that accomplished absolutely nothing, at a considerable cost. Chatham's army had never come near its objective of Antwerp and, of the 39,219 officers and men who served under his command, 106 were killed in action while 3,940 died from disease. Even those soldiers who recovered from the Walcheren fever were weak for years afterward. The ramifications of this tragic operation continued long after the last soldier left the Scheldt, as it resulted in a lengthy inquiry and directly led to the fall of Portland's government. His replacement was Spencer Perceval, a modest man and former Chancellor of the Exchequer, whom few expected to survive more than a few months in office.

Fortunately for the 2/23rd Foot, it was among the first units to return to Britain. On 6 October, too weak to march, the survivors of the five companies were taken in wagons to Flushing and put on board waiting transports that carried them to Harwich where, depending on their physical condition, they either went into hospital or joined the rump of the battalion at Horsham. Of the 456 officers and men of the 2/23rd who served on Walcheren, not a single man was lost by combat or desertion but 183 died from sickness, either on the island or in British hospitals. As late as January 1810 Wyatt reported 133 men still in hospital with only to 252 fit for duty. The 2nd Battalion took a long time to recover from the Walcheren expedition, which was its last service outside Britain.

As 1809 drew to an end, Britain's cup was bitter. The hopes raised by the Spanish insurrection and Austria's declaration of war against France had disappeared as a result of Moore's retreat to Corunna, Napoleon's victory at Wagram and the Scheldt disaster. The only seemingly good news in this catalogue of woes was that Wellesley, cleared by the Cintra inquiry, had resumed command in Portugal, levered a French army out of that country and advanced into Spain where he had gained a sterling, if costly, victory at Talavera in late July. But even this spark of hope had been extinguished when Wellesley was forced – by the inability of the Spanish to assist him, shortage of provisions and far superior enemy numbers – to retreat to Portugal in August.

After nearly sixteen years of conflict, no end of the war was in sight.

The hour I remember well,
When first she owned she loved me,
A pain within my breast doth tell
How constant I have proved me:
But now I'm bound for Brighton camp,
Kind heaven then pray guide me,
And send me home, safe back again,
To the girl I left behind me.

My mind her image must retain,
Asleep or sadly waking;
I long to see my love again,
For my heart is breaking.
Whene'er my steps return that way,
Still faithful shall she find me,
And never more again I'll stray
From the girl I've left behind me.[1]

Chapter 7

'The finest Brigade in the army'

1st Battalion, Nova Scotia, Portugal and Spain, April 1809 – May 1811

IT IS TIME NOW TO RETURN to the 1st Battalion in North America. It landed at Halifax from the Martinique expedition in April 1809 and, for the officers, one of the first steps was to catch up on recent news from Europe by reading the *Nova Scotia Gazette*. This newspaper reprinted material from British publications that, during the shipping season from April to September, arrived on a fairly regular basis. On 2 May, for example, the *Gazette* published a summary of Moore's correspondence with the government during the last months of 1808 ending with a letter written from Astorga on 31 December in which the British commander reported he had 'no option now but to fall down to the coast as fast as I am able'.[2] We have seen what resulted from that decision.

On disembarking, the officers and men of the 1/23rd Foot were relieved to learn that they had missed the worst winter in living memory. The battalion did, however, suffer considerable sickness, mostly dysentery, on its return and some uncharitable people attributed the cause to a plentiful supply of cheap rum in Halifax. Captain Jack Hill vehemently denied this charge, writing that his light company 'never were so sober', despite the fact that the locals generously plied everyone in uniform with free drinks, 'being so glad to see us back again'.[3] The troops of Prevost's division were heroes to the Haligonians, who treated them as such. On 28 April 1809, the townspeople threw a splendid ball at the Masonic Temple for the officers of the Martinique expedition in a room 'decorated with laurel, and filled with transparencies of Battles fought, and breaches mounted, and every other description of military honour'.[4] The bands of the 7th and 23rd Foot supplied the music and the festivities lasted until dawn. Five days later, a local merchant funded a similar celebration for the NCOs. Lieutenant-Governor Sir George Prevost attended briefly to give the King's health, which was followed by a toast to 'The Soldiers who did their duty!' and this was 'echoed round and round the room, every individual repeating the sentence, and many a hearty cheer followed the libation'.[5]

Halifax was a pleasant station but by the spring of 1809 the tension between Britain and the United States caused by the *Leopard-Chesapeake* crisis appeared to have died away, and the Welch Fusiliers began to wonder how long they would remain in this distant garrison. The great fear, recorded Lieutenant Thomas Browne, was that the battalion would be condemned 'to North American service for years to come' as units often remained for long periods on that continent.[6] Lieutenant Henry Blanckley, who had considerable experience in the Mediterranean where his father had served as a British consul at several places, wrote directly to the Horse Guards to point out that he was fluent in French, Spanish, Minorcan and Italian and had previous experience in the commissariat in Sicily. This being the case, Blanckley thought he 'might be of utility to my brother soldiers' in Wellington's army in Spain but assured the Duke of York that his 'sole motive' for writing to him was 'the good of my Country and the hope of being of service to it'.[7] Blanckley's offer to serve in the Peninsula was not accepted and he remained with the 1/23rd Foot, which made the best of its lot and rejoiced in the good news that instead of being sent back to provincial outposts, it would do duty in Halifax.

'We were thus again in comfortable quarters', Browne commented, 'which we enjoyed the more, from a feeling that we had done something to deserve them.'[8] Companies were rotated for duty in the outlying posts and batteries of the port, and at the prisoner of war cage on nearby Melville Island. The major event of the military day was the afternoon review on the Grand Parade when one of the regiments in garrison would be under arms for inspection and most officers attended this event with their ladies, as well as many civilians. Halifax offered such attractions as the Theatre Royal, the Museum of Wax Works, and the Melville Island prison, whose inmates manufactured and sold an amazing variety of handicrafts including beautifully-fashioned model ships made from scraps of bone. For the officers there was also a never-ending round of receptions, balls, picnics, carriage rides and frequent invitations to Government House as Sir George and Lady Prevost liked to entertain, and most Welch Fusilier officers dined at the vice-regal table. Drummer Richard Bentinck recalled that life in Halifax for the soldiers was also pleasant as those who had a good conduct record 'could at any time get leave to go fishing or have hunting excursions; fish swarming in the rivers and plenty of wolves, deer and rabbits in the woods to be had for killing'.[9] Failing that, there was always cheap drink – West Indian rum sold for as little as fifty cents (two shillings) a gallon in the town – and it was estimated that there were more than a hundred grog shops and watering holes in the port.[10]

Unfortunately, this may have caused some fusiliers to wander from the straight and narrow. Drunkenness, commented Bentinck, was 'an offence that the Colonel most disliked to see' and Ellis punished it severely.[11] When Prevost inspected the battalion in June 1809, he was complimentary, finding Ellis 'an intelligent, active and zealous officer', the subordinate officers 'intelligent and carefully instructed', and the NCOs and private soldiers 'orderly and regular in quarters.'[12] He noted,

Fusilier, 23rd Regiment of Foot, 1815
An artist's impression of a Welch fusilier in full dress uniform, c. 1815. Although the bearskin cap was part of the regiment's full dress, it appears not to have been worn on campaign and only rarely in garrison during the period, 1793–1815. (*Painting by G.K. Tipping, courtesy RWF Museum*)

Captain George W. Bayntun (1738–1806)
Bayntun served in the 23rd Foot from 1775 to 1788 and, after his retirement in 1793, had his portrait painted by Thomas Beach wearing the full dress uniform of the late 1780s. The fusilier bearskin was an expensive item, difficult to maintain, and not generally worn in the field.
(*Courtesy RWF Museum*)

Lieutenant Colonel Henry Walton Ellis (1782–1815)
Commissioned at the age of six months, Ellis actually joined the regiment as a senior lieutenant at the age of fifteen. This miniature was probably done when he assumed command of the 1st Battalion in 1807 and does not show the four head or face wounds he acquired in 1811–14. A superb commanding officer, Ellis was present at nearly every major engagement fought by the 23rd Foot between 1799 and 1815.
(*Courtesy RWF Museum*)

Eagle of the French 82nd Regiment of the Line

Surrendered at Martinique in 1809, this was one of the first Napoleonic eagles to be acquired by the British Army. It is now on display in the Royal Welch Fusiliers Museum at Caernarfon Castle in Wales. *(Courtesy RWF Museum)*

Lieutenant Colonel William Wyatt (d. 1820)

Wyatt commanded the 2/23rd Foot in the Corunna and Walcheren expeditions, contracting illnesses that later led to his early retirement from the Army. *(Courtesy RWF Museum)*

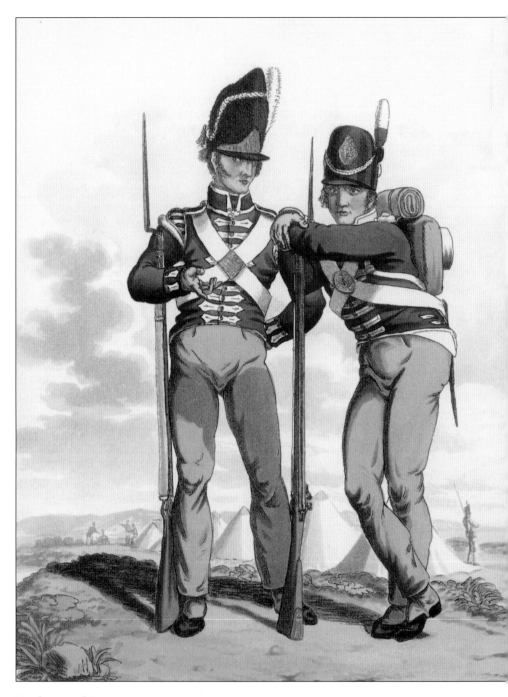

Fusilier, 23rd Foot, 1815
This period art by C. H. Smith from 1814 shows a Royal Welch Fusilier and a private of the 6th Foot
The fusilier's uniform details are correct for the late war period but Smith, like many artists, has put
the man in a bearskin, which was not worn overseas in the later years of the war.
(From Smith, **Costume of the Army of the British Empire,** *1814)*

Locking the Doors to Corunna, 1809
On the night of 17 January 1809, the 23rd Foot were the last unit to embark at Corunna. Captain Thomas Lloyd Fletcher commanded the rearguard and had difficulty locking the gate of the town leading to the harbour but, as shown in this modern painting, with the help of a corporal, he finally managed to secure it. The bearskin was not, however, worn on overseas service after 1799 although many artists depict it.
(*Courtesy RWF Museum*).

Lieutenant General Sir Galbraith Lowry Cole (1772–1842)
Cole commanded the 4th Division in which the Fusilier Brigade served between 1810 and 1814. At Albuera in 1811, he had the moral courage to disobey a direct order and launch an attack that decided the battle in favour of the allied army. (*Print after painting by Thomas Lawrence*)

Above: **Captain Gordon W. Booker (1789–1865)**
Commissioned in the 23rd Foot in 1807, Booker was badly wounded at Albuera and invalided to Britain. He rejoined the 1/23rd in 1813 and fought at Vitoria before again being seriously wounded at Roncesvalles in July and going on half pay. Booker's Peninsular letters to his fiancée are held in the regimental archives. *(Courtesy RWF Museum)*

Above left: **Bloody Albuera, 16 May 1811**
This late-nineteenth-century illustration showing the 57th Foot at Albuera is one of the few that depicts the wretched weather at the time of the action. The bloodiest battle of the Peninsular War and one of the most costly days in the history of the British Army prior to 1914, victory at Albuera was secured by the attack of Cole's 4th Division, headed by the Fusilier Brigade. *(From Marshman, Brave Deeds, 1889)*

Left: **The Looting of the Dead**
In this graphic drawing by Goya, camp followers loot and strip the dead after a battle. Such scenes occurred after every major action fought by the 23rd Foot in the Peninsula. *(Print after Goya, 'Horrors of War')*

The breach at Badajoz
Modern photograph showing the face of the Trinidad bastion which was breached by the besiegers and attacked with disastrous result by the 4th Division on the night of 6 April 1812. Gone now are the ditch, the outerworks and the many deadly obstacles created by the defenders.
(Courtesy Robert Burnham)

Flogging
Although its use has been much exaggerated, flogging was the standard corporal punishment in the British Army and for every person who wished it abolished, there was one who wanted it retained. Lieutenant Colonel Ellis of the 23rd Foot used it to maintain discipline in his battalion although he remitted most of the lashes he awarded. *(Drawing by Eugene Lelièpvre, courtesy Parks Canada)*

Salamanca

A modern photograph showing the ridge south of the village of Los Arapiles, which was attacked by the Fusilier Brigade during the battle. The fusiliers put to flight a French brigade occupying it but an enemy counter-attack caught them unprepared and they broke and ran before being re-formed and rejoining the battle. *(Courtesy Rory Muir)*

Salamanca, 22 July 1812

This painting by R. Caton-Woodville depicts the 23rd Foot engaged at close range with their opponents. The artist has depicted them in impossibly clean and neat uniforms but at least has not shown them wearing the bearskin. Note the 'flash' on the collar of the officer. *(Courtesy RWF Museum)*

Major General Robert Ross (1768–1814)
Ross assumed command of the Fusilier Brigade
in the early summer of 1813 and led it through
the last campaigns of the Peninsular War. A very
professional soldier, he is remembered today
more for his death outside Baltimore in 1814
than his service in the Peninsula.
(Courtesy Stephen Campbell of Rostrevor)

'English Troops – Campaign Baggage'
Caricature by the French artist, Eugene
Delacroix, 1815. Although there is considerable
exaggeration in the work, it was clearly sketched
from life. Throughout the period 1793–1815,
women and children accompanied the British
Army on most of its campaigns and period
commentators regarded them as a mixed
blessing. *(From **Gazette des Beaux-Arts**, 1873*

Marching to Vitoria

Thomas Rowlandson depicts troops on the march in the Peninsula. Of interest here is the number of soldiers' wives and their children, including one brawny lady on the right about to carry a young officer over the waterway. (*Author's collection*)

The 'Flash'
A sketch of Colonel Sir Thomas Pearson showing the 'flash'. The origins of this uniform distinction date to 1809 in Halifax when the regiment reluctantly obeyed a general order to cut its queues and it is still worn today by the Royal Welch Fusiliers in certain orders of dress. *(Drawing by Lieutenant General Sir Richard England, courtesy RWF Museum)*

Memorial to Colonel Sir Henry Ellis, Worcester Cathedral
Every officer and man in the 23rd Foot voluntarily gave up a day's pay to contribute to the £1,200 cost of this memorial to Colonel Ellis in Worcester Cathedral. The work of sculptor John Bacon, it shows Ellis falling from his horse while an angel hovering behind him places a laurel wreath of victory on his head.
(Photo © Sandra Taylor)

Richard Bentinck and wife in later years
Bentinck was invalided out of the 23rd Foot, much against his will, in 1823. He turned to gardening for a living but never forgot his experiences in the Great War with France. Every 18 June, on the anniversary of Waterloo, he would put on his Waterloo Medal and Military General Service Medal and make the rounds of the local gentry, soliciting donations for his private celebration of the anniversary. Richard Bentinck died at the age of eighty-eight in 1874.
(Courtesy Jonathan Crook)

Dragon Rampant in the twenty-first century
Nearly two centuries after Waterloo, the rampant Red Dragon of Wales remains the symbol of the Royal Welch Fusiliers as it is their Tactical Recognition Flash worn on certain orders of dress. The fusilier shown here is training in Afghanistan in 2007.
(Courtesy Lieutenant Colonel Nicholas Lock)

however, that in the previous eight months, there had been thirty-two regimental courts martial 'by which 101 men have been tried, 5 Sergeants and 3 Corporals reduced, 36,550 lashes sentenced and 5,950 inflicted.' These figures demonstrate that Ellis was a disciplinarian but they also indicate – as he remitted five of every six lashes given out – that he tempered discipline with humanity.

In the early summer of 1809, an important event took place in the history of the Royal Welch Fusiliers. The previous year, the Horse Guards had abolished the wearing of queues or pigtails, a practice dating back nearly a century but this order did not catch up with the 1st Battalion until after its return from Martinique. When it did, Ellis broke the news in the officers' mess one evening after dinner. Having taken an extra glass or two 'by way of softening our vexation', Thomas Browne remembered, his fellow officers immediately carried out the order using a carving knife on each other's queues before making 'a grand friz of them in the fire'.[13]

The next morning, however, there was trouble when the order was read to the men and it was not the soldiers but their wives who caused it. The wives had traditionally competed with each other to turn out the husband with the best queue and so important was this activity regarded that 'the estimation in which the women were held by the soldiers, was not by any means derived from beauty or good conduct, but was proportioned to the degree of approbation bestowed upon the heads which they had dressed'.[14] When the order to cut queues was read out, the wives assembled in small groups in the barrack yard and 'swore by oath' that 'they would murder the first operator who should dare to touch a hair of their husband's head'.[15] The adjutant reported the unrest to Ellis who was quick to put an end to it. Going directly to the barrack yard, he called out the first company and:

> … ordered a roll call of the company to see that every man was present; which was the case as it was near the dinner hour. Having ascertained this he desired them to take open order, and sending for benches from the barrack rooms had them placed behind each rank, and commanded the men to sit down. This they did in perfect silence, he then ordered off their foraging caps and sent for half a dozen hair cutters, of which there are always plenty in every Regiment. They were set to work and in less than ten minutes, nothing remained but the stump of the favourite club [queue]. The benches were then removed, ranks closed and the company dismissed.
>
> The women assembled in groups and cursed and muttered, but the eye of the commanding Officer subdued every other indication of mutiny, as he would inevitably have turned out of barracks, any of these heroines whose voice he could have distinguished.
>
> Company after company underwent the same process, and it was droll enough to see the men as they were dismissed to their barrack rooms, applying their hands to the back of their heads, to ascertain if it were a dream or a reality.[16]

This mass shearing, however, gave birth to a hallowed Royal Welch Fusilier distinction. The officers took the ribbons with which they had formerly tied their queues and fashioned them into a 'flash', or badge. This was worn on the back of the collar in the place where a small patch had been sewn to protect it from the grease and oil of the queue. We shall hear more of this practice anon.

The cutting of the queues was the perhaps most interesting happening during the 1st Battalion's 1809 service in Halifax. Otherwise, it was a pleasant round of light duties, parades, and social occasions – all great fun to be sure but there was concern that the battalion would never escape from this colonial backwater. As Captain Jack Hill commented, 'the reports of the Continental war spreading, make us look with impatience for the dispatches from Europe'.[17] During the summer and autumn, the Welch Fusiliers therefore read with interest the *Nova Scotia Gazette*'s accounts of Lieutenant General Arthur Wellesley's advance into Spain and his subsequent victory at Talavera – for which he was ennobled as the Viscount Wellington – and the 2nd Battalion's participation in the ill-fated Walcheren expedition.

In the meantime, they enjoyed life. Not a few succumbed to the blandishments of Canadian girls, whose mothers were anxious to make good matches for them because in Nova Scotia a red coat, whether commissioned or enlisted, was looked upon as a fair marital prospect. For the men, an additional inducement to matrimony was that a battalion on foreign garrison service was permitted ten wives per company rather than the six normally allowed and thus more men could legally marry. Quartermaster Sergeant Garrett Moore, who had enlisted as a private in the 23rd Foot in 1798 and risen steadily through the ranks, was one of the first to take advantage of this provision when, in July 1809, he married Mary Ferrant at Halifax. The officers were no different. His attempt to get transferred to the Peninsula not having been approved Lieutenant Blanckley consoled himself by making an excellent match with Elizabeth Foreman, daughter of one of the wealthiest merchants in Halifax. Surprisingly, that ferocious martinet but fighting soldier, Major Thomas Pearson, went to the altar with Ann Coffin of New Brunswick, the daughter of a prominent Loyalist officer. The marital tide rose so high that even the hot-tempered Major Francis Offley contemplated committing matrimony, Jack Hill reporting that Offley 'would marry, was there anything worth having' in Nova Scotia.[18]

This was rather an unkind thought on Hill's part but one should not be so surprised as, in recent years, the light company commander had become rather strange in his behaviour. 'His eccentricities', the observant Browne recorded, 'affected every thing he did, except his military duties, in all of which he was as correct as any Officer of the corps & exceedingly beloved by the soldiers of his company'.[19] For example, there was the matter of his room, which Browne entered one morning:

... to see all his clothes and every thing else belonging to him, spread out upon the Floor, a sort of Alley being left from the door to his bed. On my smiling at this arrangement he very calmly pointed out to me the great advantage that it had, over the usual custom of keeping things in boxes & portmanteaus. 'Now', says he, 'when I come into my room & want something I have only to look round about me and see at once, where it is, whilst you, I dare say, are poking half an hour or more in your box, and perhaps don't find it after all'. The Captain was quite serious, and satisfied that his wardrobe was better placed on the floor of his barrack room than it could possibly have been any where else. It was indeed a curious piece of Mosaic work, composed of coats, waistcoats, fishing rods & stockings, boots and swords, shoes and sashes. He told me also that there was another advantage attending this plan of his, which was, that he could count at any time, in about ten minutes the number of things he had in the world – that he then possessed 307 things, counting every pair of boots and gloves as two things.[20]

'I could have split my very sides with laughter', the young officer commented, but Hill 'was so grave about it, and a man at all times sensitive to ridicule'. There was also Hill's novel method of keeping his financial records on the wall of his room with red chalk as in: 'I have just lent Browne a shilling' and the date, or 'Browne has just repaid me the above'. Since officers had to pay for any damage done to their rooms before they left a station, Hill frequently had 'a bill to discharge for the fresh white-washing of his room, which he invariably did without the least dispute'.[21]

In October 1809, the battalion was again sent on outpost duty at Annapolis Royal with three companies under the command of Pearson, going farther afield to St. John, New Brunswick. Browne, who was part of Pearson's detachment, was not impressed with his new station, which he characterised as 'a miserable looking place', but found consolation in the fine shooting and fishing available in and around the town. Thus, the Royal Welch Fusiliers passed the long Canadian winter of 1809-1810.

When the weather grew warmer and the shipping season resumed and with it, the arrival of newspapers from Europe, the battalion began to grow increasingly restive. They read how Marshal André Masséna, under orders from Napoleon to invade Portugal and drive Wellington's army into the sea, was preparing for a massive offensive. In May 1810, when Edward Pakenham of the 7th Foot was promoted colonel and left for an appointment with Wellington's army, he promised the 7th and 23rd Foot that 'he would spare no exertion' to 'have them emancipated from the inactive scenes of a garrison life in North America' and transferred to the Peninsula where he 'would himself beg to have the command of us'.[22] Since Pakenham happened to be Wellington's brother-in-law, the fusiliers believed him and 'looked forwards with sincere delight to service under his command'.

In early July 1810, anxiety rose to fever pitch when the battalion returned to Halifax. The 1/7th Foot had already embarked for the Peninsula and the 1/23rd expected to follow their fellow fusiliers but were disappointed to learn they would not leave until orders had been received from Britain. Unfortunately the June mail packet, which carried official dispatches, was delayed and, when it had not appeared by the last day of July, Hill noted that his comrades were taken 'all aback' as, 'not knowing whether we are to go or stay, our situation is not very pleasant, as in this country, it is in the summer one must prepare for winter'.[23] It was early August before the packet appeared but, thankfully, it carried orders for the battalion to prepare to leave for Lisbon. There was a great celebration that night in the officers' mess, whose members drank as much of their wine stock as possible, to be spared the trouble of transporting it back across the Atlantic.[24]

There was no sign, however, of the ships that would carry the battalion to Portugal and it remained in suspense. 'We have been daily expecting to see the transports arrive that are to take us to Europe', Hill remarked at the end of August and he hardly knew 'what to write, we are in this Garrison with not very much to do'.[25] Prevost, taking advantage of the battalion's presence in Halifax, carried out its annual inspection on 2 August and praised Ellis as 'an officer of promising talents, uniformly zealous in the discharge of his duty, and judicious in the enforcement of Military Discipline'.[26] He found the field officers and captains to be, without exception, 'active and intelligent' and described the battalion as 'a good serviceable body of men, with a general appearance of health – though many are under the fixed standard' of height and whose 'conduct in quarters is orderly and soldier like'. Prevost reported that 47 men had appeared before regimental courts martial, '3 sergeants and 3 corporals reduced, 18,450 lashes sentenced and 6,975 inflicted.' It would appear that, compared to their inspection of 1809 quoted above, the battalion's discipline had improved as Ellis had handed out about half the punishment he had in 1809 and continued to remit most of it.

It was only in the first few days of October before the transports, HM Ships *Regulus* and *Diadem*, were sighted in the Eastern Passage leading to Halifax harbour. Now came a final flurry of activity, Lieutenant Browne noted, as the 'usual preparations were made', bills 'were collected and I believe paid', and 'farewells were bid to Sweethearts'.[27] On 11 October 1810 the 1st Battalion of the Royal Welch Fusiliers, 814 officers and men strong, accompanied by sixty wives and sixty-three children, embarked for Portugal.[28]

Blessed with favourable winds, the 1/23rd Foot had a good passage and, thankfully, did not experience any rough weather. Unlike their previous voyages, often made in filthy tubs chartered by the Board of Transport, *Diadem* and *Regulus* were disarmed warships, competently commanded and spotlessly clean. Royal

Navy discipline prevailed, however, and the Fusiliers seemed to be 'perpetually transgressing some little point or other of etiquette, and incurring the Captain's displeasure'.[29] On HMS *Diadem*, for example, this meant that every time Welch Fusilier officers came on deck, they had to salute the pennant flying on the main mast head; they were not to lean against the capstan nor sit on a gun carriage; assemble in groups of more than two men and, above all, never walk on the windward side of the deck which was the preserve of the captain. There were so many 'little peculiarities of the same nature' and so many breaches of naval etiquette on the part of the fusiliers that the ship's captain constantly remonstrated with Lieutenant Colonel Ellis, 'who endeavoured to find excuses for us, in our ignorance of man of war discipline'. The inevitable result, Browne noted, was that 'a sort of coolness' arose between the battalion commander and the ship's captain, 'although they did not permit it to affect their outward conduct ... on any point of duty', perhaps a tactful way of saying that the two officers barely tolerated each other.[30]

The Royal Navy's attitude towards death was straightforward and efficient. Drummer Bentinck remembered that, when one man died during the passage, he 'was sown up in a sack, almost before he was cold, with a cannon shot at his feet to sink him' and 'tilted off a plank into the sea, with a complete absence of ceremony'.[31] The man's widow, however, 'proved herself to be worthy of a soldier's wife, for she married another soon after they landed'. Another member of the fusilier family to pass away was Robert Page, a child, whose death on 20 October was briefly recorded in the muster of HMS *Diadem* accompanied by the initials, 'D.D'., or 'Discharged, Dead', after his name.[32]

By the end of October the ships reached the Azores and a further twelve days' sailing brought them to the River Tagus and Lisbon. The battalion disembarked on 13 November 1810 but did not stay long in the city. Browne recorded, that it 'was immediately supplied with camp kettles, and other necessary equipment for taking the field, the Officers purchased Mules to carry their baggage, and provided themselves with canteens, containing a few knives and forks, spoons and plates, with a drinking tin or two'.[33] Thus equipped, the 1/23rd marched from Lisbon on 16 November to join the main army.

When the Royal Welch Fusiliers arrived in Portugal, the war in the Peninsula was at a stalemate. During the previous summer, Marshal Masséna, with an army of 70,000 troops, had commenced operations intended to conquer Portugal. Moving slowly and carefully, he had taken the fortresses of Ciudad Rodrigo and Almeida, the two fortified cities that guarded the northern route into Portugal and in early September, began his advance on Lisbon. Unfortunately for the French commander, Wellington had secretly constructed the lines of Torres

The 1/23rd Foot in the Peninsula, 1810–11
Map © C. Johnson

Vedras, three belts of mutually-supporting fortifications across the northern part of the Lisbon peninsula. Lieutenant Browne, a careful observer, has left an excellent description of these defences:

> The lines of Torres Vedras extended from Alhandra on the Tagus, to the mouth of a small stream called the Sizandro. The line across the country between these points, if drawn directly, would be about twenty seven miles, but owing to the zig-zag direction of the vallies [*sic*], the line of defence was nearly forty. Every road, which could have afforded any advantage to the enemy, had been broken up, and others had been opened, to facilitate our communications with each other. Inundations had been made wherever it was possible, hills had been scarped perpendicularly, and intrenchments formed in all directions. Every approach was commanded by cannon, and redoubts had been made, capable of offering an obstinate resistance, even should the French get into their rear, and these redoubts were well provided with provisions and ammunition.[34]

Behind the first line were two others, nearly as strong. If forced to do so, Wellington intended to fall back on these defences after laying waste to the countryside outside them.

When Masséna crossed the border, it turned out exactly as the British commander had planned. Pausing only long enough to fight a rearguard action at Busaco on 27 September, which resulted in a bloody nose and heavy casualties for the enemy, Wellington withdrew behind the lines. Masséna, who had absolutely no knowledge of their existence, was amazed when he first viewed them on 14 October but immediately realised they were impregnable, given the force he had under his command. Unable to attack but reluctant to retreat, the French commander sat before the lines until mid-November before pulling back to the area around Santarem, where it was easier to procure provisions. Wellington thereupon moved north out of the lines to maintain contact but deteriorating weather ended active operations and both armies went into winter quarters.

This was the situation when the 1/23rd Foot marched from Lisbon for Azambuja, about fifteen miles southwest of Santarem. Their route took them through the village of Alhandra, which was garrisoned by a large naval shore party and the fusiliers noted the delight of the sailors who, enjoying the novelty of serving on *terra firma*, sat in the village streets, 'smoking their pipes, in venerable, velvet covered chairs, studded all over with brass nails'.[35] When it moved north of the lines of Torres Vedras the battalion marched through an area thoroughly despoiled by the French in 1808 and 1810. Lieutenant John Harrison recorded that:

> The towns represented all the horrors of War, deserted by every inhabitant, many houses unroofed and scarcely a window visible. The rich

and beautiful ornaments of the Churches and Convents all destroyed, and every place left in a most dirty and filthy description by the French. Not an article of any description to be procured nor a living animal to be seen but what belongs to the Army. We luckily took the precaution to bring a few comforts with us otherwise we should have been miserably off. ...

The French retreated in very good order, left not a vestige behind with the exception of the horses and mules which died on the road in some numbers to the great annoyance of the olfactory nerves.[36]

The soldiers were less sensitive. The battalion was often billeted in deserted and ruined churches and convents whose contents fuelled the cooks' fires. Bentinck recorded that his comrades 'burnt up carved work and polished mahogany like dried sticks' and even 'the wooden saints were powerless to protect themselves from their red-coated Protestant allies'. '"Fetch Saint Antonio here", the cook would cry out when his fire burned low or "Help me on with Saint Nicolo, Bentinck," and by their grins as the helpless "Saint" crackled into flame they might have been mistaken for a pair of gnomes cruelly tending him in purgatory.' [37]

In the last week of November 1810, the 1/23rd arrived at Azambuja and Lieutenant Colonel Ellis was delighted to learn that it would join the 1/7th and 2/7th Foot to form the Fusilier Brigade.[38] Better still, the brigade commander was none other than 'Ned' Pakenham who had fulfilled his promise made in Halifax to not only get the two fusilier battalions out of Nova Scotia but also to bring them under his command. The new brigade was attached to the 4th Division under the command of Major General Galbraith Lowry Cole. An Anglo-Irishman who had led either a brigade or division under Wellington for two years, Cole was renowned for throwing the best dinner parties in the army. The fourth element of the brigade was a company of the Brunswick Oels Jaegers, a foreign unit formed by the Duke of Brunswick, nephew of King George III. They were commonly known as the 'Black Legion' because of their black uniforms, belts and striking shakos which 'were covered at top with shiny black leather surmounted with a tuft of long black horse hair. Below was a white metal plate perforated to represent Death's head and marrow bones, the monogram of their motto -- 'No Quarter! Victory or Death!'[39] In late 1810 three of the unit's companies, armed with rifles, were distributed to British infantry brigades to improve their skirmishing capability and one came under Pakenham's command.

Its commander was 27-year-old *Hauptmann*, or Captain, Friedrich von Wachholtz, an intelligent and literate officer. The scion of a military family, von Wachholtz had entered the Prussian army as a cadet in 1798, fought against the French in the campaigns of 1806-1807 and, after the severe reduction of the Prussian army carried out at Napoleon's insistence, joined the Brunswick Oels. He was not particularly pleased at having his company attached to a British brigade and his first impression of his new superiors was not that positive:

The Duke of Wellington (1769–1852)

Wellington was respected rather than liked by his soldiers but they always knew that he would not risk their lives unnecessarily. His string of victories in the Peninsula between 1808 and 1814 and his final success at Waterloo in 1815 made him the most admired military commander of his time. (*Print after painting by Lawrence from Gleig,* The Life of the Duke of Wellington, *1864*)

> We formed a square into which General Cole and Colonel Pakenham entered. The first, the divisional commander, was a big man with a stern face, between 30 and 40, while the latter was younger, hardly in his 30s, but with an open face that appealed to me. General Cole spoke in English and I had to translate for the company. He stated that he would severely punish any man who was found looting and if the company engaged in such practices, it would be sent back to its parent regiment in disgrace. He stressed that looting was dishonourable to the character of a soldier.[40]

Irritated by Cole's abrupt manner, von Wachholtz was somewhat mollified when Pakenham, after the division commander had left the parade, 'welcomed us to his brigade with kinder words'. Pakenham himself was pleased with his new command, boasting to his brother that he had 'the finest Brigade in the Army all to Chalk, and between our selves I will prove it so'.[41]

The 1/23rd Foot remained at Azambuja until 24 January 1811 when they shifted to the nearby village of Aveiras de Cima. With the exception of some infrequent minor skirmishing, there had been little contact with the enemy for nearly two months and Lieutenant Harrison complained to his parents that his comrades were 'in such obscurity respecting the arrangements and plans of the Army, that it is almost presumption in me to offer a description that you will get more minutely and perhaps more correctly detailed in an English Paper, to which we are obliged to refer to sometimes'.[42] In late January the Fusilier Brigade was sad to see Pakenham leave for an appointment on Wellington's staff. His replacement was Major General William Houston, a somewhat elderly officer whom Harrison thought 'a pleasant old boy'.[43] The following month, however, Houston was promoted to command the newly-formed 7th Division and the brigade came under the command of Lieutenant Colonel Edward Myers of the 7th Foot, a very capable officer.

In mid-January Major General Cole formed his 4th Division in a large area of open ground to be inspected by Wellington and, for the first time, the Welch Fusiliers saw all its components on parade. The division comprised eleven battalions of infantry organised in three brigades – Myers's Fusilier Brigade (1/7th, 2/7th, 1/23rd Foot and the Brunswick rifle company); Brigadier General James Kemmis's brigade (2/27th, 1/40th, 97th Foot and a rifle company of the 60th); and Brigadier General William M. Harvey's Portuguese brigade (11th and 23rd Portuguese Regiments each of two battalions) – with a total strength of about 4,500 bayonets. All of the British units, with the exception of the 1/23rd Foot, had served in at least one campaign in the Peninsula and some, such as the 2/7th Foot, were seasoned units that had seen much action. The Welch Fusiliers were thus very much 'Johnny Newcomes' in this assembly of veterans and no doubt were the recipients of numerous jibes stressing this fact.

Although the winter of 1810-1811 was not unduly harsh, the battalion suffered considerable sickness. On 25 January 1811, Lieutenant Colonel Ellis reported 34 officers and 653 men fit for duty, 146 officers and men on the sick list, and a further 73 men, probably older soldiers unfit for active service, sent back as invalids to Britain.[44] The major malady was the traditional soldier's complaint of dysentery – as Harrison explained: 'What affects us most, are dysenteric attacks which we have all experienced more or less, and attributed by professional men more to the water than our mode of living.'[45] Harrison himself liked Portugal, finding the air 'serene and pure' but feared that 'it will never recover from the devastation of the Military operations'.[46]

In the meantime, the officers entertained themselves as best they could and Harrison recorded some of their pastimes:

> You ask me for Regimental anecdotes, which I can furnish you very little of. As for [Lieutenant James] Cane and our old Sub[altern]s, they do nothing but abuse the service from morning till night. ... [Captain Jack]

Hill is the same sterling fellow as ever, his great delight is poking after a few partridges and cocks, which bye the bye are very plentiful in this neighbourhood, but as my mother says, what's a recruiting party without a Drum and Fife, and what's partridge shooting without dogs which is the way they are obliged to sport here. And as the Irishman says, if it was not for the honour of the thing they might as well stay at home, as they generally return without a feather, and are rewarded with a good soaking.[47]

When not out shooting, and after taking 'wine very freely', Jack Hill liked to hold forth at the mess table on his favourite subject: 'the never-failing theme of the comparative merits' of Alexander, Bonaparte, Moses and Wellington as military leaders.[48] The light company commander usually 'gave the palm' to Moses, whose sanitary regulations as found in Deuteronomy 23:13, he much admired: 'And thou shall have a paddle upon thy weapon; and it shall be when thou wilt ease thyself abroad, thou shalt dig therewith, and turn back and cover that which cometh from thee.'

The soldiers had less leisure time and less enjoyable ways to spend what they did get. Many engaged in the British soldier's besetting weakness, alcohol – Bentinck remembered that wine was very cheap and his comrades could get 'as much as they could well carry at two pence a pint'.[49] The provosts maintained roving patrols in the camp lines, however, and were quick to apprehend any soldier found drunk or away from his unit without good excuse. In January 1811, Private Lewis Campbell of the battalion was apprehended by one of these patrols and arraigned before a general court martial on charges of desertion. He was found guilty and sentenced to be hanged. Luckily for Campbell, when his case was reviewed by Wellington, it was found that, although he 'was Guilty of great irregularity in straggling from his cantonments', there was not enough evidence to prove the charge.[50] Campbell was released from confinement and returned to his unit. Private Matthew Power of the 7th Foot, found guilty of the same offence, was not so fortunate. He was also sentenced to be hanged, the penalty was confirmed by Wellington and 'carried into execution' on 18 January 1811 in the presence of the assembled Fusilier Brigade.[51] Drummer Bentinck remembered the scene: 'he was accordingly taken outside the village, all the troops were paraded to witness the final punishment, in order that they might take warning by it and were formed up around an olive tree that stood on the plain' and 'the unfortunate fellow was strung up to a branch and left dangling there as a reminder of the fate of all captured deserters'.[52]

At this time a number of Welch Fusilier officers contemplated joining the Portuguese army. Two years before, it had been put under the command of Marshal of Portugal William Beresford who had carried out a thorough reform of its arming, equipping, training and administration, assisted by numbers of British officers seconded to serve with him. The results of Beresford's labour had been evident at Busaco the previous September where the Portuguese had fought so well that 'a French Officer who came with a flag of truce, asked if they were not British Troops in Portuguese Uniform'.[53] As secondment to the Portuguese army brought extra pay and usually one step in rank, it was an attractive proposition. Lieutenant Thomas Farmer explained the advantages as being that 'I do not lose my rank or promotion in my own service, and I get 8 shillings per day in addition to my pay as Lieut'.[54] The first officer to leave for Portuguese service was Major Francis Offley, who was shortly followed by Captain Peter Brown.[55] The eccentric Jack Hill, a man who always kept a sharp eye out for promotion possibilities, also began to think about the benefits of serving in a Portuguese unit.[56]

As winter turned to spring, the question on everyone's mind was when would active operations commence? It was clear that Masséna must make a move shortly as his army was melting away from lack of provisions. Harrison reported that French prisoners had 'described their Army to be in great distress. Spirits they can't get and have not had any for some time, Provisions scarce, and clothing getting very bare. Shoes are very much wanting.'[57] Wellington, impressed with the enemy's obstinacy, commented that 'It is wonderful that they have been able to remain in the country so long, and it is scarcely possible that they can remain much longer' but, 'If they go, and when they go, their losses will be very great and mine nothing' while, 'If they stay, they must continue to lose men daily, as they do now.'[58] The British commander, however, was 'determined to persevere in my cautious system', avoid a battle and let starvation do his work for him.

In early March 1811, Masséna finally realised that it was no use and quietly began to withdraw from his positions around Santarem. Bentinck commented that the French unit opposite the 1/23rd Foot made clever use of decoys:

> The hostile sentries were almost within musket shot of each other, but after the first duty, by tacit understanding, ceased to punch bullet holes into each other. One fine morning our sentry noticed that his French counterpart on the bridge kept in one attitude a remarkably long time. Growing curious, he at length shouted to him, but no word, nor motion did the Frenchman send back in reply. Our sentry began to sniff a rat and going nearer to his supposed foe took a long and careful aim at him. His bullet produced no change, though he felt certain it had hit its mark. No foe popped up his head to see why the stillness of morning was broken, but one or two of our men came out and venturing up to the rigidly erect French sentry found him literally a 'man of straw'.[59]

When Wellington learned of the French retreat on 6 March he set out in pursuit. Masséna's rearguard, however, was commanded by Marshal Michel Ney, who managed not only to delay the British advance but also to nicely judge when to retreat farther to avoid serious attack. Since Wellington's strength was about the same as that of Masséna, his intention was not so much to bring the French to battle – although he was quite willing to fight one if the opportunity should present itself – but simply to shepherd the enemy out of Portugal.

The 4th Division moved forward to Santarem on 6 March 1811 and the events of the next few days were recorded by an anonymous Welch Fusilier officer:

> Our second day's [7 March] march was to Golegao, where we found boiled beans left by the enemy, who had quitted in the morning.
>
> The third day we reached Thomar in the evening, and found that Ney had only left it in the morning – so close did we follow them up, by hard and long marches over the worst road in the world. The next night we took up our abode in the open air, in constant rain, and had nothing to cover us but our great coats and blankets – hard times!
>
> From this ground we had a forced march of thirty miles, and found nearly the whole of the British army assembled on a large plain near Pombal – our division with the light division became the advanced guard of the army.
>
> At Pombal we came up with the enemy, and drove them out that evening, but not until they had set it on fire and destroyed it completely. From this town they posted themselves very judiciously on a range of heights, with a broad river and a marsh in their front. Notwithstanding these obstacles, it was determined to attack them, and although we had marched thirty miles, it being nearly dark alone prevented us from doing it immediately.[60]

Drummer Bentinck recalled that when the battalion marched through the blazing ruins of Pombal that evening, his comrades carried 'their cartouche boxes under their greatcoats to prevent them being exploded by the sparks which rained down on them like a fiery shower'.[61]

The attack on the French position outside the town was forestalled when, leaving large campfires burning to deceive their pursuers, the enemy slipped away during the night. Wellington, however, caught up with Ney the following day near Redinha and the marshal, feeling he was being pressed too closely, resolved to fight. He took up a position around the town and his artillery, the anonymous fusilier officer recorded, was 'posted on the ridge of a hill, from whence he threw a vast deal of round shot'.[62] Wellington stationed the 3rd, 4th and Light Divisions in line on a plain before the French position and prepared to attack. When the Fusilier Brigade arrived on the field, Corporal John Cooper of the 1/7th Foot heard the orders: '"Form close column"; "Prime and load"; "fix bayonets"; "shoulder"; "slope"; "silence"; "steady";' and, finally, 'deploy into line'.[63] Preceded by a skirmish line consisting of the light companies of the three battalions and the Brunswick rifle company, all under the command of Major Thomas Pearson of the 1/23rd, the brigade then advanced. The anonymous officer takes up the account:

> The enemy's artillery played on us in high style, and many shot passed close to me. Our first line lost about 20 men killed and wounded. To have seen us deploy and march in line, as we did, you would have been highly pleased. I never saw better. The troops in the highest spirits, and to do justice to the Portuguese, they equalled us. When our first line had approached within about 400 yards, without firing but marching as steady as a rock, in ordinary time, the enemy's infantry began to retire, in double quick time, and the artillery and cavalry followed their example.
>
> They again formed on a very advantageous ground, in rear of the town which was in flames.[64]

When Wellington detached a strong force to outflank this new position, Ney decided his day was done and again slipped away. Corporal Cooper remembered that the French 'carried off their artillery at a rattling pace, followed by loud English hurrahs, and our skirmishers'.[65] During the action he had seen an unusual sight: a woman belonging to the Brunswick rifle company 'trudging boldly closely behind her husband, with a heavy load on her back, in the midst of the fire'.

The 1/23rd Foot suffered no casualties at Redinha and all who took part in it were very pleased. 'Lord Wellington has shewn himself a skilful General, and Ney has manoeuvred with great judgement', wrote the Fusilier officer, who thought his brigade's movement during the fighting 'was a beautiful sight' with 'everything so regular, as at a review in St. James's Park'.[66] Another participant thought that the army with 'colours unfurled advancing in line, and supported by solid columns of infantry and cavalry on their flanks' was 'such a sight that all former military spectacles must give way to'.[67]

As Wellington's troops followed the retreating enemy, they came across terrible scenes as the French had treated the civilian population with a violence that verged on the genocidal. Most habitations and other buildings had been deliberately destroyed; the Welch Fusiliers found a French orderly book 'containing an order to burn every town through which the rear guard passed'.[68] Men, women and children were indiscriminately murdered – in one village the French herded most of the inhabitants into a church and then set it on fire.[69] Pakenham, like many other British soldiers, was angered by these atrocious acts 'committed by these fiends of hell' and added some gruesome details: 'every Village and Town has been set fire to, all peasants taken have been killed in the most crewel manner, the women, nay even females from childhood, violated'.[70] It was his opinion that, 'if these Atrocities, and the brilliant instances of successful resistance cannot awaken the Manly feelings of Europe' to resist Napoleon's aggression then 'the world's population must prepare for degradation unknown'.

Also distressing was the way the French treated their draught animals. That the enemy was starving was evident from 'the number of horses they have left

The cruelty of the French, 1810
In this late-nineteenth-century drawing, French soldiers execute Spanish civilians
in cold blood. The war in the Peninsula between 1808 and 1814 was waged with
unrelenting cruelty by the French invaders whose repressive actions verged on the
genocidal. *(Author's collection)*

dead on the road' with steaks 'cut from their rumps', commented Harrison, but
what was worse was the fact that the French often hamstrung the wretched
creatures but left them alive.[71] Private Joseph Donaldson of the 94th Foot found
it 'pitiable' to march past these miserable animals but was also somewhat amused
by 'the position which many had taken when thus cruelly lamed' for they sat 'in
groups upon their hinder ends, staring in each other's faces, as if in deep
consultation on some important subject'.[72] What was clear to all, Harrison
commented, was that Masséna's army was in a very bad state as it left 'many men
on the road, some dying and others dead, indeed the scenes we have seen on their
retreat are too shocking to describe'.[73]

On 14 March 1811, while Wellington moved with most of the army on Casal
Novo, he ordered Cole to take the 4th Division on a flanking movement to try and
cut off the French retreat. It was gruelling but had an ultimate reward:

> We had to climb the most difficult places, and what with the heat of the
> weather, and being without provisions, I was nearly exhausted. About four
> we entered a lovely little place, Panella [Penellis], and marched on for
> Espinhal, where we arrived about six p.m. and found that General
> Nightingall's brigade had passed close to the place where Reynier was
> posted with 3,000 men, to prevent our outflanking Ney. Every oven in

the place was full of Indian corn bread, which was very acceptable to Gen. Nightingall's brigade. The enemy had even cut wood for fires, and brushwood to hut themselves, which fell to our lot.[74]

This was the 4th Division's last operation with the main army as, late in the afternoon of 15 March 1811, Cole received orders to make a forced march to the south.

These orders resulted from a disastrous occurrence that had taken place four days earlier – the French capture of the Spanish fortress city of Badajoz. Just as Ciudad Rodrigo and Almeida guarded the northern invasion route into Portugal, Badajoz and the Portuguese city of Elvas guarded the southern route. After Wellington had retreated into Portugal the previous autumn, a strong Spanish garrison had been left in Badajoz which, in late January, came under siege by French forces commanded by Marshal Nicolas Soult. When another Spanish army arrived to relieve the city, the Badajoz garrison unwisely sortied to join it, only be disastrously beaten at the Battle of Gebora on 19 February. Soult then resumed the siege but the heart had gone out of the defenders and they surrendered on 11 March. Wellington was determined to retake Badajoz and directed Marshal William Beresford to do so, giving him all the troops he could spare, including the 4th Division.

Cole wasted no time. 'On receiving the order', the anonymous Welch Fusilier officer recorded, the 4th Division 'marched until dark, when we slept on the ground, and a rainy night we had of it'.[75] By the evening of 16 March, after marching nearly thirty miles, it reached Thomar where it received a badly-needed day of rest, before moving on again. The division soon outstripped its supply lines and provisions grew scarce – the officer recalled that a 'ship biscuit lasted me four days, when I was necessitated to eat boiled Indian corn: it was the same with the men'.[76] Even worse was the fact that the soldiers' boots began to disintegrate from the lengthy marches over rough Portuguese roads – 'Our men are almost barefoot and a good deal fagged' the anonymous officer noted, 'How I have stood the fatigue and the continually sleeping out, I am astonished to think.'[77] Cooper of the 7th Foot commented that the forced marching 'over hilly stony roads without a mouthful of bread' caused much straggling as 'numbers of men unable to keep up', he noted, 'remained on the roads or in the fields'.[78] Cooper himself 'hobbled on with the column' although suffering 'dreadfully from hunger, thirst, little shoes and blistered feet'. The 1/23rd left more than a hundred men on the road but on 22 March 1811, completely spent and nearly barefoot – having covered 110 miles in just over six days – the battalion limped into Portalegre with the remainder of the 4th Division.

If the men of the division were expecting a rest, they were to be disappointed as Beresford had orders from Wellington to immediately push on to Campo Mayor, ten miles west of Badajoz. On 24 March, he set out with his entire force and by the following day, was close to his objective. By this time Soult had withdrawn to Seville but there were still substantial enemy forces in the area. The French were just in the process of pulling out of Campo Mayor and were caught with their units strung out between that place and Badajoz. Beresford therefore marched past the town and detached his cavalry to hunt down the enemy. This they did, but in a remarkably botched operation caused by a breakdown in communication between Beresford and his cavalry commander, Major General Robert Long, most of the enemy escaped into Badajoz with very few casualties. The British thereupon returned to Campo Mayor whose inhabitants, thinking the approaching columns were French, shouted 'Viva Français' but, on 'perceiving their terrible blunder they were more frightened still, thinking the British would surely make them smart worse than their foes had ever done', so promptly 'shouted, 'Viva Anglais, Viva Anglais', with even greater fervour than before'.[79]

Cheered by the welcome, the 4th Division occupied the town and some days later, received new footwear of local manufacture. These shoes 'were very clumsy and a dirty buff colour', one soldier remembered, 'and as many amongst us were without stockings, their rough seams soon made their wearers hobble like so many cripples'.[80] The Royal Welch Fusilier officers were hardly in better shape – Lieutenant Farmer confessed that he had 'not a shoe or stocking to my feet, nor a farthing to purchase them'.[81]

Before Beresford could retake Badajoz, he had to complete some preliminary steps. The city was located on the south bank of the River Guadiana, which at this point formed the border between Portugal and Spain. Since Beresford intended to besiege it from both banks, he had to get across this waterway but since the bridge at Badajoz was in the possession of the French, he had first to construct another bridge. He chose to build it at Jerumenha, about fifteen miles southwest of Badajoz, but his engineers, hampered by a lack of construction material and difficulties caused by spring floods, did not finish their task until 6 April. That day and throughout the night, Beresford marched his three divisions over the Guadiana toward the small city of Olivenza, occupied by a French garrison.

The French commandant of Olivenza, although vastly outnumbered, refused to surrender. Beresford therefore left the 4th Division – most of which was limping and not capable of swift movement – to invest the town until heavy artillery could be brought up from Elvas, and took the remainder of the army to clear the south bank of the Guadiana. On 14 April four heavy 24-pounder guns arrived and were positioned in a half-finished redoubt within good artillery range of the town walls. While the gunners laboured to get their cumbersome weapons into position, Major Thomas Pearson of the 1/23rd, acting in his usual role as the commander of the light troops of the Fusilier Brigade, took the formation's

Ox cart
The standard form of transport in the Iberian Peninsula, the unsprung ox cart, which made a wretched ambulance. Whole trains of these vehicles followed Wellington's army throughout the campaigns of 1808–14.
(*From* **Adventures of Johnny Newcome,** *1816*)

three light companies and von Wachholtz's riflemen closer to the town wall to cover them.

The guns were ready on the following morning and Cole sent a flag of truce to demand the surrender of the town. This being refused, Captain von Wachholtz recorded, the 24-pounders opened:

> ... at a point along the wall to create a breach; and very soon a few stones began to fall. They replied weakly, and without any great success. The light infantry were again called out and I had to take a platoon behind the dangerously-positioned redoubt, where three Portuguese field pieces were positioned and where it was very exposed. After a bit there was loud drumming and trumpeting from the town; we held our fire; a flag of truce came out and was taken to General Cole ... but returned in half an hour and the firing began again. Now large stones began to fall from the wall, some of them very large. This did not continue for long before the drumming was heard again from the town; a flag of truce came out and the place surrendered.[82]

Pearson's light troops were sent in to secure it, and did so to the cheers of the townspeople. Von Wachholtz, a veteran of the Prussian defeat at Auerstadt in 1806, entered Olivenza with 'the sweet thought to see Frenchmen with downcast heads' but unfortunately for the German, he was apprehended by 'a stupid Portuguese captain' who, confused by his black uniform, arrested him as a French officer. It required much lengthy and animated discussion before von Wachholtz again obtained his liberty.[83]

By now, Beresford had secured most of the southern bank of the Guadiana up to the vicinity of Badajoz and could commence siege operations against that city. Arrangements were made to bring up more heavy artillery from Elvas and the necessary materiel but progress was hampered when the Jerumenha bridge was swept away by flood water on the night of 24 April, cutting communication with the north bank. It took the hard-working engineers five days to rebuild it and, in the meantime, the 1/23rd Foot moved forward with the Fusilier Brigade, which was quartered in villages immediately south of Badajoz.

Having come through their first Peninsular campaign relatively unscathed, the battalion was in good spirits. A large draft of 9 officers and 203 men arrived from the 2nd Battalion, which made up for many of the losses the 1st Battalion had suffered since landing at Lisbon nearly six months before. Among the new arrivals were Lieutenants Samuel Thorpe, recovered from his travails of 1808 at Corunna and Walcheren, and George Browne, brother of the diarist Thomas Browne, who had recently left the 23rd for a staff appointment. Another newcomer was Lieutenant Grismond Philipps, the spendthrift subaltern from Cwmgwilly. By the end of April 1811, Lieutenant Colonel Ellis could report a strength of 41 officers and 692 men fit for duty.[84]

On 7 May 1811, marching with the 4th Division as it moved north to the Guadiana, the Royal Welch Fusiliers got their first glimpse of Badajoz, a place that would earn a grim reputation among them. Founded by the Moors, Badajoz was a strategically-placed fortress-city that had a long and violent history, having suffered at least seven previous sieges over the centuries before being taken by Soult in February 1811. It was located on high ground on the south bank of the Guadiana and connected to the opposite bank by a stone bridge, which ended in a *tête du pont* outwork. Both bridge and town were overlooked by a fort on the San Cristobal hill, located on the north bank and although it was perhaps the strongest part of the defences, it was here that Beresford made his main effort in May 1811.

In doing so, he was only obeying Wellington's orders. Having pushed Masséna out of Portugal, the British commander made a flying visit south in late April and after a reconnaissance of Badajoz, issued fairly precise instructions for Beresford directing him to take the outerworks, including San Cristobal, before trying to breach the main city wall. Suspecting that Soult would attempt to break the siege, Wellington advised Beresford that, if the French should advance, he should evacuate his siege artillery and materiel to a safe place and then concentrate his forces at the village of Albuera, sixteen miles south on the Royal Highway that led from Badajoz to Seville. Toward this end, Wellington secured a promise from the commanders of two small Spanish armies operating in the area, Generals Francisco Castanos and Joaquin Blake, to place themselves under Beresford's command. This done, Wellington returned to the north as Masséna, having re-organised his army after its disastrous retreat from Portugal, was showing signs of being about to resume the offensive.

By the end of the first week in May, Beresford had isolated Badajoz and his engineers began constructing batteries in which to place a varied collection of ancient ordnance – some pieces dating from the seventeenth century – brought from Elvas. The French commandant in Badajoz, Brigadier General Armand Phillipon, an extremely able and active officer, not only made several sorties to disrupt the besiegers' progress but kept them under constant artillery fire, which on one day cost Beresford three of his nine engineer officers. Siege operations, with their fatigue, boredom and danger, were never popular in the British army because, as one officer commented, 'death in the trenches never carries with it that stamp of glory, which seals the memory of those who perish in a well-fought field'.[85]

There was constant peril. The besiegers had to be on guard for artillery fire from the city, particularly explosive shells fired by mortars and howitzers. Fortunately, there was usually enough warning provided for the targets to take cover – a soldier in Major General Kemmis's brigade remembered that 'the dull report of the mortar announced they had left the enemy's works' and 'till they burst or fell, furnished us with ample matter for speculation, and even of mirth, at the desperate runnings on seeing them come near'.[86] The French gunners were relentless and to this same soldier, it seemed that 'wherever a group of us sought shelter, shells were almost certain of falling immediately after; and although their near approach was announced by the smoke of their fusee [fuze], and a kind of whistling noise, we were kept in a state of perpetual agitation to elude them'.[87]

By 10 May, work had progressed far enough for the construction of a battery intended to breach the walls of San Cristobal. When darkness fell that day, Phillipon mounted a sortie that was rebuffed with heavy casualties on both sides. After the firing had died away, Bentinck recalled:

> ... our main body kept out of sight and danger behind an adjacent hill, whilst strong working parties crept up to within about a quarter-of-a-mile from the walls and commenced silently and rapidly throwing up earthworks. No wonder every man wrought hard, for as soon as the gathering light in the east made them visible, the French opened upon them from every battery within reach, with the earnest endeavour to destroy both them and their dangerous works. Our sappers were withdrawn for the day, picked marksmen only being left behind the ridge they had thrown up, for the purpose of popping off the enemy's gunners.[88]

Four of the five guns in the breaching battery were dismounted. They were replaced by the morning of 12 May, only to suffer the same fate.

On this day, however, Beresford lifted the siege. He had received accurate intelligence that Soult was advancing from Seville to relieve the defenders, and ordered work to be suspended and his army, with the exception of Cole's 4th

Division, to march for Albuera. 'Numerous conjectures were formed from these movements', Harrison commented but the Fusilier Brigade remained in 'unpleasant uncertainty all the day of the 14th, that night and the following day, during which time our poor fellows were exposed to dreadful weather, and not more than a blade of grass to cover them'.[89]

Beresford had left the 4th Division behind at Badajoz to prevent the French from interfering with the removal of the siege artillery to Elvas but ordered Cole to be in readiness to march at short notice. Unfortunately, the Guadiana flooded that same day making impassable a ford near Badajoz, which the besiegers had been using to cross it. This meant that, except for the light companies of its three battalions, Kemmis's brigade on the north bank was cut off and would have to march by the bridge at Jerumenha, to catch up with the division. Around midnight of 15 May 1811, Cole received an order to march for Albuera and set out, under a downpour of rain, at about 2 a.m. with the Fusilier Brigade, Harvey's Portuguese brigade, and the orphaned light companies of Kemmis's brigade. A mistake on the part of Beresford's staff resulted in the division taking the wrong road and it was some time before Cole got back on the correct route.

It was daylight when the 4th Division neared Albuera and, as it did, the officers and men could hear a 'dull booming', which was quickly identified as artillery fire.[90] If there were any doubts remaining that action was imminent, they were quickly dispelled when the orders: '"Light Infantry to front," "trail arms," "double quick,"' were passed down the column. 'We then knew what was astir', commented Cooper of the 7th, and when the Fusilier Brigade had ascended a steep hill, they saw 'the two armies engaged below, on a plain about three quarters of a mile distant'.[91] The Royal Welch Fusiliers were about to win immortal fame in the bloodiest battle of the Peninsular War.

Upon the plains of Flanders
Our Fathers long ago,
They fought like Alexanders
Beneath old Marlborough;
And still on fields of conquest
Our valour bright has shone
'Neath Wolfe and Abercrombie
And Moore and Wellington.

Our plumes have waved in conquests
That ne'er shall be forgot,
When many a mighty squadron
Reeled backward from our shot;
In charges with the bayonet
We led our bold confreres,
For Frenchmen like to stay not
'Gainst the Royal Welch Fusiliers.

And so at Albuhera
They hoped to play their parts,
And sang 'Fal-lal-lal-lirah'
To cheer their drooping hearts;
But Britons, Welch and Paddywhacks,
They gave three hearty cheers,
And all the Frenchmen turned their backs
On the Royal Welch Fusiliers.[1]

Chapter 8

'A glorious day for the fusiliers!'

1st Battalion, Spain and Portugal, May–December 1811

WELLINGTON HAD CHOSEN THE POSITION AT ALBUERA and it was a good one. The village lay at the intersection of several roads, including the Royal Highway between Badajoz and Seville, and was situated on a low knoll about 150 yards west of the River Albuera, which itself was formed by the junction of two brooks, the Nogales and the Chicapierna, south of it. Two bridges crossed the river: an old and narrow structure near Albuera and, to the south of it, a larger bridge over which ran the Royal Highway. All these waterways were fordable to infantry but, in some places, high banks prevented the crossing of artillery and cavalry. On the west or allied side of the river lay a series of gently rolling hills running north and south, nearly bare of vegetation in May 1811, with their highest elevation being about 150 feet above the river. On the east or French side, the ground was much the same but there was a fairly extensive wood of olive and cork trees, which screened observation from the west.

On the morning of 16 May 1811, Marshal William Beresford was in command of an army of about 35,000 British, Portuguese and Spanish troops. The Spanish contingent consisted of just under 15,000 men but, as their record in combat was extremely variable, Beresford put more trust in his 10,449 British and German, and 10,201 Portuguese soldiers. These comprised Major General Lowry Cole's 4th Division, which was approaching; Major General William Stewart's 2nd British Division; a light infantry brigade of the King's German Legion; Major General John Hamilton's Portuguese division; an independent Portuguese brigade; and artillery and cavalry.

Beresford judged Albuera and its nearby bridges to be the crucial part of his position and, accordingly, placed his best troops to defend it: the German Legion brigade being positioned in the village proper while Stewart's 2nd Division was posted on the high ground immediately behind. To the north of Albuera, Beresford stationed Hamilton's division and the independent Portuguese brigade, while to the south, he placed his Spanish allies. With the

Jack Frenchman

Between 1793 and 1815, the British Army was in constant action against the armies of France. The two opponents eventually acquired a grudging respect for each other's military qualities and relations between them were usually proper and, on occasion, almost too friendly. Here a French infantry battalion advances while wearing greatcoats, the French soldier's favourite campaign dress.
(*From Detaille*, L'armée française, *1888*)

exception of the Legion battalions, all the infantry were well back from the river, with the cavalry mainly on both flanks and the artillery, thirty to forty guns in all, stationed along the line.

Marshal Nicolas Soult, Beresford's opponent, had a smaller force, 24,000 men in total, but a superior one in terms of quality and experience. Soult's 19,000 infantry were seasoned troops and he had a strong cavalry force, nearly 4,000 sabres commanded by the capable General Victor La Tour-Maubourg, and some thirty artillery pieces, under Brigadier General Charles de Ruty. Soult, a veteran of twenty-six years of military service who had risen from the ranks, was an intelligent and aggressive commander known to the British as the 'Duke of Damnation', a play upon his imperial title of *Duc de Dalmatie*, or just simply as 'General Salt'.

Whatever he was called, Soult was dangerous. Making a reconnaissance of the allied position during the evening of 15 May, he noted that Beresford's right flank was overlooked by higher ground to the south. Outnumbered, and needing to concentrate his forces at one point, Soult decided to mount an attack against this flank using the greater part of his infantry and cavalry, whose movement toward it would be masked by the woods on the French side of the river. His plan was to roll up the allied right flank and then cut the road from Albuera to Valverde, Beresford's best escape route, and either chew up his opponents at leisure or force them back in the direction of Badajoz, where they would be placed between his force and Phillipon's garrison. To fix Beresford's attention on Albuera – and thereby distract him from the French flanking move – Soult decided to open the engagement with a feint attack on the village.

This feint commenced at about 8 a.m. on 16 May. French cavalry and infantry, supported by horse artillery, moved toward the bridges and were quickly brought under long range fire from the allied artillery. It was the noise of this exchange that the 4th Division heard as it neared the scene and, on his arrival, Major General Cole sought out Beresford to get his orders. As there was heavy fighting in and around Albuera at that moment, the allied commander told him to position his troops behind Stewart's 2nd Division. When the scrapping around Albuera gradually tailed off as the French, having accomplished their purpose, withdrew, Beresford ordered Cole to station his division along the Valverde road and not to move without a direct order.[2] The division took up its assigned position and this done, the battalion commanders permitted their men to fall out of the ranks and seek some shelter from a shower of rain – Captain Friedrich von Wachholtz remembered that his company 'crawled into short bushes and sheltered ourselves as best we could'.[3] After surveying the situation, the German officer decided that 'we would either attack or be attacked.'

While Cole was carrying out this movement, Soult completed his flank march to the south behind the cover of the woods on the eastern bank of the river. Although allied observers could see troops moving through gaps among the trees, they were unsure of their direction. It was only when, preceded by a thick cavalry screen, the first massive French infantry column splashed across the Chicapierna and Nogales streams, and began to occupy the high ground behind the west bank, that Beresford realised his peril. He requested the Spanish generals to alter their position to meet this threat and then ordered Stewart to bring up his 2nd Division in support. The Spanish, not well trained, were slow to move and by the time they had realigned, La Tour-Maubourg's cavalry had brushed aside the small screen of allied mounted troops from the higher ground overlooking Beresford's right flank and de Ruty's gunners were bringing about twenty guns into position. Next, a French infantry division under General Jean-Baptiste Girard – more than 4,000 men formed in two massive columns with skirmishers in front – bore down on the Spanish, marching to the quick and insistent rhythm – ONE, two, three! ONE, two three! – of their drummers beating the *pas de charge*.

It was fortunate that a competent Spanish officer, General José Zayas, managed to deploy four regiments in line to counter this threat. Although his troops suffered heavy losses from the French artillery fire, Zayas succeeded in bringing Girard's columns to a halt with volleys of musketry. The French commander – perhaps detesting opponents whom he had seen run from many a battle – did not attempt to deploy into line but instead returned the fire from his awkward column formation, which could bring fewer muskets to bear. The exchange went on for perhaps half an hour but, inevitably, sheer numbers started to tell and Zayas' units began to melt from losses. It was at this moment that the lead elements of

Stewart's division came up. Stewart ordered the brigades of Major General Daniel Hoghton and Lieutenant Colonel Alexander Abercromby to form line behind the Spanish and prepare to replace them. Stewart, a very aggressive soldier, then moved his remaining brigade (1/3rd, 2/31st, 2/48th and 2/66th Foot) under the command of Lieutenant Colonel John Colborne in column to the right of the Spanish position, to threaten the left flank of the French column. Hoghton and Abercromby's regiments passed through the Spanish, having in many cases to elbow them out of the way as Zayas' men were determined not to take a backward step. Most of Colborne's brigade, meanwhile, deployed into line and prepared to move forward with the bayonet.

Disaster now struck. La Tour-Maubourg, seeing an opportunity, ordered a regiment of Polish lancers and two of hussars to attack the open flank of Colborne's brigade and in the smoke, mist and rain, few in the allied army noticed their approach. At the last moment, the officers and men of the 3rd Foot, Colborne's right flank unit, spotted the lancers but there was confusion as to whether they were French or Spanish and, by the time their true identity was established, it was too late. Led by the lancers, the French swept away Colborne's regiments in turn, capturing their colours. Although some of the British infantry ran together in small groups to try and make a stand, it was in vain and, in a matter of minutes, the brigade was transformed from a military formation into a mass of fugitives running for their lives. Only the 2/31st Foot, which had not deployed into line, was able to fend off the triumphant horsemen whose velocity carried them down between the Spanish line and Hoghton's brigade.

There was now a momentary lull as Beresford attempted to regain control of the situation and Girard tried to get his division moving again. Fortunately, Stewart's threatened attack on his left flank had confused the enemy commander who had not taken advantage of the cavalry charge. This permitted the brigades of Hoghton (1/29th, 1/48th and 1/57th Foot) and Abercromby (2/28th, 2/34th and 2/39th Foot) to take over the position of Zayas' decimated units. When the French infantry moved forward, instead of meeting the despised Spaniards, they encountered a solid two-rank line of British infantry whose disciplined volleys of musketry again brought them to a standstill. Girard tried to shake out his cumbersome formation into line to reply but it was no use as the British let loose 'a continuous and well directed firing of two ranks' with few rounds being lost 'on the tightly massed French column, whose only return fire, which came from its front, was light and insufficient'.[4] All attempts by Girard to deploy were to no avail and, worse still, a second French division coming up behind got mixed up with his formation, creating a confused shambles.

The musketry duel continued with heavy losses on both sides. Hoghton was killed, as were two of his battalion commanders, with the third being wounded. Major Charles Leslie of the 29th Foot thought that an 'overwhelming fire of artillery and small arms' was directed against his regiment but 'there we unflinchingly stood, and there we fell'. Whole parts of the 29th were 'swept away by sections' and the battalion 'became so reduced that it resembled a chain of skirmishers in extended order'.[5]

It was obvious to both Beresford and Soult that the deadlock could only be broken by fresh troops. Soult therefore ordered forward a strong nine-battalion brigade commanded by Brigadier General François-Jean Werlé. For his part, Beresford sent a staff officer to Major General John Hamilton with orders for him to bring up his Portuguese division but when Hamilton did not appear, Beresford went to find him. Hoghton's brigade was, meanwhile, fraying thinner by the minute and it was clear that something had to be done, and done quickly, or the battle was lost. This being the case, Lieutenant Colonel Henry Hardinge, Beresford's deputy quartermaster-general, deciding that the situation required 'an instant remedy', rode to Lowry Cole.[6]

Cole and his 4th Division had been distant spectators of the battle on the high ground to their front. Given the incessant rain showers, smoke and the contours of the ground, they could not see much of the actual fighting, which was taking place about a mile and a half from their position. They could, however, judge its intensity from the noise and the continuous stream of wounded men limping or crawling to the rear. Throughout the morning, Cole had become increasingly anxious when he received no orders from Beresford and had sent an aide to wait on the army commander but the man had not returned. When Hardinge rode up and proposed that he advance with the 4th Division, Cole was in a prickly mood and stressed he had 'positive orders *not* to leave the position in which I had been placed'.[7] The two officers got into an animated discussion, which ended when Lieutenant Colonel John Rooke, Beresford's assistant adjutant-general, arrived and Cole asked his opinion. Rooke's response was that, if Stewart was not soon reinforced, the battle was lost. This being the case, Cole decided to disobey orders and attack the French on the ridge.

To do so, his two brigades would have to cross a mile and a half of open ground, with their right flank vulnerable to cavalry. Cole therefore decided to advance in battalion columns in echelon from the left – that is, staggered back from the left to the right. This would permit quicker movement and easier deployment if it became necessary to form either line or square to counter any threat from enemy cavalry. It was a manoeuvre, he later recalled, that was 'difficult to perform correctly even in a common field-day', let alone under heavy artillery fire.[8] To strengthen his flanks, Cole placed the Loyal Lusitanian Legion of battalion size on the left and Major Thomas Pearson, with the three Fusilier Brigade light companies, the Brunswick rifle company, and the three orphan light companies from Kemmis's brigade, on his right. Support would be provided by two batteries of artillery and two brigades of British and Spanish cavalry, which would move to the right of the division.

Corporal Cooper of the 7th Foot remembered that the shout, 'Fall in Fusileers!', brought the brigade to its feet.[9] Obeying the orders of officers and sergeants, the men of the three battalions formed columns with one company behind each other, as did the two regiments of Harvey's Portuguese brigade, each of two battalions. Just as the division was forming, Lieutenant John Harrison of the 23rd Foot arrived, looking for Lieutenant Colonel Henry Ellis. That morning, the young officer had been stuck with the brigade baggage guard but had freed himself from this irksome duty and now joined his battalion. Ellis, who had no doubt that he would soon need every man who could carry a musket, told Harrison 'to go back and bring the drums up and all the spare hands I could collect from the baggage'.[10] When Harrison returned with forty men, he took over the company of Captain Jacob Van Cortland, who was acting as a field officer. When all arrangements were complete, the 4th Division, nearly 5,000 officers and men, was formed in nine distinct battalion blocks of red or blue and one of green in the case of the Lusitanian Legion. Just before Cole gave the order for the advance, Lieutenant Colonel William Myers, commanding the Fusilier Brigade, rode along its front shouting: 'It will be a glorious day for the fusiliers!'[11]

At about 1 p.m. the division advanced at the quick step of 108 paces per minute to cover the ground as fast as possible. Lieutenant Colonel Edward Blakeney, commanding the 2/7th Foot, remembered that, just as the Fusilier Brigade stepped off, the fog and rain cleared for a few minutes and he could see French infantry columns and artillery on the high ground in front and so much enemy cavalry off to the right that they seemed to be 'covering the whole plain with their swords'.[12] It was not long before the division was within range of the enemy gunners who, presented with this splendid target, made the most of it. A French artillery officer watched as the ground 'was furrowed in all directions by our projectiles and their ricochets scoured elongated gaps' through the ranks of the oncoming 4th Division.[13] Marching in the ranks of the 7th Foot, Cooper saw men 'knocked about like skittles' but proudly proclaimed that 'not a backward step' was taken.[14] For his part, Harrison had a close call when a canister bullet passed through his shako, grazing his scalp before piercing 'several folds of my pocket handkerchief which was in my cap'.[15]

Ignoring casualties, the two brigades kept moving forward. When they were just outside musket range of the French, Cole gave the order and they deployed into line, with Harvey's brigade somewhat to the rear of Myers's fusiliers. The Lusitanian Legion took post on the left flank; Pearson did the same on the right, forming his seven companies in square; and the accompanying cavalry and artillery stationed themselves to his right and rear. The division then advanced again, more slowly now, so as to maintain its dressing, all the while under relentless artillery fire. Von Wachholtz remembered that 'a round shot ricocheted diagonally through our square, took the legs off two soldiers, went through the middle, hit an officer … in the chest, and without further ado, went out on its way'.[16] The officers had trouble closing up the gap in the ranks made by this projectile as the soldiers feared 'the next round must hit the same place'.

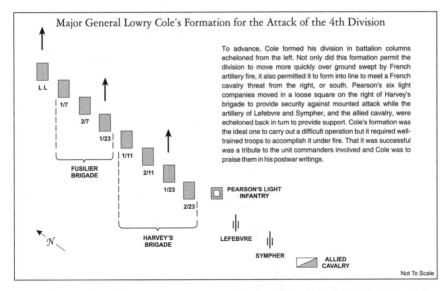

Major General Lowry Cole's Formation for the Attack of the 4th Division

To advance, Cole formed his division in battalion columns echeloned from the left. Not only did this formation permit the division to move more quickly over ground swept by French artillery fire, it also permitted it to form into line to meet a French cavalry threat from the right, or south. Pearson's six light companies moved in a loose square on the right of Harvey's brigade to provide security against mounted attack while the artillery of Lefebvre and Sympher, and the allied cavalry, were echeloned back in turn to provide support. Cole's formation was the ideal one to carry out a difficult operation but it required well-trained troops to accomplish it under fire. That it was successful was a tribute to the unit commanders involved and Cole was to praise them in his postwar writings.

LL

1/7

2/7

1/23

1/11

FUSILIER
BRIGADE

2/11

1/23

2/23

PEARSON'S LIGHT
INFANTRY

HARVEY'S
BRIGADE

LEFEBVRE

SYMPHER

ALLIED
CAVALRY

N

Not To Scale

As the British and Portuguese approached the crest of the hill, Werlé's brigade appeared on its crest. His movement had been delayed when his nine battalions had been caught up in the jumbled mass of the two French infantry divisions on the hill. It had taken time for Werlé to extricate them but he finally did so and moved forward in three distinct columns, each of three battalions. Watching the enemy approach, Major Edward Blakeney, commanding the 2/7th in the middle of the Fusilier Brigade line, thought that the 1/7th Foot on his left 'closed with the right column of the French, and I moved on and closed with the second column', while the Welch Fusiliers on the right closed with the third column.[17] The French infantry 'were formed on an eminence', Harrison later wrote:

> … and we had every disadvantage of the ground. They soon opened their fire. We returned it handsomely, came down to the charge, and cheered. They faced about after a few paces and others coming to their assistance the contest soon became general and a most determined fire kept up on both sides, so near as to be almost <u>muzzle to muzzle</u>. They again drew us on by showing us their backs, and we twice repeated our former treatment.[18]

From his position in Pearson's square on the right flank, von Wachholtz watched as the Fusilier Brigade advanced:

> … until it was perhaps 70 or 80 paces from the enemy columns, still closed for the most part. Here they halted and both sides began a dreadful session of firing that did not cease for almost half an hour. The entire field behind our line was covered with red-coated dead and wounded limping back. It was a gruesome but beautiful scene, both fire-spitting lines so close together and death with frightful roaring raging all round them.[19]

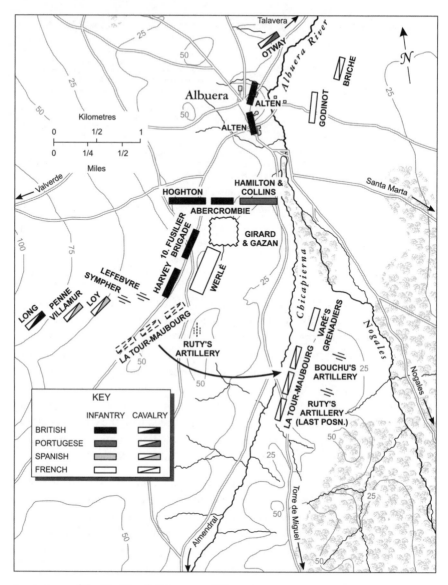

Last stage of the Battle of Albuera, 16 May 1811

While the 2nd Division and Hamilton's Portuguese Division held Girard's and Gazan's divisions in check, Cole's 4th Division mounted an attack on the French left flank. After a stiff fire-fight between the Fusilier Brigade and Werlé's brigade, the French gave way and fled to the eastern side of the Chicapierna, covered by their cavalry and artillery. *Map © C. Johnson*

The three fusilier battalions were hit by heavy artillery and musket fire but 'behaved most gloriously', in Blakeney's opinion, 'never losing their ranks, and closing to their centre as casualties occurred'.[20] The senior officers, most of whom were mounted, suffered heavily: Lowry Cole was shot off his horse and taken to the rear as were Major John Nooth commanding the 1/7th and Lieutenant Colonel Ellis of the 23rd and his adjutant, Lieutenant Robert McLelland. Myers, who ranged the length of his line encouraging his men, was shot through the stomach 'but continued, with his wonted firmness', to stay with his brigade until it became necessary to carry him to the rear.[21] Lieutenant Revis Hall, one of the shortest officers in the 1/23rd, was standing in front of Lieutenant Isaac Harris, one of the tallest, and could not help joking that 'the ball that goes over my head' would hit Harris.[22] Moments later, Hall was killed by a musket ball through the forehead. To Cooper of the 7th, the engagement resolved itself into loading, firing and advancing, all of which were punctuated by frequent commands of 'Close up' and 'Close in', as men fell on either side.[23]

The fight see-sawed back and forth but the fusiliers gradually pushed the French back. They now linked up with the right flank of Hoghton's brigade which, reinforced by the Spanish and Hamilton's Portuguese division, were holding their own. The battle was in the balance and La Tour-Maubourg, seeing that his infantry comrades needed assistance, brought his cavalry into action. The first attack, mounted by two regiments of dragoons, rode directly at Harvey's brigade, possibly thinking the Portuguese would not stand. This was a mistake as they were 'received with, and repulsed by a well directed fire' from the Portuguese infantry who 'shewed great steadiness' that 'would have done honour to the best and most experienced troops'.[24] Rebuffed, the dragoons rode off but, in a few minutes, the regiment of Polish lancers tried to repeat with the Fusilier Brigade the same success they had earlier enjoyed against Colborne. As Harrison watched, they rode towards the Welch Fusiliers' right flank but 'observing us so unshaken and so little dismayed at their fierce appearance, when within about one hundred yards, they wheeled about and we saluted their *derrières* with a smart fire'.[25] A few minutes later, Harrison received his 'reward for the day', a musket ball through the thigh, and limped back to the rear using his sword as a cane.

The duel between the Fusilier Brigade and Werlé's troops continued but the French got the worst of it, as they could not bring the same firepower to bear. From his position with Pearson, Hill could make out the fusiliers steadily advancing and soon had the satisfaction of seeing the Colours of the 23rd Foot on the summit of the hill where the French 'had not been enabled to maintain themselves'.[26] Blakeney of the 2/7th Foot remembered seeing:

> … the French officers endeavouring to deploy their columns, but all to no purpose; for, as soon as the third of a company got out they immediately ran back, to be covered by the front of the column. Our loss was, of course,

most severe; but the [three Fusilier] battalions never for an instant ceased advancing, although under artillery firing grape the whole time.[27]

When Werlé and several of his senior officers were killed or wounded, the French began to falter and, suddenly, 'gave way under the pressure of the recoiling crowd in front', and then 'the battalions next them on their left, already much thinned and disordered', followed 'the first mass of fugitives'.[28] Von Wachholtz recorded the climax of the battle:

> … we heard from our line a dull 'hurrah' that grew louder & finally became horrible and our brigade threw itself on the opposing column with the bayonet. They covered the short distance, the enemy saw the stalwart English with their long bayonets, advancing to within 15 paces, and those in the front rank began to waver, others soon followed and within a few seconds, all were gripped with disorder and speedily took flight.[29]

'It was so sudden', commented another officer as, at one moment the fighting was intense but, in the next, nothing could be seen 'but the backs of flying Frenchmen'.[30]

The French infantry, ably covered by their artillery and cavalry, made their way to the far side of the Chicapierna and Nogales streams. It was about 3 p.m. but Beresford decided not to continue the action – perhaps wisely as he had suffered just under 6,000 killed and wounded, about 17 per cent of his army – in seven hours of fighting, 4,159 of them British, or about 40% of the troops of that nation which had fought in the battle. He re-formed along the line of hills on the allied side of the river. Von Wachholtz's company, stationed where the Fusilier Brigade had fought, found the area 'covered with dead and wounded such that there were a dozen heaped together every ten paces'.[31]

The Fusilier Brigade's casualties had been horrendous – of the 2,015 officers and men it had taken into action, 1,045 had been killed or wounded, a loss rate of 52 per cent. The casualties included the brigade commander, Myers, who had been mortally wounded, and all three battalion commanders, who had been wounded. There were only two majors in the formation still standing and Pearson of the 23rd being senior, assumed command. The Welch Fusiliers had paraded 41 officers and 692 men that morning; by the late afternoon, they had lost two officers and 74 men killed, 11 officers and 246 men wounded (of whom two officers and at least 35 men later died of their wounds) and 6 men missing, a total of 339 casualties. The company of Captain William Stainforth, wounded in action, came out of it commanded by Corporal Thomas Robinson, a former weaver from Lancashire, who was promptly promoted to sergeant.[32]

*

Albuera was the bloodiest battle fought by the British army in the Peninsular campaign and one of the most costly days in that army's history prior to the First World War. The rudimentary medical services simply could not handle the numbers of wounded, including John Harrison of the 23rd Foot who hobbled:

> ... about a half a mile to the rear, when I met our Sergeant Sutler who, with the feelings and foresight of an old soldier, had brought a horse for the relief of his comrades and conveyed me about half a mile [farther] to the rear to where their baggage was then standing, where I was glad to lay down. ...
>
> Having laid in this state for nearly four hours, and seeing no chances of conveyance except my horse, there not being more than two or three waggons employed, which were obliged to attend to those in greater distress, and not admiring my berth for the night, I summed up resolution and proposed to [Second Lieutenant Robert] Castle to accompany me on a mule which he consented. With some difficulty and much pain I was mounted and we set off for Valverde.
>
> The road presented a shocking scene, numbers exerting themselves to avoid the inclemency of the night from which numbers lost their lives. Not being more than two leagues we reached Valverde soon after ten. I had previously sent my servant on to endeavour to get us an empty hovel, but this was out of the question, and we pigged in with some soldiers of the Buffs [the 3rd Foot]. Still no 'Pill' [surgeon] was to be procured, being few in number and having many subjects. ... I refreshed myself with a little tea and bread, which was all the sustenance I had that day, but notwithstanding slept pretty well on a little straw till morning.[33]

Harrison was fortunate. Most of the wounded remained on the battlefield, some for days. Cooper of the 7th and Bentinck of the 23rd both remembered that they and their comrades made some efforts to move the wounded from their regiments to the bottom of the hill and get them water but there were too many and the survivors themselves were exhausted. Bentinck commented that, as evening came on, the battalion's rations came up and the corporals of the 23rd went to get them but not knowing how many men were still alive, provided inflated numbers to the commissaries so that, for once at least, the Welch Fusiliers 'all had enough' to eat.[34] When darkness came, figures could be seen moving about the battlefield with lanterns, some trying to help the wounded, others trying to strip and loot the dead. Ignoring them, Bentinck's comrades built large fires with the stocks of hundreds of muskets lying about and then made themselves 'comfortable amongst the dead' under a downpour of rain.[35]

When Major General James Kemmis's brigade arrived on the morning after the battle, they gazed in horror at:

... the appalling sight of upwards of 6000 men, dead, and mostly stark-naked, having, as we were informed, been stripped by the Spaniards, during the night; their bodies disfigured with dirt and clotted blood, and torn with deadly gashes inflicted by the bullet, bayonet, sword or lance, that had terminated their existence. Those who had been killed outright, appeared merely in the pallid sleep of death, while others, whose wounds had been less suddenly fatal, from the agonies of their last struggle, exhibited a fearful distortion of features.[36]

This particular witness was struck by the fact that the bodies were not scattered about, as he had seen on other battlefields, but were 'lying in rows or heaps; in several places whole subdivisions or sections appeared to have been prostrated by one tremendous charge or volley'.

For his part, Soult remained in position near Albuera for two days, during which time he attempted to collect his wounded and then retreated to Seville. His casualties had been even heavier than those of Beresford, an estimated 8,000 or about a third of his force, and he had to abandon nearly a thousand wounded during his retreat.

Survivors of Albuera were amazed that they had lived through it. As it would be some time before the official casualty lists would be published, those who could write, sent short notes to their families in Britain to let them know they were alive. Among the Welch Fusilier correspondents was Lieutenant Grismond Philipps who informed his family that he had 'escaped unhurt, thank God for it, as it is Wonderful to me how I did'.[37] True to form, however, Grismond could not resist putting the touch on his father, informing him 'that from the fatigue I have undergone I have been obliged to borrow 50 dollars to buy a horse, and have [given] a Bill for the money which I trust you will have the goodness to accept'.

The official reports came later. Wellington, having himself won a notable victory at Fuentes de Onoro against Masséna on 5 May, disliked Beresford's first effort at a report, which he felt was too despondent, and directed the marshal 'to write me down a victory'.[38] Beresford did but, though he credited his success to 'the distinguished gallantry of the troops under his command', he hardly mentioned the 4th Division, particularly the Fusilier Brigade, in the action, paying more attention to Stewart's 2nd Division.[39] Furthermore, although the marshal accepted Stewart's suggestion that a sergeant be commissioned from each of the three battalions in Hoghton's brigade, he did nothing for the Fusilier Brigade although Stewart himself candidly admitted that it had 'effectually secured the victory of the day'.[40] Beresford's attitude brought a protest from Lowry Cole (who disliked him intensely) and who was in receipt of a letter from Hardinge stating that the Fusilier Brigade 'exceeded anything the usual word gallantry can convey' at Albuera and crediting Cole's 4th Division as having 'unquestionably saved the day and decided the victory'.[41] Somewhat tardily (in fact nearly a month later), Beresford agreed to commission a sergeant from each of the three fusilier battalions and, as a result, Sergeant David Scott of the 1/23rd Foot was gazetted an ensign in the 11th Foot. 'Everybody has been excessively indignant at the indifferent way Marshal Beresford passes over the Fusilier Brigade in orders', complained Harrison who felt the allied commander should have 'done us justice at first, and known how to appreciate the merits of good soldiers when they were unfortunately placed under his command'.[42]

This critical sentiment was echoed by many who had fought at Albuera and there was much relief when Wellington sent Beresford back to Portugal to assume an administrative command. One of the most vocal critics was Colonel Edward Pakenham who, although he had given up command of the Fusilier Brigade the previous January, still took a personal interest in it. Pakenham believed that, at Albuera, 'the unexampled Spirit of Wm. Myers and the Fusiliers, under Cole, not only gained the day, but prevented the annihilation of the Army' and Beresford should have acknowledged them.[43] 'The truth', Pakenham complained to his brother, 'which that marshal was unequal or unwilling to relate, would make Your Blood run Cold.'[44]

The three months that followed Albuera were relatively quiet, giving the Fusilier Brigade a chance to lick its wounds. While Pearson commanded the brigade, Jack Hill, now senior captain, took over the 1/23rd Foot, which, on 25 May, reported only 376 all ranks fit for duty. In the aftermath of Albuera the 1/7th and 2/7th Foot were amalgamated because of losses and the 1/48th Foot was brought into the brigade to keep up its strength. In that same month, Major General Edward Stopford was appointed to command the Fusilier Brigade and Pearson reverted to command the 1/23rd Foot which he did until Lieutenant Colonel Ellis returned to duty after recovering from his wound. As Pearson was the only field officer in the Welch Fusiliers, Major Francis Offley rejoined from Portuguese service to assist him. By the end of June, with many of the lightly wounded from Albuera back in the ranks, the battalion mustered 463 all ranks. In August, the unit received a large draft from the 2nd Battalion, which included Major Thomas Dalmer, five other officers and 254 men and, by the end of that month Ellis, returned to command, reported having an effective strength of 597 all ranks.

During this period, operations continued at a reduced tempo. In late May 1811, Wellington commenced the second siege of Badajoz but, frustrated by a lack of proper siege artillery, enjoyed no better luck than had Beresford. When he learned that Marshal Auguste Marmont, who had replaced Masséna, had brought his army down from the north to join Soult, Wellington lifted the siege on 10 June and withdrew to a strong position on the north side of the River Guadiana. This was not a healthy area and the army suffered much sickness – the Welch Fusiliers had nearly half their strength on the sick list in June and July 1811. When

Marmont and Soult arrived at the Guadiana, they displayed a reluctance to attack and contented themselves with a few cavalry probes before withdrawing, Marmont to the north and Soult to the south. Operations in the Peninsula now entered a state of equilibrium: Wellington could not advance because the French held the key Spanish fortresses of Badajoz and Ciudad Rodrigo while the French could not advance because Wellington held the equivalent Portuguese fortresses of Elvas and Almeida. Wellington therefore re-organised his army in preparation for a northward move with the object of taking Ciudad Rodrigo, using a new, modern siege train sent out from Britain. By 18 July, he was ready and the army marched north. Just before they set out the Fusilier Brigade was pleased when Pakenham again assumed command of the formation.

While he waited for the siege train to arrive, Wellington sent the 3rd and Light Divisions on 10 August to screen Ciudad Rodrigo and positioned the remainder of his army in positions some distance to the west of it. The 4th Division was sent to Fuente Guinaldo where they spent much of September constructing a defensive position. In the middle of that month, Marmont, reinforced by the army of General Jean Dorsenne, moved toward Ciudad Rodrigo with 58,000 troops to re-provision it. Believing that once they had completed this task, the French would withdraw, Wellington was caught off guard when Marmont sent a large cavalry force beyond Ciudad Rodrigo to make a reconnaissance. On 25 September, it attacked Major General Thomas Picton's 3rd Division at El Bodon, forcing Picton to make an epic fighting withdrawal across a plain to Fuente Guinaldo to join Wellington. When Picton's division neared the British position, Wellington ordered Pakenham to take the Fusilier Brigade out on to the plain to cover it from the enemy cavalry, which he did and the weary men of the 3rd Division got safely into Fuente Guinaldo.

On the following day, 26 September, Major General Robert Craufurd's Light Division arrived, somewhat tardily. Wellington now had nearly 15,000 men assembled but he was outnumbered by Marmont, who had the greater part of his army either in front of Fuente Guinaldo or on the march toward it. Throughout the day, the two sides stared at each other but Marmont and Dorsenne were reluctant to attack a general whose ability to choose good defensive ground was, with reason, highly respected by the French. When darkness came, it brought with it a heavy fog and at 11 p.m. Wellington, ordering fires to be lit along the line to confuse the French, put his army on the road for the village of Aldea da Ponte, about ten miles to the west.

The Fusilier Brigade acted as rearguard for this movement, Pearson's light infantry provided the rearguard for the brigade, and von Wachholtz's rifle company provided the rearguard for Pearson. The German officer, who disliked Pearson (as, indeed, did most men who served under him), resented the fact that, throughout the night, the Welch Fusilier officer constantly urged von Wachholtz' company to quicken their pace with loud shouts of 'Brunswickers, move forward!' This was all very well but since Pearson was mounted and von Wachholtz was on foot, the latter noted tartly that 'human strength is increased in those who can ride'.[45] After a twelve-hour march the brigade reached Aldea da Ponte shortly before noon. Although this place was outside Wellington's planned defensive position, it was a useful junction and he ordered Pakenham to hold it. Pakenham gave the task to Pearson who, after posting pickets, permitted his men, ravenous from the long march, to cook their dinner. Exhausted, von Wachholtz 'laid under a tree and rested; my baggage came up. I ordered coffee but I had just received the first cup when a sergeant reported to me that the light companies should fall in.'[46] His feelings still ruffled by Pearson's treatment of him, the German resolved not to hurry but 'calmly drank some cups of coffee and then went down to where the company was standing' only to learn that a French force had driven in the army's cavalry screen.

This force consisted of a brigade of cavalry and a division of infantry under the command of General Paul-Charles Thiébault. Marmont, finding that the British had slipped away during the previous night, had ordered Thiébault to maintain contact and, arriving outside Aldea, the French commander halted while he reconnoitred the ground. Aldea was situated in a gorge with a stream running through it and was flanked on both sides by rocky, wooded hills. Deciding to attack, Thiébault sent three battalions of infantry forward, one to frontally assault the village, the others to flank it on either side.

Von Wachholtz's company, positioned on the outskirts of Aldea, immediately engaged the French skirmishers. Pakenham, who had come forward, ordered the Brunswick officer to withdraw but by this time one of the French battalions had worked itself around the side of the village and the Brunswickers had to move 'at the trot'.[47] Pearson pulled his light companies out of Aldea as they were in danger of being surrounded and fell back to higher, open ground to the west. Thiébault's infantry and cavalry then triumphantly took the village and formed on its far side facing the main British position.

Wellington, deciding that the French did not pose a serious threat, directed Pakenham to retake Aldea. Forming the Fusilier Brigade in line, with Harvey's Portuguese brigade in support, Pakenham ordered an advance. Lieutenant Robert Knowles of the 7th Foot, just arrived from Britain and fighting his first battle, remembered that the brigade:

> ... advanced steadily against a heavy column of Imperial Guards [actually the grenadier companies of French line regiments], but they, perceiving our intention, retired in double quick time. Our Light Infantry poured in a dreadful fire amongst them, and numbers of them lay dead and dying on the field. They attempted to form on rising ground opposite, where our Artillery did great execution.[48]

By this time, the French artillery was also in action and took the oncoming brigade under fire. Drummer Richard Bentinck, serving in Captain Jacob Van Cortland's company of the 23rd, had a close call when he received a canister or musket ball through his shako plate which wounded him slightly, causing him to bleed 'down both sides of my head'.[49] Moments later, a round shot hit the company 'sweeping the legs off three men who stood in file' and carrying away the front of Van Cortland's stomach. With 'a convulsive motion' the company commander 'dropped his sword and placing both hands to his bowels to keep them in, staggered back' against Bentinck. The drummer helped him to the rear but they only moved a short distance before Van Cortland slumped to the ground, still vainly trying to keep his intestines inside his body. Lieutenant Colonel Ellis rode up and tried to comfort the mortally wounded man: 'Never mind, Captain, you die on the field of honour'.[50] 'Poor honour for my dear wife and children' was the captain's response and he expired shortly thereafter. Van Cortland was mourned by his fellow officers as a 'deserving and excellent' soldier who had 'signalled himself in 28 different engagements' but, as Bentinck noted, he was doubly lamented by the soldiers 'for his kindly behaviour' toward them.[51] Jacob Van Cortland was the last of the three Loyalist American officers who served with the Welch Fusiliers during the war. Major Philip Skinner had transferred to another regiment while Lieutenant Harman Visscher had drowned in the *Valk* disaster of 1799.

Forced back by Pakenham, the French abandoned Aldea. It was promptly re-occupied by Pearson with his light infantry while Pakenham kept the Fusilier Brigade behind the village in immediate support. As evening came on, everyone expected a quiet night but they were to be disappointed as, just at dusk, a fresh French division mounted a second attack against the village. Pearson's men were soon heavily engaged and von Wachholtz remembered that his company could 'clearly hear their officers' shouts of "en avant!"'[52] Bentinck recalled that at one point Pearson launched a counterattack through the village which 'bore all before it, aided by surprise and panic' but the French, 'yielding to command, got together and drove' the light infantry back.[53]

In confused fighting in and out of the houses, Pearson was hit in the leg and his horse killed under him. Unable to get out from under its weight, he shouted for assistance but, as Bentinck pointed out, although Pearson 'was a daring, able Officer', he was 'very bad with his men, flogging them terribly at the least excuse, so that he was hated by them all, though they liked well enough to follow his lead' in battle. The result was that Pearson's appeals went unheeded as the fusiliers were only 'too glad at the prospect of seeing him killed or at least taken prisoner, to do so' and therefore went on their way 'rejoicing' although they could hear Pearson shouting that he would 'tan their hides' if he ever caught them.[54] Fortunately for the enraged Pearson, someone rescued him from his plight and got him back to the British lines.

At this point, Pakenham came to the assistance of the light infantry with the entire Fusilier Brigade. Knowles commented that the brigade commander 'led us on ... under such a man cowards would fight' and that Pakenham waved his hat in the air and shouted 'Lads! Remember the Fusiliers!'[55] The 'huzza that followed intimidated the French, and they ran too fast for our bayonets, but our fire mowed them down by dozens'. Von Wachholtz now assumed command of the brigade's light infantry and positioned them behind stone walls at the outskirts of Aldea but the enemy 'appeared to be withdrawing and we therefore followed him with charged bayonets' through Aldea and, after 'a short time there, we received the order to return to our regiments and bivouac.[56] The intense little action at Aldea da Ponte cost the Welch Fusiliers a veteran officer killed, and two officers and thirteen men wounded.

Although Aldea was in British hands at the end of the fight, Wellington ordered it be abandoned as it was his intention to withdraw again that night. As the army moved off, Wellington asked Pakenham to provide a 'stop-gap regiment' as rearguard and Pakenham replied that he had already assigned the Royal Welch Fusiliers that task. 'Ah', responded Wellington, 'that is the very thing'.[57]

'Marched again at midnight', Cooper lamented, 'and stumbled on in bad roads until daybreak.'[58] By the morning of 28 September, however, Wellington had concentrated much of his army at Alfayates but, when he learned that Marmont was not pursuing but had withdrawn, he sent his troops into winter quarters on the Portuguese side of the border.

The 4th Division was stationed along the line of the River Agueda with the Royal Welch Fusiliers being billeted at the Spanish village of Barba del Puerco, west of Ciudad Rodrigo. It was here that Lieutenant John Harrison, having recovered from the wound he suffered at Albuera, found them when he rejoined in November 1811. The major topic of conversation among the officers, besides speculation as to when they would receive their pay which was months in arrears, was that Major Francis Offley had just appeared before a general court martial 'arising from a disturbance between several Portuguese Officers and him'.[59]

This event had taken place on 29 September when Offley was probably acting as brigade major. Having selected a site for the brigade camp he had ordered some fusiliers to chase away the mules and draught animals of Harvey's Portuguese brigade which were grazing on it. He did not bother to inform anyone in that formation before doing so and when some of Harvey's officers remonstrated with Offley over this high-handed act, heated words were exchanged. The Welch Fusilier officer made 'use of violent, intemperate, and threatening language and gestures', whereupon a Portuguese officer struck him. Furious, Offley drew his sword and challenged the man to a duel but calmer heads prevailing, the affray ended without bloodshed. Charges, however, were brought against Offley for 'unmilitary, scandalous, and infamous behaviour, such as is unbecoming an officer and a gentleman' including issuing a duelling challenge. On 15 October Offley pleaded 'not guilty' to all charges before a general court martial and, after deliberation, the court absolved him of 'scandalous and infamous behaviour' in 'consequence of the extreme provocation' he had 'received in being struck'. It did, however, find Offley guilty of three charges of unmilitary behaviour and sentenced him to 'be suspended from rank and pay for the space of six calendar months'. When Harrison rejoined the battalion, Offley was awaiting Wellington's review of his sentence but if the hot-tempered Offley thought the commander of the Peninsular army was going to reduce it, he was mistaken. Wellington confirmed the court's finding and Offley commenced his punishment on the first day of 1812.[60]

Francis Offley was not the only Welch Fusilier to appear before a general court martial that autumn. In October 1811, Private Richard Weeds of the 23rd Foot, Privates George Rider and Jeremiah Taylor of the 7th Foot and Private Thomas Ward of the 48th Foot were arraigned, charged with having absented themselves without leave from their camp and robbing 'from the house of a Portuguese inhabitant, near the village of Valverde, several articles of clothing'. The court dismissed the charges against Taylor and Ward after Rider confessed that he and Weeds had carried out the theft. They were both found guilty and sentenced 'to receive a corporal punishment of one thousand lashes each' although the court recommended Weeds for mercy. After reviewing the judgement, Wellington confirmed the sentence but pardoned both men because Rider had been honest and spared two innocent men from punishment. He took particular care, however, to make it 'clearly understood' that, in future', he will spare no pains to discover and bring to trial those who may injure the inhabitants of the country, and that whatever punishment the Court Martial may sentence shall in every case be inflicted'.[61]

When he rejoined that November, Harrison found the 1/23rd 'much altered' as it had 'lost some noble fine fellows, men and Officers, since the day we entered the field of Albuera' and there were 'several young gents strangers to me'.[62] This was somewhat of an understatement as, during their first year in the Peninsula, the battalion had suffered a very high rate of officer casualties. Ellis had been wounded, as had the senior major, Thomas Pearson, and the adjutant, Lieutenant Robert McClelland. Two experienced majors were now lost to the battalion, as Pearson had been invalided home and was destined for a staff position in North America, while Offley was about to be suspended.[†] Three captains had been killed in action or died of wounds (Colin McDonald, Frederick Montague and Jacob Van Cortland) while one, William Keith, had died of illness and eight lieutenants had been killed or wounded. Casualties, of course, meant promotion, particularly as vacancies resulting from active service were usually filled by seniority and not purchase. Thus, Lieutenants Alexander Gourlay, Thomas Griffith and Thomas

---

† Thomas Pearson's experiences in North America during the war of 1812-1814 with the United States, in which he fought in the four major battles of the northern theatre of that conflict and was wounded in two of them, can be found in the author's book, *Fix Bayonets! Being the Life and Times of Lieutenant-General Sir Thomas Pearson, CB, KCH, 1781-1847* (Toronto, 2006).

Hawkins attained captaincies in the battalion, with the consequent promotion of several lieutenants below them on the *Army List*.

All this was of great interest to Jack Hill, who had left the Welch Fusiliers in September for a brevet majority in the Portuguese service. An officer who calculated his promotion possibilities with great interest, Hill noted that:

> ... our senior Capt. [William Keith] then is dead of a fever & the 2nd [Jacob Van Cortland] killed by a round shot, Offley our 2nd Major has got himself into a Devil of a scrape, which is most likely to break him. From my situation as senior Cap[tai]n. and getting a majority in my own corps, it is possible. I might be order'd to the 2nd Bn which if they do not do I shall become a candidate for a Portuguese Lt. Col[onel]cy.
>
> Imagine out of our Cap[tai]ns we have 4 underground and two so badly shot through the lungs that neither are expected to live long. There are only two left out of the Cap[tai]ns we brought from America who command the flank Comp[anie]s.
>
> We have our four Majors here. Pearson is going home shot through the thigh. ... [Major Thomas] Dalmer is order'd home. ... Every thing seems quiet just now. I think the campaign might as well be considered at an end & certainly we have lost many of our best officers.[63]

For the Royal Welch Fusiliers, 1811 had been a bloody introduction to war in the Peninsula and the hope was that the new year would bring better things.

Come all you valiant soldiers and listen unto me,
Who has got an inclination to face your enemy.
Never be faint-hearted but boldly cross the main,
Come and join Lord Wellington who drubbed the French in Spain.

    With Wellington we'll go, we'll go, with Wellington we'll go,
    Across the main o'er to Spain and fight our daring foe

Early on the 22nd the battle it begun;
With courage bold both armies fought till setting of the sun.
Drawn up in line of battle great guns did loudly roar;
Balls like hailstones flew about; men bleeding in their gore.

    With Wellington we'll go, [etc.]

It's said the French in number with prisoners that were ta'en,
Amounted to twenty thousand who were in battle slain.
Six stand of colours we took, with other warlike store;
Two eagles fine in London shine, which grieves the French full sore.

    With Wellington we'll go, [etc.]

All you that wish to have a peace, from heavy taxes free,
Pray for success to Wellington and all his grand army.
May he always gain the victory so that the war might cease,
Then trade again in England would flourish and increase.

    With Wellington we'll go, [etc.][1]

Chapter 9

'We kept up a hot fire on the enemy'

1st Battalion, Portugal and Spain, November 1811 – November 1812

Although the weather was cold and wet, the Royal Welch Fusiliers' quarters from November 1811 to January 1812, near Gallegos in Portugal on the bank of the River Coa, were not unpleasant. Their billets and activities that winter were probably similar to those of their fellow fusilier regiment, the 7th Foot, as described by Lieutenant Donald Cameron of that unit:

> ... we were billeted on the inhabitants, the officers in the best houses or cottages, according to seniority, and the soldiers in the remainder. We had chimneys built, and oil-paper or sheepskin answered for glass in the windows. ... Being now in winter-quarters, every exertion was made in drilling and proficiency for the next campaign. Our volunteers were from different militia regiments and most of them were young soldiers. They were kept close at it.[2]

Lieutenant Colonel Henry Ellis would have carried out similar training in his battalion. If Ellis followed Wellington's standing orders for the Peninsular army, and he probably did, he would have staged a route march of six to eight miles at least twice a week, held frequent drills and ensured that his battalion was never 'dismissed from a parade without performing some one or other of the manoeuvres prescribed by His Majesty's Regulations'.[3] Rather than carry out all the intricate manoeuvres in the 1792 *Rules and Regulations*, Ellis and his adjutant, Lieutenant Robert McClelland, who was responsible for drilling the battalion, likely concentrated on the essentials which were defined by one knowledgeable Peninsular officer as being 'line marching, echelon movements, and formation of the square in every possible way'.[4]

We know that the officers of the 1/23rd Foot operated a regimental mess that winter as it was an expense listed by 21-year-old Lieutenant John MacDonald, from Rhue, Arisaig, Invernesshire, who arrived from the 2nd Battalion in February 1812. One of the few Scots officers in the regiment,

MacDonald complained to his brother about the high cost of going to war:

> In the first place we get three months pay in advance on leaving England to provide sea stock for the passage, &c. On joining, we are obliged to pay our mess fees which are £3. 10s, To get a sling belt and sabre which costs £8. 8s, a pair of epaulets £6. 10s and overalls, &c, &c. The 2nd battalion wearing wings, pantaloons, and regulation swords. This with ... servants wages, the wear and tear of a campaign, and being obliged to buy a whole set of cooking as well as eating utensils would take very nearly 12 months pay to be properly completed in.[5]

The officers of the 1/23rd also held at least one party that winter because Friedrich von Wachholtz, who attended, has left a description of it. As he recorded in his diary, the battalion officers, led by Henry Ellis whom the German called the 'boy colonel', assembled in the main street of a small village, each with a country girl, and 'drank grog and punch and amused themselves' by dancing with their partners. Von Wachholtz (a somewhat reserved man judging by his diary), did not join in the frivolity but did enjoy watching the girls dance the bolero 'accompanied by a basque drum beat by a maiden, castenets and hand claps to give the time'.[6]

Another member of the battalion who likely did not attend the party was Walter Bromley, the battalion paymaster, who spent part of that winter working on a book. Bromley had enlisted in 1790 and risen to the rank of sergeant in the 23rd Foot before being appointed quartermaster in 1800 and paymaster in 1805. The previous winter he had found religion, and had become involved in a project to distribute Church of England bibles and religious tracts to the Portuguese, particularly priests, and had cheerfully handed out these items to anyone who wished to receive them. Dissatisfied with military life, Bromley resigned his commission in March 1812 and returned to Britain, determined to make a living as an author. His first published work, the somewhat awkwardly titled *Treatise on the Acknowledged Superiority of the French over the English Officer in the Field. Extract from an Intended Publication called Campaigning Made Easy, Recommended to Officers going to Spain and Portugal. A Farewell Letter to the Officers of the Welch Fusiliers and an Essay on Happiness* appeared shortly afterwards. It was basically an advertising prospectus soliciting readers for the books Bromley wished to write but which, unfortunately, never saw print. Perhaps wisely, he laid down his pen and become a missionary, at first to the aboriginal people of Nova Scotia and later to those of Australia, where he accidentally drowned in 1838.[7]

Another more military activity took place that winter. On Wellington's orders, much of the army manufactured siege materiel as the allied commander was determined to have another attempt at taking Ciudad Rodrigo and actively prepared for it. When he learned that Marshal Marmont had been ordered to dispatch 16,000 men from his army to assist the French forces in Catalonia in the north-eastern corner of Spain, Wellington sensed opportunity, and rapidly assembling his army on the Agueda, moved against Ciudad Rodrigo, which was invested on 8 January 1812. The tasks of constructing trenches and batteries fell to the 3rd, 4th and Light Divisions, which each spent a day in turn at this labour. The weather was miserable but for the Welch Fusiliers, a worse problem was that provisions were so short, they christened their bivouac in a nearby woods the 'starvation camp'. A few British soldiers, discouraged and hungry, deserted to the enemy and their comrades were frequently reduced to eating acorns gathered in the woods by a detail sent out each day for that purpose. The domestic pigs, which lived on these acorns, noted Drummer Richard Bentinck, were also acquired with some stealth as:

> The men used to conceal their bayonets under their coats when they went out, and to bayonet the grunters without mercy when neither Officer nor owner was in sight, and fat pork boiled with the acorns helped them down nicely, or fried in wine, which was the one commodity that could be had almost anywhere at two pence a quart. Nor were the Officers any better off. They would look steadfastly another way if they came upon a soldier staggering under a side of pork, and a piece of it quietly dropped into their tent would seal their lips to silence.[8]

With whole divisions being used as labour parties, the works progressed quickly. Batteries were constructed for the new siege artillery, received from Britain the previous autumn, which quickly knocked breaches or ruptures in the main wall of the fortress. By 19 January all was ready and that night, the 3rd and Light Divisions assaulted Ciudad Rodrigo, taking it at the cost of 1,300 casualties including two generals, and capturing 1,300 prisoners. The triumph was soured by the behaviour of the assault troops who, having entered the city, dispersed to get drunk, loot and plunder.

A number of British deserters were found serving in the French garrison and among them was Private Thomas Jones of the 23rd Foot. They were tried by a mass court martial, found guilty and sentenced to be shot in front of their brigades, which were assembled for the purpose.[9] Drummer Bentinck was in the provost guard, which watched over Jones the night before his execution and since the man did not want to die in foreign uniform:

> [He] bought a forage jacket of Bentinck for three shillings, for that purpose. He begged for a pint of rum, but the quartermaster would not allow it, though he gave him as much food as he would eat. He was for standing in the grave to be shot, but was made to get out, and he then knelt by its side. Two soldiers fired at him, and failing to kill him he was finished by a ball through his head by the Provost Marshal's pistol.[10]

Badajoz
This view, from the north side of the River Guadiana, shows the great natural strength of the fortress-city. It was besieged three times by British forces before being finally taken in April 1812, with a fearful loss of life.
(*From Grant,* **British Battles on Land and Sea,** *1897*)

Following the execution, the Fusilier Brigade marched by the graves of the condemned in single file. Lieutenant Knowles of the 7th Foot thought 'it was the most awful sight I ever beheld' while Friedrich von Wachholtz found the entire business to be 'nauseating'.[11]

Have taken the key to the northern route into Spain, Wellington now turned his attention to Badajoz, its southern counterpart, and in late February the army marched south to the vicinity of Elvas. At this time, there were changes of command in the 4th Division. The newly-promoted Lieutenant General Lowry Cole, taken ill, was temporarily replaced by Major General Charles Colville while, at the same time, the Fusilier Brigade lost their much-liked commander, Pakenham, who took over a brigade in the 3rd Division. His replacement was Major General Barnard Bowes, a competent and aggressive officer. It took some time to assemble the ordnance and materiel necessary but by early March, Wellington was ready and on the 16th of that month, the 1/23rd Foot, 644 all ranks, moving as part of the 4th Division, invested Badajoz.

The French garrison of the city was 5,000 strong and commanded by the same Brigadier General Armand Phillipon who had rebuffed the two previous British sieges in May and June 1811. Over the last nine months, this energetic officer had worked hard to improve the city's defences. Phillipon had strengthened the walls, dug countermines, which could be loaded with explosives under the most likely approaches, and dammed up the Rivillas stream which flowed into the River Guadiana immediately east of the city walls, creating a flooded marsh that was a difficult obstacle to cross.

In contrast to the previous sieges, Wellington and his chief engineer, Lieutenant Colonel Richard Fletcher, decided to mount their main effort not on the north side of the city but against its south-eastern quarter. This would necessitate first taking an outwork, Fort Picurina, which would constitute a good position for the batteries of heavy guns that would create breaches in the main walls. The work of digging the first parallel – a trench whose axis was similar to that of the main wall of the city – was commenced and completed by a working party of no less than 1,800 men on the night of 17 March. That done, saps, or trenches dug toward the object of the attack, were started and these were constructed in a zig-zag fashion to prevent the French from firing down their length. Phillipon did everything in his power to hamper this work, sending out sorties at night to destroy the trenches, deploying small field guns outside the walls to provide enfilade fire down the line of trenches, and keeping the British working parties under constant fire with as many of the 140 guns mounted on the defences as he could bring to bear.[12]

For the Fusilier Brigade, which took a turn in the trenches approximately every third day, it was a cold, wet, miserable and dangerous period. It rained on seven of the first nine days of the siege and the parallels and saps became, at first, knee-deep and then waist-deep in water, and some collapsed. The French gunners were alert and their fire was dangerously accurate. Captain von Wachholtz saw:

> … with my own eyes a couple of heads sent to the Devil. The damned little 4-pdr. guns fired so sharp, that one scarcely saw the smoke, when the shot with a whining sound was over head. With the more respectable 12 or 24-pdrs. one had more time to get one's head under cover. The worst, however, were the shells as from them there was no place to hide.[13]

Private Richard Roberts of the 1/23rd remembered when a whistling shell landed near his working party:

> I called to the men to lie down, and we all threw ourselves on the ground in a heap. Many were above me. The moment it touched the ground, the shell burst. The groans of my wounded comrades still ring in my ears! One poor fellow had the crown of his head taken clean off; another was literally [dis-]embowelled; and others had their limbs shattered and lopped off.[14]

Undertaking backbreaking labour in conditions not dissimilar to those their descendants would experience nearly a century later on the Western Front, the

Welch Fusiliers lost 1 officer and 13 men killed, and 50 wounded between 17 March and 5 April 1812. The officer killed was Brevet Major William Potter and among the wounded was Lieutenant-Colonel Ellis, who was hit in the forehead by a musket ball, a wound that put him out of action for nearly two months. As they worked, the fusiliers' appearance became somewhat ragged, particularly as they had not received their annual clothing issue. 'We had to work very hard and the weather was so much against us as it was continually wet and the winds very stiff', Bentinck commented.[15] The fusiliers' shoes:

> ... were worn off our feet and all our clothes turned to rags with the work and the weather. Some of the men had to whip [take] their blankets that they had to lap [sew] them in to make trousers of. I myself was not as bad as a great many of them. I was not without shoes to my feet and my trousers were not so bad. I went many a time and waited until the butchers had killed the cattle and brought the hides for the men to make shoes of as we had no supply from England.[16]

Despite the weather and other problems, the siege work went forward with mathematical precision as parallels, saps and then breaching batteries were constructed each day. On 25 March 1812, Fort Picurina was taken by assault and quickly converted into a battery for the heavy guns that would breach the main walls. Five days later, fifty-two heavy guns or howitzers were firing against the Trinidad and Santa Maria bastions, the intended breaching sites. By 6 April, the hardworking gunners had cut three breaches in the main wall: that at the Trinidad bastion being nearly 150 feet wide, that at the Santa Maria bastion about 90 feet wide while a smaller rupture had been created between the two.

Wellington decided to attack that night and his plan called for five separate but linked operations. The 4th and Light Divisions would take the Trinidad and Santa Maria bastions respectively by direct assault through the breaches. To distract the defenders, the 3rd Division would feint an attack on the castle located at the north-east extremity of the city walls near the junction of the Rivillas stream and the Guadiana, while the 5th Division would feint against the San Vincente bastion in the south-west angle of the walls. These two diversions would be 'escalades' – that is, the troops would rush the walls with ladders and try to gain entrance. Finally, a small detachment of 150 men drawn from the trench guard of the 4th Division on duty that day would attack the lunette of San Roque, an outwork north-east of the main breaches, located near the dam that bottled up the Rivillas stream. The attacks were scheduled to begin at 7 p.m. but were delayed for three hours because of the need to provide more time for the assembly of the assault forces.

This delay proved fatal as it gave Phillipon time to carry out additional defence work. When darkness fell and the British artillery stopped firing at about 7 p.m., the French constructed retrenchments or temporary breastworks behind the breaches and anchored solid wooden beams, a foot square and bristling with

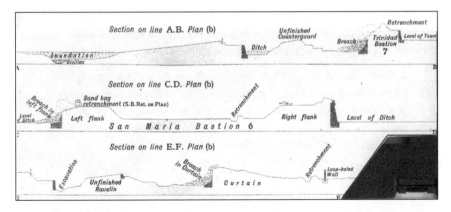

Section on line A.B. Plan (b)

Unfinished Counterguard

Retrenchment

Breach — Trinidad Bastion 7

Level of Town

Ditch

Inundation
Rivillas

Section on line C.D. Plan (b)

Breach in left flank

Sand bag retrenchment (S.B. Ret. on Plan)

Retrenchment

Left flank

Right flank

Level of Ditch

Level of Ditch

San Maria Bastion 6

Section on line E.F. Plan (b)

Excavation

Breach in Curtain

Retrenchment

Loop-holed Wall

Unfinished Ravelin

Curtain

The Breaches at Badajoz, April 1812

Cole's 4th Division attacked the breach in the Trinidad Bastion. The attackers had first to cross the flooded area of the Rivillia stream, get over a stockade, cross the flooded ditch, and then get over the unfinished counterguard before they reached the breach proper. The assault failed with heavy casualties.

(From J. W. Fortescue, History of the British Army*)*

sword blades, across their top, and strewed nail-studded planks in front of them. The breaches had earlier been mined with shells and explosive charges that could be detonated by fuzes and the defenders of the two main breaches, nearly half the garrison, were supplied with at least three loaded muskets each and also furnished with plentiful supplies of grenades, shells, explosive charges, baulks of timber, and even large rocks, to be thrown at the attackers. These last-minute preparations were concealed from the attackers by mist, which rose from the flooded Rivillas.

On the other hand, the mist also shrouded the approach of the Light and 4th Divisions to their assembly areas for the assault, located between the lines southeast of the breaches. At about 9 p.m., Corporal John Cooper of the 7th Foot remembered orders being given to 'Pile knapsacks by companies ... fall in ... and move off silently.'[17] Von Wachholtz's rifle company was in the Fusilier Brigade's advance party and the German nearly got into a fight before the shooting even started when he 'had an argument with the captain of the 60th as to who should go first, as I had more seniority in grade, but his regiment was more senior'. Major General Bowes decided against von Wachholtz and so he 'went to the artillery and took a cup of rum, with it the business seemed more dignified'.[18] Gleefully, he later added, Major General Colville noticed that the obstinate 60th captain was 'unfit for any military business' as 'he had clearly drunk too much', and the man was sent to the rear in disgrace.[19]

At about 9.45 p.m., while the four divisions were moving toward their objectives, the trench guards, 150 strong, attacked the San Rocque lunette. Captain Robert Hawtyn of the 1/23rd commanded those elements drawn from the Fusilier Brigade and Lieutenant Knowles of the 7th Foot was with him. 'After being exposed for half an hour to the hottest fire I was ever under', Knowles recalled, the attackers managed to get one ladder against the wall and:

> A Corporal was the first who got into the Fort, and was immediately killed. I was the third man who mounted the ladder. On leaping into the place I was knocked down by a shower of grape which broke my sabre into a hundred pieces. I providentially escaped without any serious injury, although my clothes were torn from my back.[20]

Close behind Knowles on the ladder was Private Roberts of the 23rd who:

> ... was in the act of placing my foot on the wall, when a stout Frenchman made a cut at my head with his sword; but at the same instant I had twelve inches of my bayonet in him, and he fell on his face on the wall. The cut I had received in my head was so severe, that but for my brass cap-plate, my skull would have been cloven in two. I lost all recollection for the moment, and tumbled off the ladder into the ditch, about twenty-five feet; and there I lay for some time. When I came to my senses, the blood was flowing very freely and blinding my eyes. Trying to staunch it the best way I could, I again scrambled up the ladder.[21]

Knowles, meanwhile, picked up his corporal's musket, 'and with the assistance of eight or ten men who had now got into the Fort, I charged along the ramparts, destroying or disarming all who opposed us'.[22] Those defenders not killed either fled to the main city walls or surrendered. The lunette taken, the attackers turned to destroying the Rivillas dam, so as to reduce the flooded area guarding the breaches.

The noise and fire of the attack on the lunette alerted the defenders who let off rockets for illumination, which revealed the main assault forces closing on the walls. Cooper remembered that the Fusilier Brigade was within 300 yards of the wall when 'up went a fire ball' that lit the 'crowded state of the ramparts, and the bright arms of our approaching columns'.[23] The defenders opened up and to von Wachholtz, the entire line of the city walls 'appeared to be spitting fire'.[24] As the leading elements of the brigade reached the breaches, 'the earth opened, as mines exploded and grenades were thrown at us' while the noise of musketry and artillery fire, combined with 'the continuous 'hurrahs', [and] the blowing of bugles created a tangled, confused effect'.[25]

Arriving at the ditch before the Trinidad bastion, the men of the Fusilier Brigade jumped down into it, those carrying grass bags to fill it and those with ladders taking the lead. They came under heavy fire, commented Cooper, as 'mortars, cannon and muskets, roared and rattled unceasingly', while mines 'ever and anon blew up with horrid noise' and to add to the din, 'there were the sounding of bugles, the rattling of drums, and the shouting of the combatants'.[26] Von Wachholtz recorded that as he approached the palisade before the ditch, 'we got a general salvo from the breach – they had been waiting for us – we could see them crowded along the line of their breastwork'.[27]

Having jumped or climbed down into the ditch the attackers moved toward the Trinidad breach and began to climb it but not a man reached the top alive, and those killed or wounded tumbled down its slope to hinder the progress of men coming behind. The defenders' musketry was relentless. Its effect was multiplied by the explosions of grenades, mines and shells, the latter being lit and simply rolled down the slope of the breach. Many officers and NCOs were killed or wounded, the attackers lost cohesion, and the 4th Division's attack degenerated into a series of unco-ordinated attempts by small groups of brave men to climb the breach and get to grips with the enemy. Lieutenant John Harrison of the 1/23rd Foot participated in one rush and was about halfway up when he 'was shot through the right arm nearly above an inch of the elbow' and 'had scarcely time to thank them for this', before he was hit again in the right shoulder, the ball passing out half way down his arm.[28] As he tumbled backwards, the young officer was hit a third time in the calf of his right leg but Harrison was lucky – he survived.

Cooper remembered that men kept entering the ditch and it 'was soon filled with a dense mass which could neither advance nor retreat' and upon which 'the enemy threw the missiles from the parapet, with a continuous fire of musketry and round shot'.[29] Some men were drowned when they fell into a deep, water-filled trench dug at the bottom of the ditch. Scaling ladders were placed across this trap but they were soon set on fire by the explosions and this, in von Wachholtz's words, 'strongly illuminated the gruesome scene'. 'The enemy's fire was so continuous', he recalled, 'that our people began to hesitate ... despite the cheers and forward movement – and the cheers were growing weaker and weaker.'[30]

Seeing it was hopeless, the surviving officers ordered a withdrawal. 'They are coming out', one of von Wachholtz's men told him, and the German 'decided to go also and gave the order to pull back'.[31] The 4th Division's attack on the Trinidad bastion had failed and the Light Division had had no better luck at the Santa Maria bastion, which was defended just as tenaciously. Wellington's main assaults had been decisively rebuffed at a horrendous cost but the two diversionary attacks were successful and after some heavy fighting, Badajoz was in British hands by the early hours of 7 April 1812.

At this point the army disgraced itself. The surviving attackers, maddened by what they had just experienced, flooded into the city to begin an orgy of looting and plundering that was to last nearly two days before it was brought under control. Cooper noted that many survivors of the 4th Division returned to the Trinidad breach and, when the sword-studded beam was removed, 'rushed into the town by thousands' and broke into any building that might contain liquor.[32] Like many of his comrades, Bentinck believed a rumour that Wellington had given the army 'twenty-four hours to plunder' but this was merely an attempt to rationalise criminal behaviour.[33] Lieutenant Thomas Browne, serving on the staff, found it difficult 'to describe the scenes of drunkenness & insubordination' which took place in Badajoz:

> ... nor can any one except those who have witnessed it, form an idea of the state of Soldiers after a successful storm. With faces as black & dirty as powder can make them, eyes red & inflamed, & with features full of wildness & ferocity, & of the insolence of victory, after a desperately contested struggle, they break into houses, ransack every spot where wine or spirits can be supposed to lie hid, & after repeated intoxicating draughts, begin their work of plunder. Woe to that unfortunate owner of a mansion, if any such remain, who attempts to remonstrate. Discipline being at an end, the whole world seems given up to their indiscriminate rage & plunder.[34]

If the excuse is made that the soldiers who engaged in this behaviour had been maddened by their experiences during the assault, it must also be stressed that the victims were innocent citizens of an allied nation.

For several days afterwards, Bentinck remembered, the army's camps resembled 'a fair with every kind of spoil, and thronged with the townspeople buying back their goods'.[35] He also pointed out that officers were involved in these transactions, although they 'did not themselves carry off the articles, but if they saw a watch, a jewel case, or any other thing they fancied, they would tell one of their men to get it for them'.[36]

Wellington now possessed Badajoz but he had paid a terrible price. The total losses during the siege were 1,035 killed, 3,789 wounded and about a hundred missing. Of these 803 had been killed and 2,858 wounded during the actual assault of 6 April. The Welch Fusiliers' share of this grim accounting was 2 officers (Captain J.H. Maw and Lieutenant George Collins) and 34 men killed and 20 missing. Fifteen officers, including Lieutenant Colonel Henry Ellis and 92 men were wounded and, of these, 2 officers (Brevet Major William Potter and Lieutenant B. Llewelyn) and 24 men later died of their wounds. Bentinck, who did not take part in the plundering, was in the detail that went to the Trinidad breach on the morning after the assault to recover the battalion's dead and wounded:

> we went out and found all the Officers we could and we brought them back to the camp and buried them. Some of them was knocked down in the trench with the men and the trench was completely filled up with dead bodies so that we could walk over the trench without difficulty. ... In our tent we mustered six out of eighteen and two of the six was wounded. I was wounded in the leg by the explosion of a shell and the Sergeant was wounded by a ball in his head. [37]

Private Roberts remembered that, on 7 April, 'all that could be mustered of my company including myself, was eight men!'[38] The Welch Fusiliers' total loss for the siege of Badajoz from 17 March to 6 April 1812, was 246 officers and men or nearly 37 per cent of the strength they mustered on the earlier date. When Lieutenant John MacDonald, recovered from a bout of illness, rejoined the battalion a few weeks later, it was small wonder that he described it as a 'skeleton'.[39]

With the key fortresses of Badajoz and Ciudad Rodrigo in his possession, Wellington now had the initiative. He could choose to move against either of the two French armies facing him – that of Marmont in the north or Soult in the south – while neither enemy commander could undertake a sustained offensive against Wellington with these two fortresses in British hands. Wellington chose to attack Marmont and, a few days after Badajoz fell, he marched his army north to the area of Agueda River, leaving a force under Lieutenant General Sir Rowland Hill to keep Soult occupied. Here he paused for some weeks to re-organise and re-supply his troops and the Fusilier Brigade went into camp around the village of Traves.

The strength of the 1/23rd Foot remained weak for some time after the siege of Badajoz. It was augmented in May 1812 by a draft of seventy-four men from the 2nd Battalion. The 1/23rd reported 331 all ranks on the 25th of that month when it was inspected at Traves by Major General William Anson, temporarily commanding the 4th Division in the absence of Colville, who had been wounded at Badajoz. Anson, who led the other British brigade in the division, apologised profusely in his report that he did not know the 1/23rd Foot well, having only joined the division a few weeks before, and had not had much to do with them since. He may also have been somewhat tentative because Ellis was at this time commanding the Fusilier Brigade, Bowes having been transferred to the 6th Division, and Anson himself was holding his first brigade command.

In any case, his report made frequent use of the qualifier 'appear'. Lieutenant Colonel Henry Ellis, Anson wrote, 'appears an active & intelligent officer;' the officers 'appear to be competent;' and the sergeants 'appear active and intelligent, obedient & respectful to their officers'.[40] Anson was thankfully more definite about the private soldiers whom he characterised as 'a good Body of men, with a general appearance of Health & cleanliness' who were 'well drilled, & well behaved'. He found that the battalion performed its field exercises 'with precision' but noted that it had not yet received its clothing for 1811 and that its muskets 'appear' to have been 'delivered at different times, & have the Marks of different Regiments upon them'. By this time, most of these weapons would have been the India Pattern musket, a shorter and lighter version of the Short Land Pattern which, originally manufactured for the East India Company's troops, was later widely issued throughout the army.[41] Anson noted that only ten offenders had come before regimental courts martial in the previous six months, an indication of good discipline but of course this did not include Private Thomas Nugent who went before a general court martial in June charged with theft and was sentenced to receive a thousand lashes, to be inflicted before the assembled Fusilier Brigade.[42]

On 13 June 1812 Wellington resumed the offensive, crossing the Agueda with 51,000 men and advancing in the direction of Salamanca, with the intention of bringing Marmont to battle. The French commander was caught by surprise as, following an abortive raid into Portugal while Wellington had been occupied with Badajoz, he had dispersed his army to re-provision. When Wellington paused after taking Salamanca on 17 June to besiege three small extemporised fortifications inside that city, however, Marmont got a chance to concentrate his scattered forces. On 20 June, he advanced close to Salamanca and there was an exchange of artillery and some skirmishing between the two armies. An unlucky round shot struck Lieutenant William Leonard of the 23rd, removing much of his upper torso and Private Richard Roberts, standing nearby, was horrified when Leonard's 'head came upon my foot'.[43] Much to Wellington's disappointment, as he had chosen a very strong position on which to fight a defensive battle, Marmont withdrew. When the Salamanca forts had fallen, Wellington pushed northeast thirty miles to the River Douro only to find Marmont, his army now assembled and nearly equal in strength, holding all the crossings.

To the puzzlement of his troops, Wellington did not attack, and the two opponents simply stared at each other across the Douro for the next two weeks. At about this time, Majors Francis Offley and Thomas Dalmer returned to the 1st Battalion. Dalmer had come out from the 2nd Battalion in 1811 but had gone back to Britain after Offley had returned from Portuguese service following Albuera. Offley, it will be recalled, had been suspended for six months. It is not known what Offley did during this period but, when his suspension terminated on 30 June, he went back to the Welch Fusiliers. As Ellis was still commanding the Fusilier Brigade Offley, being senior to Dalmer, assumed command of the 1/23rd while Dalmer took command of the brigade's light troops. At about the same time, Lieutenant General Lowry Cole returned to the 4th Division after a long absence.

For the army, the stalemate on the Douro was not an unpleasant time. Lieutenant MacDonald of the 23rd wrote to his parents that the countryside was 'most delightful', the biggest problem being the intense heat' but that was perhaps 'lucky as we sleep in the fields every night'. Provisions were good and the Welch Fusiliers were truly 'in the land of milk and honey, ... which is brought in to camp daily', living mainly on 'bread and milk as it is impossible to eat meat that has been kept for any time'. 'The army is perhaps the finest that has been in the

Peninsula', MacDonald confidently added, and he and his comrades expected 'a very active campaign'.[44]

They were therefore puzzled on 16 July when, after Marmont crossed the Douro in an attempt to outflank Wellington, the British commander ordered a withdrawal. For the next six days, the two armies engaged in a curious sidestep, often in sight of each other, as Marmont kept trying to get around Wellington's flank while the British commander moved to prevent it. By the evening of 21 July, this military minuet had brought the two armies into an area about seven miles west of Salamanca. After the sun set there was a violent thunderstorm; Lieutenant Thomas Browne recalled that 'the night grew darker & stormy, thunder rolled tremendously over our heads, & vivid flashes of lightening [*sic*] made the scene most imposing'.[45] Many soldiers took the storm to be an omen of battle on the following day – and they were right.

When the Royal Welch Fusiliers stood to their arms before break of day on 22 July 1812, dawn brought warm sunlight. The two armies were so close that, as von Wachholtz recorded, 'we heard the enemy beat reveille and assembly', but since there did not seem to be any immediate threat, the troops were dismissed to eat breakfast, get water and gather forage. The 4th Division was positioned north of the little village of Los Arapiles with the divisional light troops placed in front. Looking south from their position, von Wachholtz thought the terrain was 'extraordinary', gently rolling and undulating along a series of rocky ridges, but directly in front, two 'very high rocky hills stretch their heads upwards toward the sky'.[46] The first and closer feature was the Lesser Arapile while about a half mile beyond was the Greater Arapile. Nothing could be seen of the enemy except an occasional glimpse of moving columns in the distance and, as the morning wore on and nothing happened, the brigade light troops lay down in a field south of Los Arapiles, 'nibbled on rusks, and drank fresh water' brought to them by the villagers'.[47]

Wellington had concentrated five of his six infantry divisions south of the River Tormes within two miles of Los Arapiles, and only Pakenham's 3rd Division and some cavalry were north of the river. Most of his nearly 52,000 British and Portuguese troops were hidden from French view by low, rolling hills. Unaware of the allied position, Marmont decided his adversary was going to continue retreating and resumed his westward movement of the previous day, ordering his lead division to quicken its pace to try and cut the British communications. As Wellington did not move, however, this meant that the French commander's six divisions with 48,500 men would be marching in a spread-out formation some six miles long across the front of the British position, not more than two miles away from it.

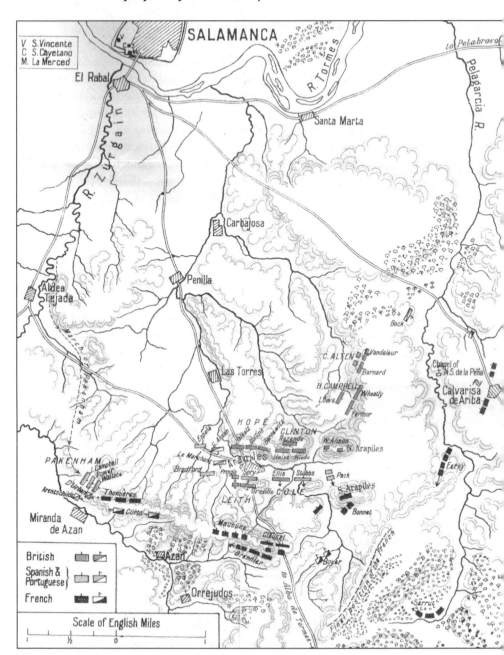

Salamanca, July 1812

Dispositions in the early stages of the battle.

(From C. W. Oman, **History of the Peninsular War***)*

Marshal Auguste de Marmont was no fool. As he could glimpse British troops in and around Los Arapiles, he ordered General Jean-Pierre Bonnet to take his division and seize the Greater Arapile to form a pivot around which he could move safely. To provide further protection he ordered General Antoine Maucune, whose division was ahead of Bonnet's in line, to take the ridge immediately south of Los Arapiles. Both officers obeyed their orders promptly: Bonnet taking the Greater Arapile and Maucune the ridge where he immediately deployed at least twenty pieces of artillery that opened fire at Los Arapiles. At this point, however, Maucune exceeded his orders and sent in light infantry to take the village.

Von Wachholtz and his company were watching a cavalry clash out on the open ground when artillery fire began to land around Los Arapiles, which was shortly followed by the appearance of French skirmishers. Dalmer commanded the Fusilier Brigade light troops and, as the enemy approached, he engaged them but, in von Wachholtz's words, 'the brave French advanced and we were soon within 100 paces of Life'. The French artillery became increasingly accurate and Dalmer's troops were forced to withdraw to the village, covered by their own artillery. Dalmer was wounded in this exchange as was Captain Thwaites of the 1/48th, the next senior, so Lieutenant George Browne of the 23rd, brother of the diarist Thomas Browne, assumed command of the light troops. As the *voltigeurs* approached Los Arapiles, the light troops 'went forward at a trot' with a 'hurra' and 'threw them back'. Once started, this scrapping continued for nearly two hours as the brigade light troops, von Wachholtz commented, 'advanced until we suffered from canister fire;' then the French 'advanced and received our pills'.[48]

It was now about 2 p.m. Wellington, who was watching the French movements through his telescope, spotted that the lead French division, commanded by Brigadier General Jean Thomières, was some distance ahead of the remainder of Marmont's army, leaving a gap between it and the next French formation. 'By God', he snapped, 'that will do' and gave immediate orders for the 3rd, 4th and 5th divisions to attack.[49]

Pakenham's 3rd Division, which had moved south of the Tormes during the morning, delivered the first blow. Forming quickly into line, it ascending the plateau across which Thomières's division was marching in column, fired several volleys, and then pushed home with the bayonet turning the surprised French division into a mass of refugees fleeing to the rear. Lieutenant General James Leith's 5th Division, to the right of the 4th Division, came into action next, advancing directly toward the ridge held by Maucune's division, pushing that officer's skirmishers back with ease and then engaging Maucune's infantry who were in solid battalion columns. As the surprised British line looked on, the French suddenly began to form squares. The reason for this was that Major General John Le Marchant had moved his heavy cavalry brigade parallel with Leith and the French, seeing the threat, formed squares to repel a mounted attack. This being the case, Leith's infantry, advancing in line, had no problem sweeping them away with musketry and the bayonet. As the French fled, Le Marchant's brigade, which had already ridden down the survivors of Thomières's division, charged and literally cut Maucune's division to pieces. Marmont's left wing had now ceased to exist.

Cole's 4th Division was ordered forward at the same time as the 5th. Von Wachholtz had been observing the battle between Leith and Maucune when behind him he saw 'our Division rush down the mountain, traverse the village [of Los Arapiles] in swarms', form 'into open columns' and fall 'into line'.[50] As Anson's brigade had been sent to the left, Cole had to carry out his attack with just Ellis's Fusilier Brigade and Colonel Thomas Stubbs's Portuguese brigade. The Fusilier Brigade was on the right and Ellis deployed with the 7th Foot, commanded by Major John Beatty, on his left, the 1/23rd under Offley in the centre, and the 1/48th under Lieutenant Colonel J.T. Wilson on the right. For his part, Stubbs placed the 11th Portuguese Infantry Regiment with two battalions on his left and the 23rd Portuguese Regiment of two battalions on his right. A British officer serving with the latter regiment remembered that, just before it moved, every officer and man 'fell to their knees to pray before advancing with great resolution'.[51]

Formed in a single line of two ranks, Cole's seven battalions, bayonets fixed and Colours uncased, advanced at the quick step 'in great order and regularity, under a heavy fire from the enemy's guns'.[52] They ascended a gentle slope and as they reached the crest, they could see five French battalions in columns with artillery in the intervals between them. Cole had ordered von Wachholtz's Brunswick rifle company to act as skirmishers for Stubbs's brigade because he had stationed the 7th Caçadores, the unit which normally performed that function, to guard his left flank. The German officer remembered that when the two brigades encountered the French just behind the crest of the hill, his men 'on my side and the French on their side, leveled their weapons at the same time and would have fired into each other's noses'.[53] Von Wachholtz was waiting for an order from Stubbs to withdraw his skirmishers so that the Portuguese infantry could fire but when that did not come and being 'between two fires' he threw himself on the ground and let the Portuguese 'pass over me, receiving only a few kicks'.[54]

The British and Portuguese let loose disciplined volleys at the French columns, who tried to return them from their clumsy formations. Both Cole and Ellis were wounded in this exchange as was Offley, commanding the Welch Fusiliers. MacDonald was grazed on the arm by one musket ball while a second struck the knot of his sash 'which was luckily tied in front, and did not penetrate the skin, though it knocked me down for a few seconds'.[55] Wilson of the 48th assumed command of the Fusilier Brigade but the loss of three senior officers at a crucial moment caused confusion. The five French battalions, a brigade from General Bertrand Clausel's division, were thrown into disarray, however, by the steady volleys from the British and Portuguese and fell back in disorder but did not break.

Seeing this, Clausel ordered forward his second brigade of five battalions, which had been stationed a few hundred yards to the rear. At almost the same time, Bonnet's division assailed the 7th Caçadores on the left flank of the division and threw it back onto the 11th Portuguese Regiment on the left of Stubbs's line. The Portuguese brigade, an eyewitness commented, suddenly 'gave way like a wave of the sea, first on their left, then by degrees all the way to the right'.[56] At the same time, Clausel's troops came up the hill toward the Fusilier Brigade 'with a brisk and regular step, and their drums beating the *pas de charge*; our men fired wildly and at random among them; the French never returned a shot, but continued their steady advance'.[57]

Most witnesses agree that the Fusilier Brigade was somewhat disordered after its initial attack when Clausel's infantry approached. A spectator in Leith's division to the right, recorded what happened next:

> The Fuzileers in this situation unsupported at the moment commenced firing without forming after the first attack. The French regiment form'd close column with the Grenadiers in front and closed the Battalions, ... They then advanced up the hill in the most beautiful order without firing a shot. ... When about 30 paces distant our men began to waver, being still firing, and not properly formed. The Ensigns advanced two paces in front [of the Fusilier Brigade] & planted the colours on the edge of the hill & Officers stept out to encourage the men to meet them. They stopt with an apparent determination to stand firm, the enemy continued to advance at a steady pace & when quite close the Fuzileers gave way.[58]

A witness serving with the Fusilier Brigade recalled that the officers of the three battalions tried to stop the its rearward drift by advancing 'in a line in front, waving their swords, and cheering their men to come on, but the confusion became a panic'.[59]

After the initial exchange of fire, Friedrich von Wachholtz had joined the 7th Foot. Watching the French columns steadily moving closer, he:

> ... expected that they would charge us but that we would throw them down the hill but to my amazement I saw first the Portuguese and then the British, despite all entreaties made, 'right about face' and rush madly back down the hill. Before I could decide if I should remain or go with them, I found myself instinctively already at the fastest gallop which I have ever made in my life. I covered an enormous distance at each stride.[60]

Seeing the 4th Division collapse, Bonnet and Clausel's troops moved forward to take advantage of the situation. Three regiments of French dragoons charged the broken brigades of the 4th Division, which hastily formed squares to repel them. Behind the enemy cavalry came two brigades of French infantry which ran straight into Major General Henry Clinton's 6th Division, advancing on

Wellington's orders, which not only stopped them cold but drove them back. While this was taking place, the officers of the Fusilier Brigade struggled to re-form its three battalions, which 'had come to their senses, and were furious with themselves for having allowed the enemy to gain the advantage'.[61] Eventually, the brigade advanced to the left of the 6th Division, moving 'up the heights under a heavy fire, without returning a shot; and drove the enemy in its front, from his ground'.[62] The brigade experienced a stiff musketry contest but, as evening came on, the French gave way and fled rearward, protected by troops who only arrived at the close of the action. It now being nearly dark and Wellington, finding it impossible to pursue the enemy, who had seemingly vanished, halted his army behind a strong picket line.

Salamanca shattered forever the belief that Wellington was a defensive-minded general. At the cost of 5,220 casualties, he had more or less eviscerated Marmont's army, inflicting 12,500 losses on it, about a quarter of its strength, one of the French casualties being Marmont, who was seriously wounded. In the words of one historian, Salamanca 'decided the Peninsular war' because it gave the British commander a moral ascendancy over his opponent that he never lost.[63] 'Splendid as are his military talents', an officer in the 4th Division noted, however, Wellington 'must consider himself in great measure indebted to his success from his good fortune in commanding the bravest Troops in the world; men who when well led on will hesitate at nothing.'[64]

Unfortunately, the price of bravery is not cheap. The three battalions of the Fusilier Brigade, which had entered the battle with 1,357 all ranks, suffered 380 casualties, causing them to be temporarily amalgamated into a single unit after the action. The Welch Fusiliers' share of the butcher's bill was Major Francis Offley and ten men killed while Lieutenant Colonel Henry Ellis, Major Thomas Dalmer, five other officers and ninety men were wounded – about a quarter of the battalion's strength.

It had been a vicious battle. One British participant thought he had never seen ground so 'strew'd with Heads, Arms, Legs, Horses' and wounded men who 'lay bleeding and groaning' and 'women screaming and crying for the loss of their husbands'.[65] Inured to such sights, von Wachholtz was on picket duty during the night that followed and he had some problems with a Portuguese officer who tried to arrest the German 'as he took me for a Frenchman from my uniform' but fortunately the matter was sorted out after considerable discussion in several languages.[66] The Brunswick officer then made his way toward an abandoned enemy artillery piece which he intended to claim for his company, but had only taken a few steps when 'up came two sergeants from the 23rd and took it as a good prize', one of twelve such guns captured at Salamanca. The French gun detachment, which had fought to the last, lay dead around their weapon and one of von Wachholtz's men asked his permission to remove the pants from the corpse of the enemy artillery officer. The German 'gave it with some distaste as if it was not my man, it would be another'.[67]

During the night, the camp followers came out to search the dead and wounded. Many of them were soldiers' wives who were soon at work 'stripping & plundering friend & foe alike'.[68] It was Lieutenant Thomas Browne's belief that these scavengers 'gave the finishing blow, to many an Officer who was struggling with a mortal wound' and that Offley, 'who lay on the ground, unable to move, but not dead', was one of them. There is no firm evidence for this statement, but since Browne was probably repeating camp gossip, there may possibly be some credence to it. Other women were stricken with grief including the beautiful young wife of a British officer missing on the field who ran around it 'wildly with her hair loose' searching with an 'earnest anxiety & a distracted air amongst the dead, & those of the wounded who had not yet been removed' and stopping at every corpse, 'the greater number of which had already been entirely stripped by the Spaniards or women of the army'.[69]

More than 8,000 men in both armies, who had been wounded during the battle, were treated by the allied medical officers. Most lay where they fell until they could be collected and transported in unsprung carts to extemporised hospitals in the surrounding villages. The medical officers worked until they dropped from exhaustion, slept and rose to work again. Amputation – which converted a complicated limb wound into one easily treated – solved the problem of too many wounded men and not enough time for proper treatment. Medical personnel had no anaesthesia available although many tried to provide alcohol to the wounded before operating but, more often than not, recourse was made to strong assistants and straps to keep the patient immobile. The scenes in military hospitals after a major battle such as Salamanca were horrific – a military surgeon of the time remembered that:

> ... nothing but the Groans, of the wounded & agonies of the Dying are to be heard. The Surgeons, wading in blood, cutting of[f] arms, legs & trepanning heads to rescue their fellow creatures from untimely deaths – to hear the poor creatures, crying – Oh, Dear! Oh Dear! Oh My God! my God! Do, Doctor, Doctor! Do cut of[f] my leg! my arm! my head! to relieve me from misery! I can't live! I can't live – would have rent the heart of Steel & shocked the insensibility of the most harden'd assassin & the cruelest savage.[70]

Surgeon George Guthrie, one of the senior medical officers of Wellington's army, treated the wounded from Albuera, Salamanca and other major battles in the Peninsula. A pioneer in combat surgery, Guthrie made careful notes about some of his cases, which included Private John Wilson of the 1/23rd Foot who was hit at Salamanca in the upper thigh by a musket ball. The wound seeming to be a simple one requiring no surgery, Wilson was bandaged and put to bed but, while making his rounds, Guthrie saw:

> ... this man sitting at night on his bed, which was on the floor, with his leg bent and out of it, another man holding a candle, and a third catching the

blood which flowed from the wound, and which had half filled a large pewter basin. A tourniquet with a thick pad was placed as high as possible on the upper part of the thigh, and the [medical] officer on duty was requested to loosen it in the course of an hour; that was done, and the bleeding did not recommence.

The next day, the patient being laid on the operation table, I removed the coagula from both openings, and tried to bring on the bleeding by pressure and by moving the limb; it would not, however, bleed. As there could be no other guide to the wounded artery, which was evidently a deep-seated one, I did not like to cut down into the thigh without it, and the man was replaced in bed, and a loose precautionary tourniquet applied. At night the wound bled smartly again, and the blood was evidently arterial. It was soon arrested by pressure.

The next day I placed him on the operating table again, but the artery would not bleed. This occurred a third time with the same result. The bleedings were, however, now almost immediately suppressed, whenever they took place, by the orderly who attended upon him; care having been taken to have a long, thick pad always lying over the femoral artery, from and below Poupart's ligament, upon which he made pressure with his hand for a short time.[71]

As Guthrie noted:

A painter could not have had a better subject for a picture illustrative of the miseries which follow a great battle, than some of the hospitals at Salamanca at one time presented. Conceive this poor man [Wilson], late at night, in the midst of others, some more seriously injured than himself, calmly watching his blood, his life flowing away without hope of relief, one man holding a lighted candle in his hand, to look at it, and another a pewter washhand-basin to prevent its running over the floor, until life should be extinct. The unfortunate wretch next him with a broken thigh, the ends lying nearly at right angles for want of a proper splint to keep them straight, is praying for amputation or for death. The miserable being on the other side has lost his thigh; it has been amputated. The stump is shaking with spasms; it has shifted itself off the wisp of straw which supported it. He is holding it with both hands in an agony of despair.[72]

Fortunately, Private John Wilson recovered from his wound.

Hampered by a shortage of cavalry, Wellington did not closely pursue his enemy's defeated army after Salamanca and it retreated rapidly to the east. When the

British commander learned that Marmont was not going to be reinforced from the other French armies in Spain, they being occupied in their own areas, he decided to move on Madrid. The army set out on 6 August and a week later entered the Spanish capital, from which Joseph Bonaparte had fled. The overjoyed inhabitants gave them a splendid reception, Lieutenant MacDonald remembering that:

> ... nothing could equal the joy of the inhabitants on seeing us enter Madrid, in fact no language that I can use can convey the least Idea of it, they surrounded us in immense crowds, embracing the soldiers, pulling the officers very nearly off their horses, & every body exclaiming, 'Viva los Inglezos'. Any unconcerned spectator would have thought them mad, the Young and Old dancing about all parts of the City, the church Bells all ringing, the Bands of the Different Regiments playing, the houses most beautifully decorated with tapestry, & at night illuminated, in fact the whole scene exceeded any description that can be given of it.[73]

Wellington himself did not remain long in Madrid. A few weeks later, he took part of his army to besiege the fortress-town of Burgos, a vital communications centre on the road to France. The other part remained in the area of Madrid with the 4th Division being camped in and around the Escurial, a Spanish royal palace.

The 4th Division enjoyed six glorious weeks at the Escurial. After 'three months marching and countermarching', MacDonald commented, it was wonderful to have a comfortable billet.[74] As Ellis had resumed command of the Fusilier Brigade after recovering from his Salamanca wound, the battalion was led by Dalmer, who had also recovered from a wound suffered in that engagement. MacDonald noted that besides himself and Dalmer, there were only four other officers with the battalion and only about 200 men fit for duty, so the prolonged rest at the Escurial was particularly welcome. The Welch Fusiliers suffered much from illness during that summer, averaging just over 400 men sick during the months of July, August and September. The Escurial had been plundered and stripped by the French but the 'most beautiful chapel & the Burial place of the Kings of Spain' remained, which MacDonald thought exceeded 'any thing of the kind perhaps in the world' was still worth visiting.[75] His biggest complaint, as usual, was money as the officers' pay was six months in arrears:

> [Those] that have money in England can not get cash for Bills, & some of them pay as high as Eight shillings for every Dollar. The [regimental] Staff have not been paid since December 1811. Now we have got a halt we are in expectation of getting some, as the great difficulty of procuring provisions on a march obliged them to give all the ready money to the Commissariat Department.[76]

One popular topic of conversation that summer was events outside the Peninsula. In May 1812 a deranged man had assassinated Prime Minister Spencer

Perceval. He was replaced by Lord Liverpool, the former Secretary for War and the Colonies, who was in turn replaced in that portfolio by Lord Bathurst, the former President of the Board of Trade, both being men determined to defeat Napoleon. Meanwhile, the Duke of York, who had resigned his appointment as commander-in-chief in 1809 after a scandal involving the alleged sale of commissions by his mistress, had returned to the Horse Guards in 1811. These three men were strong supporters of Wellington and would provide competent leadership for Britain in the latter years of the war.

In June 1812 Britain had gained both a new ally and a new enemy. Napoleon's economic policy of prohibiting trade with Britain, which had been intended to humble her by striking at her maritime commerce and had been the original reason for his involvement in the Iberian Peninsula in 1807, had created unforeseen results. On 18 June 1812 the United States, infuriated by London's policy of forbidding any neutral country to trade with the French empire or its allies and the Royal Navy's impressment of American seamen, declared war against Britain. On the other hand, Russia had also suffered from Napoleon's restrictive economic policies and Czar Alexander became increasingly restive. This led to tension with Napoleon who decided to invade Russia as a means of 'crushing England by crushing the only continental power strong enough to give him any trouble by joining her'.[77] On 24 June, after months of preparation, Napoleon marched eastward with several armies totalling nearly half a million men to commence the campaign that would ultimately lead to his downfall.

While the 4th Division enjoyed some leisure at the Escurial, Wellington was having a frustrating time at Burgos. He had not brought his siege train forward, and possessing inadequate ordnance and materiel, he spent more than a month before its walls and, despite the loss of nearly 2,000 men in a number of assaults, had nothing to show for his efforts. In the meantime, his very success had caused the French to unite against him and in October Marshal Soult came north from Andaluzia and with General Clausel (commanding Marmont's army in that officer's absence) advanced with more than 100,000 troops. In the face of these odds, Wellington decided that he had no choice but to retreat. He lifted the siege of Burgos and on the last day of October 1812, his army left Madrid watched by silent and reproachful crowds. A week later, he had re-united with Hill's force, which had come up from the south, and was positioned in a strong position in front of Salamanca. He hoped that the two French commanders would attack but they preferred manoeuvre and while Clausel faced Wellington in front, Soult began a long march around his flank, threatening his communications with Portugal.

On 15 November Wellington therefore ordered a further withdrawal to the vicinity of Ciudad Rodrigo and for four miserable, wretched days the army moved west, trudging along muddy roads under continuous rain, sleet and snow. This march was done on empty stomachs as, through incompetence, there was a total failure of the commissariat to supply rations. The nights were bitterly cold and

Bentinck recalled that when he got up one morning, 'I found nine or ten men lying around me dead and stiff.' The drummer added that, although the army was forbidden to plunder, this order was disobeyed or the soldiers would have starved, despite the fact that the men were not permitted 'to fall out of the ranks and get a drink of water by the road side' though many did and were 'flogged for it'.[78]

Punishment or not, men did leave the ranks, either too exhausted to continue, or desperate to find food. After one day of marching in particularly bad weather, Lieutenant Thomas Browne was ordered to take a wagon and collect stragglers left behind on the road. He found:

> Groupes [*sic*] of women & children & drum boys lay perishing with cold – some had already died in a sort of rolled up posture – others were not yet dead, but convulsed with a sort of hysterical laugh which sometimes precedes death – there were stout soldiers too, who had breathed their last by the roadside on that bitter night, & many a gallant spirit, that would have been unmoved in the thickest fire had been bowed down by cold & hunger.[79]

Colonel John B. Skerrett, who had assumed command of the Fusilier Brigade just before the retreat commenced, became infuriated. As he explained to von Wachholtz, Skerrett thought the British were 'the most stupid people in the world' because they did not utilise the resources of the local population to ease the situation. 'We see men dying on the side of the road', he complained, 'but we do not use the Spanish villagers' mules and carts to carry either these miserables or provisions.' It was Skerrett's belief that 'it was absolutely necessary to always consider the area where one made war as enemy country' as the 'new method of waging war absolutely demanded it'.[80] Skerrett had a point but, whenever possible, Wellington always tried to prevent undue harm coming to the civilian population – in marked contrast to the French – and this policy always paid dividends.

During the retreat, nearly 3,000 allied soldiers either died or were taken prisoner by the French who did not press the retreating British very hard but contented themselves with merely keeping in contact. The 1/23rd Foot lost one officer, Lieutenant George Farmer, who fell out with severe rheumatism, and thirty-eight men. When Wellington reached the vicinity of Ciudad Rodrigo, Marmont and Soult gave up the pursuit and both armies retired to winter quarters. A few days later, John MacDonald wrote to his father that it had been 'the first time I have been in a serious retreat & I hope it shall be the last'.[81]

Sing all ye bards with loud acclaim,
High glory give to gallant Graham,
Heap laurels on our Marshal's fame
Who conquered at Vittoria.

Triumphant freedom smiled on Spain,
And raised her stately form again,
When the British Lion shook his mane
On the mountains of Vittoria.

Let blustering Suchet crossly crack,
Let Joseph run the coward's track,
And Jourdan wish his baton back,
He left upon Vittoria.

Britannia's glory there was shewn,
By the undaunted Wellington,
An' the tyrant trembled on his throne,
When hearing o' Vittoria.[1]

Chapter 10

'We paid Jack Frenchman in his own coin'

1st Battalion, Portugal and Spain, November 1812 – July 1813

IN EARLY DECEMBER 1812, after a long and hard campaign, the 1st Battalion of the Royal Welch Fusiliers went into winter quarters at the Portuguese village of Soitella near the border with Spain. Officers and men were thankful for the respite but, for Lieutenant Colonel Henry Ellis, the end of active operations brought additional labour as he had fallen behind in his paperwork. Such important items as the regimental quarterly pay list to 24 December 1811; the officers' quarterly pay list to the same date; and the monthly returns for the period up to 24 May 1811 had not been received by the appropriate departments and 'could he please attend to them, etc'. The army postmaster was concerned about getting payment of 15 Portuguese reas each on some thirty-four letters (roughly 4s 3d) written by the officers and men of the battalion and 'could he please look into the matter' – and so on, and so on.[2]

Ellis's attention was also directed to a General Order dated 10 October 1812 stating that the 23rd Foot was among several regiments for which new clothing was being held at Lisbon. The army quartermaster 'had received no directions on the subject' and would the commanding officer of the 1/23rd Foot therefore make arrangements to ensure that every one of his fusiliers received 'his clothing at or before Christmas', which was clearly impossible, given the communications in the Peninsula.[3] The fact that his battalion had been on campaign when this order was promulgated was no excuse, it had to be obeyed. In fact, all the units in the Fusilier Brigade were looking somewhat bedraggled in the early winter of 1812/1813. Von Wachholtz recollected that at the first parade held following the retreat of November, his riflemen paraded in trousers that were holed and repeatedly patched while their company commander had been reduced to wearing knee breeches which, as he recorded in English in his diary, made it 'pretty cold'.[4]

There was one document in the pile of paperwork that annoyed Ellis as it did most other battalion commanders in the Peninsular army. This was a

'Memorandum to Officers commanding Divisions and Brigades' by Wellington, dated 28 November 1812. Although intended only for senior officers, many of them passed it on to their subordinates and its contents became public knowledge after it was published in the British newspapers. Noting the irregularities that had occurred during the recent retreat, Wellington attributed them 'to the habitual inattention of the officers of the regiments to do their duty, as prescribed by the standing regulations of the service, and the orders of this army'.[5] Regimental commanding officers, Wellington emphasised:

> ... must enforce the orders of the army regarding the constant inspection and superintendence of the officers over the conduct of the men in their companies, and they must endeavour to inspire the non-commissioned officers with a sense of their situation and authority. By these means the frequent and discreditable resort to the authority of the Provost, and to punishments by courts martial, will be prevented, and the soldiers will not dare to commit the offences and outrages of which there are so many complaints, when they well know that their officers and non-commissioned officers have their eyes on them.[6]

Henry Ellis was annoyed when he read these words as during the retreat, he had 'never slept three hours any one night' but had still managed to bring his battalion through it with minimal loss.[7] Now, 'instead of being thanked for his exertion', he and his fellow commanding officers were being subjected to harsh criticism. As for not enforcing discipline in his unit, even before Wellington had issued this order Ellis had set matters aright by court-martialling six privates for being 'drunk and disorderly' during the retreat and shortly thereafter he demoted four sergeants for 'neglect of duty on the march'.[8] His loss of thirty-eight men during the retreat was small compared to other battalions in the army – camp gossip was that Lieutenant Colonel William Grant's 1/82nd Foot – which had been attached to the Fusilier Brigade during the retreat – had lost as many as 400 men and Grant faced a court martial because of it.[9] In actual fact recent research has revealed that Grant only lost about 175 men but that is still far in excess of the losses of the 1/23rd Foot.[10]

Ellis's biggest problem, and one shared by the other commanding officers in the army, was a high rate of sickness. Lieutenant John MacDonald commented that when it went into winter quarters, the battalion was 'a skeleton' with 'not more than two hundred men' fit for duty.[11] Matters did not improve all that much over the winter as the battalion averaged about 300 men on the sick list each month, and it was only in May 1813 with the return of good weather, that the number of sick began to appreciably decline. For this reason, Ellis was glad to receive a draft of nine officers and seventy-four men from the 2nd Battalion in January 1813. As was the custom in the 1/23rd, when the 'Johnny Newcomes' arrived, the veterans taught them how to make fires, set up camp and prepare their rations. Drummer Richard Bentinck noted that the clothing of the reinforcements 'was clean and good' and 'they were quite surprised to see us in such a poor state' but 'it was not long before they was nearly as bad'.[12] Fortunately, Ellis managed to get the battalion's uniforms at Lisbon forwarded to it and by spring all his men were well clothed.

A new arrival to the Fusilier Brigade that winter was Colonel Robert Ross's 20th Regiment of Foot, which joined it in January 1813 to replace the 48th, which was transferred to Anson's brigade. Although the 7th and 1/23rd were sorry to see the men with whom they had stormed the breach at Badajoz and fought at Salamanca depart, the 20th Foot was a well-disciplined regiment that had seen considerable service and Cole had asked for it to be included in his division.[13] It had, however, recently spent much time in garrison and its officers and men had to adjust to life in the field. Major Charles Steevens of the 20th complained about the brigade's winter quarters which:

> ... were miserably cold, for the Portuguese had no idea of a comfortable fire-place, and frequently there was not a glazed window in the house; the consequence was, when we wanted light we were obliged to open a shutter instead of a window, so that we admitted cold as well as light. ... I have sometimes put oiled paper, as a substitute for glass, in the windows of my quarters, that I might enjoy light without being taxed with the cold; no such comforts anywhere, after all, as in 'Old England'.[14]

Such complaints would have surprised the two fusilier regiments – indeed MacDonald thought the Welch Fusiliers' winter quarters at Soitella

> ... perhaps the most healthy in Portugal. We are within a mile of the river Douro, in the centre of the country where you get all your port wine from & which is infinitely better here not having been mixed with any spirituous liquors. ...
>
> We have established a Dinner Mess here on the same terms as in England except the wine which we get at near sixpence a bottle, we have besides some excellent shooting with some wild boar hunting but they are very scarce and difficult of access. This is the whole of our occupation since we arrived here, which is indeed is a kind of paradise in comparison to the lives we lead when up the country.[15]

In later years, Drummer Richard Bentinck remembered Soitella with pleasure as, for about two weeks after the retreat, the officers left the men 'almost to themselves' as 'a period of indulgence' to recover from the rigours of the retreat. A number of the men in Bentinck's company had come to the end of their seven-year terms but, lured by the 16 guineas bounty offered, decided to re-enlist. This bounty was paid in gold – somewhat surprising given the perennial shortage of specie in the Peninsula. The Portuguese winesellers did not know the value of a guinea, having never seen the coin before, 'and refused to let the soldiers have much for them, but on an official proclamation of the value being made they were just as eager to get hold of them, as they had been dubious before'. With wine costing the men between two and three pence a bottle – a significantly lower price than that paid by the officers, it should be noted – Bentinck's company had several jolly weeks until the money was gone. Not at all dismayed, his comrades convinced the winesellers to accept bills or cheques drawn on Ellis and the 23rd Foot and, as the Portuguese 'could not read a word of them and the guineas had turned out so well, they were readily persuaded that these worthless scraps of paper were of equal value, notwithstanding the stipulation that they were not to present them to the Colonel till the troops were about to move'. Thus restocked with funds, Bentinck's company carried on with its jollification. In March, however, when the battalion switched its quarters from Soitella to Agodras, Ellis was surrounded by a crowd of civilians waving scraps of paper and eager for their money – and loud were their lamentations 'when he gruffly informed them' that he had no such men in his battalion as 'Sergeant Glazecap', 'Corporal Musket', and so on, 'whose names were affixed to these little bills'.[16]

The new quarters at Algodres were situated on the Spanish border and MacDonald thought them 'very inferior here to what they were down the country' at Soitella and as the billets were scattered, the officers were 'obliged to break up our mess'. The battalion, he noted, 'still continues very weak in men (being about 350 effective bayonets)'. Sickness continued to plague the army, 'especially the guards, one brigade of whom have buried six hundred men since our coming in to quarters, & the men that recover are no better than skeletons'. This, MacDonald believed, would make it 'impossible to commence the campaign before the latter end of May'.[17]

On 25 March 1813, Colonel John Skerrett, commanding the Fusilier Brigade, inspected the 1/23rd Foot at Algodres. Unlike Anson, who had carried out the battalion's previous inspection in May 1812, Skerrett was not at all tentative in his remarks. He praised Ellis for having 'bestowed the greatest attention on the Battalion' and reported:

> *Officers.* – All are equal to, and have performed, their duty with perfect zeal, a great many have been wounded, and with the exception of a few lately joined, have seen much active service, perfect unanimity prevails among them.
> *Non-Commissioned Officers.* – Very good, most of them very old soldiers, who have seen much severe service and been wounded.
> *Privates.* – A fine body of men, very stout, cleanly, and at the moment very healthy, lately they have suffered from sickness from unavoidable circumstances.[18]

Skerrett stated that the Welch Fusiliers' uniforms were new, their weapons 'fit for service', their ammunition complete, and their performance of the field exercise and movements 'perfect'. Overall the 1/23rd Foot was described as 'fit for service although weak in numbers'. Even at this date, with winter turning to spring, Ellis had 204 officers and men on the sick list out of a total strength of 649 all ranks.[19]

Turning to the subject of discipline, Skerrett noted that 'punishments appear to have been avoided as much as possible' and attached to his report a summary of the regimental courts martial held in the previous six months. During that time 50 soldiers had been tried, with 2 being acquitted, and it is notable that alcohol played a part in no fewer than 20 of the charges. Ellis had awarded a total of 8,600 lashes but had remitted 5,105 of them, further indication that he believed the threat to be as effective as the punishment. The worst malefactor – certainly the man who received the stiffest penalty – was Private John Edwards who was sentenced to 300 lashes 'for being absent without leave' on 2 February 1813 and received 150 of them. This might be an indication of the gravity of the offence or that Edwards was a repeat offender. On the other hand, Privates Ball, Collier and Edward Edwards, charged with 'destroying a pig', were sentenced to 200 lashes each but only received 30 of them. There is no doubt that discipline was strict in the 1/23rd and yet it was no stricter than other well-commanded battalions of the Peninsular army such as the 1/11th Foot which, during a similar time period, had five fewer charges but, at the same time awarded much higher punishments.[20]

There also seems to have been a shortage of officers. Of the twenty-five reported present with the battalion at Algodres, the field officers were Ellis and Major Thomas Dalmer but there were only two captains, the companies of the missing eight being commanded by lieutenants. No fewer than eight officers, including four captains, were marked as being 'absent without leave', perhaps not as grave as it sounds because given the wretched road system, they had probably been delayed returning from leave to the regiment. The curse of every battalion commander in the Peninsula (and probably since) was the number of officers on extra-regimental duty and in this respect, Ellis reported seven as absent from the unit: Majors Charles Sutton and Jack Hill were with the Portuguese army while Captains Peter Brown, Richard Hare and Richard Walker, and Lieutenants Thomas Browne and James Swayne held staff appointments.[21]

The absence of these men, mostly veterans, was in no way made up by the appearance of John Bassett, Gerald Fitzgibbon and David Satchwell, who joined the battalion as volunteers that winter.[22] Volunteers were men who had obtained a letter of reference from General Sir Richard Grenville, the Colonel of the 23rd Foot, to Ellis recommending them for a commission in the regiment. If there were no vacancies they served as privates, and if their behaviour was acceptable, Ellis might, if he wished, appoint them as second lieutenants to fill any vacancy that occurred from deaths in the field, whether by combat or sickness. These volunteers were of extremely variable quality and despite their display of initiative in getting out to the Peninsula under their own efforts, they were not all that popular with either officers or men. Lieutenant Charles Crowe of the 27th Foot in Anson's brigade commented that:

From what I have written many people would imagine that there was a great want of good feeling towards volunteers. But numerous as they were, so few had even a slight claim to notice. Generally speaking they were not gentlemanly in appearance, or manners. Some associated with the private soldiers. Others dismayed by the hardships they had to encounter left in disgust. ... If the numbers who came out and the few who obtained rank were recorded, the disproportion would be very surprising.[23]

By April 1813, it was clear that it would not be much longer before the campaign opened. When Lieutenant General Sir Lowry Cole ordered the brigades in his division to undertake route marches in heavy marching order, it 'was a plain hint of what we had to expect would take place 'ere long'.[24] Battalion drill which, in the Peninsular army, was never-ending and at least ninety minutes a day were devoted to it with brigade-level training being less frequent but at least weekly. To complement their new uniforms, the Welch Fusiliers, along with every other infantry battalion in the army, received new equipment including lighter camp kettles, and billhooks for chopping tree branches. Each soldier was issued 'a reasonable supply of necessaries, including three pairs of shoes, and an extra pair of soles and heels, in his knapsack'.[25] All very well but, as the newly-promoted Sergeant John Cooper of the 7th Foot complained, the government 'should have sent us new backbones to bear' the extra load.[26] The veteran Cooper carefully tabulated the items that he had to carry and their weight:

1 Fusee [musket] and bayonet	14 lbs.
1 Pouch and sixty round of ball [cartridge], etc.	6
1 Canteen and Belt	1
1 Mess Tin	1
1 Knapsack Frame and Belts	3
1 Blanket	4
1 Great Coat [clearly he retained his]	4
1 Dress Coat	3
1 White [fatigue] jacket	0 ½
2 Shirts and 3 Breasts	2 ½
2 Pairs Shoes	3
1 Pair Gaiters	0 ¼
2 Pairs Stockings	1
4 Brushes, Button Stick, Comb	3
2 Cross Belts	1
Pen, Ink and Paper	0 ¼
Pipe Clay, Chalk, etc	1
2 Tent Pegs	0 ½
Weight of Kit without Provisions	53 lbs [actually 49 lbs]

Extra Weight for Marching

Three days' Bread	3
Two days' Beef	2
Water in our canteens	3

61 lbs. [actually 49 lbs][27]

'Another grand and very important alteration in the materials of the army', commented Lieutenant Crowe of the 27th Foot, was the issue of tents:

> Four bell tents were delivered to each company. One for the Officers to be carried with their own baggage, and three for the use of the soldiers, to be carried by the Bât Mule in lieu of the camp kettles, who, had he been consulted, would have entered his protest against the alteration for his burden became much heavier with three tents saturated with nocturnal rains, or the very heavy dews of day break. But the increase of his burden contributed to the health of the army, and thereby its efficiency, so that this and many other hospital stations prepared by wise forethought were never filled.[28]

When Wellington reviewed the 4th Division on 10 May 1813, everyone suspected that the campaign would shortly commence. The regiments rose early so as to be ready at the appointed place at 8 a.m. when Wellington arrived. The army commander rode with Cole down the front of the entire division formed in two ranks, and then watched it advance in line a considerable distance to demonstrate its steadiness in manoeuvre. As Wellington passed in front of his Brunswick riflemen, von Wachholtz overheard him say to Cole, 'that is a good company', but was unable to hear Cole's reply.[29] 'We then marched past & went home', Lieutenant Richard Garrett of the 7th Foot complained, and 'a pretty day's work it was' as the Fusilier Brigade did not get back to its billets 'till 5 in the afternoon, so that we were out 13 hours'.[30]

Eight days later, the units of the 4th Division began to move, brigade by brigade, towards the River Agueda. They crossed it at a ford by means of boats attached to strong cables strung from bank to bank. The river was high and the current was so swift that it was, in Bentinck's words, 'hard work' to get over and some of the baggage animals belonging to the soldiers' wives were 'taken off their feet' and washed downstream.[31] By 24 May, the division was concentrated in and around the town of Legeares where to the surprise of all, the army received a considerable amount of back pay. The price of wine being what it was, Crowe noted, this windfall 'gave plenty of employment to Officers in charge of Companies all the next day' keeping order among the men.[32] Three days later, Lieutenant General Sir Thomas Graham inspected the division and Crowe recorded that the officers and men of Anson's brigade were pleased at the opportunity of seeing the Fusilier Brigade, which had a deservedly high reputation in the Peninsula army, pass in review as they 'were a fine body of men' but were 'amused and grieved' to observe 'a poor little fellow, attached as a volunteer' to the 1/23rd Foot, who 'could not keep his musket upright', struggling to keep the step in ankle-deep mud.[33]

On the following day, 28 May, the Peninsular army, 81,000 strong 'with ample material', was, in Crowe's phrase 'quietly put in motion by the master spirit of our Commander in Chief, Lord Wellington'.[34] The 1813 campaign had begun.

Although they were now on the march the Royal Welch Fusiliers, along with the rest of the army were 'completely in the dark as to the plans of the Great Lord'.[35] Wellington's strategy for 1813 derived from events in eastern Europe as London had informed him that the 'most formidable army ever collected by Bonaparte' had been 'most substantially destroyed' in Russia.[36] He thus suspected that the French emperor, faced with having to fend off Prussia and Russia, who were now moving against him, would withdraw either most or all of his forces in Spain and was somewhat surprised when this did not take place. More than 200,000 French and French-allied troops remained in the Peninsula, organised in five armies: that of Catalonia and those of the North, the South, the Centre and Portugal. Wellington did not want any three of these armies combining against him so, with the help of the Spanish guerrilla forces and the Royal Navy, he carefully planned a number of diversions in northern and southern Spain. These included amphibious raids and attacks on French communications that effectively tied up the armies of Catalonia, the North and much of that of Portugal. This still left the armies of the Centre and the South, and part of the army of Portugal, about 80,000 bayonets, which were positioned to block the British commander's 81,000 British, Portuguese and Spanish troops from advancing into central Spain.

But Wellington had no intention of playing the game according to the enemy's rules. Instead of moving into central Spain as he had done in previous years, he conceived a daring plan to send his entire army on a lengthy outflanking march north of Madrid, thus cutting enemy communications with France. At the same time, he would switch his own communications from Lisbon to ports in friendly hands on the northern coast, particularly Santander. If everything worked as planned, he would be in the rear of the French armies threatening their lifeline, while drawing his own sustenance from a shorter seaborne lifeline guaranteed by British naval superiority. Wellington began to plan this operation in February and by early May, was ready to move but was delayed by unseasonably wet weather.

For the Welch Fusiliers and the other units of the 4th Division, the great march might be said to have truly begun when they entered Spain on 28 May 1813. Three days later they crossed the River Esla and then the Douro, completely

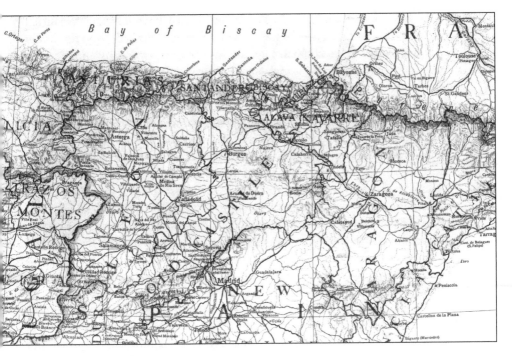

Area of Wellington's Operations, 1812–13
(*From J. W. Fortescue,* History of the British Army*)*

outflanking the French defensive lines along those waterways and forcing the enemy to fall back. The army moved on in four massive columns between ten and twenty miles apart, making it impossible for the outnumbered French to delay it by rearguard actions. They continued to withdraw – Crowe recorded that 'the French vacate the towns only a few hours before we march through' and the inhabitants greeted the allied troops with exuberant 'Vivas!'[37] On 3 June, although there was still no sign of the enemy, the 4th Division began to put out pickets at night and stand to their arms an hour before dawn, 'a most tedious and comfortless duty' as the troops had 'to stand motionless and silent in the dark on one spot, soaked by the copious dew, nothing to divert the attention but the chattering of teeth from every man'.[38] By 4 June Wellington had concentrated north of Valladolid, which had been abandoned by the enemy. This day, according to Crowe, the parties of the 4th Division sent out to gather wood had 'a very fatiguing duty' as nothing was to be found but 'bushes of wild lavender, which they pulled up by the roots' from which the scent was 'was quite overpowering while the soldiers were cooking their dinners'.[39]

It was around this time that Jack Hill returned to the Welch Fusiliers from the Portuguese army in which he had been serving since September 1811. As a brevet major, Hill had commanded the 5th Caçadores and as he had been promoted a substantive major in the British army in March 1812, he had hopes of gaining a brevet lieutenant colonelcy in the Portuguese service. It is uncertain why Hill left the 5th Caçadores to return to the 1/23rd – perhaps Ellis had asked for him or perhaps the eccentric Hill had blighted his career prospects by annoying his superiors. This latter cause is the essence of an anecdote told by a British officer who served with Hill in the Portuguese army. According to this witness, Hill had become very irritated with his brigade commander, Colonel Thomas Bradford, a somewhat fussy individual who visited Hill's camp on a daily basis and always found minor faults with its arrangement. To ward off this pest, Hill had a nearly impenetrable abbatis of tangled trees and branches constructed around his tent and when Bradford next visited, finding 'he could not penetrate the Major's [Hill's] sanctorum, he began to call for him most lustily; while the Major, pretending not to hear, continued rubbing his hands together in great glee'.[40] A few hours later an orderly arrived with a positive order from Bradford directing Hill to remove the abbatis and shortly thereafter, he was back with his regiment.

Another Welch Fusilier officer who returned to the fold at this time was Lieutenant George Farmer, missing since the retreat of the previous November. While at Valladolid, Lieutenant Thomas Browne heard a report that there was in the city a sick British officer who had been confined to bed for months, too ill to move. After considerable effort, Browne found the man in an obscure quarter in a miserable room up several flights of stairs. The sick officer was Farmer, but Browne scarcely recognised him:

> ... as his countenance & whole frame were frightfully changed by rheumatism. His body was literally doubled up, & appeared to have stiffened in that position, & his beard which had not been shaved for weeks covered the greater part of his countenance. When he saw me, he literally burst into a loud hysterical laugh, & I thought the poor fellow was mad, but when he recovered himself, he told me that the sight of a friend & brother Officer was so sudden & unexpected, that it quite overpowered him.[41]

Browne had Farmer cleaned up and moved to a better room but he was no longer physically capable of service and shortly afterwards retired from the army.

The march continued and, on 7 June 1813 the 4th Division entered Palencia to the cheers of the townspeople but it did not linger long. The division averaged between fifteen and twenty miles a day and Major Steevens of the 20th Foot recorded that:

> We used to march every morning between three and four o'clock, generally reaching our camping ground about 10 a.m. The roads were remarkably good, resembling our own in England and there were no hills. Salisbury Plain was a joke to what we met with in the country through which we passed, for the eye could not reach the extent of the plains over which we marched; they abounded with game, and at one of our

encampments I am sure that I do not exaggerate when I say, that our division killed a hundred hares.[42]

March discipline was strict in the Peninsular army and particularly so in the 4th Division. As his standing orders attest, Lieutenant General Lowry Cole intensely disliked straggling of any kind:

> On a march, one Field Officer the Adjutant and Surgeon to march in rear of their Regiments. The Commanding Officers of Companies in rear of their Companies. Officers to remain constantly at their Sections. ...
>
> No man to fall out in the rear without a ticket of permission from the Officer commanding the Company if sick he will receive one from the Surgeon. These tickets are to be returned to the Officer commanding the Corps when a man rejoins his Company. When a man is permitted to fall out on a march in consequence of sickness, or any other account, no Non-Commissioned Officer or any other person is to be left with him, as doing so weakens the Regiment still more; the Rear Guard will take care of them. When leave is granted by the Officer commanding the Company to a man to fall out to ease himself he must give his arms to be carried by the other men of the Section as the troops will have frequently leave to fall out, for this purpose leave must seldom be granted. Any man who shall obtain leave to fall out on pretence of sickness and it shall afterwards appear he was not really sick must be punished by a Court Martial or otherwise. ...
>
> The Baggage Guard will consist of a Subaltern from the Division with a Serjeant and eight rank and file from each brigade including a Corporal from each Regiment [and] will march in rear of the baggage, and must not leave behind them a sick man or straggler. The Officer will be answerable for bringing them all up, however long it may be. On the arrival of the Guard at the place of halting the sick and stragglers will be conducted to their several Corps by the Corporal of each Regiment attached to the Guard for that purpose. The men not having tickets will be given up to the Regimental Guard. ...
>
> Any man whether he shall have obtained permission or not, to fall out, who shall straggle into the villages on the line of march, or stop in those, through which the column may pass, must be made prisoner, and tried by a Drum's Head Court Martial for disobedience of orders, on the arrival of the troops at their camp or quarters, if not previously punished for the offence by the Provost Marshal.[43]

'The order of march', remembered Sergeant Cooper of the 7th Foot, 'was in sections of threes' and:

> ... the march of a brigade might be seen at a great distance, by the great cloud of dust which enveloped it. The suffering of the men in these dust clouds was dreadful, from the heat, thirst, heavy roads, tight clothing,

cross belts, and choking leather stocks. When we came to cross a stream, no halt was allowed; therefore hands or caps were dipped into the water as we went over it.[44]

Cooper also recalled that the rations usually consisted of

> ... a pound and half of soft bread, or one pound of biscuit; one pound of beef or mutton; one pint of wine, or one-third of a pint of rum; but no vegetables. ... When bread could not be obtained, we got a pint of unground wheat, or a sheaf of wheat out of the fields, or else two pounds of potatoes. No breakfasts, no suppers, no coffee, no sugar, in those days.[45]

On 10 June Wellington's advance elements were nearing Burgos, which had been evacuated by the French. By this time, the army had outstripped its supply lines, either from Santander or Portugal, and the quantity and the quality of the rations began to decline. Garrett of the 7th Foot commented that:

> Sometimes our men get two ounces of flour served out to them, other times ¼ pound of bread, other times raw wheat & sometimes nothing at all. Meat we have always got a tolerable supply of as we drive a good herd of oxen with us. Officers are equally as bad off as the men as the French have carried off everything with them or have destroyed, & although I have plenty of money I have not been able to buy a morsel with it these three days.[46]

The following day the 4th Division was ordered to leave its sick behind. There were only 53 in total and Crowe believed that this low number was 'strong proof of the indomitable spirit of the British soldier under bodily sufferings' as 'many men in the Division looked more like moving mummies than able soldiers'.[47] It was clear, however, that the continuous marching and short rations were starting to take their toll:

> We have been three days without bread or biscuit, our advance has been so rapid that the commissariat stores from the rear cannot overtake us. Consequently, an extra half pound of meat per man has been supplied. This was highly expedient but, salt, wherewith to flavour this pound and half of beef, reeking from the fresh slain bullock was not to be procured for nine days we have been destitute of this, lightly esteemed, blessing of providence. ...
>
> But the nausea with which we swallowed our soup meagre, and the sodden flesh, lacking salt, made many of us painfully sensible of its great value. The effect of the want of this important article, was that all of us suffered dreadfully from diarrhoea, our eyes, and our noses, told us how woefully some of our men were afflicted, and their pale hollow cheeks and their nether garments confirmed the fact, for the flux ran from them as they marched.[48]

It was not just men who suffered from the exertions of the long march of 1813 because it must be remembered that women were also present with the army. Some were legitimate wives, and others the companions of officers and soldiers. Thomas Browne (a bachelor) railed against these women 'who in spite of orders, threats & even deprivation of rations', insisted on marching 'in numbers, (from the depots in the rear, appointed for them)', alongside their husbands.[49] The soldier's wives were a tough breed – because they simply had to be – and possessed a rough-and-ready morality, having 'no hesitation in engaging themselves three or four deep to future Husbands' in case their current husbands were killed.[50] An officer overheard one of these seasoned campaigners reply to a soldier who had offered himself as successor to her present husband, should he fall: 'Nay, but thou'rt late, as I'm promised to John Edwards first, & to Edward Atkinson next, but when they two be killed off, I'll think of thee.'[51] Many women had children with them and despite their mixed reputation, were often surprisingly good mothers. During the advance in June 1813 an artillery officer met such a young mother of the Welch Fusiliers after he observed:

> ... in a string of crowded mules, an ass with the nicest pair of hampers I had seen. They were flat-sided, and comfortably roofed, and looked altogether so snug that I set down the owner as a more than usually knowing fellow. When I had jostled through the crowd, I turned round to look again at the ass, when to my surprise I observed in one hamper that was open in front, that it was nicely lined with scarlet cloth, and that a pretty little child was fast asleep in it. I asked the boy who was leading the ass whose it was, and found the little treasure belonged to the mess sergeant's wife of the 23rd Infantry; and the mother, a respectable-looking young woman, who was riding just by, told me she had carried the little one so for more than a year very safely.[52]

On 15 June, the 4th Division crossed the River Ebro at Puente Arenas. Over the next few days there was increased skirmishing between British advance guards and French rearguards. Joseph Bonaparte, sometime king of Spain, and his chief field commander, Marshal Jean-Baptiste Jourdan, had managed to collect 57,000 troops to defend the line of the Ebro but, as this had just been turned by Wellington, they fell back. It was elements of this force that Cole's 4th Division encountered near the town of Osma on 18 June. The divisional light infantry were in front and began skirmishing with the French tirailleurs but when enemy artillery came into action Major Frederick Sympher's brigade of King's German Legion artillery, attached to the division, came forward to reply. In the position of the 27th Foot, Crowe watched as the gunners 'galloped past us, towards some sand hills, a little in advance on our left, where in most admirable despatch, in the time that I can describe it, they halted, unlimbered their guns, the drag ropes were affixed, and the men dragging the cannons to the summit, with the ammunition wagons to a secure place a little below'.[53] 'The first gun', he noted, 'opened its fire before the second could be posted.'

The French artillery took Sympher's guns under fire and it was not long before round shot was bouncing past them down the reverse slope where the 27th Foot was positioned. 'This was the first time I was under fire, and shall never forget it', Crowe recorded, 'and the oldest soldiers in the ranks expressed their dislike to our situation'. The veterans, however, gleaned some amusement from observing the conduct of those officers who had not yet been under fire 'and expressed their opinions very unreservedly'.[54] Outnumbered, the French withdrew in good order and that night the two forces camped within sight of each other, but in the morning the enemy was gone.

Joseph Bonaparte and Jourdan, anxiously waiting for reinforcements from the Army of the North, had drawn back to Vitoria where they prepared to make a stand. On the morning of 19 June Cole advanced cautiously toward Vitoria but at about noon, he came in sight of a strong French rearguard covering some bridges over a small waterway. Lieutenant Gordon Booker of the 23rd Foot remembered that the French were found:

> ... strongly posted in a village which was situated on the slope of a hill, and there was a small river, which separated our right from their main body. The village was surrounded with rocks and broken ground and the valley which led to the river was covered with brush wood. The ridge of mountains near the base of which the village was situated was covered with wood to the very top. In the village was a bridge which was concealed from us by houses.
>
> The Fusilier Brigade was ordered to move along the ridge, with their light infantry and the Cacadores covering their front, and gradually to incline towards the village. The Right [Anson's] Brigade having a regiment and their light companies in front, moved along a road in the valley leading to the town. This brigade and the Portuguese advanced in a very gallant style and drove their light troops from an eminence where our artillery was afterward posted with some advantage. The skirmishers followed them across the ford and established themselves on the opposite bank. The French columns retired slowly on a road parallel to the ridge of the mountains which it seems took them to the Camino Real leading to Vittoria.
>
> While these operations were going on, on the right, the Fusilier Brigade carried the village, passed the bridge and got into the road by which the enemy were retiring. The whole division then moved on, supporting the light troops and succeeded in driving them from three very strong positions. We were entirely alone and it was impossible to prevent them from effecting their object which was to join the main body of the French Army.[55]

That night it rained heavily and everyone was thankful that the next day, 20 June, a halt was ordered so that those divisions in the rear could catch up. While the 4th Division enjoyed its rest, Wellington was busy reconnoitring and making arrangements for a general attack on the French position at Vitoria.

Located in a valley some eight miles wide and ten long, Vitoria was an important communications centre lying at the junction of five major roads. Assuming that Wellington would approach from the west, Joseph and Jourdan positioned their 57,000 men with 35,000 facing in that direction and the remainder covering secondary roads approaching from other directions. But Wellington had no intention of attacking where the enemy was strongest and instead divided his army into four separate columns which would move against not only both French flanks, but also their rear. The flank and rear attacks would go in first, and when they had hopefully diverted the French and drawn off the forces facing west, the 4th and Light Divisions would launch a major attack at the middle of the French line, which was posted on the far side of the winding River Zadorra.

Early in the morning of Monday, 21 June 1813, Crowe of the 27th Foot in Anson's brigade remembered that the commissary, for the first time in ten days, issued a quarter pound of bread to each man. A few days before, Crowe and a comrade had exhausted their finances by purchasing a 4 lb. loaf so were somewhat 'indifferent about breakfast, and laid ourselves down to sleep away hunger'. In a few minutes, however, the rumble of artillery roused them and it was with a 'craving' stomach that Crowe began the 'longest day I ever experienced'.[56] A few minutes later, Cole ordered the 4th Division to stand to its arms.

The artillery fire marked the beginning of Wellington's flank attacks. At about 8.30 a.m., Lieutenant General Rowland Hill attacked the heights on the left of the French line in the west and heavy fighting ensued. Sometime later, Lieutenant General Sir Thomas Graham began his attack north-west of Vitoria. Late in the morning Wellington learned that the bridge over the Zadorra at Tres Puentes was undefended and immediately ordered the Light Division to secure it, which was promptly done. He now waited for the final flanking attack, to be mounted by Lieutenant General George, Lord Dalhousie, with the 3rd and 7th Divisions against the right of the French line. Dalhousie, who had been detained by bad roads, was slow getting into position and even slower to attack, and this annoyed his subordinate, the newly-promoted Lieutenant General Sir Thomas Picton, commander of the 3rd Division, who was keen to get stuck into the enemy. The 55-year-old Picton, a native of Poyston in Pembrokeshire, had a well-deserved reputation in the Peninsular army for his choleric temper and Picton had reason to be irritable on 21 June 1813, as the day before he had been kicked by a horse and was in some pain.[57] When an aide rode up to him to inquire if he had seen

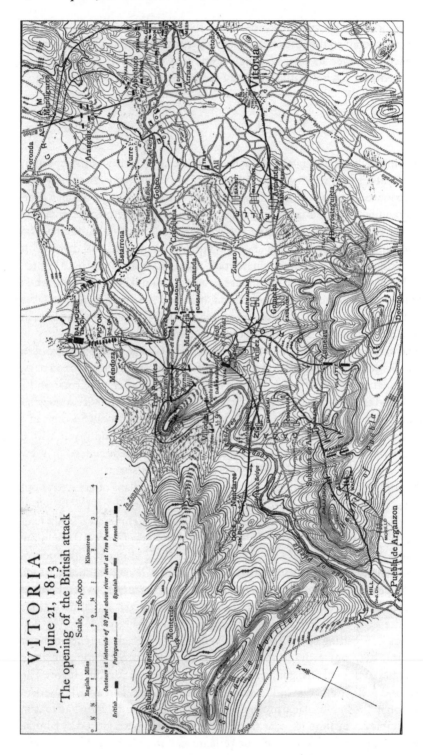

VITORIA
June 21, 1813
The opening of the British attack
Scale, 1:160,000

Dalhousie, Picton ascertained that the man was carrying orders for that officer to attack. Circumventing them, he ordered his own division to advance, riding ahead and exhorting his men with shouts of 'Come on, ye rascals! – Come on, ye fighting villains!'[58] The 3rd Division was shortly over the Zadorra and rolling up the French flank.

It was now the turn of the 4th Division. At about 3 p.m., as the outflanked French fell back from their positions near the Zadorra, Wellington ordered Cole to advance. With Skerrett's Fusilier Brigade leading, the division quickly seized a bridge over the waterway 'in their wonted gallant' fashion but most of the division opted to ford the waterway, which was not very deep.[59] Crowe recalled that, when the 27th Foot slipped down the bank, splashed across the water and then 'clambered up on the other side, assisted by those who had passed', the thirsty soldiers scooped up water in their shakos and drank it 'with avidity'.[60] Once across, the division formed on the far side and prepared to advance on the new French position in parallel with the Light Division on its left and Hill's troops on the right. As the division formed, the enemy artillery, positioned on a hill north-west of the village of Arinez, 'ascertained the range of our position', Crowe commented, 'and then rattled at us most furiously with shots and shells'.[61] Cole gave the orders and the 4th Division advanced in three distinct lines with Anson's brigade in front, followed by Skerrett's fusiliers and then Stubbs's Portuguese brigade, all screened by the divisional light troops who went in advance to deal with the French tirailleurs.

At about the same time the Light Division captured the hill from which the French artillery had withdrawn, the light troops of the 4th Division troops entered a troublesome wood in which the French appeared to be positioned, and the three brigades went forward. Major Jack Hill noted that the Fusilier Brigade;

> ... started to help the French off the field, going over hedges and ditches for near ½ a mile, we found the French, infantry and cavalry, on a small plain near a wood. The difficulties of the ground prevented the French Cavalry from doing anything. The formation of the Cavalry on our side, the bringing up of the guns, the crossing of the plain and entry of the light troops into the wood, assisted by the fire of our cannon, was very well executed.[62]

When the brigade neared the wood, Lieutenant Booker remembered, the enemy, 'when scarcely within musket shot', suddenly 'wheeled about and took to their heels'.[63] The Welch Fusiliers had never seen French troops act this way and Lieutenant John MacDonald thought that 'there never has been an instance

---

Left: **Vitoria, June 1813**
The opening of the British attack.
(*From J. W. Fortescue*, History of the British Army)

in which the French army have behaved so bad, & indeed there appeared a complete panic in the ranks', as, far from standing and 'giving us an opportunity to charge', they 'seldom allowed us to get within gunshot of them'.[64] After the Fusilier Brigade had passed the wood, Booker commented, 'a fine prospect presented itself' with the Light Division on the left 'rapidly advancing' while the Puebla heights 'on our right were covered with redcoats and the French flying in all directions'.[65] For the 4th and Light Divisions, the battle now became a steady advance as the enemy retired.

The French army was close to collapse. Aware that they were nearly surrounded, Joseph Bonaparte's men began to stream back toward the eastern end of the valley and the road to Salvatierra, the only escape route left open. When Joseph issued an order to retreat at about 5 p.m., it was meaningless, as most of his soldiers had already voted with their feet and were making away as fast as they could, having abandoned their artillery, transport, heavy equipment and much else.

As the 4th Division moved toward Vitoria, the Fusilier Brigade took the lead, the enemy always falling back before them. Shortly after this, word came down the line that 'We have taken all the enemy's guns.'[66] Near Vitoria, Booker recorded, the French rearguard attempted to make a stand 'to give time for their baggage to move out but our lines attacked their solid squares and drove them from one position to another'.[67] Skirting Vitoria, Cole directed the 4th Division along the road to Salvatierra. In doing so, it passed by a field with a magnificent bean crop and the men, most of whom had nothing to eat the entire day, 'immediately broke the ranks, dashed into the field, and came out each of them loaded with beans pulled up by the roots, which they devoured voraciously'.[68] Cole was furious at this act of indiscipline, but as Steevens of the 20th commented: 'Those who have never served on a campaign cannot be aware of the privations to be endured when soldiers are on active service; it requires rude health and strength to withstand the numerous hardships to which they are subjected.'[69]

On the far side of Vitoria, the division passed the abandoned transport and baggage of Joseph's army, which included:

> All the Baggages, Carriages, Mules & Equipage of King Joseph & his Court – the Military Chest which had arrived with the arrears of pay for the Army of the Centre only a few days before, & contained some Millions of [Spanish] Dollars in Silver & Doubloons – Coaches with their Coachmen on the Boxes or Postillions on the Horses, flogging & swearing to the utmost extent of their lungs – Ladies with imploring arms, or outstretched Infants thrusting themselves from the windows of these Coaches, or descending from the them to the ground – others on Horseback or on Mules, endeavouring in vain, to extricate themselves from the mass of impediments that blocked up their way, & to gallop off ... all these mixed up with Cannon, Tumbrils, drunken French Servants, the wounded, the dying & the dead.[70]

Vitoria
A photograph taken in the early 1960s shows the western section of the valley of the Zadorra which was the site of the battle. Enclosed by high ground on almost all sides, the valley proved a trap for the French army, which was decisively beaten in a signal triumph that ended French aspirations in Spain.
(From Weller, **Wellington in the Peninsula,** *courtesy Greenhill Publishing)*

Unfortunately, as MacDonald wistfully commented, Wellington was now riding with Cole and though, 'we repeatedly saw on each side of us carts, & wagons loaded with plates & silver', not a man fell out of the ranks 'to lay his hands on it'.[71]

> [The Fusilier Brigade] marched past all these spoils on the road, still continuing to pursue the enemy until it was dark; we were not allowed to take anything as we moved along, it was *look* at all things, but *touch* nothing, much to our disappointment of course; but such a restriction was perfectly right, so as to prevent disorder and confusion. It just shews the discipline of our men, who could pass such treasure and yet refrain from plundering.[72]

Wellington later praised the 4th Division, which 'had more opportunities to plunder than any other part of the Army', for their discipline.[73]

Unfortunately, some of the mounted units were not so well behaved and stopped pursuing the French to turn aside and plunder. Booker dryly noted that 'I am sorry to say that this baggage impeded the progress of some of our cavalry but as Lord Wellington has threatened to dismount them, they will probably get on better next time.'[74] It was on this day that the 14th Light Dragoons (now the King's Royal Hussars) acquired Joseph Bonaparte's silver chamberpot, from which they still drink champagne on special occasions. Included in the plunder was Jourdan's marshal's baton which Wellington sent to the Prince Regent who returned the favour by promoting Wellington a field marshal and sending him a British field marshal's baton, which the prince thought was a fair exchange.

Cole kept up the pursuit until dusk when, as Jack Hill recalled, 'the troops began mistaking each other' in the dark and 'the bugles sounded the close'.[75] It was another few hours before the Fusilier Brigade went into bivouac and got something to eat. Garrett of the 7th Foot happily recalled that after eighteen hours marching or fighting, he baked some coarse barley meal which he found in an abandoned French knapsack, 'into a kind of cake & baked on the fire with some beefsteak & a good cup of tea, which was the best part of the meal'.[76]

Vitoria was a signal victory for Wellington. At the cost of 5,158 killed, wounded and missing, he had inflicted 8,000 casualties on Joseph Bonaparte's army and captured 2,000 prisoners, 151 artillery pieces and 415 artillery caissons. The Fusilier Brigade's losses had been surprisingly light because as Booker remarked, 'whenever we came near the enemy they ran away from us'.[77] The brigade lost twenty-four casualties and the Welch Fusiliers' share was one man killed and three wounded.

Wellington's triumph spelled the end of Napoleon's ambitions in Spain and it also had other far-reaching results. When word of the victory arrived in Central Europe, it tempted Austria to join the coalition of Britain, Prussia and Russia against Napoleon. Already threatened by invasion on France's eastern frontiers, the French leader now faced a similar threat on his western frontier. In the Peninsular army there was considerable satisfaction after their victory – as Charles Crowe put it: 'we paid Jack Frenchman in his own coin'.[78]

When night fell, soldiers and civilians emerged to plunder. Much of the French military chest passed into private hands and Wellington only recovered a hundred thousand Spanish dollars, or £22,500, which infuriated him because of his constant shortage of specie. Not all the looters did well – a couple of cigar-smoking Spaniards ended their plundering careers when they broke into a covered vehicle that was actually a French ammunition caisson, and which exploded when one of them carelessly dropped a hot ash on its contents.[79]

On the following morning the Fusilier Brigade's bivouac area 'more resembled a Fair, than a regular encampment' with 'every man selling or buying some article of plunder'.[80] Crowe estimated that the 27th Foot acquired at least 3,000 Spanish dollars (£675) 'besides plate, regimentals, swords, fowling pieces, etc'.[81] MacDonald contented himself with a good mule and a medal of the *légion d'honneur*, which he acquired at bargain prices.[82] Not surprisingly, the soldiers' wives did well out of the business and could be seen parading about in fine muslins, 'three or four gowns one over the other, trimmed with fine lace, several pairs of earrings dangling from their ears, reticules, watches & fans as part of their costume'.[83] The contrast of this finery, Browne commented, with 'their brazen tanned faces and brawny arms' was 'ludicrous'. Browne also noted that women formed part of the plunder as 'upwards of 500 Spanish Damsels' who had been French camp followers, passed into the hands of the victors but became 'speedily reconciled to this change in their position, caused by the fortune of war'.[84] With his keen eye for detail, the young officer recorded that these new recruits 'were attired in every sort of dress that can be conceived, some in jackets above & petticoats below, others as hussars, some again in habits, others in muslin with large straw bonnets'.

The most successful plunderer in the 1/23rd Foot was Private John McLaughlan, an Irishman from Derry, who had been fortunate enough to get into the French military chest. 'He crammed every pocket, his shoes and stockings, his linings and his knapsack with gold and silver pieces', Bentinck recorded, and was seen on the night after the battle 'sorting them out on his blanket, spread on the ground'.[85] McLaughlan had too much coin to carry so he asked Ellis 'if he would kindly take charge of some of the money for him, as he could not march with it'. Ellis agreed and deposited the money in the care of George Sidley, the regimental quartermaster. Unfortunately for McLaughlan, four days after the battle, Lowry Cole issued a divisional General Order that all booty still in the possession of individuals was to be delivered to their commanding officers to be divided 'for the equal benefit of every man' in their regiments.[86] As a result, when McLaughlan went to Ellis for some of his money, he received a sharp rebuke: 'Be off you rascal, if you had been minding your duty you would have got no more than any other man.'[87] Ellis ordered Sidley to divide the money among the men in the battalion, which was done with every soldier receiving seven or eight Spanish dollars.[88] Given that the battalion's strength on 25 June 1813 was 223 men, this meant that the luckless Irishman lost as much as 1,784 dollars, or nearly £400 – rather a stiff blow for Private McLaughlan, considering that his pay was £18 5s a year.

Wellington was angered by his army's behaviour after Vitoria. 'We started with the army in the highest order', he complained', and up to the day of the battle nothing could get on better' but the looting that followed 'has annihilated all discipline'.[89] It was some time before he could get his troops moving again and when he did, he gradually herded the French armies toward their own border. Although the weather was poor, with frequent rainstorms, it was not an unpleasant time and Browne commented that the Spanish women livened the day's marches 'laughing and singing' while perched on mules and playing guitars, 'which they accompanied with pretty voices, the muleteers themselves joining in chorus, whenever their airs admitted of one, which most of them did'.[90] The female recruits acquired at Vitoria were careful to pay their respects to the British commander who, 'angry as he was to see such an increase of baggage, could not help smiling as he passed them to their loud "Viva Wellington" saluting him as he went by'.[91]

For the 4th Division, the only action in this period occurred on 25 June near Villafranca, sixty miles north-east of Vitoria. Jack Hill, commanding the light troops of the Fusilier Brigade which was in the advance, came up against a French rearguard in a valley. He drove them across it and 'up the opposite hills' where he found the enemy strongly posted and halted, waiting for the brigade to come up in support. When this did not happen, Hill 'gradually fell back in extended order, firing all the time' and his men 'behaved very coolly, and extricated themselves well, out of the scrape'.[92] On the following morning, the brigade encountered another French rearguard on a hill in front of the town of Tolosa and climbed to clear it but in Hill's words, 'a useless heavy skirmish was kept up for several hours along the woody declivities'. When Portuguese and Spanish troops began to outflank the enemy position, the French withdrew and the brigade slept in Tolosa that night.

Wellington's soldiers, having advanced nearly 300 miles in about forty days, were tired. Nonetheless, they expected that they would soon invade France to make the enemy 'feel what war is in their own country'.[93] Wellington, however, halted at the border. He had first to deal with the fortress cities of San Sebastian on the Bay of Biscay and Pamplona inland, neither of which could be left in his rear if he entered France. These places were hard nuts to crack: San Sebastian was located on a small peninsula and was very difficult to approach, while Pamplona was one of the most strongly-fortified places in Spain. Wellington did not have enough siege ordnance and equipment to tackle both at once so he opted to blockade Pamplona and besiege San Sebastian, where the engineers commenced their work on 12 July. Another reason for not continuing the advance was that Napoleon, after having won two major victories against the Russians and Prussians in May, had signed an armistice to cease hostilities until early August. Wellington knew that if the war was ended through negotiation or the armistice was extended, Napoleon would be in a position to reinforce his armies on his Spanish. This being the case, he turned his attention to the two fortresses and waited on events.

The 4th Division arrived before the walls of Pamplona in the first days of July. For nearly two weeks they served as part of the blockading force and during that time, Garrett of the 7th Foot recorded, the Fusilier Brigade used to allow the garrison to come out and cut corn without interrupting them, but the moment the French 'began to carry it away, we attacked them, though we used to lose a few by the fire from the town & after killing & wounding a good number of them in return we obliged them to drop their corn & get back in as fast as they could, which corn we carried off for ourselves'.[94]

In the first few days of July 1813 the Fusilier Brigade received a new commander when Skerrett was transferred to the Light Division. Skerrett had not been popular with either the fusiliers or Lowry Cole and he was to be even less popular in his new division.[†] His replacement was the newly-promoted Major General Robert Ross of the 20th Foot, a 47-year-old veteran with 24 years service, who had fought in Holland and Egypt, played an important role at the Battle of Maida in 1806, and had participated in Moore's campaign of 1808-1809. Ross was a fighting soldier and a dedicated and professional officer, and Friedrich von Wachholtz, who was an astute judge of character, thought highly of him.[95] Ross's regiment, the 20th Foot, however, was still regarded as an unknown quantity by the hard-bitten 7th and 23rd Foot for it had not yet seen stiff action with the Fusilier Brigade.

On 18 July 1813 the 4th Division left Pamplona and advanced to the French frontier. The Fusilier Brigade was in fine fettle. 'We have completely turned the tables on the French', boasted Lieutenant Garrett of the 7th Foot, 'instead of their hemming us up in Portugal we have kicked them out of Spain & entered the mighty France itself'.[96] After five long and bloody years, it was beginning to appear as if the war in the Peninsula would shortly be coming to a successful conclusion. 'The opinions in the army now are that we shall all be home before Christmas', John MacDonald wrote to his parents, 'as it is thought the French will send no more troops to this country'.[97]

---

† On 1 September 1813 Skerrett refused repeated requests for support from the commander of one of his rifle companies trying desperately to defend a bridge at Vera over the River Bidassoa against a superior French force. In the end, the French took the bridge and killed or wounded half the company. The Light Division never forgave Skerrett and he left that formation shortly afterward. Skerrett was killed at the siege of Bergen-op-Zoom in March 1814.

Come cheer up! cheer up! here's more news from old Spain,
Our soldiers have beat the French robbers again,
On the Pyrenees mountains, the conflict began,
Huzza, boys, huzza, the brave British have won,

   See the enemy flies, follow, Wellington cries,
   My heroes be steady, have your bayonets ready,
   A Briton in battle either conquers or dies.

Each infantry regiment (anxious to win),
With dreadful effect, frequent vollies poured in.
Then straight to the charge, the bold heroes did go,
And heaps upon heaps at their feet were laid low.

   See the enemy flies, [etc.]

In vain did old Soult try to rally his men,
We battered their breast works again and again,
Determined to conquer or die in the field,
Who savage invaders to Britain must yield.

   See the enemy flies, [etc.][1]

Chapter 11

'My people only thought of fighting'

1st Battalion, Spain and France, July 1813 – June 1814

THE DEFEAT AT VITORIA and the retreat of his armies in Spain toward their own territory in the early summer of 1813 infuriated Napoleon. He had been hoping that his recent victories against the Russians and Austrians, which had resulted in an armistice, would permit him to negotiate a peace settlement. Far from it, Wellington's victory convinced Austria, which had been hesitant to join the other allies, to contemplate going to war against him. Looking for scapegoats, Napoleon dismissed his brother Joseph and Marshal Jourdan, and replaced them with Marshal Nicolas Soult. Taking command on 11 July, Soult quickly re-organised the various French armies facing Wellington into one with nine divisions, comprising about 85,000 men. He improved his troops' tattered morale by blaming their recent misfortunes on Joseph and Jourdan. 'Soldiers', he told them, 'I sympathise with your disappointments, your grievances, your indignation' but although 'the blame for the present situation must be imputed to others', it was their task, he said, 'to repair the disaster'.[2] In an amazingly short period of time – less than two weeks in fact – thanks to the hard work of Soult and his senior officers, the French army was again ready to take the offensive.

News of Soult's activities reached Wellington who began to plan how best to meet an enemy attack. While part of his army besieged San Sebastian and part blockaded Pamplona, Wellington had deployed the remainder, about 60,000 men, along the Franco-Spanish border in a line nearly forty miles long, running from the Bay of Biscay to the vicinity of Roncesvalles. The major roads leading through the Pyrenees were held by outposts with stronger formations in the rear, ready to support them. It was Wellington's belief that if Soult did attack, it would come in the coastal area in an attempt to relieve San Sebastian, so he positioned the greater part of his forces to block such an attempt. When he received word of French movement towards the passes of Maya and Roncesvalles to the east, Wellington suspected that these were just feints to distract his attention. Soult had, in fact, decided to attack, not near the coast but through those two passes with the intention of relieving Pamplona and not San Sebastian. Soon after dawn on 25 July 1813, 21,000 French troops moved against Maya and 41,000 against Roncesvalles, which was held by Lieutenant General Lowry Cole and his 4th Division.

That same day, after receiving a warning from Wellington that Soult might attack, Cole took steps to increase his forward forces. He ordered Major General Ross to march with the Fusilier Brigade to the vicinity of the Roncesvalles pass and alerted his other two brigades, commanded by Major Generals Anson and Stubbs, to be ready to follow. Lieutenant Gordon Booker of the 23rd Foot remembered that most of the officers of the regiment had dined in the local town on the evening of 24 July and that, when they returned to their camp, they learned the brigade would parade for Divine Service at 9 a.m. in the morning so they dispersed to their tents. At about 1 a.m., 'the alarm sounded, the tents were struck and the baggage packed'.[3] As soon as he could, Ross moved off with the 7th and 20th Foot, leaving the 1/23rd, which had been tasked with bringing up the brigade baggage, in camp with orders to follow at dawn. When Ross reached the vicinity of Roncesvalles at daybreak, he sent von Wachholtz's rifle company to screen his front and then permitted his men to rest on their arms.

The Roncesvalles pass through the Pyrenees is about a mile wide and is approached by a U-shaped, shallow valley known as the Val Carlos. On either side of this valley are two long but narrow ridges, the Linduz to the west and the Altobiscar to the east, with the main road through the pass following the eastern ridge. Ross deployed on the Linduz while Major General John Byng's brigade of the 2nd Division positioned itself on the Altobiscar.

The Fusilier Brigade was just coming into position at about 6 a.m. on 25 July when Ross heard musketry from the east. He immediately pushed out the brigade light troops under Major Alexander Rose of the 20th Foot, and a short while later, Cole rode up to inform him that Anson and Stubbs's brigades were on their way, but that he should keep a sharp look-out as the French had attacked Byng's brigade on the Altobiscar. There was no sign of the enemy in front of Ross's position until late in the morning when von Wachholtz's riflemen spotted troops moving through gaps in the trees but were unable to identify their nationality. The Brunswick officer promptly reported this to Ross, who ordered him to advance and investigate these troops. Ross himself then moved forward along the Linduz ridge with the left wing of the 20th Foot and in a few minutes, von Wachholtz's company opened fire, clearly identifying the unknown troops who were, in fact, a French infantry division, which was followed by two more, the three formations having a total of 19 battalions. The French threw out a strong force of skirmishers that drove the badly outnumbered Brunswickers back and then advanced to the Linduz ridge, just as Ross was coming forward along it. Needing to gain time both to position the troops with him and to bring up support, Ross ordered Captain George Tovey to take his company of the 20th and clear away the French skirmishers. Moving at the double quick in close

Combat of **RONCESVALLES**
July 25ᵗʰ 1813
Scale of Miles
0   1   2

Val Haira

Lamartinière
Taupin
Château Fignon
Maucune
Village of Val Carlos
Vandermaesen
Leicar Atheca
Foy
Morillo
Campbells Approach
Ross
Linduz
Altobiscar
Byng
Loverdo
Roncesvalles
Reg. Leon
Country of Orbaiceta
Anson
Burguete
Stubbs
Espinal
To Pampeluna
Orbaiceta

British   Spanish and Portuguese   French

Roncesvalles, July 1813
The three battalions of the Fusilier Brigade, deployed across the Linduz Ridge, held off far superior numbers of French troops.
(*From C. Oman,* A History of the Peninsular War)

order, Tovey's men had no trouble accomplishing this task but as they did so, they ran head on into the leading company of a French battalion coming up a narrow path onto the ridge.

What happened next was a rare instance of bayonet fighting. Tovey recalled that his company:

> … paused in astonishment, for we were face to face with them, and the French officer called to us to disarm; I repeated bayonet away, bayonet away, and, rushing headlong amongst them, we fairly turned them back into the descent of the hill, and such was the panic and confusion

occasioned among them by our sudden onset, that this small party, for such it was compared to the French column, had time to regain the regiment, but my military readers may rest assured that it was required to be done in double quick.

The enemy had many killed, and the leading French officers fell close at my feet, with two others, all bayonetted. The company, with which I was the only officer present on this occasion, did not amount to more than between seventy and eighty men, and we had eleven killed and fourteen wounded.[4]

Captain Friedrich von Wachholtz, a fascinated observer of this encounter, noted that when the two bodies met face to face:

The French instinctively stepped back a pace, several of them made half a turn, as if about to give way; but their officers, some with appeals, some with threats and some with curses, kept them to their work. They stood firm, and their bayonets came down to the charge: as did those of Tovey's company. For a few seconds the two sides surveyed each other at a distance of two paces: then one French company officer sprang forward into the middle of the British, and began cutting left and right. He was at once bayoneted, and then the two sides began to fence cautiously with each other, keeping their line and not breaking forward into the enemy's ranks; it was more like bayonet drill than a charge.[5]

Tovey fell back to where Ross had posted half the 20th, and the French came on again but were stopped short by disciplined musketry. They made two determined attempts to break through Ross's line but were hampered by the fact that there was not enough space to deploy their superior numbers. The fighting went on for most of the afternoon and after the 20th had exhausted their ammunition, they were replaced by the 1/23rd Foot, which had now come up. Lieutenant Gordon Booker commented that:

There was a very high mountain in the front of our position but separated from us by a deep ravine and a very thick wood which extended about halfway up the hill on which we were posted. ... We arrived and were ordered by companies into the wood. The enemy in vain endeavoured to pass the ravine and we remained opposed to a very superior force until we had twice expended our ammunition. We were relieved by the 7th Fusiliers and about six o'clock the right [Anson's] and Portuguese [Stubbs's] brigades made their appearance.[6]

Von Wachholtz described how the Fusilier Brigade held its position:

The enemy was visible, several thousands strong, on the higher part of the spur; every half-hour or so he sent another company down to relieve his skirmishers. He always came up in detail and slowly, for there was a tiresome defile to cross, over a deep cutting in the crest, where only one man abreast could pass. We could always let the head of the attack debouch, and then attack it and throw it back on its supports.[7]

During the incessant musketry, Drummer Richard Bentinck was standing behind Private Finch of the 23rd when Finch was killed by a musket ball through the forehead. 'This poor fellow had on a pair of new shoes', which Bentinck took off his feet 'at the request of a comrade who was almost barefoot' but, minutes after the man put them on, he too was killed, rendering the shoes 'as useless to him as they now were to their late owner'.[8]

When Anson's brigade came up to support the fusiliers, Crowe of the 27th remembered, they heard 'sharp fire on all sides'. As his regiment struggled along a narrow, hilly track to take up position on a high ridge, 'the soldiers involuntarily jousting [jostling] against each other were greatly annoyed', which drew a jest from one of those irrepressible Irish wits who seemed to fill the ranks of the British army. Noting that it was Sunday, he quipped: 'Och, now, and sure this is very pretty Divine Service, and is it not? Well nivir mind boys! For who iver is kilt to day will have great advantage, for sure, ain't we half way to heaven already!'[9] When the 27th Foot reached the top of the height, their attention was riveted to the Linduz ridge, 'most gallantly contested by our Left [or Fusilier] Brigade: the possession of which would have enabled the enemy to force the whole position of our army'. From their position, Crowe and his comrades 'could see and with intense interest watch the fatal scene. It was heart rending to witness so many brave fellows fall, some to rise no more, others to [too] badly wounded to leave the field of battle, and others crawling or limping down for assistance.'[10]

The fighting continued and casualties were heavy on both sides. At one point, Ross sent Major Charles Steevens of the 20th Foot to Cole to ask for reinforcements but the divisional commander's response was blunt: 'Tell General Ross he must keep his post, for I cannot render him any assistance'.[11] To Steevens, it was remarkable that the French did not mount a major attack to drive the brigade from its position and he attributed this to the fact that the enemy thought 'we had a large reinforcement at hand, which was not the case; if, therefore, they had advanced we must, it was supposed, have given way, and it might have turned out an unfortunate day for us'.[12] In fact, the French commanders, trying to move nineteen battalions of infantry along a single track that did not deserve to be called a road, simply could not bring their superior strength to bear. When a heavy mist descended in late afternoon and brought an end to the action, there was great relief on both sides.

The French attack against the Maya pass was more successful, the enemy gaining the pass but not getting far beyond it. Although Cole had enjoyed better fortune at Roncesvalles, he was concerned that, with only 11,000 men under his command, he would be facing at least 30,000 Frenchmen in the morning. Despite the fact that he had orders from Wellington to defend the pass 'to the utmost' and knew that Lieutenant General Sir Thomas Picton was on the march with his 3rd Division to join him, Cole decided to retreat and gave the appropriate orders. 'As soon as it became sufficiently dark to screen our movements from the French sentries', Lieutenant John Bainbrigge of the 20th Foot recorded, the Fusilier Brigade 'was ordered to fall in silently, leaving a picquet with instructions to keep the men as much as possible walking about in front of the fires so as to attract the notice of any patrols of the enemy who might be on the look-out'.[13]

It was impossible to bring out the seriously wounded so they were left, wrapped in blankets, and their 'clammering and cries', von Wachholtz remembered, 'echoed in my soul'.[14] Sergeant John Cooper of the 7th Foot never forgot how, as his comrades marched past the wounded, they would ask 'Will you leave us here?'[15] But the brigade 'stole away and left them to the mercy of the enemy and the mountain wolves, not being able to take them off'. Bainbrigge of the 20th recalled that the wounded were collected and placed together and 'small cards were then pinned on their jackets, having a few words written on each in French, consigning them to the mercy of our gallant enemy'.[16] 'This appeal', he noted, 'was strictly attended to' by the enemy.

The withdrawal was a nightmare. In the dark men 'frequently fell into deep holes or stumbled over roots and boughs of trees, and unavoidably tripped up others in their fall' which, 'though trifling in themselves, caused infinite confusion and many tedious and vexatious halts'.[17] In the dark and the mist, which had now thickened, the Fusilier Brigade lost its way and had to march most of the night in single file along mountain paths. In the ranks of the Royal Welch Fusiliers, Booker recalled, Ellis 'made the men hold by each [other's coat tails] otherwise we should have lost half the Brigade'.[18] What made it worse was that the men had not eaten since the previous evening.

> We got no bread this day [complained Cooper] and our rum was purposely spilled to prevent drunkenness. This night march was horrible, for our path lay among rocks and bushes, and was so narrow that only one man could pass at a time; consequently our progress was exceedingly tedious, stopping as we did five or ten minutes every two or three yards. This was made much worse by the pitchy darkness. Many were swearing, grumbling, stumbling, and tumbling. No wonder, we were worn out with fatigue, and ravenous with hunger.[19]

By dawn, the 4th Division had reached a main road where, as the rearguards had not reported any enemy movement, Cole let them sleep for a few hours.

Lieutenant Crowe had just nodded off, the reins to his horse wrapped securely around his hand, when his slumbers were interrupted by a violent kick and a shout: 'What do you here? Why do you lie here?' The young officer jumped to his feet to find 'a stout sturdy fellow dressed in a long dark coat and a round hat' standing before him. Understandably annoyed, Crowe told the stranger:

'Keep out of the reach of my arm or I will knock you down!'

He [the stranger] drew back at this threat and demanded, 'What Regiment is this?'

I coolly answered 'We are never ashamed, it is the 27th Regiment and who the devil are you to make this demand?'

'Don't talk to me Sir! Where is the Colonel?'

'Where is he always! At his post'.

And away went Crowe's 'blustering chuffy visitor'.[20]

It was Picton, of course, and a soldier who recognised the irritable and badly-dressed commander of the 3rd Division shouted: 'Here comes old Tommy; now boys, make up your minds to fight.'[21] Picton, Bainbrigge remembered, rode up to a staff officer and demanded 'Where the devil are you going?' The somewhat flustered officer replied that the division was 'retreating, sir, by Sir Lowry's orders'. 'Then he's a d—d fool', responded Picton, 'halt your brigade instantly, the 3rd Division is coming up', and he then rode on to find Cole.[22] When the two generals met each other, the inevitable sparks flew, but Cole convinced Picton, who being senior, assumed command, that his decision to retreat was correct and the withdrawal continued. The two divisions pulled back slowly throughout 26 July and into the morning of the next day.

They were almost within range of the French guns at Pamplona when Cole noticed some fine defensive ground near the village of Sorauren and obtained Picton's permission to occupy it. This ground was an east-west ridge about a mile and a half long, and about 2,000 feet high, joined by a bridge of land to another, higher, ridge to its north. Cole deployed along this ridge with the Fusilier Brigade on his left, Major General Archibald Campbell's Portuguese brigade in his centre and Anson's brigade on his right. He stationed his main line back behind the crest, placing only his light companies on the slope of the ridge. Picton, meanwhile, stationed his division and a Spanish division somewhat to the right and considerably to the rear of Cole.

They were in position by the late morning of 27 July and watching Soult's army approaching, when Wellington arrived. The British commander had learned of Soult's attack on 25 July, nearly at the same time as a British assault on San Sebastian was repulsed with heavy casualties. Finding it difficult to get accurate information, because of the distances and slow communications, he had ridden south the previous day to visit his widespread forces and had now reached Picton. Taking in the situation quickly, Wellington sent off an order to bring up the 6th Division, his only uncommitted formation, to support Picton, and then rode to the Fusilier Brigade's position on the ridge. The troops spotted him and their cheering was so loud that Soult, on the opposite ridge, heard them and observed Wellington through his telescope. He therefore decided to delay his attack until all his troops had come up, leaving one of his senior subordinates, General Bertrand Clausel, so infuriated that he beat his own forehead with rage.

Besides a few random shots, nothing happened for the rest of that day, which both puzzled and delighted Wellington, as reinforcements were on the move towards him. Just after darkness fell, a tremendous thunderstorm swept down from the Pyrenees with such force, Bainbrigge commented that:

> Many of our cavalry horses took fright, broke away from their picket stakes, and galloped madly over the half-sleeping soldiers; many of them strayed into the enemy's lines, and several of these horses were recognised next day ridden by French staff officers. The rain now fell in torrents; in a few minutes all our fires were totally extinguished, the loud peals of thunder echoing back from rocks and ravines, became one continuous roar; the lightning was so vivid that its flashes illuminated the surrounding hills and wooded country, exhibiting in all their wretchedness the thoroughly drenched soldiers of both armies; many of whom might be seen huddled together in small parties; others, rolled in their blankets or great coats, were apparently sleeping soundly, unconscious of the raging tempest.[23]

Thankfully, 28 July 1813 dawned fair and bright. Throughout the morning Wellington and his army could observe the movements of Soult's army, which seemed to be massing, but as the hours passed with no attack, many thought the French would retreat. 'We could see the enemy very distinctly from our position', Steevens noted, 'and (with my glass) I observed Soult several times that morning'.[24]

Shortly before noon, however, Soult threw 15,000 men against Cole's position. Pushing the Fusilier Brigade light troops and some attached Portuguese caçadores in front of them, four French battalions formed in columns advanced nearly to the crest of the ridge only to be thrown back by a bayonet charge mounted by all three of Ross's battalions. Ross had just re-formed his line when a second French attack, this time mounted by five battalions, was made a little farther to his right. This, too, was thrown back down the ridge but minutes later the enemy made a third attack, this time with seven battalions formed in column and preceded by a heavy screen of skirmishers, against Campbell's Portuguese brigade to Ross's right. One of Campbell's regiments broke and fled to the rear, leaving the 7th Foot on Ross's right flank disordered and in danger. At almost the same time the five enemy battalions, which had earlier been rebuffed, re-formed and attacked the left and centre of Ross's line and forced the Fusilier Brigade back. The battle hung in the balance.

Wellington had left the defence of the ridge to Cole and his brigadiers but several times during the action he had sent Pakenham, acting as adjutant-general, to Ross 'to thank the Fusilier Brigade for their efforts'.[25] Now he intervened directly in the battle and ordered the 27th and 48th Foot of Anson's brigade to charge with the bayonet and the two regiments swept the enemy back down off the ridge. A French officer, watching this attack, recorded with admiration that

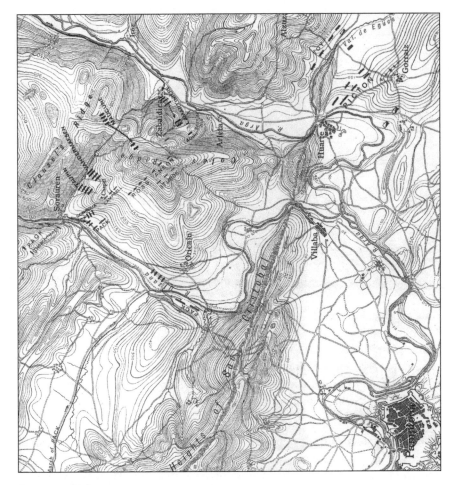

Sorauren, July 1813
Deployed somewhat in advance of Picton's main force, the 4th Division's three brigades defeated superior numbers of the enemy in a very hard-fought action.
(*From J. W. Fortescue,* **History of the British Army***)*

the two battalions 'charged at a running pace, but with such order and unity that looking on from a distance one might have thought it was cavalry galloping'.[26] The battle began to tilt in Wellington's favour. The 6th Division had earlier arrived on Cole's left flank and became warmly engaged with the French forces which had been attacking him. There was desultory skirmishing for another hour but by 4 p.m., the battle for the heights, which became known as 'Cole's Ridge' – later termed the Battle of Sorauren – had ended.

It had been a bloody business. Wellington, a man not given to exaggeration, termed it 'fair bludgeon work' and if the men of the Fusilier Brigade had scorned the French for their poor performance at Vitoria, they now changed their minds

Cole's Ridge, France
The view from the position of the Fusilier Brigade during the Battle of Sorauren,
28 July 1814, shows the ground over which the French advanced. During this very
hard-fought and bloody action, the 4th Division held off far superior numbers of
enemy troops and earned a new nickname from the army: 'The Enthusiastics'.
(From Weller, Wellington in the Peninsula, *courtesy Greenhill Publishing*)

about the quality of their opponents. They 'came on like madmen', recalled
Booker, 'huzzahing and making a dreadful noise, they were driven back three
times and suffered very much.'[27] Crowe of the 27th believed that Soult had:

> ... sent forward some of the best troops in France, in every direction
> their attacks evinced the cool firmness of well tried veterans. And his
> skirmishers were first rate marksmen. Our oldest soldiers noticed the
> above with the following characteristic remark 'Hands up soldiers! For
> there will be wigs on the green today (i.e. dead men's heads on the grass)
> Here is no child's play, for Jack Frenchman is in right earnest!'[28]i

Ellis of the 23rd took an objective view of the business:

> The battle of the 28th of July was a beautiful display of military
> manoeuvres: the enemy formed his columns in the most perfect order,
> and advanced to the attack with a rapidity and impetus apparently
> irresistible. I was in immediate support of the seventh Caçadores
> (Portuguese), who were the advanced piquet, and consequently received
> the first shock of the enemy's column. My people only thought of

fighting, and at once checked their progress. Our supports on both sides were brought up, and the contest continued with varying success till four o'clock, when the enemy withdrew, only leaving his voltigeurs in our front. We had three divisions upon us, – the fourth, fifth and seventh: the two former were chiefly opposed to the fortieth [also the 27th and 48th], who made two unheard of charges: indeed, the whole day was a succession of charges.[29]

During one of the charges, Drummer Bentinck had been wounded:

A black looking Frenchman who had skewered a Fusileer as he burst through their line, and jerked him off his bayonet dead, next lunged the weapon at Bentinck, but receiving at the moment a blow on the skull from the butt end of a musket, he fell senseless, his bayonet passing through Bentinck's thigh instead of his body. Disliking much to have 4d per day taken from his pay [for food while] being in hospital, Bentinck limped by the side of his comrades all day, with his shoe full of blood, and both trousers and stocking glued to his leg so fast with it that he had to soften them with water to get them off when evening came. He then went to the doctor and got some plaster and bandages on the wound, and as they rested for some days after this, it soon healed.[30]

'How any of us got out of this action is to me astonishing', John MacDonald commented, as the French 'kept advancing until they were overthrown down the hill again with our bayonets' but, he added proudly, the enemy 'never gained an inch of ground the whole of this day'.[31] Five French divisions had tried and failed to drive the 4th Division off its position and attacks on both Cole's flanks had also been beaten back. Soult's drive on Pamplona had been decisively checked, and his supplies running low – he had started his offensive on 25 July with only enough provisions to feed his army for four days – the French commander ordered a retreat.

On the morning of 30 July when the French began to pull back, they got a nasty surprise when they came under artillery fire. On Wellington's orders, the previous day the men of the 4th Division had, with great difficulty, dragged some light field pieces to the top of the ridge and when the enemy:

... were on the move in the morning [of 30 July] they were somewhat astonished by our firing some Shrapnell shells amongst them, as we had got a gun up on the heights early that morning. I saw the French scampering away when the first shot was fired, not expecting we could get a gun up such a height. It carried completely across the ravine, and I heard that one of the shells did great execution, killing and wounding about twenty-four men, as was reported to have been said by a French prisoner afterwards taken; and this was not at all improbable, as it pitched into a column, which it completely dispersed.[32]

Wellington then mounted a powerful attack of his own which not only inflicted heavy casualties on the French but also thoroughly demoralised them and in the following days, Soult withdrew his defeated army.

The battles in the Pyrenees from 25 to 30 July 1813 were costly to both the Fusilier Brigade and the 1/23rd Foot. The brigade lost 627 casualties of all types while the battalion lost 24 killed and 99 wounded. Ellis noted that, after these engagements, his battalion had 'only the semblance of one' as with the losses in action, sick, 'and attendants on the wounded I am reduced to one hundred and sixty bayonets'.[33] Among the dead were Captains William Stainforth and Henry Walker, and Volunteer John Bassett while among the wounded were Ellis, Booker and Lieutenant Henry Ledwith. Ledwith died of his wounds a month later, and in his place, Ellis commissioned Volunteer Gerald Fitzgibbon as a second lieutenant in the battalion. David Satchwell, the last of the three volunteers who served with the battalion during the 1813 campaign, was to be commissioned in October.

The performance of the 4th Division during the Pyrenees battles was much admired throughout the Peninsular army, which bestowed a new nickname on it. Formerly called 'The Supporting Division', it now became 'The Enthusiastics'.[34] In a similar vein, the 20th Foot, having proved itself entirely worthy of serving alongside the veteran 7th and 23rd Foot received the nickname, 'The Young Fusiliers'.[35] Steevens, who assumed command of the 20th, thought the Pyrenees campaign 'a very dismal one, for although I had great promotion, still it was in a melancholy way, by loss of old friends'.[36] A great many officers and men in the Fusilier Brigade would have echoed that sentiment.

Wellington again turned his attention to San Sebastian. Following the failed assault of 25 July, more siege guns were brought up to bombard this stubbornly-defended fortress. During these operations, the Fusilier Brigade was camped near Lesaca, about fifteen miles to the north-east. It was a very quiet time, Steevens remembered:

> ... as far as not being actually engaged with the enemy constitutes quietness; for although we were frequently advancing and taking up new positions, it did not fall to our lot to be again engaged for some little time; however, as we had a pretty fair share of honour and glory lately, it was therefore not to be expected that we could always be fighting. Sometimes we were so posted that our brigade could see what was going on among some of the other divisions, although in reality we had not much to do with it; but the country being so mountainous, a part of our army might be engaged, and we be mere spectators.[37]

By the last day of August a significant breach had been created in the walls of San Sebastian.. An assault was planned that same day and it was to be made by the 5th Division, assisted by volunteers from the 1st, 4th and Light Divisions. The 200-man detachment from the 4th Division was under the command of Major Alexander Rose of the 20th Foot, and Rose had no problem finding men willing to volunteer for this very dangerous task. Rose had a presentiment of his own death and when Steevens wished him success, the reply was 'God bless you, I shall never see you again.'[38] The assault went in and after a desperate battle, the city was taken at the cost of 2,376 British casualties. Among those killed were Rose and four soldiers of the 1/23rd while Lieutenant William Griffiths and four men of the battalion were wounded.

The same day that San Sebastian fell the Fusilier Brigade watched the Battle of San Marcial, fought between the French and Spanish, from their camp on a mountain ridge. This engagement, a French attack on the Spanish position, was a victory and the brigade were 'spectators during the whole time', Steevens commented, 'with our arms piled, and perfectly at ease'. From their position, the officers and men of the brigade 'could see a long way into France' and also 'had a fine view of the sea, being not more than a league from it'.[39] The altitude of their camp may have provided a splendid view but the weather in the mountains that autumn was miserable. The brigade's tents were 'very cold and damp at night, for the rain frequently came down in torrents, and beat through them', but as Steevens put it, 'there was nothing to do but to grin and bear it'.[40]

Three days after the fall of San Sebastian, Wellington received some very good news. Napoleon had rejected a peace settlement on the basis that France's future border would be the west bank of the Rhine – a generous offer considering his situation – and Austria had declared war against him. The armistice therefore ended and the fighting was resumed on 12 August. Although Napoleon won a victory at Dresden in the last days of August, his subordinates suffered two defeats at Katzbach and Kulm. It now appeared that the conflict would continue until the French leader was either overthrown or killed, and this being the case, Wellington began to plan an invasion of France.

Following his defeat in the Pyrenees and his repulse at San Marcial, Soult had constructed a fortified line of redoubts, some ten miles in length, along the River Bidassoa. He did not have enough force to hold the entire position in strength but, expecting that Wellington would attack either in the centre or on his left flank in the Pyrenees, he placed most of his forces in those positions. For this reason he was taken completely by surprise on 7 October 1813 when the British commander attacked and swiftly penetrated his right flank on the coast. Soult was forced to fall back to the next waterway, the Nivelle, where he began to construct a new line of fortifications along a front of about sixteen miles.

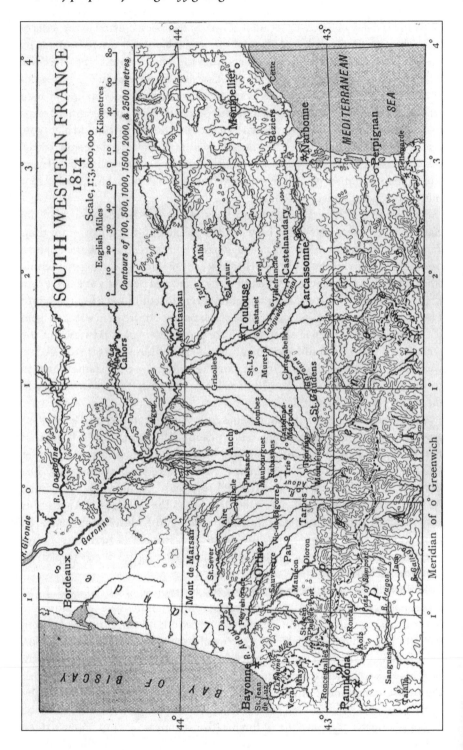

SOUTH WESTERN FRANCE
1814

Scale, 1:3,000,000

Kilometres
0 10 20 30 40 50 60 70 80

English Miles
0   10   20   30   40   50

Contours of 100, 500, 1000, 1500, 2000, & 2500 metres.

Having taken San Sebastian, Wellington waited until Pamplona, the other frontier fortress, surrendered on 31 October before making his next move. On 10 November he attacked across the Nivelle with superior forces, and after some hard fighting, again broke through the French defences. The 4th Division, which had not been involved in the Bidassoa operation, did play a minor role in the crossing of the Nivelle, being ordered to capture several redoubts around the village of Sarre. Cole formed his three brigades in three lines and it was Anson's brigade in the lead that suffered the heaviest casualties while Ross's Fusilier Brigade, being in reserve, lost only twenty-four men. MacDonald of the 23rd remembered that the 4th Division drove the enemy:

> ... from their entrenched positions with the greatest ease, indeed so much so that the rear Brigades of each Division even at the principal point of attack were never engaged. The enemy as usual rather abandoning the few tents they had, with all their heavy artillery, than wait for the arrival of half the troops that were brought against them, consequently the losses fell on a few particular regiments that led the different columns, the precipitances of their retreat & the very intersected state of the country from woods & rivers & redoubts rendered the taking of many prisoners impossible.[41]

Bentinck remembered that the victory at that Nivelle was only accomplished after a stiff fight but that, 'after the battery was taken we had a very sharp engagement' and 'drove them out of their camps and took possession of them'.[42]

Soult now pulled back to the line of the River Nive, just south of Bayonne. As Pamplona and San Sebastian had fallen, Wellington could employ his entire army against this position but, because the Nive was in flood from autumn rains, he had to wait some time before attempting a crossing. This delay was perplexing to many in the army including the Fusilier Brigade, which had not seen any really hard action since the Pyrenees battles of late July. As MacDonald commented, 'whether he thinks we had enough of fighting' in the Pyrenees 'or that the Fusiliers are scared I do not know but his Lordship has certainly taken great care of us for the last three months'.[43] More good news arrived in early November when Wellington learned of the great victory at the Battle of Leipzig fought on 18 October, at which 300,000 allied troops had inflicted a crushing defeat on Napoleon, who lost nearly two-thirds of his 190,000 men. Austrian, Prussian, Russian and Swedish armies were now advancing against France itself and Napoleon desperately tried to raise new forces. He ordered Soult to send him

---

Left: **Area of Wellington's Operations, 1813–14**
From J. W. Fortescue, **History of the British Army**

14,000 men, which put the marshal at a disadvantage, in terms of numbers, against Wellington.

The autumn weather in the Pyrenees was not very comfortable. MacDonald complained that the 'cold was intense, & raining every day' and he felt sorry for the 'poor Spaniards who have nothing but the clothes they stand in' suffered and it was 'not uncommon to see two or three dead in the morning of the guard or picquet which they furnished'.[44] On the other hand, things were not all that bad because:

> The Country about here is beautiful abounding in wood & having a number of rivers intersecting it in all directions, it appears uncommonly well cultivated & to have been very populous, but very few of the inhabitants have returned as yet, having all retired in to the interior on the day of the attack, so that we have only the walls of the houses left, in the towns the accommodation is better as a great number of the inhabitants had remained & others are coming back every day, but the most part of our Division are quartered in farm houses & the people cannot bring themselves to live with us in detached houses as yet. The language they speak is peculiar to the bordering provinces of the Pyrenees [the Basque language], and does not resemble French in the least. However the principal inhabitants can talk French very well & all seem to curse Bonaparte & his government with heart & soul.[45]

On 9 December 1813 Wellington launched an assault crossing of the Nive and secured substantial bridgeheads close to Bayonne. On the following day, Soult counterattacked but was repulsed. He renewed the offensive on 11 December and was again rebuffed, as he was at a third attack made on 13 December. During these actions, the 4th Division acted in a supporting role but as Steevens commented, it saw more marching than fighting:

> Our Division (the 4th) was quartered, for about a fortnight, at a village called Ascain, whence we marched at daylight on the morning of the 8th of December and encamped. The next morning the enemy attacked the centre of our line, and our division went in support, but the enemy were repulsed, and we were not engaged. On the 10th December the enemy attacked our left, and the day after the right of our line, but they were completely beaten in every attack they made, and retired with great loss. We had a good deal of marching, for the 4th Division were at every point where the troops were engaged, being the supporters, and therefore having to move wherever our assistance was required; consequently we had more marching than any other division. For eight days we were without our baggage, and for two or three nights without tents, exposed to rain and sometimes frost.[46]

A notable event took place on the night of 10 December when three battalions of German troops from Nassau and Frankfurt, who had been serving in the French army, crossed the lines and surrendered, on condition that they be repatriated to Germany. This was accepted and Lieutenant Colonel Ellis met them at the picket line and escorted them into the Fusilier Brigade camp. Steevens thought:

> They were very fine looking fellows, and their officers came over with them; they were without their baggage, which had been left at Bayonne; their bands were also there; however they had plenty of bugles, and took good care to blow them as soon as they were safe in our lines. It was about ten o'clock when they arrived, and we gave them a very good supper, for they got three bullocks and plenty of rum and biscuit; they were then marched to St. Jean de Luz; there were about 1300 of them, and their grenadiers were the finest men I ever saw. Some of them told me that when they went into action they used to bite off the balls and merely fire blank cartridges at us, shewing how averse they were to the French, and how much they respected our nation.[47]

Whether the German claim that they did not fire on British troops was true or not, Soult immediately disarmed most of his remaining foreign units lest they, too, abandon the imperial cause, which was clearly sinking.

The weather continued abysmal with frequent torrents of cold rain and the men of the Fusilier Brigade began to grow 'very tired of the campaign, which seemed to weary the most zealous'.[48] Wellington decided that it was time to place his army in winter quarters, and Ross's three battalions were billeted in and about the village of Arrauntz, about seven miles from Bayonne. Once settled in, the soldiers commenced the great work of 'Shoemaking and mending, & repairing Clothes' as their 'watch-coats that were worn out, & in holes, were cut up to mend red coats'.[49] The result was that 'the Men had every Colour on their backs' and 'would have done Harlequin credit'. Providentially a shipment of clothing arrived from Britain and the different regiments:

> ... were allowed to come down from the lines to St. Jean de Luz, where they arrived successively. The day they marched into St. Jean de Luz, they halted, the day after they clothed from head to foot, & the day after that, they began their march to the Army. This operation lasted, until nearly all the Army were newly clothed. The scene of this operation was not a little amusing, & the wit of the Soldiers, at thus changing as it were their skins, was exerted to the utmost. Caps, Jackets, Trowsers, everything old, was thrown away, & the Army soon appeared as gay as it had ever done. The men became comfortable & warm, & the quantity & quality of the vermin, they thus got rid of, was sufficient, as they themselves owned, to cause their becoming fat & plump in a very short time.[50]

Better still, Cooper of the 7th Foot noted, 'for the first time in the Peninsula we kept Christmas'. His comrades contributed 'some money, meat, or wine;' sheep were killed for the main course and, although cutlery was scarce, 'yet we managed to diminish the stock of eatables in quick time'.[51] For dessert, they 'had plenty of apples; and for a finish, two or three bandsmen played a merry tune, while many warmed their toes by dancing jigs and reels'. Lieutenant Thomas Browne, serving with the staff at St. Jean de Luz, was pleased that, during this winter respite, a church service was held 'every Sunday in a field near the Sea'.[52] A 'Hollow square was formed by a Brigade of Infantry quartered in the Town, & under the Colors of one of the Regiments, was placed a big drum for a reading desk' and Browne observed that the attention 'of Officers & Soldiers was exemplary, & doubly so when Psalms & Lessons were selected alluding to our situation, or to the uncertain tenure by which we held our lives'.[53]

In the first days of 1814, this pleasant sojourn was interrupted when the Fusilier Brigade was called out from its billets after Wellington became alarmed at a possible French attack. As Steevens commented:

> At eight o'clock, on the night of the 3rd January, 1814, we went away very suddenly from Arrauntz. After a few hours marching we fortunately got housed for the night, for we had left without baggage or tents. We made off again at 4 a.m. on the 4th, marched all day, and encamped at night. The next day we did the same, and on the morning of the 6th we started again to drive the enemy over the river Arran [Adour]. About three o'clock in the afternoon of that day we came up with them; they were posted on the heights at a short distance from the river; the 3rd Division was on our right and part of the 2nd Division on our left, ours (the 4th Division) being in the centre; the enemy were attacked in all three points, and in about an hour and a half they were driven across with very little loss on either side.[54]

The brigade was not involved in any fighting, he added, but it 'saw the whole business'. It now went under canvas at camps near Usteritz, six miles south of Bayonne as 'the roads became impassable, and neither army could move'.[55] The tent lines were crowded, but as MacDonald noted, were 'infinitely better than what we have been accustomed to in Portugal'.[56] The local population was friendly because they dreaded 'nothing so much as the return of the French soldiers who continue their system of plunder even in their own country'.[57] Wellington was well aware of the feelings of the French people toward their own army and wishing to gain their support, had issued a General Order before his army had crossed the border that he was 'desirous that the inhabitants should be well treated' and that his troops 'must recollect that their nations are at war with France solely because the Ruler of the French nation will not allow them to be at peace'.[58] This policy paid immediate dividends, MacDonald noting that the allied army was 'everywhere received by the inhabitants as friends come to deliver them from the tyranny of the French Army which they said was intolerable'.[59] Wellington's insistence on the proper treatment of civilians was backed up by divisional provost marshals who were swift to punish any soldier found looting, using a drumhead court martial if necessary. Drummer Bentinck saw 'a man of the 5th Regiment hanged on a tree for plundering'.[60]

In February 1814 the war again came to life. By this time the allied armies were deep in French territory although Napoleon, with flashes of his old brilliance, waged a very able defensive campaign, winning a number of small victories that caused them to halt their advance. Incredibly, the French leader spurned yet another peace offer, albeit less generous than the previous one, and vowed to continue fighting. Wellington, learning that Napoleon had ordered Soult to detach more troops to reinforce him, resolved to use his superior strength to force the French marshal away from Bayonne by mounting a major offensive west of that city. On 14 February, Lieutenant General Sir Rowland Hill advanced with 13,000 men to threaten Soult's communications and the French commander responded by switching his forces to his left flank. Once this had taken place, Wellington mounted an attack on 23 February across the River Adour west of Bayonne with 31,000 troops under the command of Lieutenant General Sir John Hope. Hope was savagely counterattacked but was able to maintain a bridgehead on the French side of the river at the cost of heavy casualties. Wellington now switched emphasis to the French left flank, east of the city, and on 24 February, he levered Soult's outnumbered forces out of their position, forcing them to withdraw. Soult took up a strong position with 36,000 men on a ridge overlooking the town of Orthez. On 27 February, Wellington attacked this position with 43,000 men and this time the 4th Division experienced serious fighting.

Cole's task was to take the village of St. Boes at the western end of the ridge. The Fusilier Brigade led the attack and Ross had little trouble in securing a church on the outskirts of the village, but when he attempted to advance through and beyond it, he was halted by heavy fire from well-served French artillery. Reinforced by a Portuguese caçadore regiment, Ross tried again but was hit in the face ('in the chops' as he put it) by a musket ball and forced to turn over command to Ellis.[61] Ellis managed to take most of St. Boes but could not advance beyond it, owing to the murderous French artillery fire. At this point the French counterattacked to regain the village, which anchored their right flank, and the battle deteriorated into severe skirmishing in the village streets. Cooper commented that his company were 'firing in rapid bopeep fashion', when some of his comrades discovered a large quantity of wine in a nearby house and 'handed it out copiously' to their comrades so that 'the game' became 'Drink and fire, fire and drink'.[62] The three battalions of the Fusilier Brigade, MacDonald proudly asserted, 'which never exceeded a thousand men kept their ground with the greatest obstinacy & even drove the enemy for a considerable distance and before any other troops had arrived to their assistance'.[63] In the end, however, it was no use and Ellis was forced to relinquish St. Boes.

The other British attacks on the Orthez ridge met with no better success and by noon the battle was a stalemate. Wellington now threw in reinforcements and attacked again in the centre and on the left, the Light Division coming up to aid Cole. In the afternoon, the French finally began to give ground and then commenced a disorderly retreat. His victory cost Wellington 2,200 casualties but he had thoroughly beaten Soult, whose armies were now not only disorganised but demoralised. The Fusilier Brigade lost 304 men in what MacDonald thought was a 'murderous action', with the Royal Welch Fusiliers' share of bill being 16 men killed, with 3 officers (Captains Henry Wynne and Charles Jolliffe and Lieutenant Isaac Harris) and 69 men wounded. 'For my part', MacDonald commented, 'I wonder how any of us escaped' but the young officer had only suffered 'a few bruises from splinters of shells & stones which everyone have received'.[64] Ross's wife, Elizabeth, was at Bilbao with their son and as soon as she learned that her husband had been wounded, she mounted a mule, 'and in the midst of rain, hail, mud, and all other accompaniements of bad weather', rode a distance of ninety miles 'over snowy mountains and bad roads to nurse him'.[65] While Ross recovered, Henry Ellis retained command of the Fusilier Brigade.

Napoleon was staring defeat in the face. Despite a number of impressive but small victories he was unable to prevent the allied armies, which vastly outnumbered his forces, closing in on Paris. Many of his subjects, weary of endless fighting, wished him gone and conditions inside France became increasingly chaotic. Even before the Battle of Orthez, Wellington had received information that the mayor of Bordeaux, one of the largest cities in France after Paris, wished to declare for the Bourbons against Napoleon. When Soult retreated eastward after Orthez, he left open the direct road between Bayonne and Bordeaux and Wellington sent Marshal William Beresford with the 4th and 7th Divisions to take possession of the city, which was done on 12 March. With Bordeaux taken, Wellington now moved south-east towards Toulouse, the other great city in the area. The army moved off on 18 March, Soult's outnumbered force retreating before them, and by 26 March the Fusilier Brigade could see the walls of the city.

Built on both banks of the wide River Garonne, Toulouse was virtually unapproachable on three sides because of the presence of that and other waterways. The best axis of attack was from the north-east, where the Calvinet ridge overlooked it but to occupy that position Wellington had first to cross the Garonne. The engineers went to work and, after a failed attempt, completed a pontoon bridge on 4 April. Part of the army now crossed over but flood water swept away the bridge and it was not until 7 April that it was again serviceable.

The Fusilier Brigade, along with the remainder of the army, was forced to wait until the engineers had finished their pounding, but as Bentinck reported, it was not an unpleasant time:

> ... we were there about three weeks. It was a very fruitful country and we got plenty of wine. It was so plentiful that we cooked our potatoes and meat in wine. Some of the men when they went into the warehouses they left the plug out and the wine was running all over the floor. When we bought it, it would not have cost more than three halfpence a pint. We always provided a little tub of wine in the tent at night so that we used to drink until we fell back. If there was any left in the morning we used to upset it and get some fresh.[66]

On Easter Sunday, 10 April 1814, the 4th Division took up positions northeast of Toulouse. Under Marshal William Beresford's command, the 4th and 6th Divisions were to attack the Calvinet Ridge, which Soult had fortified with a number of redoubts. Beresford had a long approach march and, delayed by mud, did not put in his attack until late in the morning. He formed in two lines with the 6th Division on the right and the 4th Division on the left while Cole placed Anson's brigade in his front, his Portuguese brigade in his second and Ellis's Fusilier Brigade in his third line. This done, the two divisions moved towards the ridge and were struggling up its slippery slope when they were attacked by a French division formed in columns. This was quickly beaten off but as French cavalry were moving in the open ground to Cole's left, he ordered Ellis to form the Fusilier Brigade in battalion squares to guard that flank. Both divisions came under heavy fire from 'about forty pieces of artillery (who kept playing shot, shells & Grape at us)', remembered MacDonald, but the 4th Division moved 'with as much coolness as if we were marching on parade'.[67]

Beresford delayed his final attack until he had brought up artillery and then, in mid-afternoon, both divisions moved against the Calvinet Ridge. MacDonald recalled that the Fusilier Brigade formed line and:

> advanced against some very strong redoubts which the French evacuated in the most cowardly manner. The sight was the finest that I ever saw, & every part of the army that saw it were delighted. We completely succeeded in our part & must have taken an immense amount of prisoners if our cavalry who had moved on the right bank of the Hers river, had been able to cross, but finding all the bridges destroyed they were obliged to make a great detour & were consequently late in coming up.[68]

By late afternoon it was over. Soult withdrew into Toulouse, which he abandoned the next day. As usual, the fighting had been costly, Wellington losing 4,568 men to Soult's loss of 3,236, but the Royal Welch Fusiliers' share was very light, being one man killed and seven wounded. MacDonald attributed this to the fact that the Fusilier Brigade had 'been the rear one of our division'.[69]

On 12 April 1814, the allied army entered Toulouse and that night Wellington learned of the abdication of Napoleon six days before, from Colonel Henry Cooke who had ridden hard from Paris. The Battle of Toulouse had actually been fought needlessly, although neither Wellington nor Soult were aware that the war had ended. MacDonald described the events of a momentous day:

> Before our entrance the inhabitants had all hoisted the white [Bourbon] cockade & had destroyed Bonaparte's bust which had been erected in the market place, & had openly declared for the Bourbons, so that you may conceive their joy on Col Cooke's entrance in the Theatre at night, with the official dispatches of Bonaparte having abdicated the throne in favor of Louis the XVIII. Lord Wellington immediately handed the Bulletin to the mayor who read it amidst thunders of applause. ...
>
> Thoulouse [*sic*] is a beautiful city &c the bridge is superb, but I cannot give any description till we return which we expect to do in a day or two, as this news has been sent to the French Army, & Marshal Soult is expected in town this evening to arrange matters & we are to go into cantonments until the terms are settled.[70]

True to his obstinate nature, however, Soult refused to accept that the war was over and it took five more days before he acknowledged that France had been defeated.

In the weeks that followed, the Royal Welch Fusiliers marched slowly towards the Atlantic coast. By the end of May 1814 they were billeted in a village with the interesting name of Condom and from there they proceeded to Blancquefort, outside Bordeaux. The Peninsular army now began to break up as the Portuguese regiments prepared to march for their own country while the British units either embarked to return to Britain or fight in the American war. The 7th Foot was selected for American service but, much to the chagrin of the 1/23rd Foot, they were not chosen, as only the strongest regiments were taken and the battalion's strength – just 450 men on 25 May – was considered too weak.[71] As regiments departed and veteran divisions and brigades were disbanded, it was a sad time for many as old friends and comrades parted. It was made sadder when Wellington ordered that none of the faithful Portuguese and Spanish women who had campaigned with the army for years were to be permitted to embark, with the exception of a few 'who have proved themselves useful and regular' who might accompany their soldier consorts 'with a view to their being ultimately married'.[72] The remainder were consigned to the care of the Portuguese army who escorted them to their native regions. Many of these poor unfortunates had to be separated from their menfolk by force, and their lamentations were awful.

The Royal Welch Fusiliers' turn to leave came surprisingly quickly. On 14 June the 1/23rd Foot, 569 all ranks with 36 wives and children, boarded the 74-gun ship, HMS *Egmont* at Pauillac in the Gironde estuary.[73] 'You may easily conceive the joy of both the officers and men', Lieutenant John MacDonald commented, 'the greatest part of the latter being six years on service' abroad.[74]

When wild war's deadly blast was blawn,
And gentle peace returning,
Wi' many a sweet babe fatherless,
And many a widow mourning,
I left the lines and tented field,
Where long I'd been a lodger,
My humble knapsack all my wealth,
A poor and honest sodger.

The wars are o'er, and I'm come home,
And find thee still true-hearted;
Tho' poor in gear, we're rich in love,
And mair we'se ne'er be parted.
Quo' she, my grandsire left me gowd,
A mailen plenished fairly;
And come, my faithful sodger lad,
Thou'rt welcome to it dearly!

For gold the merchant ploughs the main,
The farmer ploughs the manor;
But glory is the sodger's prize;
The sodger's wealth is honour:
The brave poor sodger, ne'er despise,
Nor count him as a stranger;
Remember he's his country's stay
In day and hour o' danger.[1]

Chapter 12

'And gentle peace returning'

1st and 2nd Battalions, Britain,
June 1814 – March 1815

HIS MAJESTY'S SHIP EGMONT made good time from France and arrived at
Plymouth on 25 June 1814. Just before the Royal Welch Fusiliers landed, Drummer
Richard Bentinck remembered, the men were issued new white fatigue jackets and
trousers and threw their old garments overboard 'as they was all filth and dirt'.[2] Ten
days later, the 1/23rd Foot set out for Gosport, their new station. Moving by way
of Ivybridge, Bridport, Dorchester and Southampton, the battalion marched
through scenic countryside and, better still, it enjoyed a tremendous reception from
the civilian population as, after more than two decades of war, all Britain was in a
festive mood. In every city, town and village there were celebrations – parades,
banquets, toasts, bonfires, sermons, processions, speeches, and illuminations – to
mark the end of the war. London hosted the Czar of Russia, the King of Prussia and
the old and ferocious Field Marshal Gebhard von Blücher, the senior Prussian
general, who paid the British capital the supreme compliment of saying that it would
be a fine place to sack. The greatest reception, however, was accorded to the newly-
named Duke of Wellington, who landed at Dover two days before the 1/23rd Foot
disembarked at Plymouth to be lionised by the entire nation.

As the battalion marched east through Devon, Dorset and Hampshire,
Bentinck fondly recalled in later years, it was:

> ... cheered, fed and regaled as though each man of it were some illustrious
> hero; until it seemed like dreamland to the poor fellows after having had
> years of fighting and starving and marching in inhospitable climes. ...
>
> In almost every town they passed through they were treated to as much
> meat and drink as they could use by their fellow countrymen, who were
> not only joyful at peace, but delighted to have amongst them the gallant
> soldiers who had won it for them. ...
>
> At length, however, these hospitable potations interfered so much with
> the men's marching that the Officers began to put a stop to them when

they could ... Still the men got plenty of grog given to them when their day's duties were over. The townspeople would make bonfires, get the soldiers to fire volleys of blank cartridges and then roll out barrels of beer for the general delectation.[3]

When the 1/23rd arrived at Southampton, it found several militia regiments camped near the city. Lieutenant Colonel Henry Ellis took up his headquarters in the best hotel and:

> ... the faithful Regimental Colours were as usual displayed from his windows. These colours the Regiment had had all through the Danish campaign, their Canadian sojourn, the Martinique invasion and the Peninsular War; and shot, shell, sword cuts, weather and battle smoke had reduced the once gay banners to what seemed like a few discoloured rags fluttering from a pole. A number of jealous Militiamen hooted and made fun of these war torn symbols saying they were not worth putting up. There upon a gentleman in the crowd gathered around began indignantly to denounce their conduct, [and] in the course of an inspiring speech pointed out that the tattered aspect of the flags was their greatest honour and amid the cheers of the crowd, wound up by making a collection for the Fusileers. Upwards of fifty pounds was soon contributed in response.[4]

The public-spirited man attempted to present the sum collected to Lieutenant Colonel Ellis but he 'declined to accept it, on the grounds that the men, if they got any drink would end up fighting with the Militiamen'. Finally, on 16 July, having enjoyed a thoroughly marvellous triumphal procession along the south coast, the 1/23rd Foot marched into the New Military Barracks at Gosport.

Gosport was also the station of the 2/23rd Foot, currently under the command of Brevet Lieutenant Colonel Thomas Dalmer. For the first time in their history, both battalions of the regiment were stationed together and their respective commanding officers referred to them 'by the pleasant appellation of 1st and 2nd of Welch'.[5] The 1st Battalion also re-united with the regimental Goat, who had not accompanied them overseas in 1808 but had remained in Britain under the care of either the 2nd Battalion or one of the Welsh militia regiments.

It is time to catch up with the activities of the 2nd Battalion, which we last encountered in late 1809 when it returned from the disastrous Walcheren expedition. The battalion had remained at Horsham, trying to recover its strength, until February 1810 when it made its way in gradual stages to Portsmouth to embark in April of that year for the Channel Islands where it served until August 1811. It was then transferred to Wales, becoming the first battalion of the regiment, in the 122 years since it had been raised, to serve in the country whose name it bore. The 2nd Battalion served mainly at Haverfordwest in Pembrokeshire, until April 1813 when it changed stations no less than four times in eight months before ending up at Berry Head in Devon. Here it remained until

February 1814 when it moved to Winchester for four months before shifting to Gosport.

The 2nd Battalion's strength during these years was fairly weak, ranging from 115 to 379, primarily because its function was to recruit and train men for the 1st Battalion and, between 1810 and late 1813, it had sent nearly 600 officers and men to the Peninsula. Its service in Wales accelerated the process by which the Royal Welch Fusiliers became more Welsh. At its annual inspection carried out at Haverfordwest in July 1812, the inspecting officer noted that, of a total enlisted strength of 150 men, no fewer than 98 were 'Welch'. In 1813, after receiving 263 volunteers from the militia, its regimental return for 25 June described 7 officers and 108 men as being 'Welsh' while in February 1814, 6 officers and 123 men were listed as being 'Welch' – evidence that even in the regiment itself there existed doubt over the correct way to spell the word.

On 24 October 1814, as part of the general reduction of the army, the 2/23rd Foot was disbanded. Most of its officers were placed on half pay while 447 men were transferred to the 1st Battalion. At the same time, efforts were made to discharge men who were physically unfit or below the fixed standard of a minimum height of five feet, five inches although, as Bentinck commented, some of the shorter men 'had proven to be the best soldiers in the Regiment'.[6] During the previous decade, inspecting officers had frequently observed that the height of the enlisted men in the 23rd Foot was shorter than average. It should be noted that, at this time, it was generally believed that Welshmen were not as tall as men from other areas of the British Isles and some years after the Great War with France had ended, one officer argued that the army's minimum standard of height for recruits – which was five feet, five inches – was 'much too high for Welchmen, although necessary for English, who below a certain height are seldom strong'.[7] He noted that:

> The Carmarthenshire Militia was the shortest but broadest-shouldered corps in the Kingdom. …Will any man say that a Merthyr miner of five feet two would not outrun in light, outmarch in heavy marching order, or outfight hand to hand, – and the confidence of superiority in hand-to-hand fighting, generally prevents the necessity of its employment, – any Manchester weaver or Cockney counter-jumper of six feet three, without chest, loins, or sinews?[8]

When the reduction was complete, the Royal Welch Fusiliers became a single battalion regiment with a strength of 1,197 men, twenty-one over the authorised establishment.

In 1814 the army did not issue medals to its enlisted personnel for either gallantry or good behaviour and many regimental commanding officers compensated for this oversight by awarding their own decorations. Ellis was one of them and, as he had returned to Britain, he arranged for the manufacture and presentation of medals to soldiers who had displayed meritorious and distinguished conduct in Egypt, Denmark, Martinique and the Peninsula. These

Regimental Medals, 1814
Immediately after returning to
Britain in the summer of 1814,
Colonel Ellis ordered new Colours
to replace those carried by the
1/23rd since 1806, which had been
reduced to rags. He also had struck,
probably at his own expense, silver
medals for the men of his battalion
who had served with it since 1801,
listing the actions at which they
had been present. (*Tancred,*
Historical Record of Medals)

medals were cast in silver and engraved on one side
with the coronet, feathers and motto of the Prince of
Wales and on the other, with the names of the battles
in which the man had served, surrounded by a laurel
wreath. They were designed to be worn with a ribbon
which was probably scarlet with blue edging.
Unfortunately there is no extant record of the names
of the men who received these decorations.[9]

That autumn, leave was granted to every soldier
who had been with the 1st Battalion when it had
sailed to North America in 1808, among them
Richard Bentinck, who drew £9 back pay and set out
for his native village of Bacton in Suffolk. In the eight
years he had been abroad, Bentinck had never written
to his parents and was not even sure they were still
alive, but made the 150-mile journey in five days,
helped by the occasional ride on farmers' wagons.
When he arrived, his mother at first did not recognise
the young soldier of 22, whom she had last seen as a
16-year-old boy, but was overjoyed to find him alive.
Bentinck's father having died, she had married a farm
labourer and this man introduced the drummer to the
wealthy farmer who was his employer, 'a jovial and
kind hearted figure' who was fascinated with
Bentinck's war stories, 'plying the narrator with good
meat and drink meanwhile'. He offered Bentinck
work with the harvest and the young man 'thoroughly
enjoyed himself' until his two months of leave were
over.[10] When the job was done, the farmer held a
party for his labourers and their families and, as
Bentinck recalled, there was 'plenty of beer and we
began to drink to his health and wife and family' but,
although most of those present 'had not finished
drinking their health when they were quite drunk', the veteran Bentinck 'sat there
to the last and we were invited to go the next day and finish what was left'.[11] When
he made his way back to Gosport to rejoin the battalion, Bentinck was richer by £3
and had acquired a liking for 'simple farm life'.

Henry Ellis also took leave that autumn. He had been promoted colonel in June
and made a Knight Commander of the Bath so it was as Colonel Sir Henry Ellis
that he travelled to his family's estate at Kempsey, four miles from Worcester. Ellis
was well known to the people of that city and area and they decided to honour him
with a piece of engraved silverware 'as a Tribute of Respect considered due to him
for his gallant Conduct during a period of upwards of fifteen years arduous Service

in the Defence of his Country'.[12]. On the afternoon of 26 December 1814, the Worcester *Herald* reported, a ceremony took place in the town hall of the city. Ellis arrived with the Earl and Countess of Coventry and their family:

> On their appearance, the recruiting parties in this city, stationed at the entrance-door of the Guildhall, by the considerate and commendable zeal of Capt. Sanderson, presented arms, the band playing God Save the King. Colonel Ellis was ushered into the Council Chamber, where he was received by the Mayor and Body Corporate. the rest of the august party moved forward to the assembly-room. In a few minutes, Colonel Ellis, attended by many members of the Corporation, and numerous friends, made his entré amidst an unanimous burst of applause, and to which manifestation of approbation he repeatedly bowed.[13]

The Earl of Coventry then presented Ellis with a silver-gilt cup[†] 'completed with singular taste and elegance' which stood 'on a handsome pedestal' and contained 'many military devices, the arms of the Colonel and the City of Worcester.'[14] In presenting the gift to Ellis, the earl noted that it was 'a testimony' of his 'meritorious services as repeatedly displayed in the defence of your country.' In responding, Ellis acknowledged that he was:

> ... more indebted to the assistance of my officers and men, than to those personal merits you have been kind enough to attribute to me.
>
> Happily placed at the head of a most distinguished corps, I had only to attach myself to their fate, assured that their enthusiastic bravery would lead to an honourable result. To their exertions I shall ever attribute the distinctions you have this day conferred upon me.

The Mayor then bestowed the Freedom of the City of Worcester on Ellis and, when the speeches were finished, he left the town hall while the cup 'was taken by two sergeants (and a guard with fixed bayonets) to the shop of Mr. Powell, a local jeweller where it was to be on display', as the 'bells of the various churches were rung in his honour'.[15] Ellis and a large party dined that evening at Croome, the nearby estate of the Earl of Coventry.

In his absence, the 23rd Foot at Gosport was under the command of Lieutenant Colonel Dalmer. Among the newcomers from the now defunct 2nd Battalion were two young Welshmen, Privates Thomas Jeremiah and Lewis Griffiths. Jeremiah was one of twelve children of a farmer in Goytre near Pontypool, Monmouthshire, who, having too many mouths to feed, had sent him at the tender age of ten to earn his living as an indentured farm labourer. Jeremiah was working on a farm near Abergavenny in late 1812 when he 'became much taken up with the dashing appearance' of a recruiting party from the Welch Fusiliers 'and formed many an excuse for to go to town' and view 'those gallant sons of Mars whose Military and

---

† This cup is currently on display in Royal Welch Fusilier Museum in Caernarfon Castle.

soldierlike appearance was striking, attractive and pleasing to my young and susceptible mind'.[16] Not surprisingly, the recruiting sergeant found young Jeremiah easy prey and he enlisted in the 2nd Battalion in November 1812.

Like so many young men before and after, Thomas Jeremiah found that his dreams of martial glory did not correspond with reality in the army. Lieutenant Colonel William Wyatt, having never fully recovered from the Walcheren expedition, had retired and had been succeeded in command of the 2nd Battalion by Major John Leahy, who had seen service with the 1st Battalion in the Peninsula. In Jeremiah's opinion, Leahy was a tyrant who made frequent use of flogging to maintain discipline, Jeremiah himself being sentenced by a regimental court martial to receive 300 lashes for being ten minutes late back to his quarters after tattoo. He received 75 of them. Jeremiah claimed that Leahy became 'so notorious' in the army that 2/23rd could not get any more volunteers from the militia, 'particularly the Welsh Militias from whence we their country regiment used to be furnished with [the] best and Hardiest men in the army'.[17] This was probably an exaggeration but there is no doubt that Leahy was not a popular officer and there was much rejoicing in the early summer of 1814 when Dalmer, 'an officer & soldier and a gentleman', whose 'disposition was diametrically opposite' to Leahy, assumed command. The soldiers were so happy that they took to chalking 'Long life to Colonel Delmare, and down with the tyrant' in large letters on their barrack doors and other conspicuous places in their quarters. As was intended, these graffiti infuriated Leahy who 'sought very diligently after the authors of those libels but all in vain'.

For his part, Lewis Griffiths was a labourer from Tal-y-llyn, Merionethshire, who had been drafted into the Royal Merionethshire Regiment of Militia, which had been sent to Ireland in June 1811 and stationed in Granard, County Longford. There Griffiths met and married a young woman named Jane Drumble in a whirlwind romance. Many years later Jenny, as she was usually known, remembered that Lewis Griffiths:

> ... first saw me in the church at Granard, in Ireland, when I was about fourteen years of age. He afterwards made my acquaintance by meeting me on my way home from school. As my mother and sister lived out of the town I remained at school all the week and went home on Saturday evenings. When he met me I told him I should be blamed if I was seen walking with him; and that if he insisted on going in the same direction he must walk on the other side of the hedge. He remarked that the road was free. 'Very well', I said, 'if it is free I will walk on the other side of the hedge and you can walk on the road'. He then came on with me about a mile and a quarter. After he knew how I went home from school he often met me, and it was in that way we became intimately acquainted one with another. My parents knew nothing of our acquaintance.
>
> Some time after, the company in which he served had orders to leave the town. Before he went he told me many times that he did not care what

they did with him if I did not go with him. When he was about to leave he sent letters to me in which he said he knew he should be flogged, but he would never go until he had seen me; so I thought I would just go to him and bid him goodbye. No one belonging to me knew that I went. When I saw him I said, 'Well, Lewis, I am come to bid you good bye'. 'No Jane', he replied, 'I will never go while I live if you don't come with me'.[18]

Lovelorn, Griffiths went to Lieutenant Colonel Vaughan, his commanding officer, and asked permission to marry. Vaughan interviewed Jenny and finding that she was a decent young woman – which was not always the case with the prospective wives of soldiers – ordered the banns to be posted 'twice in one day and once the next, because the men were leaving the town; and we were married in Granard Church'.[19] The wedding probably took place in late 1813 and Jenny, then about sixteen years of age, was carrying the couple's first child when Lewis Griffiths enlisted in the 23rd Foot for seven year's service on 6 April 1814 which, ironically, was the same day Napoleon abdicated, bringing an end to the war.

Although he was no longer a major player on the world stage, the former emperor of the French was never far from anyone's mind during the first months of peace . Under the terms of his abdication, Napoleon had been exiled to the Mediterranean island of Elba and provided with an army of a thousand men and two small warships to keep up imperial appearances. His replacement as head of state was Louis XVIII, brother of the monarch who had been executed in 1793, who had spent much of the intervening period in Britain as a guest of the Crown. Not many, including his own people, liked the overweight and ineffectual Louis but he was really the best of a number of bad options. The restoration of the monarchy in France was only one of a myriad of problems facing European nations in the aftermath of hostilities and to resolve them, representatives from the major states and principalities travelled to an international congress convened in Vienna in September 1814. The five major powers – Austria, Britain, France, Prussia and Russia – promptly fell out over the question of the future of Poland and the solution of this issue exercised their representatives through much of the winter of 1814-1815.

Europe was at peace but Britain was still at war with the United States. In July 1814, diplomats from the two nations began discussions at Ghent intended to resolve the conflict but, in the meantime, owing to the end of the greater war in Europe, Britain was in a position to reinforce her forces in North America. Most of the troops went to Canada where the local commander, Lieutenant General Sir George Prevost, had conducted a defensive campaign for two years against repeated American invasion attempts. A smaller force, under the command of Major General Robert Ross, former commander of the Fusilier Brigade, was sent to the Chesapeake Bay area on the Atlantic coast. In August 1814, still not fully recovered from the wound he had suffered at Orthez the previous February, Ross brushed aside an American army at the Battle of Bladensburg and occupied Washington. A later attempt to take Baltimore, however, ended when Ross was killed while carrying out a reconnaissance of the enemy defences.

Wellington had wisely refused any command in North America so to replace Ross, London's choice fell on Major General Sir Edward Pakenham, another former commander of the Fusilier Brigade. Pakenham, who had no illusions about the difficulties he faced, had earlier expressed the hope that he had 'escaped America and shall consider myself vastly fortunate in having been spared from such a Service'.[20] In October 1814, Pakenham sailed for New Orleans, which the senior naval officers in North American waters, inspired by the prize money they would acquire if the city fell, had urged on the government as a worthwhile objective.[21] He arrived there on 23 December 1814, one day before a peace treaty was signed between Britain and the United States. Having no knowledge of this, on 8 January 1815 Pakenham launched an attack against a well-fortified American defensive position outside New Orleans, which was repulsed with heavy British casualties, himself among them. The 7th Foot, the Welch Fusiliers' old Peninsular comrades, lost a hundred officers and men in this sad affair whose purpose, Wellington believed with reasonable grounds, was only plunder.[22] 'Had Wellington been there', Sergeant Cooper of the 7th commented, 'the Americans would have had less to boast of.'[23]

When news of this defeat reached Britain in March 1815, Lieutenant John MacDonald commented that, if the 1/23rd Foot had 'thought themselves particularly unlucky in being left when the 7th embarked' for North America, 'they now think otherwise' and added that Colonel Henry Ellis was 'in very low spirits' from the news of Pakenham's death as the two men 'had been always inseparable'. Besides, MacDonald added, there was 'every chance of a new field being opened for us on the Continent from having this moment learned of Bonaparte landing in France'.[24]

It was true. While the diplomats had danced, dallied and debated at Vienna, Napoleon had kept a close eye on events on the mainland and, learning that there was much dissatisfaction in France, particularly among his former soldiers, he had decided to make one last throw of the dice. On 1 March 1815, he landed in France with his thousand men; ten days later he was in Lyons and ten days after that he was back in Paris. Having reclaimed power, Napoleon immediately began to organise for war, while at the same time loudly proclaiming his peaceful intentions. In response, the nations at Vienna declared him an outlaw and began to mobilise. Wellington was appointed allied commander in the Low Countries and the British government began to assemble forces to be dispatched to him.

One of the first units selected was the 23rd Foot. There was the usual last minute rush to get things ready and Ellis transferred the Goat to the keeping of the depot company under Captain John Harrison – 230 invalids and recruits – which would remain behind in Gosport. Ellis also left behind the Colours of the 1st Battalion, as they were little more than rags and took, instead, the Colours of the disbanded 2nd Battalion, which were in much better condition. This exchange caused grumbling among the veterans of the 1st Battalion who 'said they would rather fight under their own old rags than under the finest flags in the Army'.[25] On 24 March 1815, the Royal Welch Fusiliers, 'about seven hundred as fine men as ever fixed bayonets', embarked for the continent.[26]

Thanks to the conscientious efforts of regimental historians we have enough reliable information to provide some description of the officers and men of the Royal Welch Fusiliers who participated in the last campaign of the Great War with France.[27]

Beginning with the officers, Colonel Ellis had nearly eighteen actual years in the army, having served in every major campaign in which the 1/23rd had participated from the Helder in 1799 to the Peninsula in 1814. His two senior subordinates, Brevet Lieutenant Colonels Thomas Dalmer and Jack Hill, had eighteen and nineteen years of service respectively, with Hill's record being almost identical to Ellis while Dalmer did not fight in Martinique or in some of the actions in the Peninsula. The regimental adjutant, Lieutenant John Enoch, and quartermaster, George Sidley, had somewhat less experience, eight and seven years respectively but, as both were commissioned from the ranks, they had previous service as enlisted men.

Of the ten company commanders or senior lieutenants commanding companies in the absence of the actual commanders, all had an average of nine years of service and Francis Dalmer and Joseph Hawtyn were brevet majors. Four had been with the regiment in Martinique and nine with it in the Peninsula, including six who had fought at Albuera. The fourteen first lieutenants had an average of five and a half years of service, with ten having served in the Peninsula and five of those having fought at Albuera. As might be expected, the four second lieutenants were less experienced, all having been commissioned in 1813 and none apparently having fought in the Peninsula.

Turning to the enlisted personnel, the staff NCOs – the regimental sergeant-major, quartermaster-sergeant, paymaster-sergeant, armourer-sergeant and the two drum majors – were an average of thirty-four and a half years old in 1815 and had about eleven and a half years in service. As an indication of the promotion patterns in the British army of the period, it had taken these men on average fifteen months to reach corporal's rank, another fifteen months to reach sergeant's rank but a little over seven years more to attain staff rank. The sergeants were, on average, thirty-three years old and had an average of ten and a half years of service while the corporals were somewhat younger, averaging just over twenty-eight, and possessing a little over eight years service. The private soldiers were younger still, an average of just under twenty-five years of age, with about four and a half years service. Only 8.6 per cent of the private soldiers had enlisted prior to 1804,

26 per cent had enlisted between 1805 and 1809 while the great majority, 68 per cent, had enlisted between 1809 and 1814. As a matter of interest, the average height of a soldier in the Welch Fusiliers was between five feet, six inches and five feet, eight inches and, despite the discharge of men below the fixed standard of height in the previous year, there were still more than a hundred men in the regiment under the required standard of five feet, five inches.[28]

In terms of origins, based on the data for 666 soldiers, 59.4 per cent (396) were from England, 30.9 per cent (206) from Wales, 8.4 per cent (56) from Ireland, 0.8 per cent (5) from Scotland with three men – one British North American, one Italian and one Dane – coming from outside the British Isles. The prime recruiting ground for the 23rd Foot was northern Wales and the adjacent English counties, particularly Lancashire which contributed no less than 114 men, or about one of six in the unit. The greater part of the Welsh recruits, 155 of 206, came from the counties of Cardiganshire, Denbighshire, Merionethshire, Montgomeryshire and Pembrokeshire. In 1815 just over a fifth (136 of 672) of the men had previous military experience, predominantly in the militia (110 men) although only twenty-eight of the former militiamen can be positively traced to Welsh militia regiments.

Information exists on the civilian occupations of 586 men in the regiment in 1815. Well over half had worked in unskilled occupations prior to enlistment, most calling themselves 'labourers' which should be read as 'agricultural labourers' or farm hands. The next three major occupational groupings (construction/building trades, iron/metal trades and textile/clothing trades) account for most of the men, 178 in total, who claimed to have had crafts or trades. Another 72 men described themselves as having had such specialised occupations as baker, barber, bookbinder, butcher, clothier, coach maker, cordwainer (shoe maker), hatter, locksmith, papermaker, potter, stocking weaver, tailor, trunk maker, vice maker and watchmaker. The term 'skilled craft or tradesmen' has to be viewed with some caution, however, as it becomes clear when looking at the ages of men who described themselves as carpenters, blacksmiths or tailors – trades that require considerable training – that they could not have completed the necessary apprenticeships when they enlisted. They were probably unskilled help or runaway apprentices and, although the army was forbidden to enlist such men, this regulation was often ignored.

Three of these specialised occupations bear closer examination: tailors, cordwainers or shoemakers and weavers. Tailoring and shoemaking are trades that are affected by economic downturns, which may have forced these men into the army, if they were skilled. It is more likely, however, that they were unskilled assistants or, in the case of cordwainers, actually itinerant cobblers. As for weavers and others engaged in the clothing and textile occupational group the advent of industrialisation in the late eighteenth century destroyed its traditional structure, which had hitherto been based on skilled craftsmen working in their own homes. The new factories with their machines created massive unemployment and the number of weavers and textile tradesmen in the British army was very high – something well known to recruiters who cheerfully signed them up.

In sum, when the 23rd Regiment of Foot boarded the transports, *Ariel*, *Percival* and *Poniana*, at Gosport in March 1815, Colonel Sir Henry Ellis was a fortunate commanding officer as he led a veteran unit composed largely of men who had seen considerable service. It was a far different regiment than that which had sailed for the West Indies in March 1794 under the command of his father.

When it embarked, the 23rd Foot was bound yet again for the Downs off Deal on the Kent coast. Private Thomas Jeremiah remembered that when the men were issued sixty rounds of ball cartridge just before leaving, the young soldiers who had never seen action acquired 'cannon fever' but the 'cheerful and undaunted advice' of the veterans 'dispelled their tremendous fears'.[29] The regiment reached the Downs on 27 March but a Channel gale, which lasted two days, delayed their departure for Ostend, their next destination. Several ships dragged their anchors and were forced to cut their cables to avoid running onto the notorious Goodwin Sands. Lieutenant MacDonald recorded that his vessel 'drifted a considerable distance but a third anchor brought her up again and we rode it pretty well' which was a happy situation 'for we had twenty officers packed together in one little cabin, the greatest part of course quite sick, and not able to go on deck, much less ashore, from the violence of the wind and rain'.[30] Two days later, the regiment was transferred to several small sloops to make the run for Ostend, which it reached on 30 March.

It was at this point that Jenny Griffiths and her six-month old daughter, Margaret, were nearly parted from Lewis. As she later commented:

> There came orders from the general that no women with young children should be allowed to disembark. I was the fourth woman on the list. When the men were landing my husband was standing by the side of the ship. 'Now, Lewis Griffiths, disembark', the Colonel [Ellis] said. 'All right', my husband replied, but did not go. 'Why don't you disembark, Lewis Griffiths; what are you waiting for?' 'For Jane to come too, Sir'. 'Well, then', said the Colonel, 'go on, Jane'.[31]

And she did.

The Royal Welch Fusiliers were back on the continent with the express purpose, as Lieutenant Colonel Jack Hill put it, of ensuring that 'Bonaparte & his friends' were 'swept from the face of the earth'.[32]

Our plumes have waved in conquests
That ne'er shall be forgot,
When many a mighty squadron
Reeled backward from our shot;
In charges with the bayonet
We led our bold confrères,
For Frenchmen like to stay not
'Gainst the Royal Welch Fusiliers

And what could Bonapart-ee,
With all his cuirassiers,
In battle do at Waterloo,
'Gainst the Royal Welch Fusiliers?
And ever sweet the drum shall beat
That march into our ears,
Whose martial roll awakes the soul
Of the Royal Welch Fusiliers.[1]

Chapter 13

'Remember the old times boys, this is their last try'

The Waterloo Campaign, 1815

OSTEND WAS ALL CONFUSION, confusion caused not only by the numbers of troops disembarking in this small port but also by fears of a French attack. Although recently made part of the Netherlands, Belgium had been French for a generation and there was considerable support for Napoleon, so much so that Lieutenant John MacDonald commented that on the day the Welch Fusiliers disembarked, there 'was a diligent search for spies' but 'though every body knew they were numerous still they could not be made out'.[2] The 23rd Foot did not linger long – on 31 March 1815, it embarked on canal boats and had a pleasant inland voyage to Bruges and then marched to Ghent, arriving on 3 April. Here it remained nearly three weeks, occasionally mounting guard at the residence of Louis XVIII who had taken refuge in the city, before moving on to billets in the East Flanders town of Grammont, about twenty-five miles west of Brussels. A Scotsman, MacDonald found the humidity of the low-lying countryside uncomfortable but retained 'the Highland custom' of having a 'wee drop' first thing in the morning to ward off sickness and was only 'sorry I am not able to smoke any tobacco, as it must also be a preservative'.[3]

The question on everyone's mind, particularly the Peninsular veterans, was the whereabouts of Wellington. The Anglo-Dutch army assembling in Belgium was under the nominal command of the Prince of Orange, the 23-year-old heir to the Dutch throne, but one British veteran remembered his comrades constantly complaining that 'surely we shall not be led to battle by that boy'.[4] The day the troops learned that 'Nosey' was indeed back to lead them was a memorable one and that evening, this same soldier recalled, 'was spent by reminding each other of the glorious deeds done in the Peninsula, mingled with song and dance, good hollands [gin] and tobacco'.[5]

Wellington was less happy with the situation he found on his arrival. He had asked the government for 40,000 British troops but since many of the veteran units were still on their way back from North America, what he got was about

24,000 British and King's German Legion infantry padded out with a mixture of Belgian, Brunswick, Dutch and Hanoverian units, many of which were either raw recruits or had recently fought in Napoleon's army. With his usual attention to detail, Wellington mixed reliable and unreliable troops together, placing veteran units alongside green units. As part of Lieutenant General Sir Charles Colville's 4th Division, the 23rd was brigaded with the 51st Foot, a light infantry regiment which had seen considerable Peninsular service, and the 3/14th Foot, an inexperienced and young battalion nicknamed the 'Peasants' because it included more than 300 'Buckinghamshire lads fresh from the plough'.[6] As he was the senior battalion commander, Colonel Hugh Mitchell of the 51st took command of the brigade.

Wellington appointed Peninsular veterans to senior positions throughout his army and among them was Lieutenant General Sir Lowry Cole who received a division. When he learned of this appointment, Cole wrote to Wellington to ask for some of the regiments he had commanded in Spain – the 7th, 20th, 23rd and 40th Foot – to be placed in his formation. If this was done, Cole would 'feel much gratified and obliged' as their officers were men 'who are well acquainted with me and whose merits I can appreciate'.[7] In response, Wellington, lamenting the fact that he no longer commanded his old Peninsular army, paid the Royal Welch Fusiliers a fine compliment:

> I wish I could bring everything together as I had it when I took leave of the Army at Bordeaux, I would engage that we should not be the last in the race: but as it is I must manage matters as well as I can and you may depend upon it, I will give you as many of your old troops as I can lay my hands upon.
>
> I saw the 23rd the other day and I never saw any regiment in such order. They were not strong [in numbers] but it was the most complete and handsome military body I ever looked at.[8]

Grammont was a pleasant billet. Mitchell was able to carry out an intensive training programme consisting of two to three hours of battalion drill four days a week and brigade level exercises on two days. This work began at dawn but was usually over by 9 a.m. and thereafter the officers and men had much leisure time. MacDonald recorded a typical day for the Welch Fusilier officers:

> We rise every morning at five to exercise the men for the campaign. At eight come home and breakfast, after breakfast take a book from a very good little library in the house and stroll into the garden. Here we romp among the groves & banks till you choose to sit and eat fruit, of which there is the greatest abundance, the same as in England. About two, lounge out [to] pay your visits & return at four to dress for dinner at the mess. At seven we generally ride out in the country for an hour or two, from nine to eleven always with the family, who are never alone, sometimes in one house, sometimes in another.[9]

Private William Wheeler of the 51st Foot commented that the soldier's day was also pleasant:

> As soon as we rise a cup or two of good coffee. Eight o'clock breakfast on bread and butter eggs and coffee. Dinner meat and vegetables, dressed various ways, with beer, afterwards a glass of Hollands grog and tobacco, evening, sallad [*sic*], coffee, etc. then the whole is washed down by a settler with Hollands grog, or beer with a pipe or two, then off to bed.[10]

The soldiers got on well with the civilians on whom they were billeted and helped out the local farmers to the extent that, when the brigade left Grammont, the men 'had weeded the flax and the corn, and the potato crop of that year was entirely of their planting'.[11] Relations of another kind were also common. 'There are some very pretty young women here', Wheeler noted:

> ... some of them are got very much attached to our men, and I doubt not when we move there will be an augmentation in the number of women [with his regiment]. I must here observe that your humble servant does not intend to get entangled with any of them. It might be all very fine in its way and no doubt there are many sweets in having a pretty lovely young woman for a comrade, but then, I know from observation that there is an infinite number of bitters attending it, a soldier should always be able to say when his cap is on, his family is covered, then he is as free as air.[12]

In late May 1815, the soldiers got a change from drill and agriculture when the brigade was ordered to fill in holes and level hills near Grammont for a grand review of the army's mounted troops by Wellington and Field Marshal Blücher, the Prussian commander. This event took place on 23 May and Private Thomas Jeremiah, a fascinated spectator, recorded that when a trumpet sounded the command, 'prepare to mount', all 'was silent as the grave, not a word; we could hear a pin fall when in an instant 18 thousand men were in their saddles and steady'.[13] Major Edwin Griffith from Flintshire, on parade with the 15th Hussars, was more nonchalant, recording that the 'heat of the day was very great, not a cloud in the sky, or a breath of air stirring, all of which added to the brilliancy & beauty of the scene though it roasted us all to death'.[14]

Henry Ellis, a much-decorated veteran wounded many times in action, was regarded with awe by the younger officers in the brigade. He had brought his nephew, Edward Ellis, along as a volunteer and Ensign George Keppel of the 14th Foot, not quite sixteen and with just two months service, learned much about the commanding officer of the 23rd from Edward. Keppel remembered Henry Ellis as 'a light-hearted man, of an affectionate disposition, and much loved by officers and men'.[15] Private Jeremiah echoed these sentiments, describing his battalion commander as a man who was respected by his superiors, loved by his officers and 'feared by his men, so that the whole regiment lived in harmony under his mild administration and although that he ruled with an iron rod, it was covered with velvet'.[16] Jeremiah never forgot the day when two privates of the 23rd, having been sentenced to 300 lashes each by a regimental court martial, were punished. Lest the flogging upset the sensibilities of the local civilians, Ellis marched the battalion out of Grammont into a farm field to carry out the sentence. The first man to be punished, Jeremiah recorded:

> ... one of those hardy Welsh mountaineers who generally have more courage than judgement, received 3 hundred lashes in the usual manner. As terrible as this punishment was it could not as much extract one sigh from this hardy Briton, the next was a man of more delicate feeling for he shouted loud before the lash had touched him but the word was that he cried out in Welsh which caused us all to blush to think that the Irish and English [in the battalion] should ridicule us because that one Welsh could not stand the lash, but to prove them wrong, the man who had already received his punishment volunteered to take this fellows punishment so he should not disgrace the hardy Welsh by cringing from the lash. Our good and kind colonel wisely observing the effect this fellow's conduct had on all the young Welsh lads, caused him to be taken down and took him by the ear and gave him such a kick as became a coward who could not stand his punishment without disgracing his country.[17]

As May turned to June, rumours abounded that the French were on the move. 'We have reports every day about the commencement of the campaign', MacDonald commented, 'but nothing certain.'[18] Given the sympathies of a great part of the Belgian population, Napoleon had accurate intelligence about his opponents and was aware that the allies were preparing to launch a major invasion of France but, as Austria and Russia were still mobilising, he resolved to attack Blücher and Wellington with the object of taking Brussels and gaining time in which he could negotiate a favourable peace. In early June, he concentrated 120,000 men, mostly veteran troops, on the Belgian border to oppose Wellington with about 92,000 men and Blücher with about 113,000. The French emperor stood a good chance of success if he fought each of his opponents separately, but would have considerably less chance if they combined against him. Napoleon's plan was therefore to defeat them in detail and on 15 June 1815 he crossed the River Sambre at Charleroi with the intention placing his force between the two allied armies. Because he had to cover several different axes of advance, Wellington had dispersed his Anglo-Dutch forces across southern Belgium but, when he learned of the French advance late that same day, he issued orders for his scattered units to move to a general rendezvous at Quatre Bras near Charleroi.

At about 8 a.m. on Friday, 16 June 1815, a dispatch rider brought Mitchell orders for his brigade to set out immediately for Enghien, about twenty miles to the east. When Keppel of the 14th Foot, (who must have overslept) appeared on parade that morning, he found his battalion 'in heavy marching order, and all ready for a start'.[19] The Welch Fusiliers were assembled for exercise when Ellis received his marching orders and he gave them ten minutes to collect their kit, advising them to take three days' rations. Most men, Bentinck recalled, 'trusting to the continued kindness of the inhabitants, and little dreaming of the coming needs', did not bother to load themselves with the extra weight of food.[30] 'During this time', remembered Jeremiah, Grammont 'was crowded with horse and foot, regiment after regiment of cavalry and artillery came thundering through the streets, all blazing with anxiety to meet the French this day'.[21]

Mitchell ordered the women of the brigade to be left behind but young Jenny Griffiths, determined to remain with Lewis, appealed to Ellis for permission to accompany her husband. He advised her to return to the depot company in Britain, promising that he would send for all the regimental women once the campaign was over but Jenny obstinately persisted and the good-natured Ellis, impressed by her loyalty, finally said, 'In the name of God go with your husband'... Every indulgence that can be given you shall be given.'[22] Jenny and her nine-month-old daughter were with the 23rd Foot when Mitchell's brigade marched out of Grammont, the drums and fifes of the three battalions playing 'The girl we left behind us', amid the 'cheers of the men and the wailing of the women'.[23]

The day proved to be blazing hot and Ellis gave permission for men to remove their thick, red wool coatees and march in their white fatigue jackets, a cooler garment. When he reached Enghien in the late afternoon, Mitchell received new orders to make for Braine-le-Comte, ten miles to the east and, as the brigade moved in that direction, the sounds of artillery fire could be heard from the south-east. It was dark before it got to Braine, which they marched through before camping overnight in a field on its outskirts. As most of the men had no provisions, they went to sleep hungry that night, after marching nearly thirty miles.

The artillery fire heard during the afternoon of 16 June came from two separate battles being fought that day. Shortly after crossing the Sambre, Napoleon had divided his army, sending Marshal Michel Ney with two of his five corps to seize the vital crossroads at Quatre Bras while he attacked Blücher's army at Ligny, eight miles to the east. After some hard fighting, the emperor managed to defeat Blücher who was forced to retreat but Ney had less success at Quatre Bras where he was stubbornly resisted by a portion of Wellington's troops, who managed to hold this vital position against superior forces. On the morning of 17 June, however, when Wellington learned of Blücher's defeat, he had no choice but to withdraw before Napoleon brought his entire army against him. This order was given in the late morning and the allies moved north to a position that Wellington had selected near the forest of Soignes, about twelve miles south of Brussels. There, he had informed Blücher, he would stand and fight if the Prussian

The Waterloo Campaign, June 1815
As part of Mitchell's Brigade, the 23rd Foot marched from Grammont via Enghien and Braine-le-Comte to Nivelles and then near Waterloo on 16–17 June.
(From J. W. Fortescue, **History of the British Army***)*

commander would send at least one corps to assist him. For his part, Napoleon proved remarkably slow on 17 June and Wellington's withdrawal was not seriously harassed by the French. Convinced the Prussians were retreating to the east, the emperor contented himself with detaching Marshal Emmanuel Grouchy with 33,000 men to follow them while he moved on Brussels with the greater part of his army.

That same day, 17 June 1815, Mitchell's brigade near Braine-le-Comte stood to its arms at dawn and at 6 a.m., resumed its march. The brigade commander had received new orders to head for Nivelles, ten miles to the east, and the marching this day was at first very slow as the route lay along a narrow, secondary road but by midday the brigade reached that town. Nivelles was crowded with troops, civilians and wagons full of wounded from the action at Quatre Bras moving through it in all directions. Mitchell halted for some time in the streets to let a brigade of Belgian cavalry pass through his ranks, thinking they were changing position. In fact, as Wheeler noted, 'they were running away, helter skelter, the Devil take the hindmost' although he and his comrades were delighted when one of the Belgians dropped a purse, which they quickly scooped up.[24] It was nearly mid-afternoon before Mitchell could get clear of Nivelles and, once out of the town, Ellis ordered the Welch Fusiliers to put on their 'fighting coats', the red coatee that was the well known and respected hallmark of British infantry.[25] The brigade now moved north along a good paved road, 'intermixed with Cavalry, guns, stores, and baggage of all descriptions'.[26]

More artillery fire was heard, nearer this time. It was caused by the enemy's dilatory harassment of Wellington's rearguards, which were moving just behind the brigade. It was a hot and humid day and toward evening, a terrific thunderstorm broke and torrential rain poured down on the marching column. 'What a sight', Wheeler of the 51st commented, 'even to we old campaigners, but more particularly to the young soldiers' with the cavalry 'retiring in sullen silence as often as opportunity served would wheel round to check the enemy ... rain beating with violence, guns roaring, repeated bright flashes of lightning attended with tremendous volley of Thunder that shook the very earth and seemed to mock us with contempt.'[27]

The rain was so heavy that 'all we had about us was completely soaked', Jeremiah complained, but that was not 'the greatest of our thoughts, for hunger bites harder than a wet shirt' and the Welch Fusiliers had definitely begun 'to feel the wolf biting'.[28] There was general relief when, in the early evening, the rain not only stopped but the brigade turned off the main road and halted in an extensive field of mature rye. Here it received a liquor ration, or rather half a ration, each officer and man being in turn presented with a little 'tin-pot full' of gin.[29] 'This was poor comfort' after two days of marching without food, remarked Jeremiah, but he found it funny to see some of the Welch Fusiliers, 'for not having anything on the stomach', fall down drunk after taking what amounted to three 'table spoonfuls of spirits'.[30] Questions put to the other troops in the vicinity about the location and the possibility of procuring food brought the response that the brigade was south of Brussels, that a nearby hamlet was called Merbe Braine, and that there might be food in a small town about three miles away with the pleasant English-sounding name of Waterloo.

As soon as the brigade fell out, officers and men began a hunt for something to eat. Wheeler and his comrades made for Waterloo where they used part of the contents of the purse they had acquired to purchase a good supply of bread, cheese, brandy and gin from a storekeeper. Ellis also sent a detail into Waterloo to see if he could procure food for his men and Jenny Griffiths decided to join it:

> I left the baby in the arms of my husband and accompanied them to see if I could get any victuals. I first of all went into a liquor shop to see if I could get some beer and some spirits, but the keeper said he could not spare any, as he had not got a 'tot' for each of the men. ... I went to another

house and saw half a loaf of black bread on the table, not worth twopence-
halfpenny. I asked, 'What do you want for that?' and the woman replied
that I should not have it for one hundred pounds. Dr Smith [Surgeon
Thomas Smith] afterwards saw me and asked what I wanted. I told him
that I had tried to get a quart of beer and a noggin of gin, but I said I should
be satisfied with a pint of beer, as it would make a nice drink for Lewis. Mr
Sealey [probably Quartermaster George Sidley], an officer, said he would
give up his own allowance before I should go without any. Having been
served with a pint of beer and some gin, he asked me if there was anything
else I wanted. I replied that I had wanted some bread. We then went to the
house where I saw the half loaf on the table, and before the woman could
say a word he put his hand in his pocket for a franc piece, flipped it
towards her, and was gone in an instant with the bread, leaving her crying
out that an English officer was robbing her.[31]

Jenny proudly took her shopping back to camp but, when she laid the loaf on the
ground for a minute, someone 'whipped it away', leaving her and Lewis hungry.
At least they had some drink to warm them and it was needed as the rain, which
had ceased for a few hours, 'came again with increased violence, ... accompanied
by thunder and lightning'.[32]

That night the brigade lay on its arms in a muddy field of trodden rye. Young
Ensign Keppel of the 14th Foot, soaked to the skin, tried to stay awake under the
downpour but, at length, stretched himself out in the mud on the slope of a hill,
which 'was like lying in a mountain torrent'.[33] In the lines of the 51st, Wheeler
and his comrades, well fortified with food and liquor, spent the night sitting on
their knapsacks while 'water ran in streams from the cuffs of our Jackets', being,
as one remarked, both 'wet and comfortable'.[34]

The dawn of Sunday, 18 June 1815, came around 4 a.m. About an hour later, the
rain tailed off and, along with the men of two armies, the Welch Fusiliers, soaked
and numb from cold, roused themselves and began to clean their weapons before
standing to arms. Since action this day was likely, the company officers inspected
their men's ammunition to ensure they had sixty dry rounds of ball cartridge and
made good any deficiencies from the supply that accompanied the battalion. After
they were stood down, many men scattered to look for food, some using bayonets
to dig up potatoes in a nearby field, eating them raw, or attempting to cook them,
while others chewed on ears of rye to ease their hunger pangs. Thomas Jeremiah
and a comrade were lucky – not only did they find an abandoned wagon with a
large cask of flour and filled their knapsacks, they also discovered wine, brandy and
some silver coin in the cellar of an empty residence.[35] Drummer Richard Bentinck

was also fortunate for he found some beer in a cottage and drank about a quart of it which filled his stomach 'for a while for it was both a meal and a drink'.[36]

Doors, shutters and furniture from nearby buildings provided fuel, and fires were soon alight, both for warmth and to cook anything acquired. Some of the fusiliers had found a pig, which they slaughtered and began to boil in a camp kettle. They offered a piece to Jenny Griffiths but her stomach rebelled at eating nearly raw meat and she refused it, despite her hunger.[37] Jeremiah mixed his flour with wine and brandy to make cakes which he laid on the cinders of a fire to bake and, very shortly, had 'no less than half the regiment looking as if they would rob me of what I had so much trouble in getting'. He sold one of the half-baked items to an officer for two silver coins but the 'man had not gone many yards before some of his comrade officers robbed him of the greatest part of it'.[38] Mary Baker, wife of Private Richard Baker from Somerset – for Jenny Griffiths was not the only woman with the regiment that day – started some 'taters' boiling in a kettle. A hungry officer asked her for one, which she gave him but shortly afterward, Jenny remembered, when orders came to fall in, 'one of the soldiers kicked over the kettle with the potatoes, and I don't think she got one of them'.[39]

It was now about 9 a.m. and Ellis had the 23rd Foot in battalion column, ready to march. He took the opportunity to ride down the front of his regiment and, as described in the prologue to this book, warn them that action was imminent and exhort them to live up to their fine record earned in many previous battles. Standing near Lewis Griffiths in No. 7 Company was his 17-year-old wife Jenny holding their nine-month-old daughter. Many years later, Jenny recalled that Lewis was not afraid because he was convinced that 'no one would kill him' but two other men in his company, for whom Jenny did washing, said to her, 'You will never have to wash for me again' and these predictions came true.[40] Jenny remained with her husband even after orders came for the battalion to move and when it did, she walked beside him, holding her baby.

The 23rd Foot did not have far to go, about a thousand yards. Earlier that morning Wellington had received Blücher's assurance that he would come to his assistance and Wellington's plan was to fight a defensive battle until the Prussians arrived. He had selected an excellent position to do so – a ridge about three miles long running generally east to west with a fairly steep front slope but a much gentler reverse slope. A lateral country road ran along much of its length which offered a convenient and protected route for the movement of troops and guns. Two major north-south routes intersected this road: the Brussels-Genappe highway at about the centre of the ridge and, to the west, the Nivelles highway. These joined near the farm of Mont St. Jean, some thousand yards to the rear of the ridge. Wellington placed his main line along the ridge but also garrisoned three good defensive positions that lay in front of it. On the left or east flank were several small villages and farms; in the centre beside the Brussels-Genappe highway was the large, enclosed farm of La Haie Sainte; and on the right or western flank bordering the Nivelles highway was the Château de Hougoumont, a substantial collection of farm buildings with an enclosed orchard on its east side. In front of the ridge lay a gentle, shallow valley, about 1,200 yards wide, bordered on its south by a second, higher ridge which was in the possession of the French.

On the morning of 18 June 1815, Wellington had about 73,000 troops and 192 guns, a fairly strong force, but the quality of these troops was variable. In the fight that lay ahead, he could only really count on his 25,000 British and King's German Legion infantry because many of the Belgian, Brunswick, Dutch, Hanoverian and Nassau units were green and untrained. Knowing full well Napoleon's reputation for manoeuvre, he suspected that the emperor might try to move around his right flank. For this reason, he had stationed 17,000 additional troops at Halle about eight miles north-west of Hougoumont, too far distant to be brought into action. Wellington placed his artillery just forward of the crest of the ridge, with good fields of fire to his front, and his infantry and cavalry on its reverse slope, with skirmishers and pickets on its forward slope. His chosen position offered protection for infantry from direct artillery fire while its flanks and front were secured by strongpoints, and the terrain would 'channel' any attack into a very narrow corridor between them. The entire allied line, from the farm hamlets on the east to the western flank beyond the Nivelles highway, was less than three miles in length.

Mitchell's brigade was nominally part of Colville's 4th Division, which had been sent west to Tubize, about three miles south of Halle. As this brigade included two veteran battalions from the Peninsula, the 23rd and 51st Foot, Wellington detached it from its parent formation and used it to buttress his right flank. Five companies of the 51st and the light company of the 14th were placed to the west of the Nivelles road along a continuation of the sunken lane or 'covered way', as it is referred to in most accounts of the battle, that ran behind Hougoumont. The remaining five companies of the 51st Foot were positioned about 200 yards behind in support while the 14th Foot was placed farther to the rear just south of Merbe Braine. The Welch Fusiliers were placed in the second line of the main position on the reverse slope of the ridge, immediately behind Major General Sir John Byng's Guards brigade, whose light companies formed part of the garrison of Hougoumont. Lieutenant Fensham's light company of the 23rd was stationed forward in the covered way behind the château with its right flank on the Nivelles highway, parallel to a company of the 51st, whose left flank rested on it. Immediately upon coming into position, both companies constructed an abattis or barrier of tangled small trees and branches across the highway to discourage its use by French cavalry plainly visible not 500 yards to the south.

It was some time after 9 a.m. when Mitchell's brigade took up its assigned positions. Ellis left the 23rd in column of companies as it was a useful formation

The 23rd Foot at Waterloo, 1815
Stationed on the right flank of the main line, immediately behind Hougoumont,
the regiment's position can be located today by two trees in the immediate vicinity.
Note the profile of the ridge, with a steep angle on its front slope and a gentler
angle on its reverse, which provided protection from French artillery fire during the
action. (*Courtesy Dominique Timmermans and http://napoleon-monuments.eu*)

for movement or deployment – and because there were so many regiments on
the reverse slope, space was at a premium – and told his men to sit. By this time
the rye, nearly five to six feet high in places, had been beaten down by troops,
horses and wagons and mixed with ankle-deep mud from the previous night's
storm to form a wet mat. The sun was out, however, and the ground was
beginning to dry.

Jenny Griffiths still refused to leave her husband. He became exasperated
with her to the point of swearing 'Damme, stand back!' but this only brought
a retort from the young woman that it was not a good time for Lewis to
profane as he might soon appear before his maker.[41] 'Jane', responded Lewis,
'Don't be afraid, and don't be troubled. I may be wounded. Damn the French;
they never made a ball yet that will kill a man.' Ellis came over to the couple
with Surgeon Thomas Smith and the two men finally convinced Jenny to go
to the rear by appealing to her maternal instincts: 'if anything happens to that
baby in your arms you will never forgive yourself'.[42] This tipped the balance
and the young woman reluctantly agreed to accompany Smith to a church
(probably in the nearby village of Braine l'Alleud) where he planned to set
up a dressing station.

After that, there was nothing to do but wait so the Welch Fusiliers sat on the
trampled grain and watched as the allied army came into position. In Jeremiah's
words, it was 'one of the most cheerful and glorious sights that ever a British

soldier saw', to witness thousands of men 'moving with the regularity of a mass line, every regiment moved as steady as if on a parade in St. James's Park'.[43]

About two miles south of where Private Thomas Jeremiah from Pontypool was sitting on wet, muddy ground, Napoleon Bonaparte, emperor of France, was making plans to destroy him and his comrades. Napoleon had about 77,000 men and 266 pieces of artillery that morning but, unlike Wellington's multi-national patchwork quilt of an army, they were almost all veteran troops. He was confident that after the beating he had given them at Ligny two days before, the Prussians were retreating to the east and Grouchy's 33,000 men could occupy them long enough for him to finish off Wellington. When he carried out a reconnaissance of the allied position shortly before 9 a.m., Napoleon was pleased that his enemy had apparently decided to stand and fight. He shrugged off advice from several of his senior officers who had encountered Wellington in battle that it was not wise to attack him on defensive ground of the British general's choosing and that manoeuvre was the best option. Instead, the French commander decided on a massive, straightforward assault on the centre of the ridge, coupled with a subsidiary strike at Hougoumont. These attacks were planned for 9 a.m. but were delayed as some French units had not yet arrived and the wet ground made it difficult to bring artillery into position. Nonetheless, as the time went by, sweating French gunners dragged more than 120 artillery pieces through the mud into positions where their fire could soften up the allied line on the ridge.

For Wellington's army, the wait ended around 11.30 a.m. when, as Keppel of the 14th Foot remembered, 'a single cannon-shot was fired; a pause of two seconds was distinctly perceptible, and then arose a roar of artillery, which did not cease for the next eight hours'.[44] Most of the French artillery fired at the area of the crossroads but several batteries, estimated by one gunner officer stationed on the crest of the ridge, approximately in front of the 23rd Foot, as being twenty-two guns, 'all of which were well served and annoyed us considerably', fired directly at Hougoumont and any troops visible near it.[45] Out of sight on the reverse slope of the ridge, the Welch Fusiliers were not exposed to the full fury of this bombardment but the occasional round shot that came over the crest did bounce through their ranks, killing one officer and a number of men. Ellis therefore formed the battalion in a two-rank line parallel to the ridge so that fewer casualties would be caused by any shot that struck it.[46]

The 14th Foot suffered worse. They had moved closer to Hougoumont when the French attack on the château commenced at about midday. Captain William Turnor of that regiment remembered that, just after the battalion formed square to fend off cavalry should they get through the troops in front, they came under fire from two enemy guns that seemed to concentrate their fire against it.[47] Understandably, Keppel took a very particular interest in these guns, 'heightened by the consciousness that I formed part of that living target against which their practice was pointed'.[48] When French skirmishers engaged the troops defending the covered way, the young officer recorded:

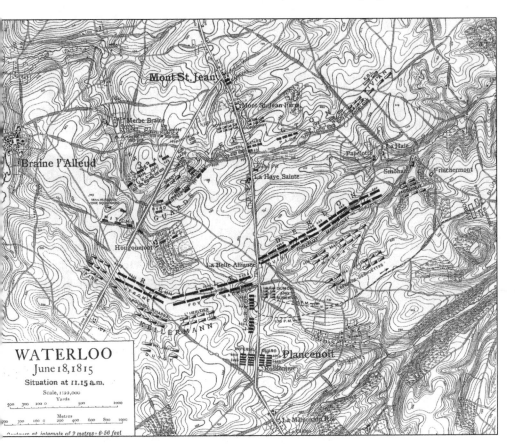

Waterloo, 18 June 1815: Initial Dispositions
From J. W. Fortescue, **History of the British Army**

... a bugler of the 51st, who had been out with the skirmishers, and had mistaken our square for his own, exclaimed, 'Here I am again, safe enough'. The words were scarcely out of his mouth, when a round shot took off his head and spattered the whole battalion with his brains, the colours and the ensigns in charge of them coming in for an extra share. One of them, Charles Fraser, a fine gentleman in speech and manner, raised a laugh by drawling out, 'How extremely disgusting!' A second shot carried off six of the men's bayonets, a third broke the breastbone of a Lance-sergeant (Robinson), whose piteous cries were anything but encouraging to his youthful comrades. The soldier's belief that 'every bullet has its billet', was strengthened by another shot striking Ensign Cooper, the shortest man in the regiment and in the very centre of the square. These casualties were the affair of a second. We were now ordered to lie down.[49]

As Napoleon brought more guns into action the bombardment increased in tempo and continued until about 1.30 p.m. when it lifted for a few moments as the major French attack was delivered against the centre of Wellington's line. By this time, Napoleon had learned that Prussian cavalry, the vanguard of Blücher's army, was visible two miles to the east but, instead of shifting his army to meet this threat, he sent four divisions of infantry, 16,000 bayonets, against the ridge. Initially, they met with some success but a counterattack ordered by Wellington and mounted by Thomas Picton, still wearing his disreputable greatcoat and round hat, threw the French back and their ruin was completed by a devastating charge made by the British heavy cavalry. The irascible Picton was unfortunately killed at the head of his troops, where he would have wished his end to come. The French rallied and came on again, only to be thrown back a second time.

It was now about 3 p.m. and a lull ensued. Wellington took the opportunity to pull the units which had repulsed the recent attack back to the reverse slope of the ridge and shift other units, replacing shaken units with fresh troops. The fighting at Hougoumont had continued almost without pause for nearly three hours and Wellington reinforced the defenders with much of Byng's Guards brigade and moved up the Welch Fusiliers to replace them on the right flank of the main line. They were still positioned on the reverse slope of the ridge and not visible to the French gunners so Ellis re-formed the battalion in column of companies. At about 4 p.m., the French artillery fire, which had tailed off during the previous hour, increased in tempo. Shortly thereafter, a warning was passed along the ridge: 'Prepare to receive cavalry!'

By this time Napoleon had given tactical control of the battle to Marshal Michel Ney. The emperor was becoming increasingly worried about his right flank, where strong columns of Prussian infantry were now visible, moving out of the woods in the direction of the village of Plancenoit. Ney, a brave but rashly aggressive general, decided to mount a massed cavalry attack and nearly four 4,000 horsemen formed to advance on the allied line between La Haie Sainte and Hougoumont, a very narrow front of about 700 yards. The massing of such large numbers of mounted troops was clearly visible to Wellington and he ordered his infantry to form square, and his gunners to fire as long as possible at the cavalry before sheltering with the infantry. On receipt of this order, Ellis formed the Royal Welch Fusiliers into a square, four ranks deep on all sides, with the first two ranks kneeling.

Shortly after 4 p.m., the French cavalry advanced and there was much relief in the allied ranks when they did so, as the enemy guns ceased firing. Those men on the ridge who could see into the valley, were entranced by the grandeur of the scene as thousands of mounted troops wearing blue, white, green and red uniforms moved in squadrons toward them. The left flank units of the oncoming cavalry were from Napoleon's Imperial Guard, the Chasseurs à Cheval in green and the Chevaux-léger-lanciers in red. As they came over the brow of the hill, the gunners fired a last round and then ran back to the squares with their loading implements, throwing themselves flat on the ground in front of their infantry comrades. Having passed the guns, the French horsemen now flowed around the squares. It was 'at this trying moment', recalled Jeremiah, that Ellis told the Welch Fusiliers 'to wait well for his word of command and which was strictly obeyed until they were within 30 or 40 paces of us when we opened a most destructive fire' on the green and red clad horsemen.[50] Drummer Bentinck, serving with the Grenadier Company, remembered it this way:

> We had to form a square pretty quick against them and they came up to us within about twenty yards. The Colonel gave us orders not to fire on them until he gave the orders. There they gazed on us on all sides but when they found that they could not enter they turned round to go back. We then got orders to open fire on them and we shot a great many horses from under them. We took a number of men prisoner but did not kill that many.[51]

Always keeping at least half the muskets on any one face of the square loaded, Ellis then fired by half companies at the horsemen who, unwilling to impale themselves on the bristling bayonets, contented themselves with riding around the perimeter of the square, some of the lancers futilely jabbing with their weapons at the infantry. Then, having accomplished nothing, the French rode back over the ridge; the allied gunners returned to their weapons and fired canister at them as they withdrew. When the enemy cavalry were gone, however, the French guns started up again and their fire was very effective against infantry in squares, even if the enemy gunners could not always see their targets.

For this reason, there was relief when the French returned and the artillery ceased. This time they were cuirassiers and carabineers – big men on big horses wearing steel or brass helmets and chest armour – as well as light cavalry. Captain Cavalié Mercer, whose troop of horse artillery had just come into position about 250 yards east of the Welch Fusiliers, has left a graphic description of this attack:

> On they came in compact squadrons, one behind the other, so numerous that those of the rear were still below the brow [of the hill] when the head of the column was but at some sixty or seventy yards from our guns. Their pace was a slow but steady trot. None of your furious galloping charges was this, but a deliberate advance, at a deliberate pace, as of men resolved to carry their point. They moved in profound silence, and the only sound that could be heard from them amidst the incessant roar of battle was the low thunder-like reverberation of the ground beneath the simultaneous tread of so many horses...
>
> I thus allowed them to advance unmolested until the head of the column might have been about fifty or sixty yards from us, and then gave the word, 'Fire!' The effect was terrible. Nearly the whole leading rank fell at once; and the round-shot, penetrating the column carried confusion throughout its extent.[52]

The surviving cuirassiers rode around the squares – Bentinck watched as they 'drew up looking for a gap in the line of bayonets bristling before them' but at 'every shoulder hunched a comrade and each soldier stood like a rock'.[53] The French horsemen circled around and, after Ellis gave the order to fire, Bentinck noted that few of the French were killed 'though some were knocked down off their mounts by the force of the bullets which were unable to penetrate chain mail or brass'. When the cuirassiers wheeled away, Ellis put another volley into them and Bentinck 'counted upwards of 40 poor horses left lying on the plain, besides many that could not limp away'. It was a hard battle on horses and Jack Hill lost his mount, 'Honesty', when a roundshot 'carried off a fore leg, a shell destroyed the saddle but did not kill, he got also a musket shot in the chest & poor fellow he bled to death'.[54]

Once the enemy cavalry had withdrawn, the bombardment resumed and the Welch Fusiliers began to suffer a steady stream of casualties from round shot and shells: Major Joseph Hawtyn, commanding the Grenadier Company, and Captain Charles Jolliffe, commanding No. 8 Company, were killed, while Regimental Sergeant-Major David Morrissey, Lieutenant John Clyde of No. 3 Company and Sergeant John Hudson of No. 1 Company were mortally wounded. The gaps in the ranks were closed up by the officers and NCOs and the dead dragged out of the square, while the wounded were brought into its centre. Assistant Surgeon John Monroe did what he could for them until such time as they could be evacuated to extemporised dressing stations set up in nearby villages and farmhouses.

It was not long before the French were back. This time, Mercer commented, their attack was preceded by 'a cloud of skirmishers, who galled us terribly by a fire of carbines and pistols at scarcely forty yards from our front'.[55] Again, the horsemen surrounded the squares, taking casualties but unable to do anything more. Ellis had his battalion well in hand, delivering the rate of fire he saw fit on the targets he saw fit to choose, always keeping loaded muskets ready – just in case. When the French withdrew, the gunners again returned to work, firing canister into their retreating ranks.

About a hundred cuirassiers, understandably reluctant to risk this gauntlet of fire, tried to escape by riding south along the Nivelles road. They encountered the abattis the light companies had constructed and immediately came under heavy and accurate aimed fire from the road's defenders. Lieutenant Alexander Brice, who had assumed command of the Welch Fusilier light company after Lieutenant George Fensham had been killed, believed that 'scarcely a man succeeded in making his escape'.[56] Private William Wheeler, who was with the 51st company on the other side of the Nivelles road, agreed with this assessment as he 'went to see the effects our fire had, and never before beheld such a sight in as short a space, as about an hundred men and horses could be [seen] huddled together, there they lay'.[57]

Again, the French cavalry came up the ridge, slower this time but accompanied by horse artillery and skirmishers to soften up the allied gunners and infantry.

Ellis had just shouted to his men, 'Remember the old times boys, this is their last try', when he was hit in the chest and reeled in the saddle.[58] 'Feeling himself faint from loss of blood', an eyewitness recorded, Ellis 'calmly desired an opening might be made in the square, and rode to the rear but a short distance from the field he was thrown from his horse while in the act of leaping a ditch'.[59] He was later found and taken to a nearby house to have his wound dressed. Dalmer assumed command of the 23rd, which again came under artillery fire as the cavalry withdrew.

They returned yet again and the entire business was repeated, with no more success for the French than before. It was possibly during this charge that Jack Hill was hit. As he commented:

> I went to the front face of the square, in order to try to bring some musket fire to bear on the Enemy, in endeavouring to get through the close ranks I got the grape shot [actually canister] in my shoulder & five other wounds in my face. I knew when I got the bullets in my face but do not recall when the grape hit me. When I fell & they came round me & said 'he has got a ball through his right eye'. Col Dalmer asked me some questions, I said I had got just as much as I could carry off, & that I thought pretty nearly enough to finish me.[60]

Believed to be mortally wounded, Hill was carried to the rear.

Although they were doing their best to kill them, many in Wellington's army admired the bravery of their opponents. 'The French fought with desperation', Turnor of the 14th remarked, and the cavalry 'particularly distinguished themselves, and charged our infantry when in squares of battalions, four, five, six times, but they were not to be broken'.[61] At one point, in the middle of one of the attacks, a British officer remembered shouting, 'By God! those fellows deserve Bonaparte, they fight so nobly for him' and later wrote that 'I had rather have fallen that day as a British infantry-man, or as a French cuirassier, than die ten years hence in my bed.'[62] In all, Ney eventually sent sixty-seven squadrons from twenty regiments – nearly 9,000 sabres – at Wellington's line and there is no reliable record as to how many charges these men made. Estimates range from three to more than twenty but there is, however, general agreement that the cavalry attacks ceased at about 6 p.m.

Shortly after the French horsemen withdrew for the last time, Ney succeeded in taking the farmhouse of La Haie Sainte, placing Wellington in a difficult position. At the same time, a strong force of French infantry, cavalry and light artillery put in a last attack on Hougoumont, where there had been nearly constant fighting for six hours. Part of this force moved east of the château toward the ridge and, as Lieutenant Robert Holmes of the Welch Fusiliers recalled, the 23rd and 71st Foot advanced some way down the forward slope to meet it:

I only recollect one attack of Infantry (in column) during the day, which did not alter our formation. Some Regiment in our rear, I think the 71st, deployed into line and advanced with the 23rd Square (a [71st] wing on each flank) some distance down the slope of the hill. The [French] Infantry having given way a charge of Cavalry immediately followed. The [71st] Regiment in line ran into square to our right, a little in advance and nearer to the garden of Hougoumont.[63]

The enemy having been repelled and the two battalions coming under heavy artillery fire as well as musketry from the area of Hougoumont, they resumed their former position on the ridge.

It was now approaching 7 p.m. and Wellington's army was exhausted. Its spirits, however, were cheered by the sight of Prussian troops attacking the village of Plancenoit, two miles south-east. Blücher's army, delayed by bad roads, had been slow to arrive but Napoleon no longer had any doubt that his object of defeating the two allied armies separately had utterly failed and that he was facing a disaster. His best option at this point would have been to withdraw, link up with Grouchy and hope for better things on another day. Instead, he decided to make one last attack with his best troops, the Imperial Guard, most of which had been held in reserve, in a final attempt to break Wellington's army.

In preparation, the French artillery increased their rate of fire and heavy enemy masses were observed moving down into the valley in front. At about 7.30 p.m., preceded by a thick screen of skirmishers and supported on their flanks by such cavalry and infantry as could be collected, eight battalions of the finest infantry in the French army moved steadily in columns toward the ridge, their drums beating the insistent rhythm of the *pas de charge*. Three battalions halted but five continued up the front slope of the ridge, taking heavy casualties from allied artillery. Fully expecting that Napoleon would at some point commit these veteran troops, Wellington had positioned some of his best remaining units to meet them and what followed was a repetition of so many battles in the Peninsula where unshaken British infantry in line defeated French infantry, even superb infantry, in column.

The attack failed totally and the repulse of the Imperial Guard broke the spirit of Napoleon's army. It began to stream southward down the highway to Genappe, completely routed, just as the Prussians broke through at Plancenoit. Wellington now ordered a general advance and his weary soldiers pushed on as far as Rossomme, a distance of about four miles. At this point, about 9.30 p.m. the Prussians took over the pursuit and gleefully harassed the wretched French throughout the night, destroying any possibility of Napoleon re-organising his army. The emperor escaped on horseback and arrived at Paris two days later where he attempted to raise a new army. In ten hours of heavy fighting he had lost all his artillery and 36,000 soldiers killed, wounded and captured. Allied losses were not nearly as high; Wellington suffering about 15,000 killed and wounded and Blücher about 7,000 losses.

The Welch Fusiliers took no part in the repulse of the Imperial Guard although they were able to catch occasional glimpses of it through the smoke. When the order came to advance, recorded Lieutenant Holmes, the battalion 'deployed and advanced in line; but finding nothing to oppose us, we wheeled by Companies to the right and moved in column' to a point about 300 yards short of the inn of Belle Alliance on the southern ridge.[64] Bentinck remembered that the battalion captured many prisoners during this time, and being very hungry, he 'opened one of the prisoners knapsacks to see what I could get and I found two loaves of bread. I took them and gave one to my comrades and ate the other myself.'[65]

Although they were not as heavily engaged as many other regiments at Waterloo, the Welch Fusiliers' losses were not light. Of the 711 officers and men present with the Colours that morning, 14 had been killed and 87 wounded, or about 14 per cent of the unit. Among the wounded were the commanding officer, the second major and Private Lewis Griffiths of No. 7 Company. By any standard the 23rd Foot had done its duty and done it well – holding the right flank of the main line throughout the latter stages of the battle – and it was an exhausted and hungry battalion that camped on the slope of a ridge where Napoleon had stood during the day. It is quite possible that their bivouac that night resembled that of another British battalion at the end of the battle, which an officer found fast asleep 'wrapped in their blankets with their knapsacks for pillows' and there 'they lay in regular ranks, with the officers and sergeants in their places, just as they would stand when awake'.[66]

One hopes that the fusiliers slept soundly as the aftermath of Waterloo was dreadful. Nearly 52,000 men lay dead and wounded in an area of about six square miles and the shooting had hardly ended before the scavengers – soldiers, camp followers and civilians – moved among them, looking for loot and plunder. Most of the men lying on the ground were French, as the allied wounded were the first to be removed but no such succour was available for the enemy. In their extremity, many begged passing British soldiers to kill them to relieve their pain – 'Ah, Monsieur, tuez moi donc! Tuez moi, pour l'amour de Dieu!'[†] – but it was nearly three days before those who survived received medical attention.[67] The allied wounded were more fortunate as the army and the people of Brussels transported many into that city, where they received treatment in its hospitals.

When the battle was over, Jenny Griffiths searched for Lewis only to be told that he had been hit and taken to Brussels. She picked up her baby and walked to that place to find him:

† 'Sir, please shoot me! Shoot me, for the love of God!'

I searched for him all Sunday night, but saw no sign of him. Then all day on Monday I went through about 300 rooms where the wounded soldiers lay, but I could not find him, not withstanding numbers told me they had seen him coming. On Tuesday morning [20 June 1815] I found out that there were some hospitals I had not visited, so I went through them nearly all without success. I then went to the Elizabeth Hospital, and as I went up one flight of the stairs I saw a Sergeant Stanley [Sergeant Thomas Winstanley] and his wife. His wife said to me, 'Now you are here sit down and have your breakfast'. I replied, 'No, I will not take bit nor sup until I know whether Lewis Griffiths is dead or alive'. 'Well, then', she said, 'you must not leave me until Stanley gets his returns, and then you will know who is killed and who is alive'. She then went down stairs; and who should she meet but Lewis Griffiths, who had heard that I had come there for him. She left him outside the door, and came in and said, 'Well, I have heard that your husband has gone to Antwerp'. 'Then I will go too', I said, 'I will never taste anything until I have seen whether he is alive or not'. He then opened the door and entered the room. The little baby said, 'Da-da', and I then saw it was my husband.[68]

Jenny remembered that, when she first saw her husband again, he looked different, as 'when he went into the battle his face was as red as a rose, but it was now as white as paper'. Griffiths had been hit in the shoulder by a musket ball which had shattered, and the surgeons had extracted seven fragments from his wound. The re-united family remained in Brussels for a month while Lewis convalesced.

Jack Hill, believed to be mortally wounded, amazingly survived and three weeks after the battle, was well enough to describe his wound in a letter:

The 4¾ ounce ball (iron grape) entered under the collarbone & came out through the blade bone behind. The wound behind is beginning to heal & the discharge is trifling, the front wound still continues to discharge very much. He is a most confounded ugly fellow, with a nasty red & bazomed face as big as a tea cup. I have had a great deal to do to keep body & soul together, & have never yet been out a bed, except when assisted by these people for the Doctors to dress me twice a day. ...

In case I get over this, I think I shall make a campaign at the Horse Guards & try what they will do for me. I think it most probable I shall get '[£]300 a year for this wound, as I do not conceive it possible that the arm can be reestablished.[69]

Henry Ellis was not as fortunate. During the night of 19 June, the hut in which he was laying caught fire and, although he was rescued by Assistant Surgeon John Monroe, the shock was too much and Ellis died two days after the battle. His last words, according to an anonymous Welch Fusilier officer – probably Surgeon

Monroe – were 'I am happy – I am content – I have done my duty.'[70] He was mourned by every officer and man in the 23rd Foot and the same correspondent remembered how one private reacted:

> Among several of the soldiers of his regiment, who were at the farmhouse with him, mortally wounded, and inquiring anxiously after their Colonel, there was one who supported a very bad character, and he had been frequently punished. To this man I said, to learn his attachment, – 'He is just dead; but why should you care? You cannot forget how oft he caused your back to be bared?' 'Sir', replied he, his eyes assuming a momentary flash and his cheek a passing glow, 'I deserved the punishment, else he would never have punished me'. With these words, he turned his head a little from me, and burst into tears'.[71]

Colonel Sir Henry Walton Ellis was buried with full military honours at the base of the windmill in Braine l'Alleud, a nearby village. Ellis had never married but did have a relationship with a woman named Elizabeth Gore, by whom he had two sons. He left the greater part of his estate to them and ironically, one of the men named in his will as a guardian for his eldest son was Major Francis Offley, killed at Salamanca nearly three years before. Henry Ellis was thirty-two at the time of his death.

On the day after the battle, Blücher and Wellington began their advance on Paris. Mitchell's brigade was ordered to march to Nivelles, a tedious journey as nearly the whole of Wellington's army was moving down one road. Ensign Keppel recalled with amusement that when the 14th Foot entered Nivelles, many of the young Buckinghamshire lads 'had decked themselves in the spoils of the vanquished, and presented a motley group of Imperial cuirassiers, hussars, and grenadiers a cheval' with one young man wearing the 'cumbrous' and profusely-decorated hat of a tambour major, or drum major.[72]

The army moved, by way of Mons, Valenciennes and Le Cateau, to Cambrai – names which would become all too familiar to a later generation of British soldiers – until 23 June when a halt was called to give straggling units a chance to catch up. Lieutenant John MacDonald took the opportunity to let his family know that he had survived the battle of Waterloo:

> I have but a moment to inform you that I am still in the land of the living after one of the most glorious actions that the English Army ever fought. I am quite distressed that I have not been able to write home but I hope you will not lose a moment to inform them of the reason, for I assure [you] we have been marching or in motion from twelve to fourteen hours

every day since we left Grammond [*sic*] & the weather is quite wet, and we have not a particle of baggage, indeed I am much afraid our regiments [baggage] is lost as we had further to come than any other part of the Army, and of course were the last.[73]

Wellington now had to deal with the French frontier fortresses and Colville's division was tasked with taking Cambrai. Colville decided to try a surprise escalade rather than a formal siege and sent two of his brigades to one side of the city to carry out the actual attack, and Mitchell's brigade to the other to make a feint. John MacDonald recounts what happened:

> We entered this city last night at eight o'clock by Escalade & felt proud in our being the first regiment in the square, which however occasioned us to remain as guards all night, after a very handsome compliment by General Colville, to protect this town. We entered with very little loss as nothing can stop our fellows now. We got over two parapets and a dry & wet ditch with amazing rapidity, placed the Ladder and was in the city before any of the [divisional] staff had any idea of our having arrived at the outerworks, as we were only intended to have made a feint.[74]

The governor and garrison withdrew to the citadel where they negotiated a surrender that took place on 25 June. Private Wheeler of the 51st recorded that 'His pottle belly' Louis XVIII was on hand for the ceremony and 'blubbered' over the citizens of the town 'like a big girl for her bread and butter, called them his children, told them a long rigmarole of nonsense about France, and his family, about his heart, and about their hearts, how he had always remembered them in his prayers, and I don't know what'.[75]

Wellington enjoyed similar success with the other fortresses and those that did not surrender were simply blockaded by second line troops while the main army moved towards the French capital. By this time, Blücher's Prussians had taken the lead in what had become a race to be the first to get to Paris. Blücher, however, enjoyed the advantage of being able to supply his army by requisition, or simply taking what he needed from the countryside while Wellington, as had been his custom in the Peninsula, issued strict orders about the correct treatment of civilians. These orders were backed up by provost marshals who were quick to punish any soldier found looting and who, as Keppel remarked, were unpopular with both officers and men. The young officer remembered the time one of these detested men rode by his battalion, to a great deal of 'hissing, hooting, and yelling'.[76]

> [Keppel] looked round to see the object of such universal execration, and beheld, mounted on a grey pony, a hideous-looking man with an enormous head, a pale pasty complexion, small cunning grey eyes, and a disagreeable expression of countenance. His cocked hat, silk sash, and silver epaulette bespoke him to be an officer, but no dress could have

made him look like a gentleman. It was the Provost Marshal. He was accompanied by half a dozen drummers who held on to his horse by straps attached to his saddle. They were in the lightest marching order, carrying nothing but their drum cases, which were slung across their shoulders. These, I was told, contained either cat-o'-nine-tails or some well-soaped ropes with nooses all ready for immediate use.[77]

By the end of June, commented MacDonald, the 23rd Foot were starting to look and feel a little worn:

We have spent a miserable ten days since this campaign commenced, we have been marching so rapidly that we have never seen our baggage. Conceive an unfortunate Christian marching twelve to fourteen hours every day, sleeping without any covering in a wet field, raining regularly every night, not able to cook any provisions, should you be so fortunate to find any, which with such immense armies is not very easy, without a change of linen and beards like turks. With all this you can hardly form an idea of the figures we were yesterday in entering here, still the army all healthy and need hardly add in the best spirits.[78]

On 3 July 1815, MacDonald noted that the Welch Fusiliers were only four miles from Paris and 'the army will be much disappointed if they do not take it by storm, though for my part I hope not'.[79] The French capital surrendered on the following day and, although it was several months before the last of the troops loyal to Napoleon laid down their arms, the war finally came to a definite end.

As for Napoleon Bonaparte, the man who had disturbed the peace of Europe for so long, he was rejected by his own people. Four days after Waterloo, he was forced to abdicate and fled to Rochefort in western France, hoping to find a vessel on which to escape to the United States. Instead he found a British ship of the line, HMS *Bellerophon*, and surrendered to her captain, handing him a letter for the Prince Regent seeking protection from 'the most powerful, the most constant and the most generous of my enemies'.[80] The British government's response was to exile him on the South Atlantic island of St. Helena, where he died in 1821.

Between 1792 and 1815, it has been estimated that nearly six million people in Europe and elsewhere died from the nearly incessant series of wars.[81] For Britain, it has been calculated that in 240 months or twenty years of actual fightin between February 1793 and July 1815, 210,000 soldiers and sailors lost their lives. Adjusted for population size, this mortality rate is nearly comparable to British losses in the First World War.[82] Thus, if for no other reason, the conflict waged by Britain during those long and bloody years can with some considerable justification be called the Great War with France.

Come all you jolly soldier-boys and listen unto me,
While I sing to you a story of warlike history.
And the glories of a Regiment I will to you unfold,
Old Cambria's pride, her Fusiliers, and Britain's boast of old.

At Bunker's Hill and Guildford, where every foot of ground,
Was covered by a deadly fire from lurking ambush found;
The Fusiliers closed up their ranks and manfully came on,
But mourn'd o'er smitten comrades when the feaful work was done.

O then, my lads, let's prove to all tha twe are well inclined,
To uphold the reputation of the gallant Corps we've joined,
Be obedient to your Officers, and orderly in town,
Be a credit to your Regiment, and shame offenders down.[1]

'The deeds of the good old Fusiliers done due justice'

The Fates of Men, a Woman and a Regiment, 1815–2010

THE CAMP OF THE BRITISH ARMY at Paris was situated outside the city in a lovely wooded area, the Bois de Boulogne, near the River Seine. Although officers could freely enter the French capital, only 100 men per battalion were permitted to visit it each day and they had to be back in their lines by sunset. Drummer Richard Bentinck, who went several times to gaze at the sights, found the inhabitants 'very civil' but 'did not entirely escape the gay dissipation for which they have always been so notorious'.[2] On the other hand, Parisians were frequent visitors to the British camp and Bentinck thought some of the 'young lasses' were 'truly the most engaging devils I ever saw'. Well housed and well fed, Wellington's men were in good spirits in the summer of 1815.

The 23rd Foot spent nearly six months outside Paris. In November, Captain John Harrison joined from Britain with new Colours and Drummer Bentinck remembered that on the evening of the day the Colours arrived they were 'wetted' so freely 'with grog that some of the men did not stand exactly in line on the morning's parade'.[3] It is likely that Harrison brought the Goat with him as, hostilities being ended, the four-legged pride of the Welch Fusiliers could now resume his rightful place at the head of the regiment.

In the autumn of that year, the Royal Welch Fusiliers received a unique honour when a General Order was issued directing that 'each non-commissioned officer and Soldier of the Regular Army shall be provided with a book, calculated to shew the actual state of his accounts'.[4] A sample of the proper form and how it was to be completed was included with the order and it was filled in as follows: 'Thomas Atkins, Private, No. 6 Company, 1st Batt. 23d Regt. Foot'. Where born, 'Parish of Odiham, Hants'.[5] In the years that followed, the name 'Thomas Atkins' was invariably used in the directions for filling out military paperwork, and through frequent usage became 'Tommy Atkins' or 'Tommy', the universal nickname of the British soldier. There have been a number of theories advanced as to why the 23rd Foot was honoured in this manner but the most plausible is that Lieutenant

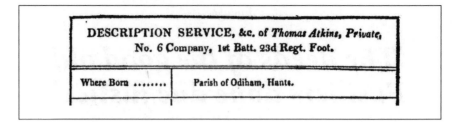

DESCRIPTION SERVICE, &c. of *Thomas Atkins, Private,*
No. 6 Company, 1st Batt. 23d Regt. Foot.

Where Born .... | Parish of Odiham, Hants.

Tommy Atkins – Royal Welch Fusilier
The section of the soldier's paybook, first introduced in 1815, which shows Private Thomas Atkins – first of the name – as being a member of the 23rd Foot. Of the many theories advanced as to why the regiment was chosen for this singular honour, the most probable is that the officer who promulgated this document – Lieutenant General Harry Calvert, the Adjutant-General of the Army – was a former Welch Fusilier officer. (*Courtesy Richard Sinnett*)

General Sir Harry Calvert, the Adjutant-General, whose department was responsible for the 1815 order, had served in the 23rd Foot from 1778 to 1790.[6] Thus, it could be argued that the first 'Tommy' was a Royal Welch Fusilier – at least on paper.

In January 1816, as part of the British occupation army in France, the 23rd Foot moved to the area around Valenciennes, being billeted in villages outside that town. As the first anniversary of Waterloo approached, the officers gave much thought to the best way of celebrating the event but decided against holding a full-scale banquet 'as it might appear as if we meant to crow over and insult the feelings of the French'.[7] Instead, they settled on marking the occasion 'in a jovial but not in a tumultuous manner', with horse races, 'gambols', a champagne picnic on the grass and dancing. 'Every thing went off in excellent style', one officer recorded, and about sixty people 'sat down to dinner, when many appropriate toasts, and songs to correspond, were given'. The regimental band provided the music and it is likely that Bentinck, – who had given up his drum after he had been made a private but remained a member of the band – was present, playing a serpent, a precursor of the modern tuba. Dancing, which commenced after the dinner, 'was kept up with great spirit' and 'as soon as the English Ladies retired, the village girls threw off their sabots, and tripped it until a late hour'.[8]

One of the songs sung that evening was a specially-composed tribute to Colonel Ellis but the Royal Welch Fusiliers also preserved his memory in a more substantial form. Every officer, NCO and private soldier in the regiment voluntarily gave up one day's pay toward the £1,200 cost of a magnificent monument to their beloved commanding officer, which was placed in Worcester Cathedral. The work of John Bacon the younger, who had completed similar projects in St. Paul's Cathedral, it portrays Ellis in the act of falling, mortally wounded, from his horse while an angel stands behind holding a laurel wreath over his head and a fusilier kneels alongside. It was the Welch Fusiliers' tribute of their 'respect and affection to the memory of a leader, not more distinguished for valour and conduct in the field, than beloved for every generous and social virtue'.[9]

So time passed – actually rather pleasantly – for the Welch Fusiliers until 23 August 1817 when the kindly Lieutenant Colonel Thomas Dalmer retired. The enlisted fusiliers, Private Bentinck prominent among them, were aghast when his replacement turned out to be none other than Colonel Thomas Pearson, that ferocious martinet but fine fighting soldier whom they had last seen at Aldea da Ponte in September 1811. In the intervening years, Pearson had rendered distinguished service in British North America, fighting in the four bloodiest battles of the northern theatre of the American war and being wounded in two of them. Pearson's last wound, a musket ball in the head, had put him out of action for nearly a year but now he was back, slightly battered but as determined as ever to maintain the strictest discipline. As Bentinck commented, he wasted no time – when two fusiliers were late coming on parade at Pearson's first inspection, they went before a regimental court martial which awarded them 200 lashes each. 'When the flogging was over', Bentinck lamented, Pearson issued a warning: 'I have only opened one eye yet; I'll warm your jackets if I have to open the other. If you behave yourselves I'll be as good as Colonel Ellis, if you don't, I will be the Devil himself.'[10]

Bentinck, who firmly believed that Pearson was the devil incarnate, may have exaggerated but there is no doubt that under his command, the Royal Welch Fusiliers became an exemplary regiment. The general officers who carried out its annual inspections during Pearson's time in command were, without exception, laudatory. As one of many examples, consider the comments made by Major General Sir Colquhoun Grant after inspecting the regiment in June 1823:

> A most exact and strictly enforced discipline is maintained in this excellent Corps, which in parade appearance, and field manoeuvre, is not perhaps to be surpassed by any Battalion in the British service. ...
>
> It will suffice to say that numerous as my inspections have been for the last three years, I have seen no corps surpass and scarcely any equal the Fusiliers, in appearance, movements and discipline.[11]

Pearson may have been an ogre – at least to soldiers such as Richard Bentinck – but he was apparently a jovial member of the officers' mess. Captain George Beauclerk, who served with the 23rd Foot in the late 1820s, characterised his comrades 'as sincere, warm, and attached' men 'as ever pushed the merry bottle round a mess-table'. 'To see the splendid and truly hospitable board' of the mess, Beauclerk enthused, 'laden with its costly plate, and surrounded by such a blaze of manly perfection, arrayed in the splendid uniform of the corps, and to hear the merry laugh and joke pass round in harmony, while good humour still lurked among the dregs of the last bottle was one of the most exhilarating and gratifying sights that the eye of a British soldier can witness'. Beauclerk praised Pearson for 'encouraging the social union of the mess-table, without endeavouring to check that liberal and independent conversation'.[12]

In November 1818, the 23rd Foot left France for Ireland where it served for five years before being posted to Gibraltar, and there it remained until 1830, except for a brief one-year deployment to Portugal. When the regiment received new Colours in 1826, they bore most of its recent Battle Honours: 'MARTINIQUE 1809', 'ALBUHERA',[†] 'BADAJOZ', 'SALAMANCA', 'VITTORIA', 'PYRENEES', NIVELLE', 'ORTHES', 'TOULOUSE', 'PENINSULA', and, of course, 'WATERLOO'. The 23rd had earlier received 'EGYPT' and the 'SPHINX', and when an Honour for 'CORUNNA' was promulgated in 1835, it was added to the Colours. The Welch Fusiliers' application for 'CIUDAD RODRIGO', was refused, however, by the Horse Guards, as although they were present at that siege, they did not participate in the actual assault.

In July 1830 Pearson was promoted to major general and bade goodbye to the regiment in which he had served for twenty-seven years. In a farewell letter to the officers, the irascible Pearson came perilously close to betraying evidence of humanity when he assured them that, 'in those instances when in the execution of public duty I may intentionally have given pain, the fault has proceeded from the head, and not from the heart'.[13] Be that as it may, it is certain that there was many a dry eye among the soldiers on the day the old fire-breather turned over command. Thomas Pearson was the last of the five young officers commissioned in the late 1790s – Thomas Dalmer, Henry Ellis, Jack Hill, Francis Offley and Pearson himself – who had led the Welch Fusiliers through their hardest wartime fighting. Ellis and Offley had been killed in action while Dalmer and Hill had, by 1830, left the service.

Pearson's replacement was Lieutenant Colonel John Harrison. Harrison had joined the regiment in 1805 and had fought in Denmark, Copenhagen and the Peninsula, being so badly wounded at Badajoz in 1812 that he lost the use of his right arm and received a disability pension of £100 per annum for his suffering. When he took command in 1830 there were still ten officers serving who had seen action during the Great War with France: Harrison, Major William Ross, Captains George Feilding and Robert Holmes, Lieutenants Edward Ellis, John Enoch and William A. Griffiths, Surgeon Thomas Smith, Quartermaster Garrett Moore and Paymaster George Dunn. Of these, the oldest was Moore who had enlisted as a private in 1798 and had been commissioned in 1827. With the exception of Surgeon Smith and Edward Ellis, all these men had been wounded, some severely. Edward Ellis, the nephew of Henry Ellis, had fought at Waterloo as a volunteer and had been commissioned after the battle.[14]

---

† The correct spelling, of course, is Albuera but apparently some clerk at the Horse Guards got it wrong and, as a result, the battle has frequently been spelled Albuhera in the English-speaking world. The same case holds true for the Battle Honours, VITTORIA and ORTHES, which properly should be spelled Vitoria and Orthez.

In 1831, when the regiment was stationed in Ireland, Harrison read a book that made him think 'myself young again'.[15] This was the third volume of William Napier's *History of the War in the Peninsula*, which contained a description of the Battle of Albuera. As Harrison wrote to his mother:

> We are jogging on here in a tolerable smooth way, myself with more occupation and responsibility than ever, which compels me to put in motion all the benefit of my past experience and the little activity I have left in my 44th year in my crippled crazy frame, which bye the bye I feel a little pride in, notwithstanding, when perusing the 3rd volume of Napier's work, just come out, to see the deeds of the good old Fusiliers done due justice to in history. You should read what he says of our conduct when grappling with the Flower of the French Army at Albuera.[16]

The passage which excited Harrison's enthusiasm was Napier's description of the attack of the Fusilier Brigade at Albuera. Although not strictly accurate in terms of historical fact, it is nonetheless a remarkably fine and justifiably famous piece of prose:

> Such a gallant line, issuing from the midst of the smoke, and rapidly separating itself from the confused and broken multitude, startled the enemy's heavy masses, which were increasing and pressing onwards as to an assured victory: they wavered, hesitated, and then vomiting forth a storm of fire, hastily endeavoured to enlarge their front, while a fearful discharge of grape from all their artillery whistled through the British ranks. Myers was killed, Cole, the three colonels, Ellis, Blakeney, and Hawkshawe, fell wounded, and the fuzileer battalions, struck by the iron tempest, reeled, and staggered like sinking ships. But suddenly and sternly recovering, they closed on their terrible enemies, and then was seen with what a strength and majesty the British soldier fights. In vain did Soult, by voice and gesture, animate his Frenchmen; in vain did the hardiest veterans, extricating themselves from the crowded columns, sacrifice their lives to gain time for the mass to open out on such a fair field; in vain did the mass itself bear up, and fiercely striving, fire indiscriminately upon friends and foes, while the horsemen hovering on the flank threatened to charge the advancing line. Nothing could stop that astonishing infantry. No sudden burst of undisciplined valour, no nervous enthusiasm, weakened the stability of their order; their flashing eyes were bent on the dark columns in their front, their measured tread shook the ground, their dreadful volleys swept away the head of every formation, their deafening shouts overpowered the dissonant cries that broke from all parts of the tumultuous crowd, as slowly and with a horrid carnage, it was pushed by the incessant vigour of the attack to the farthest edge of the height. There, the French reserve, mixing with the struggling multitude, endeavoured to

sustain the fight, but the effort only increased the irremediable confusion, the mighty mass gave way and like a loosened cliff went headlong down the steep. The rain flowed after in streams discoloured with blood, and fifteen hundred unwounded men, the remnant of six thousand unconquerable British soldiers, stood triumphant on that fatal hill![17]

Lieutenant Colonel Harrison occupies a special place in the history of the Royal Welch Fusiliers as the man who preserved the 'Flash', their famous uniform distinction. It will be recalled that when the 23rd Foot was ordered to cut its queues in 1809, the officers took the black ribbons which had been used to secure this appendage and fixed them to the back of their collars. It is not known why they did this but resistance to officially-directed change in matters of tradition has always been a hallmark of the Welch Fusiliers – witness their obstinate clinging to the archaic spelling, 'Welch', when the wider world switched to 'Welsh'. The officers wore the 'Flash' from 1809 onward and nobody commented on it until October 1834 when Major General Thomas McMahon, after inspecting the regiment, observed this 'superfluous decoration', and ordered its 'immediate abolition'.[18] Harrison sought the help of the Colonel of the Regiment, Lieutenant General Sir Willoughby Gordon, and Gordon went to a power higher than a mere major general – actually the highest in the land. Thus, on 28 November 1834, he informed Harrison that King William IV 'has been graciously pleased to approve of the Flashes now worn by the officers of the 23rd Foot, or Royal Welsh Fusileers, being henceforth worn and established as a peculiarity whereby to mark the Dress of that distinguished Regiment'.[19] Nothing more was heard on the matter from Major General McMahon.

After 32 years of service, Harrison relinquished command to Lieutenant Colonel William Ross in 1837. Ross had served with both the 14th and 17th Foot during the war and had transferred to the 23rd Foot in 1820. By this time the only wartime veteran officers left were Major Robert Holmes, Captain John Enoch, Quartermaster Garrett Moore and Paymaster George Dunn. In 1839, learning that Ellis's grave site at Braine l'Alleud in Belgium had become dilapidated, Ross and his officers had it refurbished and placed a marble memorial in his memory in the church at Waterloo.

When the 23rd Foot was re-organised into a 1st Battalion and a Reserve Battalion in 1842, Lieutenant Colonel Robert Holmes took command of the Reserve Battalion. First commissioned in the regiment in 1811, Holmes had served in the Peninsula and at Waterloo, and been wounded several times. There were now very few wartime veterans left. In 1844, Quartermaster Garrett Moore retired after 46 years of service with the Royal Welch Fusiliers, a record that is not likely to be equalled or beaten.

After 1815, the Goat accompanied the Welch Fusiliers wherever they served and was present on parade at all major ceremonial functions and when one animal took his heavenly discharge, he was replaced by another. The 1st Battalion was in

Barbados in 1844 when its current Goat expired and Queen Victoria, on learning of this sad happenstance, kindly presented each battalion of the regiment with a fine animal from the Royal Herd at Windsor. Since that time, the Goats of the regular battalions of the Royal Welch Fusiliers have, whenever possible, come from the same source and are officially known as 'Her Majesty's Goat' although it is not entirely certain whether this title improves their behaviour.

As has been discussed above, the British army did not reward the good conduct or valour of its soldiers with medals during the war with France but most good regiments, the Welch Fusiliers among them, made up for this official neglect by awarding regimental medals. In 1816, at the suggestion of the Duke of Wellington, the government decided to confer a medal on every officer and soldier who had fought at Waterloo. The creation of this medal heightened the army's awareness of the need to recognise the service of those who fought in earlier engagements and in 1847, after a long delay, the Military General Service Medal was struck to record the engagements that had taken place between 1793 and 1814, with clasps to record twenty-nine separate battles or major actions fought in those years. Seven Royal Welch Fusiliers received twelve such clasps, one received eleven and eight received ten.[20]

In 1849 there was great sadness in the regiment when Lieutenant Colonel Holmes died after 38 years' service. By now, the only wartime officer still serving was Paymaster George Dunn, who had been with the 23rd Foot since 1813. Dunn was still with the regiment when he died at the age of sixty-one in 1850, tragically 'hanging himself while in an unsound state of mind' in Plymouth.[21]

Four years later, Major Daniel Lysons and the men of No. 1 Company, 1st Battalion, Royal Welch Fusiliers, were the first British soldiers to set foot on the Crimean peninsula.

Thus, the Welch Fusiliers soldiered on during the decades that followed the Great War with France – but what became of those whose words have helped tell their story during that conflict?

Starting with Richard Bentinck – he met and married a local girl when the 23rd Foot was stationed in Ireland. Unfortunately, when the Welch Fusiliers were preparing to transfer to Gibraltar in 1821 the medical officer diagnosed Bentinck as consumptive and refused permission for him to embark. Colonel Pearson (the same ogre Bentinck so often complained about) argued unsuccessfully that if Bentinck truly was consumptive he would be better off in a warm climate. Sadly, Bentinck was discharged as 'unfit for service' in October 1823 and not having served enough time (twenty-one years) to receive a full pension, he was awarded just 9d per day. He returned to his native Suffolk where he became a gardener but was unable to support a growing family that ultimately comprised ten children, he later moved to the Midlands where the wages were better, and ended up in Heywood near Manchester. In 1856 Bentinck joined a party of pensioners who travelled to Manchester for the unveiling of a memorial to Wellington and at the ceremony, beat the 'Fall In' with the same drum sticks he had carried at Waterloo.[22] In 1867 Bentinck's pension was raised an additional 3d per day and although always reluctant to talk about his own exploits, the old veteran loved 'to discourse' about the 'campaigning days' of 1807-1815. Every 18 June, he would put on his medals and make the rounds of the local gentry to remind them it was Waterloo day, cheerfully accepting any donations to support his personal celebration of the anniversary. Richard Bentinck died in 1874 at the age of eighty-eight and his headstone describes him as 'A Waterloo Hero of the 24th Regiment of Foot', an egregious error that must make the old soldier rest uneasy.[23]

Badly wounded at Albuera in 1811 and in the Pyrenees battles of 1813, Lieutenant Gordon Booker returned to Britain where he married his fiancée, Loveday Sarah Glanville, with whom he had corresponded throughout his time in the Peninsula. Booker never rejoined the Welch Fusiliers and in 1826 changed his surname to Gregor to honour a bequest from a relative. He applied for, and received the Military General Service Medal with clasps for Martinique, Albuera, Vitoria and the Pyrenees. Gordon Gregor died in 1865 at the age of seventy-six.[24]

Thomas Browne, the industrious diarist, remained on the staff until he went on half pay in the early 1820s. He moved back to his native Flintshire where he was made High Sheriff in 1824. Through seniority, Browne continued to be promoted and reached the rank of lieutenant general in 1854, a year before his death at the age of seventy-two. Browne's first two wives died in childbirth but he had two sons by his third wife, one of whom became a major general. His brother, George, who commanded the Fusilier Brigade light troops at Salamanca and was badly wounded with the 23rd Foot at the Pyrenees in 1813, went on half pay in 1814 and served as the Commissioner of the Dublin Metropolitan Police until 1858. George Browne died in 1879 at the age of ninety-one. Their poet sister, Felicia Hemans, resided with George after separating from her husband and died in Dublin in 1831.[25]

Sergeant John Cooper of the 7th Foot returned from the American war in June 1815 and was discharged as he was a limited service (seven years) man. He tried several times to get a pension for the wounds he had suffered but was not successful until 1865, when he received a shilling per day. In 1869 Cooper published his memoirs, which provide a rare and colourful glimpse into the life of the common British soldier in the Great War against France. Cooper complained that soldiering in the 1860s was 'mere child's play compared with what it was from 1800 to 1815'.[26]

Lieutenant Charles Crowe of the 27th Foot, who left an engaging memoir of his service in the 4th Division in 1812-1813, suffered from health problems caused by his Peninsular service and went on half pay after the war. He married and returned to his native Suffolk, where he died in 1854 at the age of sixty-nine.[27]

Thomas Dalmer remained on half-pay from 1817, when he left the 23rd Foot, until 1847 when he was appointed Colonel of the 47th Foot. He was promoted by seniority to major general in 1838 and lieutenant general in 1851, although he never served in any official capacity. Thomas Dalmer died at his home in Hawkhurst, Kent, in 1854.[28]

Colonel Sir Henry Walton Ellis had never married but, as mentioned earlier, had two sons by a woman named Elizabeth Gore. The Duke of Wellington procured commissions for them and the elder, Francis Joyner Ellis, reached the rank of major before he died in Burma in 1840, while the younger, Henry, died while on passage home from India.[29]

Private Lewis Griffiths was discharged from the Welch Fusiliers in April 1821 and he and his wife Jenny returned to Tal-y-llyn where Lewis obtained work in a nearby quarry. The couple had four more children but in 1837 Jenny was left destitute when Lewis was killed in an accident. Some years later, she married a John Jones but it was not a happy relationship and she supported herself and her family by taking in washing. Her second husband having died, Jenny was nearly blind and living in poverty in 1879 when a reporter from the *Cambrian Record* took down her life story. Jenny Jones died in 1884, aged about 88, and is buried in the churchyard of St. Mary's Church in Tal-y-llyn. Her grave is marked by a fine headstone erected by 'a friend' and the inscription notes that 'she was with her husband of the 23rd Royal Welch Fusiliers at the Battle of Waterloo and was on the Field Three Days'. Jenny is remembered by the Welch Fusiliers at their annual St. David's Day dinner when the band plays the air, 'Jenny Jones', to accompany one of the traditional toasts of the occasion.[30]

Lieutenant Colonel John C. Harrison retired from the army in 1837 and lived with his wife, whom he had married in 1820, at his home, Mount Radford, in Exeter. Harrison died in 1871 at the age of eighty-three. He is always remembered in the Welch Fusiliers as the 'saviour' of the 'Flash'.[31]

The delightfully eccentric Lieutenant Colonel Jack Hill recovered sufficiently from his Waterloo wounds to rejoin the regiment outside Paris in the late summer of 1815. According to family legend, one day Hill was escorting two young ladies, the Turner sisters, along the banks of the Seine, to visit Lieutenant Ralph Smith, who was engaged to one of the girls. The trio encountered a soldier bearing a mattress and when Hill asked whom this was for, he got the reply that it was for Lieutenant Smith, who was on guard duty. 'Carry on', said Hill, 'But dip it in the river first.'[32] This must have impressed the non-engaged sister, Jane, as she married Hill in 1823 and the couple had five sons and two daughters. His wounds continuing to plague him, Jack Hill applied for, and received a disability pension of £300 per year in the same year as his marriage. He spent the remainder of his life at Totnes in Devon and died suddenly in January 1838, at the age of fifty-nine. He is buried in the churchyard of St. Mary's Church in Hennock, where his father was vicar for half a century, and there is a marble tablet dedicated to him inside the church.[33] One of Jack Hill's sons became a general after seeing much service in India and there remains a strong military tradition among his descendants – as this book went to print, Major Edward Hill, a direct descendant of Jack Hill, is commanding a company of the Royal Welch Fusiliers in Afghanistan.[34]

Found medically 'unfit for service', Thomas Jeremiah was discharged from the Welch Fusiliers in May 1837 after serving 25 years. He received a testimonial from Captain John Enoch, the adjutant, as 'a steady, sober and well behaved soldier'. Jeremiah had married and he and his wife had five children. In November 1847 he was appointed Superintendent of Police at Brynmawr, Breconshire, but an injury suffered on duty in 1856 left him permanently lame. Jeremiah then became Inspector of Weights and Measures for Breconshire and held that post until he died in 1868. He spent much time writing a memoir of his military life and experiences at Waterloo, which was recently published.[35]

Ensign George Keppel of the 14th Foot, which fought alongside the 23rd at Waterloo, stayed in the army after 1815 but later went into politics, serving two terms as a Member of Parliament. He married in 1831 and had four daughters and one son. Through seniority, he gained steady promotion and ultimately reached the rank of general. On the death of his older brother Keppel became the 6th Earl of Albemarle, but to the end of his days never forgot his youthful experiences at Waterloo and his memoirs, published in 1876, contain an excellent description of the battle. Keppel died in London at the age of ninety-one in 1891.[36]

Corporal Samuel Mason, the Worcestershire labourer who enlisted in the 23rd Foot in February 1794 and fought in every campaign in which the Welch Fusiliers participated between that date and Waterloo, was promoted sergeant in December 1815. He was discharged at the age of forty-seven in May 1818 with a pension of 10d. per day and later became a pensioner at the Chelsea Hospital. In terms of length of wartime service, his closest competitor in the 23rd Foot was Drummer William Mawson, also a labourer from Worcestershire, who enlisted six months after Mason in August 1794 and survived all the way to Waterloo. Mawson was discharged in May 1820 as being 'Old, worn out and Rheumatic'.[37]

Lieutenant John MacDonald of the 23rd Foot, the Scotsman who believed a 'wee drop' in the morning warded off illness, was promoted captain in 1827 and became paymaster of the regiment the following year. MacDonald married at Gibraltar in November 1829 but sadly died a few months later at the age of thirty-eight.[38]

Thomas Pearson commanded various administrative districts in Ireland from 1830 onwards and was promoted to lieutenant general in 1841. Pearson retired from the army in 1843 to live in the village of Sandford Orcas in his native Somerset. He seems to have had financial problems in his later years as he endorsed an American patent medicine, 'Swaim's Celebrated Panacea', which claimed to cure 'Incipient Consumption, Scrofula, General Debility, White Swelling, Rheumatism, Diseases of the Liver and Skin, and all Diseases arising from impurities of the Blood and the Effects of Mercury'.[39] His wife, Ann, lived apart from her husband in later years – which is entirely understandable – but

Pearson visited her annually at her residence in Bath. Thomas Pearson died in Bath in 1847 and is buried with his wife in the crypt of St. Swithin's Church in that city. He left his widow a passable wine cellar and very little money but her circumstances were eased by a general officer's widow's pension.[40]

Richard Roberts, who survived a perilous crossing of the North Atlantic in 1808, as described in Chapter Five, was discharged from the Welch Fusiliers in 1827 after eighteen years of service. In 1848 he was appointed Keeper of Caernarfon Castle but was dismissed in 1851 because of his attitude toward visitors, particularly 'painters, teetotallers and American tourists to whom he was downright rude'.[41] During his time in this post, Roberts made a little money on the side selling a 'List of Different Actions' in which he was engaged for six pence.[42] Roberts was still alive as late as 1862 as his memoirs of his wartime experiences – including his claim to have personally killed several senior French officers – were published that year in a periodical called *The Workman's Friend*. Be that as it may, Roberts received three regimental medals for Copenhagen, Martinique and the Peninsula, and the Military General Service Medal with eleven clasps.[43]

Lieutenant Colonel Charles Steevens of the 20th Foot, who had fought with the Fusilier Brigade in 1813-1814, retired from the army in 1818. Two of his sons were commissioned and both died on active service, one in the Crimea and one in the Indian Mutiny. Steevens devoted some of his later years to writing a memoir of his Peninsular experiences, which was published after his death in 1861 at the age of eighty-four.[44]

Lieutenant Samuel Thorpe of the Welch Fusiliers, the 16-year-old officer who participated in the retreat to Corunna and was wounded twice at Albuera, transferred to the 39th Foot in 1812. He was badly wounded at Toulouse in 1814 but recovered in time to fight that summer in North America. Thorpe retired on half pay as a captain in 1820 but returned to full pay as a brevet major in 1831 before retiring again in 1840 to Chishurst, Hertfordshire. An application to become Chief Constable of Hertfordshire was unsuccessful and Thorpe spent much of his later life as the Secretary of the Foreign Aid Society. He wrote a memoir of his military experiences, which was published after his death in 1852.[45]

Friedrich von Wachholtz, the German rifle company commander who fought with the Fusilier Brigade in the Peninsula, returned to Brunswick in February 1814. He married, was promoted major and fought at Quatre Bras and Waterloo in 1815. He continued in Brunswick service, reaching the rank of major general in 1835, and died at the age of fifty-eight in 1841. His diaries, covering his service with the Brunswick Oels from 1808 to 1813, were later published.[46]

In 1828 William Wheeler of the 51st Foot, who fought alongside the 23rd at Waterloo, was invalided from the army at the age of forty-three. His letters to his family in Britain were finally published in 1951.[47]

*

As far as can be established, the longest-surviving Welch Fusilier veteran of Waterloo was Private John Jeremiah from Goitre in Monmouthshire. Jeremiah had volunteered into the 23rd Foot in 1813 from the Monmouthshire and Brecon Volunteers, and fought in No. 1 Company during the battle. He served seven years in the regiment before being discharged in 1820 and died at the age of ninety-four in 1887.[48]

Two years later the Royal Welch Fusiliers marked their 200th anniversary. The 1st Battalion was serving in India and the 2nd Battalion in Ireland and, according to the regimental records, the celebrations were rather muted. This was not the case, however, when the regiment reached its 300th birthday in 1989, as the occasion was marked by many special events, including formal parades, commemorative services, dinners and ceremonies. The centrepiece of the festivities was a pageant held at Powis Castle, just outside Welshpool, Powys, the ancestral seat of the Herbert family, one of whose members first raised the regiment in 1689. The Queen took the salute and in her address, noted the Royal Welch Fusiliers' magnificent heritage as told in the Battle Honours 'displayed so proudly before you on the Colours' which 'are a record of true bravery, loyalty and service'.[49] Many such Honours had been added since 'WATERLOO' including 'ALMA', 'LUCKNOW', 'RELIEF OF LADYSMITH', 'MARNE 1914', 'GALLIPOLI 1915-1916', 'SOMME 1916', 'REICHSWALD', 'CAEN' and 'KOHIMA' – to name but a few of many – as the history of the Royal Welch Fusiliers since 1815 is largely a history of almost every major battle or campaign fought by the British army.[†]

On 1 March 2006, St. David's Day, the Royal Welch Fusiliers ended 317 years of existence as an unamalgamated infantry regiment when they joined the Royal Regiment of Wales (former 24th and 41st Foot) to create a new entity, The Royal Welsh. The former 23rd Foot is now officially 1st Battalion The Royal Welsh (Royal Welch Fusiliers) but continues to maintain its cherished traditions. 'Billy' or 'Her Majesty's Goat' still leads the battalion on ceremonial occasions; the leek is still eaten on St. David's Day; and the 'Flash' is worn on certain orders of dress, not only by officers but, since 1900, by all members.

Finally, *Y Ddraig Goch*, the rampant Red Dragon, is not only displayed on the Regimental Colour as it was at Waterloo, today it is the Tactical Recognition Flash worn on the right arm of every Royal Welch Fusilier in combat dress. As such the Dragon Rampant forms a direct link between the modern Welch Fusiliers and the men of the 23rd Regiment of Foot who fought at Albuera, Alexandria, Badajoz, Martinique, the Pyrenees, Salamanca, Waterloo – and so many other places – during the Great War with France, 1793-1815. The Royal Welch Fusiliers continue to serve Sovereign and nation – long may they do so.

---

† Those interested in learning more about the history of this magnificent regiment are advised to read M. Glover and J. Riley, *'That Astonishing Infantry': The History of The Royal Welch Fusiliers, 1689–2006* (Pen and Sword Books, 2008).

Abbreviations

Acc.	Accession
Adm	Admiralty
AL	*Army List*
Albemarle	George Thomas, Earl of Albemarle, *Fifty Years of My Life* (3rd edn, London, 1877)
Bentinck 1	Richard Bentinck, 'The Life and Career of Richard Bentinck', unpublished manuscript, Woodbridge Library, Suffolk
Bentinck 2	Richard Bentinck, [Memoirs of military career], *Heywood Advertiser*, May-August 1873
Browne	Roger .N. Buckley, ed., *The Napoleonic War Journal of Captain Thomas ... Browne* (London, 1987)
CO	Colonial Office
Cooper	John S. Cooper, *Rough Notes of Seven Campaigns, 1809-1815* (London, 1869)
Crowe	Charles Crowe, 'Letters and Diary from the Peninsula ... 1812-1813-1814' (unpublished)
DNB	*Dictionary of National Biography*
Dyott	R.W. Jeffrey, ed., *Dyott's Diary, 1781-1815, ... the Journal of William Dyott* (2 vols., London, 1907)
Fortescue	John W. Fortescue, *A History of the British Army* (13 vols., London, 1899-1930)
GO	General Order
Gomm	F.C. Gomm, ed., *Letters and Journals of ... William Maynard Gomm, 1798-1815* (London, 1881)
Graves	Donald E. Graves, *Fix Bayonets! The Life and Times of Lieutenant-General Sir Thomas Pearson, 1781-1847* (Montreal, 2006)
HK *Medals*	Norman Holme and E.L. Kirby, *Medal Rolls. 23rd Foot. Royal Welch Fusiliers* (London, 1978)
Jeremiah	Gareth Glover, ed., *Short Account of the Life ... of Private Thomas Jeremiah ... 1812-1837* (London, 2008)
JSAHR	*Journal of the Society for Army Historical Research*
Kirby *ORWF*	E.L. Kirby, *Officers of The Royal Welch Fusiliers ... 1689-1914* (Capel Curig 1997)
MG	Manuscript Group
NAB	National Archives of Britain, Kew
NLAC	National Library and Archives of Canada, Ottawa
Oman	C. Oman, *A History of the Peninsular War* (7 vols., London, 1902-1930)
Reg Recs	A.D.L. Cary and S. McCance, *Regimental Records of the Royal Welch Fusiliers ...* vol. 1, 1689–1815 (London, 1921); vol. 2, 1815-1914 (London, 1923) Reprinted 1995

RG	Record Group
RWFM	Royal Welch Fusiliers Museum
Steevens	N. Steevens, ed., *Reminiscences of My Military Life ... Colonel Charles Steevens* (Winchester, 1878)
Thorpe	Samuel Thorpe, *Narrative of Incidents in the Early Life of ... Samuel Thorpe* (London, 1854)
USJ	*United Service Journal*
vol	volume
Wachholtz	H.C. von Wachholtz, ed., 'Auf der Peninsula 1810 bis 1813. Kriegstagebuch des Generals Friedrich Ludwig v. Wachholtz', *Beihefte zum Militär-Wochenblatt*, 1907, 259-326
WD	John Gurwood, ed., *The Dispatches of Field Marshal the Duke of Wellington, 1799-1818* (13 vols., London, 1834-1839)
WGO	*Official General Orders of the Duke of Wellington ...* (10 vols., London, 1811-1818)
Wheeler	Basil Liddell Hart, ed., *The Letters of Private Wheeler, 1809-1828* (London, 1951)
WO	War Office
WSD	Arthur R. Wellington, ed., *Supplementary Dispatches ... of Field Marshal Arthur, Duke of Wellington, 1797-1815* (14 vols., London, 1858)
YDG	*Y Ddraig Goch* (The Red Dragon), journal of the Royal Welch Fusiliers

Notes

Prologue *pages 1–8*

Unless otherwise noted, this prologue is based on
M. Adkin, *The Waterloo Companion* (London,
2001); Bentinck 2, 25 July 1873; J. Chambers,
Biographical Illustrations of Worcestershire
(Worcester, 1820), 577; D. Dundas, *Rules and
Regulations for the Formation, Field-Exercise, and
Movements of His Majesty's Forces* (London, 1798);
Jeremiah, 21-23; J. Harris, 'Worcester Honours a
Brave Soldier'; *Reg Recs*, vol. 1, 277-284; H.T.
Siborne, ed., *The Waterloo Letters* (1891, reprinted
London, 1983); and H. Torrens, *Field Exercise and
Evolutions of the Army* (London, 1824). Information
on officers and men of the 23rd Foot at Waterloo
from HK *Medals*.

1. Whereas it may seem strange to open a book
   about a Welsh regiment with a quote from
   'Scots Wha Hae', the famous poem by Robert
   Burns, the connection is to the battle of
   Waterloo. According to an eyewitness, during a
   lull in the fighting a voice in the ranks of the
   92nd Foot was heard singing these verses,
   'which produced the most powerful effect on
   the hearts of our brave fellows'. See J.A. Hope,
   *Military Memoirs of an Infantry Officer, 1809-
   1816* (Edinburgh, 1833), 482.
2. Bentinck 2, 25 July 1873.

Chapter 1 *pages 9–23*

Unless otherwise noted, this chapter is based on
Fortescue, vol. 3, 501-547; Graves, 13-21; Alan J.
Guy, 'The Army of the Georges 1714-1783', in
David Chandler, editor, *The Oxford History of the
British Army* (Oxford, 2003); *Reg Recs*, vol. 1, 153-
193. Information on the service, organisation,
tactical doctrine and training of the British army,
1783-1793, and on the purchase system, is from J.
Houlding, *Fit for Service: The Training of the British
Army. 1715-1795* (Oxford, 1981).

1. 'The Soldier's Complaint', a broadside ballad
   dating from the late eighteenth century.
2. Inspection return, 14 May 1784, *Reg Recs*, vol. 1,
   186.
3. M. Glover and J.P. Riley, 'That Astonishing
   Infantry' The History of the Royal Welch Fusiliers,
   1689-2006 (Barnsley, 2008), 17-44.
4. G.A. Steppler, 'The British Army on the Eve of
   War', in A.J. Guy, ed., *The Road to Waterloo*
   (London, 1990), 4-5.
5. C.M. Clode, *The Military Forces of the Crown;
   Their Administration and Government* (2 vols.,
   London, 1869), vol. 1, 230.
6. Fortescue, vol. 3, 527.
7. D. Dundas, *Principles of Military Movements,
   Chiefly Applied to Infantry* (London, 1788), 13,
   14.
8. D. Dundas, *Rules and Regulations for the
   Formations, Field-Exercise, and Movements, of His
   Majesty's Forces* (London, 1792), 4.
9. It is important to understand that Dundas's
   1792 *Regulations* were the basis for all
   subsequent manuals issued during the period,
   1792-1815, including J. Le Marchant,
   *Elucidation of Several Parts of His Majesty's
   Regulations for the Formations and Movements of
   Cavalry* (London, 1798), *Light Infantry Exercise,
   as ordered by His Majesty's Regulations for the
   Movements of the Troops* (London, 1797); and F.
   de Rottenburg, *Regulations for the Exercise of*

Riflemen and Light Infantry, and Instructions for their Conduct in the Field (London, 1798). 10. *Reg Recs*, vol. 1, 188.

11. *Reg Recs*, vol. 1, 188.

12. *Reg Recs*, vol. 1, 188.

13. Houlding, *Fit for Service*, 306, quoting from NAB, WO 27, vol. 61.

14. Inspection Report, 22 May 1788, in *Reg Recs*, vol. 1, 188.

15. Information on Balfour from Kirby *ORWFM*; statistics of officers' service from *ALs*, 1783-1793.

Chapter 2 *pages 22–35*

Unless otherwise noted, this chapter is based on the following sources: A. Bryant, *The Years of Endurance* (London, 1948), 78-263; M. Duffy, 'The Caribbean Campaigns of the British Army 1793-1801', in A.J. Guy, ed., *The Road to Waterloo* (London, 1990), 23-31; Fortescue, vol. 4, part 1, 350-384, 426-496; Graves, 7-62; and *Reg Recs*, vol. 1, 190-202.

1. 'Why, Soldiers, Why' dates from the early eighteenth century and was very popular during the Napoleonic period, see L. Winstock, *Songs & Music of the Redcoats* (London, 1970), 58.

2. Fortescue, vol. 4, part 2, Appendix 940.

3. E. Cashin, *Governor Henry Ellis and the Transformation of British North America* (Athens, GA, and London, 1994), 230-231; Kirby *ORWF*.

4. Kirby *ORWF*; *AL*, 1793-1795.

5. Bradford to Williamson, 30 Dec 1794, in *London Gazette*, 14 Mar 1795.

6. H. Ross-Lewin, *With The Thirty-Second in the Peninsular and other Campaigns* (Dublin, 1904), 22-23.

7. Dyott, vol. 1, 109.

8. D. Geggus, 'Yellow Fever in the 1790s: The British Army in Occupied Saint Domingue', *Medical History*, vol. 23 (1979), 38-39.

9. Quoted in Geggus, 'Yellow Fever', 5310. Geggus, 'Yellow Fever'.

11. Losses of the 23rd Foot in the West Indies from *Reg Recs*, vol. 1, 191-195. General army losses from N. Cantlie, *History of the Army Medical Department* (2 vols., London, 1974), vol. 1, 230; Duffy, 'Caribbean Campaigns', 29-31; and Fortescue, vol. 4, 564-566.

12. Kirby *ORWF*.

13. NAB, WO 12, vol 3961; *AL* 1796,1797; Kirby *ORWF*; Obituary, *Gentleman's Magazine*, July-Dec 1854, 626.

14. On Offley's father, Major General F.J. Needham, see *DNB*, vol. 14. General

Needham's grandmother was Mary Offley and his son therefore received the name Francis Needham Offley. Francis Offley seems to have been raised at one of his father's properties at Wareseley in Cambridgeshire as there is a tablet to him in St. James, the local church. On his illegitimacy, see NAB Prob 31, vol 1105, containing his will probated by the Prerogative Court of Canterbury, where he is described as 'Francis Needham Offley, bastard, bachelor'.
   On the other officers, see NAB, WO 12, vol 3961; *AL* 1796,1797; and Kirby *ORWF*.

15. On Henry Ellis's date of joining and family, see NAB: WO 12, vol 3961; WO 17, vol 125; *AL*, 1796, 1797; Harris, 'Worcester Honours a Brave Soldier'; Kirby *ORWF*.

16. RWFM, Acc. 3777, Hill to father, n.d. 1796.

17. On Thomas Pearson and his family, see Graves, 26-32. On the dates of joining of Hill and Pearson, see WO 12, vol. 3961; *AL*, 1796,1797; and Kirby *ORWF*.

18. Glover and Riley, *'That Astonishing Infantry'*, 279-280.

19. On the work of the Duke of York, see R. Glover, *Peninsular Preparation: The Reform of the British Army 1795-1809* (Cambridge, 1963).

20. RWFM, Acc. 3777, Hill to mother, 10 Aug [n.d. but probably 1797].

21. RWFM, Acc. 3777, Hill to mother, 10 Aug [n.d. but probably 1797].

22. Kirby *ORWF*.

23. R.E.R. Robinson, *The Bloody Eleventh* (Exeter 1988), 267-275.

24. *Reg Recs*, vol. 1, 198.

25. On the Loyalist background of Skinner, Van Cortland and Visscher, see E.A. Jones, *The Loyalists of New Jersey* (Newark, 1927); L. Sabine, *Biographical Sketches of the Loyalists of the American Revolution* (2 vols., Boston, 1864), vol. 2, 376-377; and J.R. Simms, *The Frontiersmen of New York* (Albany, 1883), 327-329.

26. Robinson, *Bloody Eleventh*, 272-273.

27. Inspection Report, 4 Oct 1798, *Reg Recs*, 197-198.

28. Dyott, vol. 1, 129.

29. Graves, 49-52.

30. RWFM, Acc. 3777, Hill to unknown, 5 Sep 1799.

31. RWFM, Acc. 3777, Hill to unknown, 5 Sep 1799. Hill's reference to a round hitting the bearskin of his helmet is not a reference to a bearskin fusilier cap but to the bearskin brush of a Tarleton helmet which may have been worn by the light company of the 23rd and some of

the officers.

32. W. Surtees, *Twenty-Five Years in the Rifle Brigade* (1833, reprinted London, 1996), 26.

33. RWFM, Acc. 3777, Hill to Secretary of the Commander-in-Chief, Feb 1800.

Chapter 3 *pages 36–49*

Unless otherwise noted, this chapter is based on Fortescue, vol. 4, part 2, 769-869; Graves, 62-77, P. Mackesy, *British Victory in Egypt* (London, 1995); and *Reg Recs*, vol. 1, 202-209.

1. 'Abercrombie's Glory', a broadsheet ballad dating from 1801 or 1802. 2. Kirby *ORWF*.

3. Earl of Ilchester, ed., *The Journal of ... Lady Holland* (2 vols., London, 1908), vol. 2, 62.

4. Gomm, 46.

5. Gomm, 47.

6. Gomm, 49.

7. RWFM, Acc. 3777, Hill to mother, 11 Jan 1801.

8. NLAC, MG 24, F70, Diary of Thomas Evans, 18 Nov 1800.

9. RWFM, Acc. 379. G. Mackenzie to father, 26 Mar 1801.

10. J.F. Maurice, ed., *Diary of Sir John Moore* (2 vols., London, 1904), vol. 2, 3-4.

11. NLAC, MG 24, F70, Diary of Thomas Evans, 22 Jan 1801.

12. RWFM, Acc. 3777, Hill to mother, 11 Jan 1801.

13. Seaman John Nichol, quoted in H. Baynham, *From the Lower Deck* (London, 1969), 29.

14. Maurice, ed., *Diary of Moore*, vol. 2, 3-4.

15. J. Browne, *A History of the Highlands and the Highland Clans* (vol. 4, Glasgow, 1840), 198.

16. Maurice, ed., *Diary of John Moore*, 4.

17. Browne, *History of the Highlands*, vol. 4, 198.

18. Maurice, ed., *Diary of John Moore*, 4-5.

19. J. MacDonald, 'Sir Ralph Abercromby by a Contemporary', *Blackwood's Magazine*, (Dec. 1915), 843-844.

20. B. Miller, *The Adventures of Sergeant Benjamin Miller* (Dallington, 1999), 19.

21. Browne, *History of the Highlands*, vol. 4, 201.

22. RWFM, ACC. 3777. J.H. Hill, Statement of Service, c. 1816.

23. RWFM, ACC. 3777. J.H. Hill, Statement of Service, c. 1816.

24. Browne, *History of the Highlands*, vol. 4, 203.

25. Maurice, ed., *Diary of John Moore*, vol. 2, 17.

26. RWFM, Acc. 379. G. Mackenzie to father, 26 Mar 1801.

27. Kirby *ORWF*; RWFM, Acc. 379. G. Mackenzie to father, 26 Mar 1801.

28. Dyott, vol. 1, 168.

29. Miller, *Adventures*, 20.

30. NLAC, MG 24, F70, Diary of Thomas Evans, 30 April 1801.

31. NLAC, MG 24, F70, Diary of Thomas Evans, 16 May 1801.

32. Miller, *Adventures*, 23.

33. H. Bunbury, *Passages in the Great War with France. 1799-1810* (1854, reprinted London, 1927), 102.

34. War Office, Circular Letter, 6 July 1802, in *Reg Recs*, vol. 1, 207.

35. Gomm, 49.

36. RWFM, Acc. 3777, Hill to mother, 25 Dec 1801.

37. RWFM, Acc. 3777, Hill to mother, 25 Dec 1801.

38. RWFM, Acc. 3777, Hill to mother, 25 Dec 1801.

39. R.H. Patterson, *Pontius Pilate's Bodyguard* (Edinburgh, 2000), 120.

40. Patterson, *Pontius Pilate's Bodyguard*, 120.

41. 'Standing Orders in the Garrison of Gibraltar, 1803', *JSAHR*, vol. 2 (1922), 89.

42. 'Standing Orders in the Garrison of Gibraltar', 126.

43. 'Standing Orders in the Garrison of Gibraltar, 1803', 181.

44. 'Standing Orders in the Garrison of Gibraltar, 1803', 183.

45. 'Standing Orders in the Garrison of Gibraltar, 1803', 183.

46. G. Glover, ed., *Memoir of the Military Career of John Dayes* (Cambridge, 2004), 7.

47. Miller, *Adventures*, 30.

48. Miller, *Adventures*, 30.

49. NAB, WO 27, vol 87, Inspection Report, 23rd Foot, 4 Mar 1803.

Chapter 4 *pages 50–67*

Unless otherwise noted, this chapter is based on Ian Beckett, 'The Amateur Military Tradition', in D. Chandler, editor, *The Oxford History of the British Army* (Oxford, 2003), 132-160; A. Bryant, *Years of Victory* (London, 1944); Fortescue, vol. 5; Graves, 79-109; P. Haythornethwaite, *The Armies of Wellington* (London, 1998), 43-56; and *Reg Recs*, 208-218.

1. Welsh Fusilier song believed to date from the 1790s, *YDG*, Feb 1924.

2. The *Cambrian*, 31 Aug 1804, quoted in B. Owen, *Welsh Militia and Volunteer Corps 1757-1908. 2. The Glamorgan Regiments of Militia* (Caernarfon, 1990), 50.

3. RWFM, Acc. 3777, Hill to mother, 28 June 1803.

4. RWFM, Acc. 3377, Hill to mother, 28 June 1803.

5. RWFM, Acc. 3777, Hill to father, 8 Sep 1803.

6. RWFM, Acc. 3777, Hill to father, 8 Sep 1803.

7. RWFM, Acc. 3777, Hill to mother, 21 Dec 1803.

8. RWFM, Acc. 3777, Hill to mother, 18 Apr 1804.

9. RWFM, Acc. 3777, Hill to mother, 30 June 1804.

10. Kirby *ORWF*.

11. RWFM, Acc. 3777, Hill to mother, 18 Apr 1804.

12. Glover, *Peninsular Preparation*, 229-230.

13. Glover, *Peninsular Preparation*, 249-250.

14. NAB, WO 4, vol. 193, Circular Letter, 19 Apr 1804.

15. RWFM, Acc. 3777, Hill to mother, 18 Apr 1804.

16. *AL*, 1804-1807.

17. Thomas Jackson quoted in Owen, *The Glamorgan Regiments of Militia*, 50.

18. J. Shipp, *The Path of Glory* (London, 1969), 3.

19. Recruiting bounty from Bentinck 2, 9 May 1873; list of necessaries from 'His Majesty's Warrant Concerning Necessaries, 14 January 1792' in *Standing Orders and Regulations for the Army in Ireland* (Dublin, 1794), 1.

20. The proper legal procedure for attestation is delineated in *Instructions to Officers Employed on the Recruiting Service* (London, 1806), 19-21.

21. *Instructions ... Recruiting Service*, 18-19.

22. *Instructions ... Recruiting Service*, 51-52.

23. P.J. Haythornthwaite, *Armies of Wellington* (London, 1994), 76-79; *Return of the Number of Men Who Extended Their Services from the Militia to The Regular Army in the Years 1807, 1808, & 1809 in Accounts and Estimates, Army Returns, etc.,*(London 1810).

24. Inspection Report, 3 June 1807, in *Reg Recs*, vol. 1, 217.

25. Regimental Orders, 1807, 2/23rd Foot, quoted in *Reg Recs*, vol. 1, 217.

26. *AL*, 1805, 1806, 1807; Kirby *ORWF*.

27. Inspection Report, 5 Dec 1806, *Reg Recs*, vol. 1, 213.

28. In 1804 the Welsh militia regiments in service were the Royal Anglesey Fusiliers; Monmouth and Brecknock Militia; Royal Cardiganshire Militia; Royal Carmarthenshire Fuzileers; Royal Carnavon Fuzileers; Royal Denbighshire Militia; Royal Flint Fusiliers; Royal Glamorganshire Militia; Royal Merionethshire Militia; Monmouth and Brecon Militia; Royal Montgomeryshire Militia; Royal Pembrokeshire Fuzileers; and Royal Radnorshire Militia.

29. *Reg Recs*, vol. 1, 216. On the increasing proportion of Welshmen in the ranks of the 23rd Foot, see *Reg Recs*, vol. 1, 213-275, Inspection Reports for the 1/23rd Foot, 10 Aug 1808; 2/23rd Foot, 5 Dec 1806, 3 June 1807, 26 Mar 1809, 16 May 1810, 27 and 28 July 1812,

Regimental Monthly Return, Feb 1814.

30. Bentinck 1; Bentinck 2, 9 May 1873.

31. Bentinck 2, 9 May 1873.

32. Bentinck 2, 9 May 1873.

33. Bentinck 2, 9 May 1873.

34. Thorpe, 1.

35. Thorpe, 3.

36. Thorpe, 5-6, 7-8.

37. Thorpe, 13-14.

38. R. Goodridge, ed., 'Letters Home', *The Waterloo Journal*, vol. 21, no 2 (Aug 1999, 21-22, G. Philipps to J.G. Philipps, 24 Aug 1809.

39. 'Letters Home', 22, G. Philipps to J.G. Philipps, 12 Sep 1809.

40. 'Letters Home', 22, List attached in G. Philipps to J.G. Philipps, 12 Sep 1809.

41. 'Letters Home', 22, G. Philipps to J.G. Philipps, 11 Oct 1809.

42. 'Letters Home', 22, G. Philipps to J.G. Philipps, 10 Feb 1810.

43. 'Letters Home', 22-23, G. Philipps to J.G. Philipps, 27 Feb 1810.

44. 'Letters Home', 23, G. Philipps to J.G. Philipps, 27 Mar 1810.

45. 'Letters Home', 23, Wyatt to J.G. Philipps, 29 Aug 1810.

46. 'Letters Home', 23, G. Philipps to J.G. Philipps, 8 Oct 1810.

47. E.L. Kirby, 'The Youth who was to save our Flash', *YDG* (Mar 1979).

48. RWFM, Acc. 3777, Hill to mother, 7 Oct 1804.

49. RWFM, Acc. 3777, Hill to mother, 7 Oct 1804.

50. One Peninsular officer thought the matter of sea stock was 'shameful' as the officers were usually hurried on board their ships and then had no chance to purchase it. See Anonymous, *Military Adventures of Johnny Newcome* (London, 1816), 11.

51. Obituary, *The Gentleman's Magazine*, Jan-June 1821, 375; Kirby *ORWF*.

52. Browne, 73.

53. There are unfortunately very few references to the Goat during the period, 1793-1815. The animal's presence on operations overseas is not noted in any of the correspondence or memoirs by Welch Fusilier officers and men but Drummer Richard Bentinck saw the animal with the 2/23rd Foot in England in 1807 and there is a secondary source that states it was with a Welsh militia regiment in 1814. It would appear that the animal was left at home during the war and did not accompany the regiment overseas.

54. RWFM, Acc. 1335, Harrison to father, 20 Nov 1807.

55. RWFM, Acc. 1335, Harrison to father, 20 Nov

56. RWFM, Acc. 1335, Harrison to father, 20 Nov 1807.
57. RWFM, Acc. 1335, Harrison to father, 20 Nov 1807.
58. RWFM, Acc. 1335, Harrison to father, 20 Nov 1807.
59. Gomm, 85.
60. Gomm, 85.
61. RWFM, Acc. 1335, Harrison to father, 20 Nov 1807.
62. Browne, 64.
63. RWFM, Acc. 1335, Harrison to father, 20 Nov 1807.
64. Kirby, *ORWF; AL*, 1807, 1808.

Chapter 5 *pages 68–83*
Unless otherwise noted, this chapter is based on Graves, 113-132; and *Reg Recs*, vol. 1, 218-225.

1. 'The British Bayoneteers', sung to the tune of 'The British Grenadiers', was popular with the army during the Napoleonic period, see Winstock, *Songs & Music of the Redcoats*, 111.
2. Browne, 67.
3. On life at Colchester during the winter of 1807-1808, see Browne, 67-68.
4. Bentinck 2, 16 May 1873.
5. Browne, 68.
6. Browne, 68-69.
7. *Rules and Regulations for Cavalry* (London, 1795), 74, quoted in Glover, *Peninsular Preparation*, 221.
8. B. Cuthbertson, *A System for the Complete Interior Management and Oeconomy of a Battalion of Infantry* (London, 1779), 113. Although Cuthbertson wrote before the war of 1793-1815, the information in his book still applied to the British army of the later period.
9. Cuthbertson, *Interior Oeconomy*, 113.
10. Cuthbertson, *Interior Oeconomy*, 113.
11. P. Compton, *Colonel's Lady and Camp-Follower: The Story of Women in the Crimean War* (London, 1970), 23.
12. H. De Watteville, *The British Soldier* (London, 1954), 124.
13. Crowe, 3 May 1814.
14. Cuthbertson, *Interior Oeconomy*, 19.
15. Major Patterson of 50th Foot, quoted in De Watteville, *British Soldier*, 180.
16. D.L. Graves, *In the Midst of Alarms* (Montreal, 2007), 162-165.
17. Adjutant General, *Regulations for Regimental Surgeons, &c., for the Better Management of the Sick in Regimental Hospitals* (London, 1799), 13.

18. *General Regulations and Orders for the Army, 1811*, General Order, 10 Apr 1813, 370.
19. General Order for Troops destined for Continental Service, 15 Apr 1807, quoted in Glover, *Peninsular Preparation*, 221n.
20. *General Regulations and Orders, 1811*, 255.
21. *General Regulations and Orders, 1811*, 256.
22. *General Regulations and Orders, 1811*, 258.
23. A broadsheet ballad of the Napoleonic period contained in R. Palmer, ed., *The Rambling Soldier* (London, 1985), 250.
24. Browne, 69.
25. RWFM, Acc. 3777, Hill to brother, 24 Feb 1808.
26. Browne, 73.
27. Browne, 69-70.
28. *Regulations to be Observed by Troops Embarked in Transports for Service Abroad* (London, 1795), 8-9.
29. *Regulations ... Troops Embarked in Transports*, 13.
30. *Regulations ... Troops Embarked in Transports*, 8.
31. *Regulations ... Troops Embarked in Transports*, 16.
32. Browne, 71.
33. Dyott, 34.
34. Dyott, 30.
35. R. Roberts, 'Incidents in the Life of an Old Fusilier', *The Workman's Friend*, 1862, 10.
36. Roberts, 'Incidents', 11.
37. Roberts, 'Incidents', 11.
38. RWFM, Acc. 3777, Hill to Humphries, 1808.
39. Browne, 78-79.
40. On Browne's activities in Nova Scotia, see Browne, 77-84. On the 1/23rd Foot in the colony generally, see RWFM, Acc. 3777, Hill letters of n.d. [June], July, 24 July , 23 Oct and 29 Nov, all 1808.
41. RWFM, Acc. 3777, Hill to mother, 24 July 1808.
42. RWFM, Acc. 3777, Hill to mother, 29 Nov 1808.
43. Inspection Report, 10 Aug 1808, *Reg Recs*, 218.
44. Browne, 84.
45. RWFM, Acc. 3777, Hill to mother, 29 Nov 1808.
46. Browne, 93.
47. Browne, 93.
48. On Martinique, see Fortescue, vol. 7, 11-17. On Pakenham and Ellis, see RWFM, Acc. 5935, MacDonald to father, 13 Mar 1815.
49. Journal of Lieutenant J. Harrison, quoted in R. Broughton-Mainwaring, *Historical Record of the Royal Welch Fusiliers ...* (London, 1889), 121. Unfortunately, Harrison's journal of the Martinique expedition, which was extant in the late 19th century, has unfortunately since

disappeared.

50. Prevost to Beckwith, 2 Feb 1809, *London Gazette*, 25 Mar 1809.
51. Harrison Journal in Broughton-Mainwaring, *Historical Record*, 122.
52. New York *Times*, 13 January 1878.
53. Browne, 117-118.
54. Harrison Journal, Broughton-Mainwaring, *Historical Record*, 122. Harrison says the tablet was placed in the 'Dutch Church' in Halifax, this is now St. George's Church.
55. Browne, 110.

Chapter 6 *pages 84–107*

Unless otherwise noted, this chapter is based on A. Bryant, *Years of Victory*, (London, 1944), 255-296, 324-334; Fortescue, vol. 6, 291-414, vol. 7, 60-96; Oman, vol. 1, 486-602; and *Reg Recs*, 219-221, 225-233.

1. 'The Soldier's Death', a broadsheet ballad, c. 1809-1810, quoted in Palmer, ed., *The Rambling Soldier*, 248.
2. Gomm, 131.
3. Thorpe, 19.
4. Thorpe, 19.
5. Thorpe, 19-21.
6. G. Glover, ed., *From Corunna to Waterloo* (London, 2007), 47.
7. Glover, *Corunna to Waterloo*, 66.
8. Thorpe, 26.
9. Thorpe, 27.
10. C. Hibbert, ed., *The Recollections of Rifleman Harris*, (London, 1970), 69
11. Thorpe, 27.
12. Thorpe, 28-29.
13. Quoted in Bryant, *Years of Victory*, 256.
14. Thorpe, 31.
15. H.M. Dawson, ed., 'Diary of the Operations in Spain under Sir John Moore', *Journal of the Royal Artillery Institution*, vol. 38, no 22 (Dec 1907), 7. The diarist is Captain A. Wall, RA.
16. Thorpe, 30.
17. Captain J. Stirling, 'Memoir of Campaign of 1808 in Spain', quoted in Maurice, ed., *Diary of John Moore*, vol. 2, 376.
18. R. Ker Porter, *Letters from Portugal and Spain ...* (London, 1809), 235.
19. Thorpe, 31-32.
20. A. Neale, 'The Spanish Campaign of 1808', in *Memorials of the Late War* (2 vols, Edinburgh, 1831), vol. 1, 176.
21. General Order, Benevente, 27 Dec 1808, in J. Moore, *A Narrative of the Campaign of the British Army in Spain* (London, 1809), 176-177.

22. Neale, *Spanish Campaign*, 182.
23. C.W. Vane, *Story of the Peninsular War* (New York, 1848), 150.
24. Thorpe, 33-34.
25. General Order, 30 Dec 1808, in Moore, *Narrative*, 184-185.
26. *Hamilton's Campaign with Moore and Wellington* (Troy, NY, 1847), 40.
27. T. Pococke, *Journal of a Soldier of the 71st, or Glasgow Regiment* (Edinburgh, 1819), 72.
28. A. Schaumann, *On the Road with Wellington* (1924, reprinted London, 1999), 111.
29. R. Blakeney, *A Boy in the Peninsular War*, (1899, reprinted London, 1989), 49-50.
30. Blakeney, *Boy in the Peninsular War*, 51.
31. M. Loyd, trans., *New Letters of Napoleon I* (London, 1898), 112, Napoleon to Fouche, 1 Jan 1809
32. Schaumann, *On the Road with Wellington*, 119-120.
33. Steevens, 69.
34. Thorpe, 36-37.
35. Neale, *Spanish Campaign*, 190.
36. Steevens, 71.
37. Ker Porter, *Letters*, 266.
38. Thorpe, 44.
39. Thorpe, 44.
40. General Order, Lugo, 6 Jan 1808, in Moore, *Narrative ...*, 194.
41. General Order, Lugo, 6 Jan 1808, in Moore, *Narrative ...*, 194.
42. *Hamilton's Campaign*, 48-49.
43. Thorpe, 41.
44. Thorpe, 44.
45. Neale, *Spanish Campaign*, 190.
46. Dawson, ed., 'Diary of the Operations', 1.
47. Thorpe, 45-46.
48. Blakeney, *Boy in the Peninsular War*, 90-92.
49. Moore, *Narrative*, 204.
50. Thorpe, 49.
51. Thorpe, 72.
52. Fortescue, vol. 6, 375.
53. Thorpe, 50.
54. Schaumann, *On the Road with Wellington*, 134.
55. Thorpe, 50-51.
56. Steevens, 74.
57. Thorpe, 53.
58. Vane, *Story of the Peninsular War*, 141.
59. Pococke, *Journal*, 95-9660.
60. Thorpe, 57.
61. Blakeney, *Boy in the Peninsular War*, 124.
62. W. Dent, quoted in M.R. Howard, 'Medical aspects of Sir John Moore's Corunna Campaign, 1808-1809', *Journal of the Royal Society of Medicine*, vol. 84 (May 1991), 300.

63. Thorpe, 73.
64. NAB, WO 27, vol 94, Inspection Return of 2/23rd Foot, Horsham, 11 May 1809.
65. Steevens, 80.
66. Blakeney, *Boy in the Peninsular War*, 128
67. Hibbert, ed., *Recollections of Rifleman Harris*, 114
68. Steevens, 81.
69. Gomm, 124.
70. R. Henegan, *Campaigns with the Field Train* (1846, reprinted London, 2007), 63.
71. Thorpe, 61.
72. Thorpe, 62.
73. D. Yarrow, ed., 'A Journal of the Walcheren Expedition', *Mariner's Mirror*, 61 (1975), 153.
74. Thorpe, 61.
75. Hibbert, ed, *Recollections of Rifleman Harris*, 115
76. M.R. Howard, 'Walcheren 1809: a medical catastrophe', *British Medical Journal*, vol. 319 (1999), 1642-1645.
77. Thorpe, 65.
78. Dyott, 287.
79. Fortescue, vol. 7, 90.
80. Fortescue, vol. 7, 89.

Chapter 7 *pages 108–131*

Unless otherwise noted, this chapter is based on Graves, 149-181; Oman, vol. 4, 1-90, 131-205, 247-287; and *Reg Recs*, 235-239.

1. The words of 'The Girl I Left Behind Me', the traditional 'loath-to-depart' song of the British army, played when a regiment left its station for the last time, date to the mid-eighteenth century. See Winstock, *Songs & Music of the Redcoats*, 67-68.
2. Nova Scotia *Gazette*, 2 May 1809.
3. RWFM, Acc. 3777, Hill to mother, 30 Apr 1809.
4. Browne, 113.
5. NLAC, MG 29, A9, Diary of Anne Elinor Prevost, 3 May 1809.
6. Browne, 122.
7. Newberry Library, MS 5029, Blanckley to commander-in-chief, 18 July 1809.
8. Browne, 113.
9. Bentinck 2, 23 May 1873.
10. Graves, 114-115.
11. Bentinck 2, 9 May 1873.
12. NAB, WO 27, vol. 94, Inspection Report, 1/23rd Foot, 27 June 1809.
13. Browne, 114-115.
14. Browne, 114.
15. Browne, 115.
16. Browne, 115-116.
17. RWFM, Acc. 3777, Hill to mother, 30 Apr 1809.
18. RWFM, Acc. 3777, Hill to Humphreys, 12 June 1808.
19. Browne, 113.
20. Browne, 112-113.
21. Browne, 113.
22. Browne, 122.
23. RWFM, Acc. 3777, Hill to mother, 31 July 1810.
24. Browne, 122.
25. RWFM, Acc. 3777, Hill to mother, 30 Aug 1810.
26. NAB, WO 27, vol. 98, Inspection Report, 1/23rd Foot, 1 Aug 1810.
27. Browne, 123.
28. NAB: Adm 37, vol. 2639, Ship's Muster, HMS *Regulus*, Oct 1810; Adm 37, vol. 2754, Ship's Muster, HMS *Diadem*, Oct 1810.
29. Browne, 123.
30. Browne, 123.
31. Bentinck 2, 23 May 1873.
32. NAB, Adm 37, vol. 2754, Ship's Muster, HMS *Diadem*, Oct 1810.
33. Browne, 132.
34. Browne, 132-133.
35. Browne, 134.
36. RWFM, Acc. 1335, Harrison to father, 26 Nov 1810.
37. Bentinck 2, 23 May 1873.
38. WGO, vol 2, GOs, 12 Nov 1810; GO, 17 Nov 1810.
39. Crowe.
40. Wachholtz, 262.
41. T. Pakenham, ed., *Pakenham Letters. 1800 to 1815* (London, 1914), 64, Pakenham to brother, 29 Dec 1810.
42. RWFM, Acc. 3335, Harrison to father, 26 Nov 1810.
43. RWFM, Acc. 3335, Harrison to father, 8 Feb 1811.
44. Strength return, 25 Jan 1811, in *Reg Recs*, vol. 1, 235.
45. RWFM, Acc. 3335, Harrison to mother, 21 Dec 1810.
46. RWFM, Acc. 3335, Harrison to mother, 21 Dec 1810.
47. RWFM, Acc. 3335, Harrison to father, 8 Feb 1811.
48. T. Bunbury, *Reminiscences of a Veteran* (2 vols., London, 1861), vol. 1, 201.
49. Bentinck 2, 23 May 1873.
50. *WGO*, vol. 3, GO, 21 Jan 1811.
51. *WGO*, vol. 3, GO, 16 Jan 1811.
52. Bentinck 2, 23 May 1873.
53. RWFM, Acc. 3335, Harrison to father, 27 Oct 1810.
54. RWFM, Acc. 5257, Farmer to brother, 26 Dec 1810.
55. *WGO*, vol 2, GO, 15 Dec 1810; vol 3, GO, 17

May 1811.

56. RWFM, Acc. 3777, Hill to mother, n.d. 1811 but after July.

57. RWFM, Acc. 3335, Harrison to father, 9 Feb 1811.

58. *WSD*, vol. 7, 1-2, Wellington to Wellesley-Pole, 8 Dec 1810.

59. Bentinck 2, 23 May 1873.

60. *Reg Recs*, 236-237, letter by anonymous officer, 17 Mar 1811. Although the identity of the writer is not given, the similarity of style and thought with that of Lieutenant John Harrison indicates that he is most likely the author.

61. Bentinck 1.

62. Letter dated 17 Mar 1811, in *Reg Recs*, 236.

63. Cooper, 52.

64. Letter dated 17 Mar 1811, in *Reg Recs*, vol. 1, 237.

65. Cooper, 52.

66. Letter, 17 March 1810, in *Reg Recs*, vol. 1, 237.

67. Jenkinson to anonymous, 21 Mar 1811, in *WSD*, vol. 7, 85..

68. Letter by anonymous officer, 17 Mar 1811, in *Reg Recs*, vol. 1, 238.

69. C. Hibbert, ed., *A Soldier of the Seventy-First* (London, 1975), 56.

70. Pakenham, ed., *Letters*, 76, Pakenham to brother, 16 Mar 1811.

71. RWFM, Acc. 1335, Harrison to father, 17 Mar 1811.

72. J. Donaldson, *Recollections of An Eventful Life* (1825, reprinted Staplehurst, 2000), 106.

73. RWFM, Acc. 3335, Harrison to father, 17 Mar 1811..

74. Letter dated 17 Mar 1811, in *Reg Recs*, vol. 1, 238.

75. Letter dated 17 Mar 1811, in *Reg Recs*, vol. 1, 238.

76. Letter dated 17 Mar 1811, in *Reg Recs*, vol. 1, 238.

77. Letter dated 17 Mar 1811, in *Reg Recs*, vol. 1, 238.

78. Cooper, 53.

79. Bentinck 2, 23 May 1873.

80. J. Emerson, 'Recollections of the Late War', in W.H. Maxwell, ed., *Peninsular Sketches*, (2 vols., London 18145), vol. 2, 208.

81. RWFM, Acc. 5257, Farmer to brother, 3 Apr 1811.

82. Wachholtz, 267.

83. Wachholtz, 268.

84. Strength return, 1/23rd Foot, 25 April 1811, in *Reg Recs*, vol. 1, 239.

85. C. Boutflower, *Journal of an Army Surgeon* (Staplehurst, 1997), 89.

86. Emerson, 'Recollections', in Maxwell, ed., *Peninsular Sketches*, vol. 2, 224.

87. Emerson, 'Recollections', in Maxwell, ed., *Peninsular Sketches*, vol. 2, 225.

88. Bentinck 2, 30 May 1873.

89. RWFM, Acc. 3335, Harrison to mother, 24 May 1811..

90. Wachholtz, 270.

91. Cooper, 59.

Chapter 8 *pages 132–151*

Unless otherwise noted, this chapter is based on G. Dempsey, *Albuera 1811* (London, 2008); Graves, 183-282; Oman, vol. 4, 363-403, 542-607; and *Reg Recs*, 240-245.

1. A Welch Fusilier version of 'The British Grenadiers' current in the early 19th century, see J.P. Riley, compilor, 'Songs and Music of The Royal Welch Fusiliers', (Wrexham, 1996).

2. Letter by Cole, *USJ*, 6 Jan 1841.

3. Wachholtz, 271.

4. *Victoires et Conquêtes ... des Français, de 1792 à 1815* (vol. 20, Paris, 1820), 223.

5. C. Leslie, *Military Journal of Colonel Leslie* (Aberdeen, 1887), 222.

6. H. Hardinge, letter in *USJ*, Oct 1840, 247.

7. L. Cole letter 6 Jan 1841 in *USJ*, Apr 1841, 540.

8. L. Cole letter 6 Jan 1841 in *USJ*, Apr 1841, 540.

9. Cooper, 60.

10. RWFM, Acc. 3335, Harrison to mother, 24 May 1811.

11. Anonymous, 'Life of Sir William Myers', *Royal Military Chronicle*, Oct 1811, 473.

12. E. Blakeney letter, *USJ* April 1841, 538.

13. E. Lapène, *Conquête d'Andalousie*, (Paris, 1823), 163.

14. Cooper, 60.

15. RWFM, Acc. 3335, Harrison to mother, 24 May 1811.

16. Wachholtz, 272.

17. E. Blakeney letter, *USJ* April 1841, 539.

18. RWFM, Acc. 3335, Harrison to mother, 24 May 1811.

19. Wachholtz, 272.

20. E. Blakeney letter, *USJ*, April 1841, 539.

21. Anonymous, 'Life of Sir William Myers', *Royal Military Chronicle*, Oct 1811, 469-474.

22. S. Hall, *Retrospect of a Long Life* (New York, 1883), 588-589. 23. Cooper, 61.

24. Beresford to Wellington, 18 May 1811, *WD*, vol. 7, 588.

25. RWFM, Acc. 3335, Harrison to mother, 24 May 1811.

26. RWFM, Acc. 3777, Hill to unknown, 22 May

1811.

27. E. Blakeney letter, *USJ* April 1841, 539.
28. C. Oman, ed, 'Albuera Once More', *The Army Quarterly*, vol. 24 (Apr 1932), 340.
29. Wachholtz, 272-273.
30. C. Oman, ed, 'Albuera Once More', 340.
31. Wachholtz, 273.
32. Casualty figures from Graves, 254-255. On Robinson, see *Reg Recs*, vol. 1, 242 and HK *Medals*.
33. RWFM, Acc. 3335, Harrison to mother, 24 May 1811.
34. Bentinck 1.
35. Bentinck 2, 30 May 1873.
36. Emerson, 'Recollections', in Maxwell, ed., *Sketches*, 234.
37. 'Letters Home', G. Philipps to J.G. Philipps, 19 May 1811.
38. P. Stanhope, *Notes of Conversations with the Duke of Wellington, 1831-1851* (New York, 1973), 90.
39. Beresford to Wellington, 20 May 1811, in *WD*, vol. 7, 588.
40. Stewart to Beresford, 26 May 1811, in R. Cannon, *Historical Records of the Seventh Regiment of Foot* (London, 1847), 63.
41. Hardinge to Cole, 24 May 1811 in M. Cole and S. Gwynn, eds., *Memoirs of Sir Lowry Cole*, (London, 1934), 77
42. RWFM, Acc. 3335, Harrison to father, 22 June 1811.
43. Pakenham, ed., *Pakenham Letters*, 100, Pakenham to brother, 5 June 1811.
44. Pakenham, ed., *Pakenham Letters*, 105, Pakenham to brother, 3 July 1811.
45. Wachholtz, 277.
46. Wachholtz, 277.
47. Wachholtz, 278.
48. R. Knowles, *War in the Peninsula* (1913, reprinted Staplehurst, 2004), 35.
49. Bentinck 1.
50. Bentinck 1, also Bentinck 2, 30 May 1873.
51. Letter by anonymous officer of the 23rd Foot, Sept 1811, in *Reg Recs*, vol. 1, 245; and Bentinck 2, 13 June 1873.
52. Wachholtz, 279.
53. Bentinck 2, 13 June 1873.
54. Bentinck 2, 13 June 1873.
55. Knowles, *War in the Peninsula*, 35.
56. Wachholtz, 279.
57. Broughton-Mainwaring, *Historical Record*, 128
58. Cooper, 69.
59. RWFM, Acc. 3335, Harrison to father, 5 Nov 1811.
60. *WGO*, vol. 4, GO, 1 Jan 1812.

61. *WGO*, vol. 3, GO, 14 Oct 1811.
62. RWFM, Acc. 3335, Harrison to father, 5 Nov 1811.
63. RWFM, Acc. 3777, Hill to William, 18 Oct 1811.

Chapter 9 *pages 152–175*

Unless otherwise noted, this chapter is based on R. Muir, *Salamanca 1812* (New Haven, 2001); Oman, vol. 5, 157-582, vol. 6, 1-180; and *Reg Recs*, vol. 1, 245-255.

1. 'Lord Wellington for ever, huzza!', broadsheet ballad dating from 1812 sung to the tune of 'The Brags of Washington', see Palmer, *Rambling Soldier*, 177-178.
2. Lieutenant D. Cameron, 'Journal of the Peninsular War', quoted in P. Groves, *Historical Records of the 7th or Royal Regiment of Fusiliers* (Guernsey, 1903), 130.
3. *WGO*, vol 1, GO, 31 Oct 1809; vol. 3, GO, 15 Apr 1811; and vol. 4, GO, 22 Aug 1812
4. W. Grattan, *Adventures with the Connaught Rangers, 1809-1814* (London, 1902), 87.
5. RWFM, Acc. 5935, MacDonald to brother, 19 Feb 1812.
6. Wachholtz, 283-284.
7. *Dictionary of Canadian Biography*, vol. 7; Kirby ORWF.
8. Bentinck 2, 20 June 1873.
9. *WGO*, vol. 4, GO, 17 Feb 1812.
10. Bentinck 1.
11. Knowles, *War in the Peninsula*, 51; Wachholtz, 284.
12. My account of the siege of Badajoz in 1812 is based on J.T. Jones, *Journals of Sieges carried on under The Duke of Wellington ...* (2 vols., London, 1827), vol. 1, 156-244.
13. Wachholtz, 284-285.
14. Roberts, 'Incidents', 22.
15. Bentinck 1.
16. Bentinck 1.
17. Cooper, 75.
18. Wachholtz, 286.
19. Wachholtz, 286-287.
20. Knowles, *War in the Peninsula*, 59-60.
21. Roberts, 'Incidents', 22.
22. Knowles, *War in the Peninsula*, 60.
23. Cooper, 75.
24. Wachholtz, 287.
25. Wachholtz, 287.
26. Cooper, 75.
27. Wachholtz, 287.
28. RWFM, Acc. 3335, Harrison to mother, 23 Apr 1812.

29. Cooper, 76.
30. Wachholtz, 287.
31. Wachholtz, 287.
32. Cooper, 76.
33. Bentinck 1.
34. Browne, 152-153.
35. Bentinck 2, 13 June 1873.
36. Bentinck 2, 13 June 1873.
37. Bentinck 1.
38. Roberts, 'Incidents', 22.
39. RWFM, Acc. 5935, MacDonald to father, 12 June 1812.
40. NAB, WO 27, vol. 26, Inspection Report, 1/23rd Foot, 25 May 1812.
41. D. Bailey and D. Harding, 'From India to Waterloo: The "India Pattern" Musket', in Guy, ed., *The Road to Waterloo*, 48-57.
42. *WGO*, vol. 4, GO, 2 June 1812.
43. Roberts, 'Incidents', 23.
44. RWFM, Acc. 5935, MacDonald to father, 12 June 1812.
45. Browne, 166.
46. Wachholtz, 292.
47. Wachholtz, 292.
48. Wachholtz, 294.
49. H. Reeve, ed., *The Greville Memoirs* (8 vols., London, 1888, vol. 4, 40.
50. Wachholtz, 295.
51. Captain Barralier, 'Adventure at the Battle of Salamanca', *USJ*, Oct 1851, 274.
52. C.B. Vere, *Marches, Movements, and Operations of the 4th Division* (1812, reprinted London, 2003), 34-35.
53. Wachholtz, 295.
54. Wachholtz, 295.
55. RWFM, Acc. 5935, MacDonald to father, 26 July 1812.
56. P. Bainbrigge, 'The Staff at Salamanca, *USJ*', Jan 1878, quoted in Muir, *Salamanca*, 149.
57. G. Wrottesly, ed., *The Life and Correspondence of Field Marshal Sir John Burgoyne* (2 vols., London, 1864), vol. 1, 204, Burgoyne to sister, 25 July 1812.
58. Letter from unknown officer in the Fusilier Brigade, National Army Museum 6807-333, quoted in Muir, *Salamanca*, 148-149.
59. Wrottesly, ed., *Life and Correspondence of Burgoyne*, vol. 1, 204, Burgoyne to sister, 25 July 1812.
60. Wachholtz, 297.
61. Wrottesly, ed., *Life and Correspondence of Burgoyne*, vol. 1, 204, Burgoyne to sister, 25 July 1812.
62. Vere, *Marches ... of the 4th Division*, 35.
63. M Glover, *Wellington as a Military Commander* (London, 1968), 132.
64. Boutflower, *Journal of an Army Surgeon*, 149.
65. R. Davies, 'A Sussex Soldier of Wellington', *Sussex County Magazine* (Feb-Apr 1928) quoted in Muir, *Salamanca*, 219.
66. Wachholtz, 297.
67. Wachholtz, 297-298.
68. Browne, 174.
69. Browne, 173.
70. W. Beaumont, 'General Notebook', 27 Apr 1813, in G Miller, ed., *William Beaumont's Formative Years* (New York, 1946), 46.
71. G. Guthrie, *Commentaries on the Surgery of War* (London, 1855), 219-220
72. Guthrie, *Commentaries*, 221.
73. RWFM, Acc. 5935, MacDonald to father, 25 Aug 1812.
74. RWFM, Acc. 5935, MacDonald to father, 25 Aug 1812.
75. RWFM, Acc. 5935, MacDonald to father, 25 Aug 1812.
76. RWFM, Acc. 5935, MacDonald to father, 25 Aug 1812.
77. M. Glover, *The Napoleonic Wars* (London, 1979), 164.
78. Bentinck 1.
79. Browne, 197.
80. Wachholtz, 307.
81. RWFM, Acc. 5935, MacDonald to father, 26 Nov 1812.

Chapter 10 *pages 176–199*

Unless otherwise noted, this chapter is based on Oman, vol. 4, 181-193, 299-469; and *Reg Recs*, vol. 1, 255-259. Information on sickness in the Peninsular army, November 1812 to May 1813, extracted from A. Bamford, 'The British Army on Campaign 1808-1815: Manpower, Cohesion, and Effectiveness', unpublished PhD thesis, University of Leeds, 2009.

1 'The Battle of Vittoria'', an 1813 broadside ballad sung to the tune, 'The Love of It', and attributed to William Glenn.
2. *WGO*, vol 4, GOs, 2 September, 23 September and 1 Dec 1812.
3. *WGO*, vol. 4, GO, 10 Oct 1812.
4. Wachholtz, 309.
5. Oman, vol. 6, 157-158, 'Memorandum to Officers commanding Divisions and Brigades', 28 Nov 1812.
6. Oman, vol. 6, 157-157, 'Memorandum to Officers commanding Divisions and Brigades', 28 Nov 1812.
7. RWFM, Acc. 2686, Booker to unknown, 28 Feb 1812.

8. NAB, WO 27, vol. 102, Inspection Return of 1/23rd Foot, 12 Apr 1813.

9. Wachholtz, 309.

10. Figures on losses in the retreat from Bamford, 'The British Army on Campaign 1808-1815: Manpower, Cohesion, and Effectiveness'.

11. RWFM, Acc. 5935, MacDonald to father, 26 Nov 1813.

12. Bentinck 1.

13. B. Smyth, *History of the XXth Regiment* (London, 1889), 362, Memoir of Bainbrigge.

14. Steevens, 89-90.

15. RWFM, Acc. 5935, MacDonald to father, 8 Feb 1813.

16. Bentinck 2, 27 June 1813.

17. RWFM, Acc. 5935, MacDonald to father, 5 April 1813.

18. NAB, WO 27, vol. 102, Inspection Return of 1/23rd Foot, 12 Apr 1813.

19. NAB, WO 27, vol. 102, Inspection Return of 1/23rd Foot, 12 Apr 1813.

20. NAB, WO 27, vol. 102, Inspection Return of 1/23rd Foot, 12 Apr 1813. Between Dec 1811 and May 1812, forty-five men of the the 11th Foot went before regimental courts martial and the maximum punishment awarded was eight hundred lashes, see Robinson, *Bloody Eleventh*, vol. 1, 401.

21. NAB, WO 27, vol. 102, Inspection Return of 1/23rd Foot, 12 Apr 1813.

22. *Reg Recs*, vol. 1, 262-264.

23. Crowe, 2 June 1813.

24. Crowe, n.d. probably Apr 1813.

25. Maxwell, ed, *Peninsular Sketches*, vol. 2, 29.

26. Cooper, 527.

27. Cooper, 5-6.

28. Crowe, n.d. but probably April 1813.

29. Wachholtz, 312.

30. A.S. White, ed., 'A Subaltern in the Peninsular War', *JSAHR*, vol. 13 (1934), 14, Garrett to C. Bentinck, 10 May 1813.

31. Bentinck 2, 4 July 1873.

32. Crowe, 19 May 1813.

33. Crowe, 27 May 1813.

34. Crowe, 27 May 1813.

35. RWFM, Acc. 2685, Booker to Sarah, 30 May 1813.

36 *WSD*, vol 7, 502, Bathurst to Wellington, 22 Dec 1812.

37. Crowe, 1 June 1813.

38. Crowe, 3 June 1813.

39. Crowe, 4 June 1813.

40. Bunbury, *Reminiscences of a Veteran*, vol. 1, 200-201.

41. Browne, 208.

42. Steevens, 93-94.

43. Crowe, Standing Orders, 4th Division, c. May 1813.

44. Cooper, 145.

45. Cooper, 147.

46. White, ed., 'Subaltern in the Peninsular War', 16, Garrett to C. Bentinck, 20 June 1813.

47. Crowe, 13 June 1813.

48. Crowe, 13 June 1813.

49. Browne, 174.

50. Browne, 174.

51. Browne, 174.

52. E. Sabine, ed., *Letters of Colonel Augustus Simon Frazer* (London, 1859), 138-139.

53. Crowe, 17 June 1813.

54. Crowe, 17 June 1813.

55. RWFM, Acc. 2686, Booker to Sarah, 14 June 1813.

56. Crowe, 21 June 1813.

57. Capt. T. Edwardes Tucker's Diary', *West Wales Historical Records*, vol. 10, (1924), 93, 20 June 1813.

58. H.B. Robinson, *Memoirs of Lieutenant-General Sir Thomas Picton* (2 vols., London, 1836), vol. 2, 210.

59. Crowe, 21 June 1813.

60. Crowe, 21 June 1813.

61. Crowe, 21 June 1813.

62. RWFM, Acc. 3777, Hill to mother, n.d., 1813.

63. RWFM, Acc. 2686, Booker to unknown, 10 July 1813.

64. RWFM, Acc. 5935, MacDonald to father, 1 July 1813.

65. RWFM, Acc. 2686, Booker to unknown, 10 July 1813.

66. RWFM, Acc. 3777, Hill to mother, n.d., 1813.

67. RWFM, Acc. 2686, Booker to unknown, 10 July 1813.

68. Steevens, 96.

69. Steevens, 97.

70. Browne, 213-214.

71. RWFM, Acc. 5935, MacDonald to father, 1 July 1813.

72. Steevens, 96.

73. RWFM, Acc. 2686, Booker to Sarah, 25 June 1813.

74. RWFM, Acc. 2686, Booker to unknown, 10 July 1813.

75. RWFM, Acc. 3777, Hill to mother, n.d. 1813.

76. White, ed., 'Subaltern in the Peninsular War', 17, Garrett to C. Bentinck, 20 June 1813.

77. RWFM, Acc. 2686, Booker to Sarah, 25 June 1813.

78. Crowe, 21 June 1813.

79. Henegan, *Campaigns with the Field Train*, 167.

80. RWFM, Acc. 5935, MacDonald to father, 1 July 1813.
81. Crowe, 22 June 1813.
82. RWFM, Acc. 5935, MacDonald to father, 1 July 1813.
83. Browne, 219-220.
84. Browne, 220.
85. Bentinck 2, 4 July 1873.
86. Crowe, 25 June 1813.
87. Bentinck 2, 4 July 1873.
88. Bentinck 2, 4 July 1873.
89. Quoted in Glover, *Wellington as Military Commander*, 111.
90. Browne, 220.
91. Browne, 220.
92. RWFM, Acc. 3777, Hill to mother, n.d., 1813.
93. RWFM, Acc. 5935, MacDonald to father, 1 July 1813.
94. White, ed., 'Subaltern in the Peninsular War', 20, Garrett to C. Bentinck, 21 July 1813.
95. Wachholtz, 319.
96. White, ed., 'Subaltern in the Peninsula War', 19-20, Garrett to C. Bentinck, 13 July 1813.
97. RWFM, Acc. 5935, MacDonald to father, 1 July 1813.

Chapter 11 *pages 200–223*

Unless otherwise noted, this chapter is based on Oman, vol. 6, 557-740, vol. 7, 1-62, 110-405, 433-512; and *Reg Recs*, vol. 1, 260-272.

1. 'Battle of the Pyrenees', a broadside ballad of 1813 sung to the tune of 'Heart of Oak'.
2. Quoted in Oman, vol. 6, 587-588.
3. RWFM, Acc. 2686, Booker to Collins, 11 Aug 1813.
4. Letter of G. Tovey, in Smyth, *History of the XXth Regiment*, 368-369.
5. Wachholtz, 322.
6. RWFM, Acc. 2686, Booker to Sarah, 27 July 1813.
7. Wachholtz, 322. 8. Bentinck 2, 4 July 1813.
9. Crowe, 25 July 1813.
10. Crowe, 25 July 1813.
11. Steevens, 102.
12. Steevens, 102-103.
13. Smyth, *History of the XXth Regiment*, 350, Memoir of Bainbrigge.
14. Wachholtz, 324.
15. Cooper, 91.
16. Smyth, *History of the XXth Regiment*, 350-351, Memoir of Bainbrigge.
17. Smyth, *History of the XXth Regiment*, 351, Memoir of Bainbrigge.
18. RWFM, Acc. 2686, Booker to Collins, 11 Aug 1813.
19. Cooper, 91.
20. Crowe, 25 July 1813.
21. Smyth, *History of the XXth Regiment*, 352, Memoir of Bainbrigge.
22. Smyth, *History of the XXth Regiment*, 352, Memoir of Bainbrigge.
23. Smyth, *History of the XXth Regiment*, 352, Memoir of Bainbrigge.
24. Steevens, 105.
25. RWFM, Acc. 2686, Booker to Collins, 11 Aug 1813.
26. Oman, vol. 6, 674, quoting J.B. Lemonnier-Delafosse, *Souvenirs Militaires*, (Le Havre, 1850), 227-228.
27. RWFM, Acc. 2686, Booker to Collins, 11 Aug 1813.
28. Crowe, 28 June [July] 1813.
29. Ellis to Harrison, July 1813, in *Reg Recs*, vol. 1, 261-262.
30. Bentinck 2, 11 July 1873.
31. RWFM, Acc. 5935, MacDonald to brother, 4 Sep 1813.
32. Steevens, 106.
33. Ellis to Harrison, July 1813, in *Reg Recs*, vol. 1, 261-262.
34. W. Tomkinson, *The Diary of a Cavalry Officer* (1894, reprinted Staplehurst, 1999), 133.
35. Smyth, *History of the XXth Regiment*, 362, Memoir of Bainbrigge. In 1881 the 20th Foot assumed the title, The Lancashire Fusiliers, and in 1968 became part of The Royal Regiment of Fusiliers, which also incorporated the old 7th Foot.
36. Steevens, 107.
37. Steevens, 107-108.
38. Steevens, 112.
39. Steevens, 110.
40. Steevens, 112.
41. RWFM, Acc. 5935, MacDonald to father, 26 Nov 1813.
42. Bentinck 1.
43. RWFM, Acc. 5935, MacDonald to father, 26 Nov 1813.
44. RWFM, Acc. 5935, MacDonald to father, 26 Nov 1813.
45. RWFM, Acc. 5935, MacDonald to father, 26 Nov 1813.
46. Steevens, 114-115.
47. Steevens, 115-116.
48. Steevens, 116.
49. Bentinck 2, 18 July 1873.
50. Browne, 255.
51. Cooper, 107.
52. Browne, 256.

53. Browne, 256.
54. Steevens, 117-118.
55. Steevens, 118.
56. RWFM, Acc. 5935, MacDonald to brother, 23 Jan 1814.
57. RWFM, Acc. 5935, MacDonald to brother, 23 Jan 1814.
58. *WGO*, vol. 5, GO, 9 July 1813.
59. RWFM, Acc. 5935, MacDonald to father, 5 Mar 1814.
60. Bentinck 2, 18 July 1873.
61. Ross to Ned, 12 Mar 1814, in Smyth, *History of the XXth*, 323.
62. Cooper, 110-111.
63. RWFM, Acc. 5935, MacDonald to father, 5 Mar 1814.
64. RWFM. Acc. 5935, MacDonald to father, 5 Mar 1814.
65. Ross to Ned, 12 Mar 1814, in Smyth, *History of the XXth*, 323.
66. Bentinck 1.
67. RWFM, Acc. 5935, MacDonald to father, 13 Apr 1814.
68. RWFM, Acc. 5935, MacDonald to father, 13 Apr 1814.
69. RWFM, Acc. 5935, MacDonald to father, 13 Apr 1814.
70. RWFM, Acc. 5935, MacDonald to father, 13 Apr 1814.
71. Bentinck 1.
72. *WGO*, vol. 6, GO, 26 Apr 1814.
73. NAB, Adm 37, vol. 3950, Ship's Muster, HMS *Egmont*, 25 May 1814.
74. RWFM, Acc. 5935, MacDonald to father, 25 June 1814.

Chapter 12 *pages 224–235*

Unless otherwise noted, this chapter is based on *Reg Recs*, vol. 1, 271-277.

1. 'The sodger's return', a traditional ballad with words by Robbie Burns, see Winstock, *Songs & Music of the Redcoats*, 113-115.
2. Bentinck 1.
3. Bentinck 2, 25 July 1873.
4. Bentinck 2, 25 July 1873.
5. Jeremiah, 11.
6. Bentinck 2, 25 July 1873.
7 'Fluellyn' in Coulburn's *United Service Magazine* 1845, vol 3, 282-284
8 'Fluellyn' in Coulburn's *United Service Magazine* 1845, vol 3, 282-284
9. The Royal Welch Fusiliers Museum holds regimental medals awarded to Privates Samuel Haughton, Alexander Mackie, Richard Roberts and Evans Williams. None have ribbons but it appears that most regimental medals seem to have been suspended by a scarlet ribbon edged blue, see L. Smurthwaite, 'Glory is Priceless!: Awards to the British Army During the French Revolutionary and Napoleonic Wars', in Guy, ed. *The Road to Waterloo*, 164-183.
10. Bentinck 2, 25 July 1873.
11. Bentinck 1.
12. Worcester *Herald*, 31 Dec 1814.
13. Worcester *Herald*, 31 Dec 1814.
14. Worcester *Herald*, 31 Dec 1814.
15. Worcester *Herald*, 31 Dec 1814.
16. Jeremiah, 6-7.
17. Jeremiah, 8.
18. 'Jenny Jones of Talylyn: Recollections of Waterloo', *The Cambrian*, 26 May 1876.
19. Jones, 'Recollections'.
20. Pakenham to mother, 6 June 1814, in T Pakenham, ed., *Pakenham Letters*, 248.
21. R. Reilly, *The British at the Gates* (Toronto, 2002), 171-176.
22. Reilly, *British at the Gates*, 362-363.
23. Cooper, 134.
24. RWFM, Acc. 5935, MacDonald to father, 13 Mar 1815.
25. Bentinck 2, 25 July 1873.
26. RWFM, Acc. 5935, MacDonald to father, 23 Mar 1815.
27. The section that follows is largely extracted from information on officers and men contained in N Holme and EL Kirby, *Medal Rolls. 23rd Foot – Royal Welch Fusiliers. Napoleonic Period. With Biographical Notes on Officers, N.C.O.s and Men* (Caernarfon and London, 1978). Holme and Kirby based their research on NAB, WO 100, vol. 15A, the 'Waterloo Roll'; vol. 1 and 6, Military General Service Medal; Regimental Pay Lists in the RWF Museum and WO 25, vols. 347-350, Regimental Description and Succession Books, 1798-1838.
28. On the heights of men in the 23rd Foot, see NAB, WO 27, vol. 129, Inspection Report, 1/23rd Foot, Oct 1814.
29. Jeremiah, 13.
30. RWFM. Acc. 5935, MacDonald to father, 3 Apr 1815.
31. Jones, 'Recollections'.
32. RWFM, Acc. 3777, Hill to father, n.d. [possibly 29 Mar 1815].

Chapter 13 *pages 236–259*

Unless otherwise noted, this chapter is based on M. Adkin, *The Waterloo Companion*; Fortescue, vol. 9; and *Reg Recs*, vol. 1, 276-290.

1. Regimental song dating to the post-1815 period in J.P. Riley, comp., 'Songs and Music of the Royal Welch Fusiliers'.

2. RWFM, Acc. 5935, MacDonald to father, 3 Apr 1815.

3. RWFM, Acc. 5935, MacDonald to father, 3 Apr 1815.

4. Wheeler, 160, 8 Apr 1815.

5. Wheeler, 161, 29 May 1815.

6. Albemarle, 90.

7. Cole to Wellington, 28 May 1815, in *Reg Recs*, vol. 1. 288-289.

8. Wellington to Cole, 2 June 1815, in *Reg Recs*, vol. 1, 289.

9. RWFM, Acc. 5935, MacDonald to sister, 13 June 1815.

10. Wheeler, 162, 29 May 1815.

11. Albemarle, 93.

12. Wheeler, 162, 29 May 1815.

13. Jeremiah, 18.

14. Glover, ed., *From Corunna to Waterloo*, 258.

15. Albemarle, 92.

16. Jeremiah, 18-19.

17. Jeremiah, 19.

18. RWFM, Acc. 5935, MacDonald to sister, 13 June 1815.

19. Albemarle, 94.

20. Bentinck 2, 25 July 1873.

21. Jeremiah, 19.

22. Jones, 'Recollections'.

23. Albemarle, 94.

24. Wheeler, 169, 19 June 1815.

25. Jeremiah, 20.

26. Wheeler, 169, 29 June 1815.

27. Wheeler, 169, 19 June 1815.

28. Jeremiah, 20.

29. Albemarle, 95.

30. Jeremiah, 21.

31. Jones, 'Recollections'.

32. Albemarle, 96.

33. Albemarle, 96.

34. Wheeler, 170, 19 June 1815.

35. Jeremiah, 21-22.

36. Bentinck 1.

37. Jones, 'Recollections'.

38. Jeremiah, 23-24.

39. Jones, 'Recollections'.

40. Jones, 'Recollections'.

41. Jones, 'Recollections'.

42. Jones, 'Recollections'.

43. Jeremiah, 24.

44. Albemarle, 100.

45. H.T. Siborne, ed., *The Waterloo Letters*, (London, 1891), 189, Bull to Fraser, 24 June 1815.

46. Bentinck 2, 25 July 1873.

47. Albemarle, 101-102.

48. Albemarle, 102.

49. Albemarle, 105.

50. Jeremiah, 28.

51. Bentinck 1.

52. C. Mercer, *Journal of the Waterloo Campaign* (London, 1927), 174-175.

53. Bentinck 2, 25 July 1873.

54. RWFM, Acc. 3777, Hill to Ley, 7 July 1815.

55. Mercer, *Journal*, 173.

56. Siborne, ed., *Letters*, 312, Holmes to Siborne, 29 Apr 1835.

57. Wheeler, 173, 23 June 1815.

58. Bentinck 2, 25 July 1873.

59. *Reg Recs*, vol. 1, 283-284.

60. RWFM, Acc. 3777, Hill to Ley, 7 July 1815.

61. Albemarle, 106.

62. C.H. Churchill to H Churchill, 24 June 1815, in H.A. Bruce, ed., *Life of General Sir William Napier* (2 vols., London, 1864), vol. 1, 179-180.

63. Siborne, ed., *Letters*, 312, Holmes to Siborne, 29 Apr 1835.

64. Siborne, ed., *Letters*, 312, Holmes to Siborne, 29 Apr 1835.

65. Bentinck 1.

66. Mercer, *Journal*, 186.

67. Mercer, *Journal*, 187.

68. Jones, 'Recollections'.

69. RWFM, Acc. 3777, Hill to Ley, 7 July 1815.

70. *Reg Recs*, vol. 1, 285.

71. *Reg Recs*, vol. 1, 285.

72. Albemarle, 109.

73. RWFM, Acc. 5935, MacDonald to sister, 23 June 1815.

74. RWFM, Acc. 5935, MacDonald to mother, 25 June 1815.

75. Wheeler, 176, 25 June 1815.

76. Albemarle, 113.

77. Albemarle, 113.

78. RWFM, Acc. 5935, MacDonald to mother, 25 June 1815.

79. RWFM, Acc. 5935, MacDonald to brother, 3 July 1815.

80. Bonaparte to the Prince Regent, 13 July 1815, in Glover, *Napoleonic Wars*, 222.

81. On the loss of life because of war during the period, 1792-1815, see S. Dumas, K.. Vedel-Petersen and H. Westergaard, *Losses of Life Caused by War* (Oxford, 1923).

82. Major Greenwood, 'British Loss of Life in the Wars of 1794-1815 and in 1914-1918', *Journal of the Royal Statistical Society*, vol. 105 (1942), 1-16.

Epilogue *pages 260–272*

Unless otherwise noted, this epilogue is based on
Reg Recs, vol. 1, 284-291, and vol. 2, 1-48, 157-159.

1. Welch Fusilier regimental song from Riley,
   'Songs and Music of the Royal Welch Fusiliers'.
2. Bentinck 2, 1 August 1873.
3. Bentinck 2, 1 August 1873.
4. General Order, 31 Aug 1815, contained in
   R.J.M. Sinnett to author, 18 June 2007; R.
   Graves letter to the *Times*, 24 Sep 1957.
5. A sample of this type of form is reproduced as an
   illustration in this book.
6. Kirby, *ORWF*; memoir of General Sir Harry
   Calvert, USJ, (1829), pt 1, 26-30.
7. *Reg Recs*, vol. 2, 2, letter by anonymous author,
   20 June 1816. The author was probably Surgeon
   J. Monroe.
8. *Reg Recs*, vol. 2, 2, letter by anonymous author,
   20 June 1816.
9. *Reg Recs*, vol. 1, 284; Harris, 'Worcester
   Honours a Brave Soldier'.
10. Bentinck 1.
11. *Reg Recs*, vol. 2, 13-14.
12. G. Beauclerk, *A Journey to Marocco in 1826*
    (London, 1828), 342-343.
13. *Reg Recs*, vol. 2, 20-21, Pearson to Ross, 3 Aug
    1830.
14. On Harrison, see Kirby *ORWF*. Details of
    officers' careers in 1829 in NAB, WO 25, vol.
    789, Statement of the Service of the Officers of
    the 23rd Regiment, n.d. (c. 1829).
15. RWFM, Acc. 1335, Harrison to mother, 18 Apr
    1831.
16. RWFM, Acc. 1335, Harrison to mother, 18 Apr
    1831.
17. W. Napier, *History of the War in the Peninsula ...
    Volume 3* (London, 1833), 545-547.
18. *Reg Recs*, vol. 2, 404.
19. NAB, WO 3, vol. 87, Hill to Gordon, 28 Nov
    1834.
20. HK *Medals*.
21. *The Times*, 27 Dec 1850.

22. Rochdale *Observer*, 6 Sept 1856.
23. Bentinck 1; Bentinck 2, 22 Aug 1873.
24. Kirby *ORWF*; E.L. Kirby, 'The Puzzle of a
    Bundle of Love Letters and an MGSM', *YDG*,
    vol. 21 (1978), 4.
25. Browne, 41-42; E. Walford, ed., *Hardwicke's
    Annual Biography for 1856* (London, 1856).
26. Cooper, 15, 140-141.
27. Crowe biographical details from .
28. Kirby *ORWF*.
29. *DNB*, vol. 6; Harris, 'Worcester Honours a
    Brave Soldier'.
30. Jones, 'Recollections'.
31. Kirby, *ORWF*.
32. E. Case, ed., *Letters to a Vicarage* (Exeter, 1988).
33. Kirby *ORWF*; and information provided to
    author by R.J.M. Sinnett.
34. Family information on Jack Hill's descendants
    from Mr. Rupert Hill.
35. Jeremiah, 3.
36. *DNB*, vol. 31.
37. HK *Medals*; and NAB, WO 97, vol. 430, Chelsea
    Pension records for Mason.
38. Kirby *ORWF*; Obituary in *Blackwood's
    Edinburgh Magazine*, vol. 28, (1830), 967.
39. Copy of advertisement in author's collection.
40. Graves, 414-422.
41. HK *Medals*, 179.
42. The Royal Welch Fusiliers Museum has a copy
    of Roberts's 'List of Different Actions'.
43. Roberts, 'Incidents in the Life'.
44. Steevens, i-ii, 124.
45. Thorpe, introduction.
46. Wachholtz, 259-260. Friedrich von Wachholtz's
    experiences from the time he left Prussia in 1809
    to his arrival in the Peninsula in 1810 can be
    found in Friedrich von Wachholtz, *Aus dem
    Tagebuche des Generals Fr. L. von Wachholtz*
    (Braunschweig, 1843).
47. Wheeler, 8-9.
48. HK *Medals*.
49. Glover and Riley, *Astonishing Infantry*, 290-291.

Bibliography

PRIMARY SOURCES

Archival

Library and Archives of Canada, Ottawa

    Manuscript Group 24, F70, Diary of Lt. Thomas Evans

    Manuscript Group 29, A9, Diary of Anne Elinor Prevost

National Archives of Britain, Kew, Surrey

    Admiralty 37, Ship's Musters

    Probate 31, Records of the Prerogative Court

    War Office 4, Secretary-at-War, Out-Letters

    War Office 12, Muster Books and Paylists

    War Office 17, Monthly Returns

    War Office 25, Registers and Description Books

    War Office 27, Inspection Reports

    War Office 97, Chelsea Pension Records

    War Office 100, Waterloo Roll

Royal Welch Fusiliers Museum and Archives, Caernarfon

    Accession 379, G. Mackenzie papers

    Accession 1335, J. Harrison papers

    Accession 2686, G. Booker papers

    Accession 3777, J. Hill papers

    Accession 5257, T. Farmer papers

    Regimental Scrapbooks and Albums

    Ms. Memorial of Service of Colonel T. Dalmer

Woodbridge Library, Suffolk

    Richard Bentinck, unpublished manuscript, 'The Life and Career of Richard Bentinck'

Newspapers and Periodicals

Gentleman's Magazine.

London Gazette

London *Times*

New York *Times*
Nova Scotia *Gazette*
Rochdale *Observer*
Worcester *Herald*

Published Official Documents

Accounts and Estimates, Army Returns, etc., London: Parliament, 1810

Kent, Duke of, F.R. Gascoigne, ed., 'Standing Orders in the Garrison of Gibraltar, 1803', *Journal of the Society for Army Historical Research*, vol. 2, (1922), 126, 181-183

Loyd, M., translator, *New Letters of Napoleon I. Omitted from the Edition Published under the Auspices of Napoleon III.* London: W. Heinemann, 1898

Wellington, Duke of, *General Orders. Spain and Portugal, ... 1809, 1810, 1811, 1812.* London: T. Egerton, 1810-1813

——, J. Gurwood, ed., *The Dispatches of Field Marshal the Duke of Wellington During His Various Campaigns in India, Denmark, Portugal, Spain, The Low Countries and France*, London: 13 vols., W. Clowes, 1834-1839

——, A.R. Wellington, ed., *Supplementary Despatches, Correspondence, and Memoranda of Field-Marshal Arthur, Duke of Wellington K.G.*, London: John Murray, 15 vols., 1858-1872

Period Military Regulations, Treatises and Technical Literature

Adjutant General, Britain, *Regulations to be Observed by Troops Embarked in Transports for Service Abroad.* London: War Office, 1795

——, *Light Infantry Exercise, as ordered by His Majesty's Regulations for the Movements of the Troops.* London: War Office, 1797

——, *Regulations for Regimental Surgeons, &c., for the Better Management of the Sick in Regimental Hospitals.* London: War Office, 1799

——, *Instructions to Officers Employed on the Recruiting Service.* London: War Office, 1806

——, *General Regulations and Orders for the Army, 1811.* London: War Office, 1816.

Adjutant General, Ireland, *Standing Orders and Regulations for the Army in Ireland.* Dublin, 1794-1800, reprinted London: John Muller, 1969

Cuthbertson, Bennett, *A System for the Complete Interior Management and Oeconony of a Battalion of Infantry.* London: J. Millan, 1779

Dundas, David, *Principles of Military Movements, Chiefly Applied to Infantry.* 1788, reprinted Cambridge: Trotman, 2002

——, *Rules and Regulations for the Formations, Field-Exercise, and Movements, of His Majesty's Forces.* London: J. Walter, 1792

James, Charles, *The Regimental Companion, Containing the Pay, Allowances and Relative Duties of Every Officer in the British Service.* London: T. Egerton, 3 vols, 1811

Le Marchant, John, *Elucidation of Several Parts of His Majesty's Regulations for the Formations and Movements of Cavalry.* London: T. Egerton, 1798

Rottenburg, Francis de, *Regulations for the Exercise of Riflemen and Light Infantry, and Instructions for their Conduct in the Field.* London: T. Egerton, 1798

Torrens, Henry, *Field Exercise and Evolutions of the Army.* London: W. Clowes, 1824

War Office, Britain, *A List of all the Officers of the Army and the Royal Marines on the Full and Half-pay.* London, 1783-1815

Published Memoirs, Diaries, Journals and Correspondence

Albemarle, Earl of, (G.T. Keppel), *Fifty Years of My Life.* London: 3rd ed., Holt, 1877

Anonymous, *Military Adventures of Johnny Newcome.* 1816, reprinted London: Methuen, 1904

Bainbrigge, J., memoir in B. Smyth, *History of the XXth Regiment.* London: Simpkin, Marshal, 1889

Barralier, Captain, 'Adventure at the battle of Salamanca', *United Service Journal*, Oct 1851, 274-277

Baynham, H., *From the Lower Deck*. Barre, Mass: Barre Publishing, 1970

Beauclerk, G., *A Journey to Marocco 1826*. London: Poole and Edwards, 1828

Beaumont, W., 'General Notebook', 1813, in G Miller, ed., *William Beaumont's Formative Years*. New York: Schumann, 1946

Bentinck, R., *Heywood Advertiser*, May-August 1873

Blakeney, E., letter, *United Service Journal* (April 1841), 538.

Blakeney, R., *A Boy in the Peninsular War*. 1899, reprinted London: Greenhill, 1989

Boutflower, C. *Journal of an Army Surgeon*. 1912, reprinted Staplehurst: Spellmount, 1997

Browne, T., R.N. Buckley, ed., *The Napoleonic War Journal of Captain Thomas Browne*. London: Army Records Society, 1987

Bunbury, H., *Passages in the Great War with France. 1799-1810*. 1854, reprinted London: Peter Davies, 1927

Bunbury, T., *Reminiscences of a Veteran*. London: 2 vols, C. Skeet, 1861

Burgoyne, J., G. Wrottesley, ed., *The Life and Correspondence of Field Marshal Sir John Burgoyne*. London: 2 vols., Richard Bentley, 1864

Cameron, D., 'Journal of the Peninsular War', quoted in P. Groves, *Historical Records of the 7th or Royal Regiment of Fusiliers*. Guernsey: F.B. Guerin, 1903

Cole, L., letter, *United Service Journal* (6 Jan 1841), 347

——, letter, *United Service Journal* (19 Mar 1841), 540

——, M. Cole and S. Gwynn, eds., *Memoirs of Sir Lowry Cole*. London: 2 vols., Macmillan 1934

Cooper, J.S., *Rough Notes of Seven Campaigns, 1809-1815*. 1869, reprinted Staplehurst: Spellmount, 2002

Davies, R., 'A Sussex Soldier of Wellington', *Sussex County Magazine* (Feb-Apr 1928)

Dayes, J., G. Glover, ed., *Memoir of the Military Career of John Dayes*. Cambridge: Trotman, 2004

Donaldson, J., *Recollections of An Eventful Life*. 1825, reprinted Staplehurst: Spellmount, 2000

Dyott, W., R.W. Jeffrey, ed., *Dyott's Diary, 1781-1815. A Selection from the Journal of William Dyott*. London: 2 vols, Constable, 1907

Emerson, J. 'Recollections of the Late War', in W.H. Maxwell, ed., *Peninsular Sketches*. 1815, reprinted Cambridge: Trotman, 1998

Frazer, S., E. Sabine, ed., *Letters of Colonel Sir Augustus Simon Frazer*. London: Longman, Brown, Green, Longman & Roberts, 1859

Garrett, R., A.S. White, ed., 'A Subaltern in the Peninsular War', *Journal of the Society for Army Historical Research*, vol. 13 (1934), 4-21

Gomm, W., F.C. Carr-Gomm, ed., *Letters and Journals of Field Marshal Sir William Maynard Gomm, 1798-1815*. London: Johm Murray, 1881

Grattan, G. *Adventures with the Connaught Rangers, 1809-1814*. 1902, reprinted London: Greenhill, 1989

Greville, H. Reeve, ed., *The Greville Memoirs*. London: 3 vols., Longman, Green, 1875

Griffith, E., G. Glover, ed., *From Corunna to Waterloo. The Letters and Journals of Two Napoleonic Hussars*. London: Frontline, 2007

Guthrie, G. *Commentaries on the Surgery of War in Portugal, Spain, France and the Netherlands*. Philadelphia: J.P. Lippincott, 1877

Hall, S. *Retrospect of a Long Life*. New York: Appleton, 1883

Hamilton, A.P., *Hamilton's Campaign with Moore and Wellington*. Troy, NY: author, 1847

Hardinge, H, letter, *United Service Journal* (18 Oct 1840) 247

Harris, B., C. Hibbert, ed., *The Recollections of Rifleman Harris*. London: Cassell, 1970

Henegan, R.D., *Campaigns with the Field Train*. 1846, reprinted Leonaur, 2007

Hibbert, C. ed., *A Soldier of the Seventy-First*. London: Cassell, 1975

Hill, J., E. Case, ed., *Letters to a Vicarage*. Exeter: Oriel Press, 1988

Holland, E., Earl of Ilchester, ed., *The Journal of Lady Holland*. London: 2 vols, Longman, Green, 1908

Hope, J.A., *Military Memoirs of an Infantry Officer, 1809-1816*. Edinburgh, author, 1833

Jeremiah, T., G. Glover, ed., *Short Account of the Life of Private Thomas Jeremiah*. Cambridge: Trotman, 2008

Jones, J. 'Jenny Jones of Talylyn: Recollections of Waterloo', *The Cambrian*, 26 May 1876

Jones, J.T. *Journals of Sieges carried on under The Duke of Wellington in Spain during the Years 1811 and 1814*. London: 2 vols., Egerton, 1827

Ker Porter, R., *Letters from Portugal and Spain*. London: Longman, Hurst, Rees & Orme, 1809

Knowles, R., *War in the Peninsula: the Letters of a Lancashire Officer*. 1913, reprinted Staplehurst: Spellmount, 2004

Leslie, C., *Military Journal of Colonel Leslie*. Aberdeen: University Press, 1887

Mercer, C., *Journal of the Waterloo Campaign*. London: Peter Davies, 1927

Miller, B., *The Adventures of Sergeant Benjamin Miller*. Dallington: Naval & Military Press, 1999

Moore, James., *A Narrative of the Campaign of the British Army in Spain*. London: T. Johnson, 1809

Moore, John, J.F. Maurice, ed., *Diary of Sir John Moore*. London: 2 vols., Macmillan, 1904

Neale, A., 'The Spanish Campaign of 1808', in *Memorials of the Late War*. Edinburgh: Constable, 1831.

Pakenham, E., T. Pakenham, ed., *Pakenham Letters. 1800 to 1815*. London: private, 1914

Philipps, G., R. Goodridge, ed., 'Letters Home', *The Waterloo Journal*, vol. 21, no 2 (Aug 1999), 20-26

Pococke, T., *Journal of a Soldier of the 71st, or Glasgow Regiment*. Edinburgh: William & Charles Tait, 1819

Roberts, R., 'Incidents in the Life of an Old Fusilier', *The Workman's Friend*, No. 1, 1862, 10-23

Ross-Lewin, H., J. Wardell, ed., *With The Thirty-Second in the Peninsular and other Campaigns*. Dublin: Figgis, 1904

Schaumann, A., *On the Road with Wellington*. 1924, reprinted London: Greenhill, 1999

Schepeler, A. von, C. Oman, ed, 'Albuera Once More', *The Army Quarterly*, vol. 24 (1932), 337-342

Shipp, J., *The Path of Glory*. London: Chatto & Windus, 1969

Siborne, H.T. ed., *The Waterloo Letters*. 1891, reprinted London: Greenhill 1983

Stanhope, P., *Notes of Conversations with the Duke of Wellington, 1831-1851*. New York: Da Capo, 1973

Steevens, C., Nathaniel Steevens, ed., *Reminiscences of My Military Life by Colonel Charles Steevens*. Winchester: Warren & Son, 1878

Surtees, W., *Twenty-Five Years in the Rifle Brigade*. 1833, reprinted London: Greenhill, 1996

Thorpe, S., *Narrative of Incidents in the Early Life of Samuel Thorpe*. London: Seeley, 1854

Tomkinson, W., *The Diary of a Cavalry Officer*. 1894, reprinted Staplehurst: Spellmount, 1999.

Tucker, T.E., 'Capt. T. Edwardes Tucker's Diary', *West Wales Historical Records*, vol. 10, (1924)

Vere, C.B., *Marches, Movements, and Operations of the 4th Division*. 1812, reprinted Cambridge: Trotman, 2003

Wachholtz, F. von, H.C. von Wachholtz, ed., '"Auf der Peninsula 1810 bis 1813." Kriegstagebuch des Generals Friedrich Ludwig v. Wachholtz', *Beihefte zum Militär-Wochenblatt*, 1907, 259-326

——, *Aus dem Tagebuche des Generals Fr. L. von Wachholtz*. Braunschweig: F. Bieweg, 1843

Wall, A., H.M. Dawson, ed., 'Diary of the Operations in Spain under Sir John Moore', *Journal of the Royal Artillery Institution*, vol. 38, no 22 (Dec 1907), 1-18

Wheeler, W., B.H. Liddell Hart, ed., *The Letters of Private Wheeler, 1809-1828*. London: Michael Joseph, 1951

Yarrow, D., ed., 'A Journal of the Walcheren Expedition', *Mariner's Mirror*, 61 (1975), 183-189

SECONDARY SOURCES
Published Books

Adkin, M., *The Waterloo Companion*. London: Aurum, 2001

Anonymous, *Victoires et Conquêtes des Français, de 1792 à 1815*. Paris: 27 vols, Panckoucke, 1820

Broughton-Mainwaring, R., *Historical Record of the Royal Welch Fusiliers*, London: Hatchard, 1889

Browne, J., *A History of the Highlands and the Highland Clans*. Glasgow: A. Fullerton, 1840

Bruce, H.A., ed., *Life of General Sir William Napier*. London: 2 vols., Murray, 1864

Bryant, A., *The Years of Endurance, 1793-1802*. London: Collins, 1942

——, *The Years of Victory, 1802-1812*. London: Collins, 1944

Cannon, R., *Historical Records of the Seventh Regiment of Foot*. London: Furnivall & Parker, 1847

Cantlie, N., *History of the Army Medical Department*. London: 2 vols., Churchill, Livingstone, 1974

Cary, A.D.L. and S. McCance, *Regimental Records of the Royal Welch Fusiliers (Late the 23rd Foot)*. Vols. 1 and 2. London: Forster, Groom and the Royal United Service Institution, 1921, 1923; reprinted by the Regiment, 1995

Cashin, E., *Governor Henry Ellis and the Transformations of British North America*. Athens, GA: University of Georgia, 1994

Chambers, J., *Biographical Illustrations of Worcestershire*. Worcester: Walcott, 1820

Chandler, David, ed., *The Oxford History of the British Army*. Oxford: University Press, 2003

Clode, C.M., *The Military Forces of the Crown; Their Administration and Government*. London: 2 vols., John Murray, 1869

Compton, P., *Colonel's Lady and Camp-Follower: The Story of Women in the Crimean War*. London: Robert Hall, 1970

Dempsey, Guy, *Albuera, 1811: The Bloodiest Battle of the Peninsular War*. London: Frontline, 2008

De Watteville, H., *The British Soldier*. London: J.M. Dent, 1954

Dictionary of Canadian Biography. Volume 5. Toronto: University of Toronto, 1976

Dumas, S., K. Vedel-Petersen and H. Westergaard, *Losses of Life Caused by War*. Oxford: University Press, 1923

Fortescue, J., *A History of the British Army*. London: 13 vols., McMillan, 1899-1930; reprinted Naval & Military Press, c. 2004

Glover, M., *Wellington as a Military Commander*. London: Penguin, 1968

——, *The Napoleonic Wars*. New York: Hippocrene, 1978

Glover, M. and J.P. Riley, *'That Astonishing Infantry' The History of the Royal Welch Fusiliers, 1689-2006*. Barnsley: Pen and Sword, 2008

Glover, R., *Peninsular Preparation: The Reform of the British Army 1795-1809*. Cambridge: University Press, 1963

Graves, Donald E., *Fix Bayonets! The Life and Times of Lieutenant-General Sir Thomas Pearson, 1781-1847*. Montreal: Robin Brass, 2006

Graves, Dianne L., *In the Midst of Alarms: Women in the War of 1812*. Montreal: Robin Brass, 2007

Groves, P., *Historical Records of the 7th or Royal Regiment of Fusiliers*. Guernsey: F.B. Guerin, 1903

Guy, A.J., ed., *The Road to Waterloo*. London: National Army Museum, 1990

Haythornthwaite, P.J., *The Armies of Wellington*. London: Arms & Armour, 1994

Holme, N. and E.L. Kirby, *Medal Rolls. 23rd Foot – Royal Welch Fusiliers. Napoleonic Period. With Biographical Notes on Officers, N.C.O.s and Men*. Caernarfon and London: Royal Welch Fusiliers & Spink, 1978

Houlding, J., *Fit for Service: The Training of the British Army. 1715-1795*. Oxford: University Press, 1981

Jones, E.A., *The Loyalists of New Jersey*. Newark: New Jersey Historical Society, 1927

Kirby, E.L., *Officers of The Royal Welch Fusiliers. 1689-1914*. Capel Curig: author, 1997

Lapène, E., *Conquête d'Andalousie*. Paris: Anselin & Pochard, 1823

Mackesy, P., *British Victory in Egypt*. London: Routledge, 1995

Muir, R., *Salamanca 1812*. New Haven: Yale University, 2001

Napier, W., *History of the War in the Peninsula*. Volume 3, London: Thomas & William Boone, 1833

Oman, C., *A History of the Peninsular War*. 7 vols, 1902-1930, reprinted London: Greenhill, 1995-1998

Owen, B., *Welsh Militia and Volunteer Corps 1757-1908. 2. The Glamorgan Regiments of Militia*. Caernarfon: Palace Books, 1990

Palmer, R., ed., *The Rambling Soldier*. London: Penguin, 1985

Patterson, R.H., *Pontius Pilate's Bodyguard. A History of the Royal Scots*. Edinburgh: The Royal Scots, 2000

Reilly, R., *The British at the Gates*. Toronto: Robin Brass, 2002

Robinson, H.B., *Memoirs of Lieutenant-General Sir Thomas Picton*. London: 2 vols., R. Bentley, 1836

Robinson, R.E.R., *The Bloody Eleventh*. Exeter: The Devon and Dorsetshire Regiment, 1988

Sabine, L., *Biographical Sketches of the Loyalists of the American Revolution*. Boston: 2 vols., Little, Brown, 1864

Simms, J.R., *The Frontiersmen of New York*. Albany: G.C. Riggs, 1883

Smyth, B., *History of the XXth Regiment*. London: Simpkin, Marshall, 1889

Stephen, L. & S. Lee, *Dictionary of National Biography*. London: 65 vols, Oxford: University Press, 1885-1900

Vane, C.W., *Story of the Peninsular War*. New York: Harper, 1848

Walford, E., ed., *Hardwicke's Annual Biography for 1856*. London: Hardwicke, 1856

Winstock, L, *Songs and Music of the Redcoats*. London: Leo Cooper, 1970

Published Articles

Anonymous, 'Life of Sir William Myers', *Royal Military Chronicle* (Oct 1811), 473

——, 'Memoir of General Sir Harry Calvert', *United Service Journal*, (1829), pt 1, 26-30

——, 'In the Reign of King George. An Old Recruiting Song', *Y Ddraig Goch*, vol 1, no. 6 (Feb 1924, 205

'Fluellyn', anonymous letter in Coulburn's *United Service Magazine*, vol 3 (1845), 282-284

Geggus, D., 'Yellow Fever in the 1790s: The British Army in Occupied Saint Domingue', *Medical History*, vol. 23 (1979), 38-39

Greenwood, Major, 'British Loss of Life in the Wars of 1794-1815 and in 1914-1918', *Journal of the Royal Statistical Society*, vol. 105 (1942), 1-16

Hodge, W.B., 'On the Mortality arising from Military Operations', *Journal of the Statistical Society*, vol. 19 (1856), 219-271

Howard, M.R., 'Medical aspects of Sir John Moore's Corunna Campaign, 1808-1809', *Journal of the Royal Society of Medicine*, vol. 84 (May 1991), 299-302

——, 'Walcheren 1809: a medical catastrophe', *British Medical Journal*, vol. 319 (1999), 1642-1645

Kirby, E.L., 'The Puzzle of a Bundle of Love Letters and an MGSM', *Y Ddraig Goch*, vol. 21 (Mar 1978), 212-215

——, 'The Youth who was to save our Flash', *Y Ddraig Goch*, vol 22 (Mar 1979), 54-56

MacDonald, J., 'Sir Ralph Abercromby by a Contemporary', *Blackwood's Magazine*, (Dec. 1915), 843-844

MacDonald, John. Obituary in *Blackwood's Edinburgh Magazine*, vol. 28, (1830), 967

Unpublished Titles and Internet Sources

Bamford, A., 'The British Army on Campaign 1808-1815: Manpower, Cohesion, and Effectiveness', unpublished PhD thesis, University of Leeds, 2009.

Crowe, C., 'Letters and Diary from the Peninsula ... 1812-1813-1814', available on *www.jjhc.info/crowecharles1855.htm*

Harris, J., 'Worcester Honours a Brave Soldier', typescript, c. 2003

Riley, J.P., 'Songs and Music of the Royal Welch Fusiliers'. Photocopy, n.p. c. 1996

Index

The author and the publishers
gratefully acknowledge the assistance
given by The Royal Welch Fusiliers
in the production of *Dragon Rampant*.

The Royal Welch Fusiliers Museum is situated in historic
Caernarfon Castle in Gwynedd, North Wales. On display
are artefacts relating to Colonel Sir Henry Ellis and his
comrades during the Great War with France, 1793–1815,
including the keys to Corunna, period uniforms,
armament and equipment, portraits of Ellis and his
contemporaries, and their medals.

For further information about the Royal Welch Fusiliers
Museum and about the history of one of the most
distinguished regiments in the British army, visit the
Fusliiers' website at
<http://wwww.rwfmuseum.org.uk>